Lecture Notes in Computer Science 8569

Commenced Publication in 1973
Founding and Former Series Editors:
Gerhard Goos, Juris Hartmanis, and Jan van Leeuwen

T0236158

Jordi Cabot   Julia Rubin (Eds.)

Modelling Foundations and Applications

10th European Conference, ECMFA 2014
Held as Part of STAF 2014
York, UK, July 21-25, 2014
Proceedings

 Springer

Volume Editors

Jordi Cabot
AtlanMod team (Inria, Mines Nantes, LINA)
École des Mines de Nantes
Computer Science Department
4, rue Alfred Kastler
44307 Nantes Cedex 3, France
E-mail: jordi.cabot@inria.fr

Julia Rubin
IBM Research
Haifa University Campus
Mount Carmel
Haifa 31905, Israel
E-mail: mjulia@il.ibm.com

ISSN 0302-9743   e-ISSN 1611-3349
ISBN 978-3-319-09194-5   e-ISBN 978-3-319-09195-2
DOI 10.1007/978-3-319-09195-2
Springer Cham Heidelberg New York Dordrecht London

Library of Congress Control Number: 2014943043

LNCS Sublibrary: SL 2 – Programming and Software Engineering

Typesetting: Camera-ready by author, data conversion by Scientific Publishing Services, Chennai, India

Printed on acid-free paper

Springer is part of Springer Science+Business Media (www.springer.com)

Foreword

Software Technologies: Applications and Foundations (STAF) is a federation of a number of leading conferences on software technologies. It was formed after the end of the successful TOOLS federated event (http://tools.ethz.ch) in 2012, aiming to provide a loose umbrella organization for practical software technologies conferences, supported by a Steering Committee that provides continuity. The STAF federated event runs annually; the conferences that participate can vary from year to year, but all focus on practical and foundational advances in software technology. The conferences address all aspects of software technology, from object-oriented design, testing, mathematical approaches to modelling and verification, model transformation, graph transformation, model-driven engineering, aspect-oriented development, and tools.

STAF 2014 was held at the University of York, UK, during July 21–25, 2014, and hosted four conferences (ICMT 2014, ECMFA 2014, ICGT 2014 and TAP 2014), a long-running transformation tools contest (TTC 2014), eight workshops affiliated with the conferences, and (for the first time) a doctoral symposium. The event featured six internationally renowned keynote speakers, and welcomed participants from around the globe.

The STAF Organizing Committee thanks all participants for submitting and attending, the program chairs and Steering Committee members for the individual conferences, the keynote speakers for their thoughtful, insightful, and engaging talks, the University of York and IBM UK for their support, and the many ducks who helped to make the event a memorable one.

July 2014   Richard F. Paige

Preface

The European Conference on Modelling Foundations and Applications (ECMFA) is a premier conference dedicated to advancing the state of knowledge in the area of Model-Driven Engineering (MDE) – a paradigm based on the use of models for the specification, design, analysis, synthesis, deployment, testing, and maintenance of complex systems. MDE relies on exploiting models and automation to achieve significant boosts in development productivity and quality.

In the past 9 years, ECMFA has provided a venue for interaction among researchers and practitioners interested in MDE. The conference engages the key figures from industry and academia in a dialog which results in stronger and more effective practical application of MDE, hence producing more robust software based on state-of-the-art research results.

The 10th edition of the conference was held during July 21–25, 2014, as part of the STAF federated event organized by the University of York, United Kingdom. The Program Committee received 58 full paper submissions – 49 for the Foundations Track and 9 for the Applications Track. Each paper was reviewed by 3 or 4 Program Committee members and papers with controversial rankings were discussed online. As the result, 14 Foundations Track papers and 3 Applications Track papers were accepted for presentation at the conference and publication in the proceedings, resulting in an acceptance rate of 29% for the Foundations Track, 33% for the Application Track.

Papers were received from authors in 16 countries and covered a large spectrum of MDE topics including model provenance, model transformations and code generation, model synthesis, model-driven testing, formal modeling approaches, business process modeling, usability of models and more. We thank the authors for contributing to the conferences and allowing us to shape an interesting and inspiring program this year.

We are also grateful to the ECMFA 2014 keynote speakers, Marsha Chechik from the University of Toronto and Darren Buttle from ETAS for accepting our invitation and for their enlightening talks.

We thank the STAF 2014 and ECMFA 2014 organizers, as well as the sponsors of the conference, for their support. In particular, we appreciate the help of Richard Paige – the STAF 2014 general chair, Abel Gómez – the publicity chair, and Jérémie Tatibouët's – the web chair. Last but not least, we thank the Program Committee members for providing their expertise and timely reviews to ensure the scientific quality of the programme. Their helpful and constructive feedback to all authors is most appreciated.

July 2014

Jordi Cabot
Julia Rubin

Organization

Program Committee

Shaukat Ali	Simula Research Laboratory, Norway
Terry Bailey	Vicinay Cadenas, Spain
Behzad Bordbar	University of Birmingham, UK
Goetz Botterweck	Lero, Ireland
Alessandro Bozzon	Delft University of Technology, The Netherlands
Marco Brambilla	Politecnico di Milano, Italy
Jean-Michel Bruel	IRIT, France
Javier Luis Canovas Izquierdo	Inria and Ecole des Mines de Nantes, France
Michel Chaudron	Chalmers and Gothenborg University, Sweden
Robert Clarisó	Universitat Oberta de Catalunya, Spain
Tony Clark	Middlesex University, UK
Manuel Clavel	Universidad Complutense de Madrid, Spain
Philippe Collet	Université Nice Sophia Antipolis - CNRS/I3S, Spain
Benoit Combemale	IRISA, Université de Rennes 1, France
Diarmuid Corcoran	Ericsson AB, Sweden
Arnaud Cuccuru	CEA LIST, France
Marcos Didonet Del Fabro	Universidade Federal do Paraná, Brazil
Gregor Engels	University of Paderborn, Germany
Robert France	Colorado State University, US
Mathias Fritzsche	SAP AG, Germany
Jesus Garcia-Molina	Universidad de Murcia, Spain
Martin Gogolla	University of Bremen, Germany
Jeff Gray	University of Alabama, US
Michael Grossniklaus	University of Konstanz, Germany
Esther Guerra	Universidad Autónoma de Madrid, Spain
Philip Harris	United Technologies Research Center, Ireland
Oystein Haugen	SINTEF, Norway
Reiko Heckel	University of Leicester, UK
Andreas Hoffmann	Fraunhofer FOKUS, Germany
Zhenjiang Hu	National Institute of Informatics, Japan
Muhammad Zohaib Iqbal	National University of Computer and Emerging Sciences, Pakistan
Teemu Kanstren	VTT, Finland
Dimitris Kolovos	University of York, UK
Thomas Kuehne	Victoria University of Wellington, New Zealand

Additional Reviewers

Abdeen, Hani
Arendt, Thorsten
Arifulina, Svetlana
Brunelière, Hugo
Canovas Izquierdo, Javier Luis
Christ, Fabian
Cleophas, Loek
Corley, Jonathan
Costa Silva, Gabriel
Cánovas, Javier
Dajsuren, Yanja
Dania, Carolina
De Carlos, Xabier
Engelen, Luc
Fazal-Baqaie, Masud
Garcia de Dios, Miguel Angel
Hilken, Frank
Iovino, Ludovico
Joncheere, Niels

Jordan, Howell
Khan, Uzair
Kirch, Dennis
Krikava, Filip
Martínez, Salvador
Matragkas, Nicholas
Mayerhofer, Tanja
Mellagard, Niklas
Mijailovic, Zarko
Ogunyomi, Babajide
Pleuss, Andreas
Plotnikov, Dimitri
Raco, Deni
Soeken, Mathias
Tisi, Massimo
Vaupel, Steffen
Wang, Shuai
Williams, James

Explicating and Reasoning with Model Uncertainty

Marsha Chechik

University of Toronto
Toronto, Canada
chechik@cs.toronto.edu

Abstract. *"The reality of today's software systems requires us to consider uncertainty as a first-class concern in the design, implementation, and deployment of those systems"*
David Garlan [4].

Uncertainty has been studied in many software engineering contexts, such as self-adaptive systems [3], probabilistic systems [5], requirements engineering [10], risk management [6] and others. In this talk, I focus on the problem of *uncertainty that the modeler has about the different aspects of software*. Such uncertainty is (a) *reducible*, i.e., it concerns things that are not inherently unknowable, and (b) *epistemic*, i.e., it is caused by a particular stakeholder's lack of knowledge, as opposed to being a property of the world.

Model uncertainty can be introduced into the modeling process in many ways: alternative ways to fix model inconsistencies [9, 2, 12], different design alternatives [13, 8], modeler's knowledge about the problem domain [14], multiple stakeholder opinions [11], etc. Instead of waiting until uncertainty is resolved or forcing premature design decisions, we propose to defer the resolution of uncertainty for as long as necessary, while supporting a variety of transformation and reasoning operations that allow modelers to "live" with this uncertainty. In this talk, I survey some of our recent work on creating, transforming, and reasoning with models containing uncertainty. I also discuss the relationship between our treatment of model uncertainty and the popular alternatives: underspecification and non-determinism (and their close relatives, "I don't know" and "I don't care").

Our specification of models with uncertainty implicitly encodes a set of alternative possible models, where we are not sure which is the correct one. This notion has been introduced in behavioural modeling [7], but we expanded it to arbitrary modeling languages. Thus, such models with uncertainty can be thought of as "plural". Interestingly, plural models can capture a variety of other SE concepts: products in a product line, models adhering to a metamodel, member models in a megamodel [1]. I further describe how this analogy enables us to lift our uncertainty results to these domains.

Acknowledgements. This is joint work with members of the Modeling Group at the University of Toronto and specifically, with Michalis Famelis, Rick Salay, Alessio DiSandro.

References

1. Bezivin, J., Jouault, F., Valduriez, P.: On the Need for Megamodels. In: Proc. of OOPSLA 2004 Workshop on Best Practices for Model-Driven Soft. Development (2004)
2. Egyed, A., Letier, E., Finkelstein, A.: Generating and Evaluating Choices for Fixing Inconsistencies in UML Design Models. In: Proc. of ASE 2008, pp. 99–108 (2008)
3. Esfahani, N., Kouroshfar, E., Malek, S.: Taming Uncertainty in Self-Adaptive Software. In: Proc. of ESEC/FSE 2011, pp. 234–244 (2011)
4. Garlan, D.: Software Engineering in an Uncertain World. In: Proc. of FoSER 2010, pp. 125–128 (2010)
5. Hinton, A., Kwiatkowska, M., Norman, G., Parker, D.: PRISM: A Tool for Automatic Verification of Probabilistic Systems. In: Hermanns, H., Palsberg, J. (eds.) TACAS 2006. LNCS, vol. 3920, pp. 441–444. Springer, Heidelberg (2006)
6. Islam, S., Houmb, S.: Integrating Risk Management Activities into Requirements Engineering. In: Proc. of RCIS 2010, pp. 299–310 (2010)
7. Larsen, K.G., Thomsen, B.: A Modal Process Logic. In: Proc. of LICS 2088, pp. 203–210 (1988)
8. Mashiyat, A., Famelis, M., Salay, R., Chechik, M.: Using Developer Converstions to Resolve Uncertainty in Software Development: A Position Paper. In: Proc. of ICSE 2014 Workshop on Recommendation Systems for Soft. Eng. (2014)
9. Nentwich, C., Emmerich, W., Finkelstein, A.: Consistency Management with Repair Actions. In: Proc. of ICSE 2003, pp. 455–464 (2003)
10. Noppen, J., van den Broek, P., Aksit, M.: Software Development with Imperfect Information. J. Soft Computing 12(1), 3–28 (2007)
11. Sabetzadeh, M., Nejati, S., Chechik, M., Easterbrook, S.: Reasoning about Consistency in Model Merging. In: Proc. of LWI (2010)
12. Van Der Straeten, R., Pinna Puissant, J., Mens, T.: Assessing the Kodkod Model Finder for Resolving Model Inconsistencies. In: France, R.B., Kuester, J.M., Bordbar, B., Paige, R.F. (eds.) ECMFA 2011. LNCS, vol. 6698, pp. 69–84. Springer, Heidelberg (2011)
13. van Lamsweerde, A.: Requirements Engineering - From System Goals to UML Models to Software Specifications. Wiley (2009)
14. Ziv, H., Richardson, D.J., Klösch, R.: The Uncertainty Principle in Software Engineering (1996)

Under the Hood: Model-Based Development in the Automotive Industry

Darren Buttle

ETAS GmbH
Stuttgart, Germany

Abstract. It is over 30 years since the first car with a programmable microcontroller rolled off the production line and onto the highway. Today's vehicles include an astonishing amount of software. Everything from seemingly trivial applications, such as turning on the trunk light, to more obviously complex applications, such as adaptive cruise control, deliver significant parts of their functionality through software.

The automotive industry was an early convert to model-based software development - it enabled engineers in classical engineering domains to leverage the flexibility and cost reductions that software control promised. By the late 1990's, code generated from physical system models could be found in series production vehicles. Increasing application complexity, coupled with reduced time to market demands, have continued to drive adoption of model-based development. In some vehicle domains, notably power train and chassis control, model-based development is the dominant software development paradigm.

In this talk, we'll look "under the hood" at model-based software development in the automotive industry and consider:

- Where is model-based development used?
- What specific challenges are presented by the domain?
- Which technologies have proven successful?
- What are the current trends and tomorrow's challenges?

We'll draw on our experience as one of the early providers of model-based software development tools and offer our perspective gained from over 20 years or involvement in vehicle projects. Join us for the ride!

Table of Contents

Foundations

Applications

Efficient Model Synchronization
with View Triple Graph Grammars

Anthony Anjorin*, Sebastian Rose, Frederik Deckwerth, and Andy Schürr

Technische Universität Darmstadt
Real-Time Systems Lab.
Merckstr. 25
64283 Darmstadt, Germany
`name.surname@es.tu-darmstadt.de`

Abstract. Model synchronization is a crucial task in the context of Model Driven Engineering. Especially when creating and maintaining multiple suitable abstractions or *views* of a complex system, a *bidirectional transformation* is required to keep all views and the corresponding system synchronized by automatically propagating changes in both directions. Triple Graph Grammars (TGGs) are a declarative, rule-based bidirectional transformation language, which can be used to support model synchronization. In practice, most TGG tools restrict the supported class of TGGs for efficiency reasons. These restrictions are, however, seldom intuitive and are often difficult to understand and adhere to, especially for non-experts. *View* Triple Graph Grammars (VTGGs) are a restricted form of TGGs, which can be highly optimized for efficient view update propagation. We argue that the restrictions posed by VTGGs are explicit and intuitive for users, as they can be adequately motivated based on the main application scenarios for VTGGs. In this paper, we present for the first time a *formalization* of VTGGs, stating precisely the advantages and limitations of VTGGs as compared to TGGs, and backing our claims with initial runtime measurements from a practical case study.

Keywords: model driven engineering, bidirectional model transformation, triple graph grammars, view triple graph grammars.

1 Introduction and Motivation

It is usually impossible to invest the time required to gain a deep understanding of a *complete* system and, therefore, a crucial task is focusing on relevant aspects with task-specific *views*. Although views are crucial for productivity, maintaining a view *manually* is infeasible for most practical applications. Generated, read-only views are also unsatisfactory as an important requirement is being able to apply changes to the underlying system at the level of abstraction provided by

* The project on which this paper is based was funded by the German Federal Ministry of Education and Research, funding code 01IS12054. The authors are responsible for all contents.

J. Cabot and J. Rubin (Eds.): ECMFA 2014, LNCS 8569, pp. 1–17, 2014.

the view. In general, a *bidirectional transformation* is required to keep all views synchronized by automatically propagating *updates* in both directions.

In a *Model-Driven Engineering* (MDE) context, *Triple Graph Grammars* (TGGs) are a rule-based, formally founded bidirectional model transformation language [8], which can be used to keep two different but related models synchronized [8]. TGGs can be used to specify views, but supporting *lightweight*, i.e., simple but very efficient, view update propagation is challenging as no restrictions are made and arbitrary source and target (i.e., view) structures are allowed. In application scenarios where the target model is, however, clearly a *view* of the source, i.e., a true abstraction/simplification, certain restrictions apply naturally to the structure of the view and can be exploited to enable efficient view update propagation. Examples include (i) reducing the complexity of a transformation by applying suitable views, and (ii) using (a chain of) views to provide a common abstraction on different structures, so that the same transformations can be applied to them. In both cases, the subsequent transformations must be able to treat views exactly as normal models, leading naturally to a set of restrictions, e.g., that nodes in the view can be created in any order. In cases where these restrictions apply, *View Triple Graph Grammars* (VTGGs), first introduced by [7], can be used as a restricted form of TGGs to realize truly lightweight views of source structures, which are specially optimized for efficient update propagation.

In practice, all TGG tools we are aware of pose certain restrictions on the class of supported TGGs to guarantee efficient synchronization (depending on the size of changes and not on the size of models). These restrictions are, however, seldom intuitive for users, i.e., are typically technical and cannot be directly motivated from the supported application scenarios. In this paper, we (i) argue that the restrictions for VTGGs are intuitive for users as they are directly connected to their intended usage, (ii) present for the first time a formalization of VTGGs as a restricted form of TGGs, giving straightforward proofs for the expected formal properties according to [8]. Furthermore, we clarify the exact difference between TGGs and VTGGs with a qualitative and quantitative comparison.

Section 2 presents our running example, explaining intuitively how VTGGs can be used for view specification and synchronization. Section 3 compares our approach to related work, Sect. 4 formalizes VTGGs as a restricted form of TGGs, and Sect. 5 provides runtime measurements from our case study. Section 6 concludes with a summary and an overview of future work.

2   Running Example

Our running example is inspired by a real-world project in which a client-server application is developed using the Eclipse Rich Client Platform (RCP) as a basis for the client. An Eclipse RCP ecosystem consists of multiple *plugin projects* (folders in the filesystem) in a *workspace* (the root folder). Figure 1 depicts such a project (Reservation) to the left. Every project contains a source folder src with Java code and other resources (e.g., icons), and a plugin.xml file. All concepts described so far are supported by the standard Java *Package Browser*.

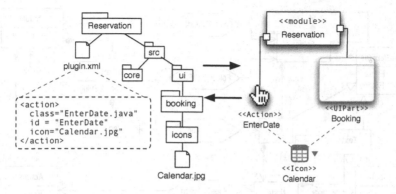

Fig. 1. Example for source and view models in the running example

Some high-level concepts used by developers are depicted to the right of Fig. 1: *Modules* represent business related containers such as the Reservation module, which provides all functionality related to the domain concept "reservation". A module consists of *UI parts*, i.e., aspects relevant for the user interface such as icons and dialogues. Modules also contain units of functionality referred to as *actions*, which can be related with an icon in the user interface, e.g., the EnterDate action, which is visualized with the Calendar icon in the UI part Booking. Note the depicted action fragment in the plugin.xml file and the folder structure, which correspond to the action and the UI part in the Reservation module, respectively. Representing projects using these high-level concepts not only supports communication amongst domain experts, but also provides a compact representation and enforces conventions that hold for all projects/modules.

2.1 Models, Metamodels, and Model Transformation

A *model* is a graph, i.e., a structure consisting of objects and links, with source and target functions connecting links to their source and target objects, respectively. Relationships between models are formalized as graph morphisms, which are structure preserving maps between graphs, i.e., maps that preserve how links are connected to objects. The conformance relationship between a model and its *metamodel* is a graph morphism "type" between one graph (the model) and another graph (the metamodel). Objects and links in metamodels are referred to as *classes* and *associations*, respectively. This algebraic formalization of MDE concepts can be extended to include further details such as type preserving morphisms, attributes (which are also typed), inheritance and abstract classes [6].

The metamodels for our running example are depicted in Fig. 2. The *source metamodel* on the left represents a simple tree structure, which can be extracted from an Eclipse project using standard parsers to produce trees from the folder structure and the different files. Concepts include, therefore, Folders, Files, and labelled Nodes with Attributes. On the right, the *view metamodel* represents the high-level concepts: Modules and Actions that reference Icons in a UIPart. The metamodel in the middle is referred to as the *correspondence metamodel* as it

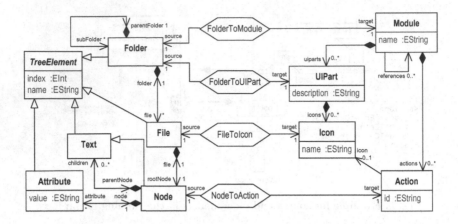

Fig. 2. Triple of metamodels for the running example

states which source and target elements correspond to each other. Note that correspondence types are depicted as hexagons only to improve readability.

A *model transformation* takes an input model M_I and produces an output model M_O. In a rule-based approach, this is formalized as *applying* a transformation *rule* r to the input model M_I. The rule $r = (L, R)$ consists of a precondition L and a postcondition R, which are both *patterns* that have to be mapped to actual model elements when applying the rule. The result of this mapping is referred to as a *match*. If a match $m(L) \subseteq M_I$ can be determined for the precondition L in the input model M_I, the rule r can be applied by replacing the precondition by the postcondition to yield the output model M_O.

2.2   View Specification with VTGG Rules

The formalization of rule-based model transformation mentioned above can be extended to *triples* of models, i.e., the precondition L and postcondition R of rules are triples of source, correspondence and target patterns. Such triple rules are referred to as *VTGG rules*, which specify a view by describing how the view model evolves *together* with related correspondence and source models.

The first step in specifying a view with a VTGG is to describe what it means to instantiate all concrete classes in the view metamodel, i.e., to create objects in the view. Such rules are referred to as *class rules* and exactly one class rule is required for every concrete (non-abstract) class in the view metamodel. Let us refer to this requirement as *Restriction 1*. Figure 3 depicts the class rules for the running example using a compact notation that combines L and R in the following manner: *Created* elements (green with a ++ stereotype) are created by the rule to fulfil the postcondition, i.e., are in $R \setminus L$, while *context* elements (black without any stereotype) constitute the precondition L. Regard the rule ModuleRule, which states that creating a module in the view corresponds to creating a root folder (folder) with an XML file (plugin, root) and a source folder structure (srcFolder, core, ui). Simple attribute conditions can be in-lined in nodes such

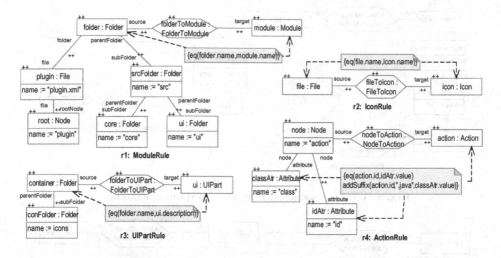

Fig. 3. VTGG class rules for the running example

as name:="plugin" in root, or specified with a separate, bidirectional constraint language such as for eq(folder.name, module.name), which can be extended to include complex user-defined constraints [1]. VTGG class rules only create elements without demanding any context, meaning that view objects can always be created in any order. Let us refer to this requirement as *Restriction 2*.

After defining how view objects can be created, the next step in the process is to describe what it means to *connect* existing view objects, i.e., to create *links* in the view by instantiating associations in the view metamodel. Such rules are referred to as *association rules* and exactly one association rule is required for every association in the view metamodel. This is an extension of *Restriction 1*.

Figure 4 depicts the association rules for the running example. In contrast to class rules, association rules contain context elements (black without any stereotype), which must have already been created with other rules before the association rule can be applied (precondition must be fulfilled). Association rules are only allowed to augment the view by creating a link between two existing view objects. For example, ModuleUIPartRule connects a Module with a UIPart. In the source model, association rules can create an arbitrary structure as long as the required context follows from the existence of the view objects. For ModuleUIPartRule, this means that the required folder structure (folder, srcFolder, uiFolder) and container folder are guaranteed to exist as they are created together with module and ui by the corresponding class rules. This is an extension of *Restriction 2*. The complete specification comprises two further association rules, r_7 and r_8, for the remaining two associations in the view metamodel.

As the view is typically an abstraction of the source, the final step is to specify in exactly what ways the source can evolve *without* affecting the view. These rules are referred to as *idle rules* and can either be *class idle* or *association idle*, depending on the required context. Figure 5 depicts two idle rules for the running example. IdleModuleRule is an idle class rule and allows the addition of

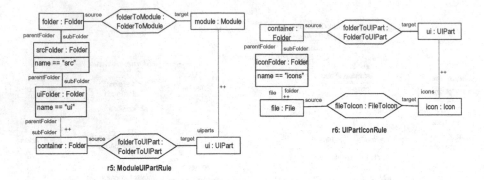

Fig. 4. VTGG association rules for the running example

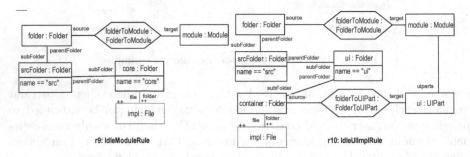

Fig. 5. VTGG idle rules for the running example

arbitrarily many implementation files to the core source folder without affecting the view in any way. Idle class rules can only require context provided by a class rule, implying that the created elements (impl in the case of IdleModuleRule) must be deleted together with the required view object (module). IdleUIImplRule is an idle association rule, which allows the addition of implementation files for a UIPart. Idle association rules can require context provided by an association rule, and in this way, IdleUIImpRule enforces that a UIPart can only be implemented if it is already part of a module. This has consequences that should be discussed with domain experts, e.g., the implementation of a UIPart must be deleted as soon as it is detached from its Module in the view to retain consistency.

2.3   Model Synchronization with VTGGs

To explain intuitively how VTGGs can be used for synchronization, Fig. 6(a) depicts a source model with a corresponding view model, both annotated with labels to denote VTGG rule applications. Fig. 6(b) depicts the corresponding rule application *dependency* graph, which is used to explain the synchronization algorithm. The following concrete scenario could have led to this triple: A user started with a source model consisting of a root folder Reservation with a plugin.xml file and src, src/core and src/ui subfolders. The user now decides to create

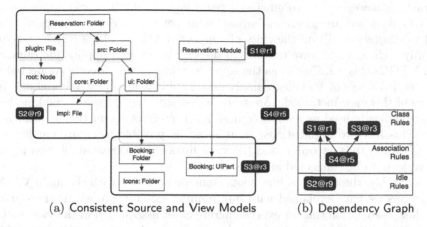

(a) Consistent Source and View Models   (b) Dependency Graph

Fig. 6. Exemplary transformation sequence for the running example

a view model via a *forward transformation*, i.e., a source-to-view transformation, which parses the source structure and creates a Reservation module in the view. This first step (S1) is consistent with the application of the VTGG rule r1 in the simultaneous build-up and the result is labelled with S1@r1 in Fig. 6(a). The user now adds an implementation file to the core folder and updates the view by repeating the forward transformation. The source structure is parsed as S1@r1, S2@r9, meaning that the view remains unchanged (S2@r9 is an application of an idle class rule and does not change the view). The user now creates a UIPart in the view named Booking and adds it to the Reservation module. These view updates are reflected in the source model via a *backward transformation*, i.e., a view-to-source transformation, which creates the corresponding source structure resulting in a triple now consistent with the rule application sequence S1@r1, S2@r9, S3@r3, S4@r5. Finally, the user deletes the Reservation module from the view. This view update is propagated using the rule application dependency graph (Fig. 6(b)). To "reverse" S1@r1 (i.e., to delete the Reservation module), all dependent rule applications have to be recursively reversed first. This means that S2@r9 (all implementation files in the core folder), as well as S4@r5 (all incident links in the view) must be reversed first, resulting in a triple consistent with S3@r3. Due to the restricted structure of VTGG rules, the dependency graph always consists of three levels as depicted in Fig. 6(b). Changes in the view are thus guaranteed by construction to have a "local" influence (to only affect dependent rule applications on lower levels).

2.4 VTGG as Restricted TGGs

Based on our example, we can now list and discuss (for now informally, cf. Sect. 4.2 for the formalization) the main restrictions posed by VTGGs. Theoretically, TGGs can be used directly (without any restrictions) to specify views.

In practice, however, due to efficiency requirements of real-world applications, all TGG tools we are aware of impose some set of restrictions (typically related to *confluence* [6]) on the class of supported TGGs. These restrictions are typically technical and have nothing to do with a focussed application domain. With VTGGs this is different, as the set of restrictions are directly connected to the intended usage of VTGGs, namely establishing a *new* view metamodel. Instances of this view metamodel are to be indistinguishable from normal models, and are typically used as a suitable high-level interface for further transformations. This has two implications: (i) it must be possible to create single view objects in an arbitrary order, and (ii) view links can be created as soon as the view objects to be connected are present.

Remarkably, these core requirements coincide perfectly with the main VTGG restrictions we have explained with our running example so far: (i) there must be a class/association rule for every concrete class/association in the view metamodel (Restriction 1), and (ii) class rules do not require context elements, while association rules only demand context guaranteed by the class rules for the corresponding source and target classes of the association in the view. A consequence is that association rules cannot depend on other association rules (Restriction 2). Both restrictions are exploited to control ripple effects of update propagation, i.e., VTGG rule dependency graphs always consist of three levels with dependencies allowed only to lower levels. The corresponding limitation of VTGGs, compared to TGGs, is that every instance of the view metamodel can be generated by the VTGG, i.e., the user has no means of constraining the induced view language in any way. VTGGs are, therefore, not suitable when this is required.

A further optimization employed by VTGGs follows from the fact that the view language is being newly specified and that it is thus allowed to add extra technical references as required to the view metamodel. In stark contrast, TGGs aim to be non-invasive and can be used for existing and unchangeable metamodels. Being able to manipulate the view metamodel means that the extra correspondence model can be reduced to a set of references leading directly from view to source elements. This is a technical point and has no effect on the formalization but is still an important VTGG restriction/optimization with a substantial effect on efficiency. Finally, as there are no idle view rules, the view can always be created from the source. This indicates a clear focus on optimizing the backward propagation (propagating changes to the view), which is greatly simplified and can be efficiently implemented as the structure of all rules on the view side is kept very simple. Forward propagation can be realized with a standard TGG algorithm either in batch (the view is re-created completely from scratch) or incremental mode (the old view is updated). We do not aim to replace TGGs and an ideal combination would be to use VTGGs as a preprocessing step for TGGs, i.e., to retrieve high-level views of low-level source and target models, before using TGGs to synchronize the views, leading to clearer, more concise TGG rules. In general, although VTGGs limit expressiveness (the language of allowed view models cannot be restricted, e.g., the running example would not be a VTGG if the roles of view and source were swapped), they provide an efficient means of simplifying (modularizing) TGG or standard graph transformation rules that can operate on these views exactly as if they were normal, stand-alone models.

3   Related Work

In this section, we classify related approaches into three main groups corresponding to the following questions:(1) How is our approach to VTGGs different from that of [7]? (2) What connections and parallels exist to the *Asymmetric Delta Lens* (ADL) framework? (3) How does the alternative definition of views in the algebraic graph transformation framework compare to ours?, and (4) What other view specification approaches, less related to VTGGs, exist?

(1) Materialized vs. Non-materialized Views: The basic idea of VTGGs for the specification of views is introduced in [7]. The *class adapter* pattern, employed by [7], alters the *source metamodel*, introducing inheritance relationships so that certain source elements can additionally take on the role of view elements. Although this enables efficient memory usage via *non-materialized views*, i.e., views that do not exist as separate models but are rather represented as an additional *role* taken on by certain elements in the source model, it complicates view composition as it is unclear how to successively adjust the inheritance relationships appropriately. In contrast to [7], our approach uses the *object adapter* pattern, maintaining our view as a lightweight wrapper for the source model. Our approach results in *materialized views*, i.e., a separate view model, and is a good compromise as the views can still be kept lightweight, e.g., by keeping all attribute values in the source model and computing attribute values for the view on demand. Furthermore, in contrast to [7], we provide a constructive formalization of VTGGs in the context of TGGs [8], which is useful as a basis for concrete VTGG implementations.

(2) Connections to the ADL Framework: Compared to (V)TGGs, the Asymmetric Data Lens (ADL) framework [4] is a more generic and abstract formalization of bidirectional transformations. The framework captures the intuitively expected behaviour of views with a set of *lens laws*. Due to its generality, it offers a formal foundation that can be used to draw parallels between very different approaches. This higher level of abstraction is, however, not only an advantage as it is impossible to formulate, e.g., a precise notion of efficiency such as in the TGG framework. For the reader versed in both frameworks, the following points give a brief overview of connections and differences:

1. The "sanity" laws from the ADL framework (incidence and identity preservation) are fulfilled for (V)TGGs by exploiting the correspondence model and do not have to be demanded explicitly.
2. Correctness for (V)TGGs corresponds to *PutGet* (correctness of backward propagation) in the ADL framework and is also used to fulfil the compositional laws. (V)TGG are, however, potentially more flexible (non-functional) and **get** is allowed to be a relation and not a function (there can be multiple consistent triples for the same source model).

3. Completeness for (V)TGGs is implicitly demanded in the ADL framework by requiring totality for **get** and **put** on the source and view model spaces.
4. Further (V)TGG properties such as efficiency or expressiveness are irrelevant in the abstract ADL setting.

(3) Views in the Algebraic Graph Transformation Framework: The algebraic graph transformation framework of [6] is extended and generalized in [5], defining typed graph morphisms between *different* type graphs and *different* data signatures, used to specify the direct connection between a view and its corresponding source. In contrast, our TGG-based formalization uses correspondence elements, i.e., a separate model, to formally specify the connection between view and source. A view itself is, therefore, not the direct result of a transformation rule, but is defined by the rules of the VTGG and the induced consistency relation. Although [5] provides the basis for a potentially simpler formalization of view specification frameworks, our TGG-based approach can make use of the substantial existing TGG formalization, and can be realized as an extension/adaptation of our existing TGG implementation.

(4) Other Approaches to View Specification: The need for views in an MDE context has led to an Eclipse project *EMF Facet*[1] that allows the specification of queries on models using Java or XPath. Compared to our rule-based, declarative VTGG approach, such queries in Java / XPath are often rather low-level and the derived EMF facet views are read-only. With a clear focus on modularity, views are used in [11] to hide details and to establish interfaces between modules. The main motivation is the modelling of large and distributed systems, where dependencies are to be reduced as much as possible. Although VTGGs can also be used for modularization and defining interfaces, our main motivation is rather to provide an efficient suitable abstraction for further manipulation with TGGs or normal graph transformations. Compared to [11], views with VTGGs are specified with an explicit set of declarative rules, while [11] uses a high-level mapping from which required transformations for the view are automatically derived. The latter is, consequently, on a more abstract level but is less expressive. In the domain of database engineering, specifying a view as a set of queries is a mature and established practice with a solid formal foundation [3]. In other domains, bidirectional programming languages [12], as well as lens implementations for strings [2] are used to support view specification. As a realization of the *viewpoint* framework presented in [10], Xlinkit [9] provides a declarative, rule-based means of specifying views on XML files. In an MDE context, however, where typed graph structures are used as models, approaches such as TGGs/VTGGs, which directly support *graph patterns* in rules are probably more natural/intuitive for view specification.

4   Formalization of VTGGs as Restricted TGGs

A *VTGG* consists of a triple of metamodels (e.g., Fig. 2) and a set of triple rules (e.g., Fig. 3, Fig. 4, and Fig. 5), which describe the *simultaneous evolution* of

---

[1] http://www.eclipse.org/proposals/emf-facet/

triples of source, correspondence and view models. This induces a *consistency relation* in the following manner: A pair of source and view models are consistent, if and only if a triple consisting of the source and view models connected with a *correspondence model* can be created using rules in the VTGG.

This consistency relation is used to automatically derive *operational* transformations that support incrementally propagating changes to the view back to the source and vice-versa. As VTGGs are designed to optimize the *incremental backward transformation* (view to source), we shall concentrate on this in the following. All other operational transformations can be derived as for standard TGGs and we refer to [8] for arguments concerning formal properties that also apply to VTGGs, which are TGGs with additional restrictions.

After introducing necessary fundamentals on TGGs, we shall first formulate precisely the set of structural restrictions on VTGG rules, and then use these restrictions to argue formal properties of incremental view updates with VTGGs.

4.1 Preliminaries

In the following, we consider VTGGs as TGGs with a set of restrictions on the set of rules. There exists a rich formal foundation for TGGs based on algebraic graph transformation [6] and we refer to, e.g., [8] for further details.

Triple Graph Grammar: A $TGG = (\mathcal{M}, \mathcal{R})$ consists of a triple of meta-models (source, correspondence and target) $\mathcal{M}$, and a set $\mathcal{R}$ of rules. Each rule $r = (L, R) \in \mathcal{R}$, $L \subseteq R$ consists of a precondition L and postcondition R, both being triples of source, correspondence and target patterns. As explained in Sect. 2, a rule is applied by mapping the precondition to elements in an input model, i.e., determining a match, which is replaced with the postcondition.

Formal Properties of TGGs: TGG rules describe the simultaneous evolution of triples of models but can be operationalized and used to derive unidirectional forward (source to target) and backward (target to source) transformations. The TGG is also used as a contract that stipulates the expected behaviour of the bidirectional transformation realized with the forward and backward transformations derived from the TGG [8]. In the following we only formulate the laws for the incremental backward transformation as this is what is optimized for VTGGs and must thus be shown to be sound:

Correctness: Correctness demands that the derived backward transformation only creates *consistent* triples, i.e., triples that can be generated by the TGG.

Given a $TGG = (\mathcal{M}, \mathcal{R})$, where $\mathcal{M} = \mathcal{M}_S \leftarrow \mathcal{M}_C \rightarrow \mathcal{M}_T$, let $\mathcal{L}(TGG)$ denote the set of all models that can be derived using rules in $\mathcal{R}$, and $\mathcal{L}(\mathcal{M})$ the set of all model triples that conform to the metamodel triple $\mathcal{M}$.

Let Δ_T denote the set of *all supported changes* $\delta_T = M_T \leftarrow M_T^- \rightarrow M_T^+ \in \Delta_T$, which can be applied to a source model M_T by deleting all elements in $M_T \setminus M_T^-$ and adding all elements in $M_T^+ \setminus M_T^-$.

Let $BT : \mathcal{L}(TGG) \times \Delta_T \rightarrow \mathcal{L}(\mathcal{M})$ denote the *incremental* backward transformation derived from the TGG, a partial function which maps a model triple

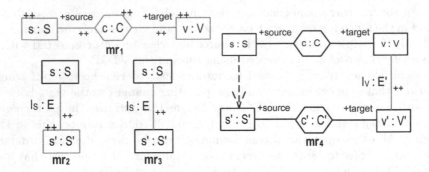

Fig. 7. Meta-rules used to specify the allowed structure of VTGG rules

$M_S \leftarrow M_C \rightarrow M_T \in \mathcal{L}(TGG)$, and a change to the target model $\delta_T = M_T \leftarrow M_T^- \rightarrow M_T^+ \in \Delta_T$, to an updated triple $M'_S \leftarrow M'_C \rightarrow M_T^+ \in \mathcal{L}(\mathcal{M})$.

BT is *correct* iff it produces model triples in $\mathcal{L}(TGG)$, i.e., $range(BT) \subseteq \mathcal{L}(TGG)$.

Completeness: As a backward transformation can be trivially correct by rejecting all input, it is important to demand completeness, i.e., that the derived backward transformation be able to handle *every* input for which there exists a consistent output, i.e, an appropriate triple in $\mathcal{L}(TGG)$.

BT is *complete* iff $\forall M_S \leftarrow M_C \rightarrow M_T \in \mathcal{L}(TGG), \forall M_T \leftarrow M_T^- \rightarrow M_T^+ \in \Delta_T,$ $\exists M'_S \leftarrow M'_C \rightarrow M_T^+ \in \mathcal{L}(TGG) \Rightarrow BT(M, \delta_T) \in \mathcal{L}(\mathcal{M})$ is defined.

Efficiency: An *incremental transformation BT* that propagates a source model change by changing the target model incrementally, is efficient if its runtime is independent of the size of the models and depends only on the scope of influence of the change, i.e., all elements that must be re-translated due to the change.

4.2   VTGGs as Restricted TGGs

Given a $TGG = (\mathcal{M} = \mathcal{M}_S \leftarrow \mathcal{M}_C \rightarrow \mathcal{M}_T, \mathcal{R})$, let the target metamodel $\mathcal{M}_T$ be referred to in the following as the *view metamodel*, denoted as $\mathcal{M}_V$. To define the allowed structure of VTGG rules, Fig. 7 depicts four *meta-rules* mr_1 – mr_4. These meta-rules will be used as building blocks to construct the allowed patterns that comprise VTGG rules, substituting the types S, S' with types from the source metamodel, V, V' with types from the view metamodel, and C, C' with types from the correspondence metamodel as required. Meta-rules are depicted using the compact notation (merging L and R), while the actual rules generated by applying meta-rules are built up explicitly by specifying L and R separately.

For a meta-rule mr, let $\mathcal{L}(mr)$ denote the set of triples that can be generated by applying mr on the empty triple (denoted as $\emptyset$) with types from $\mathcal{M}$, i.e.: $\mathcal{L}(mr) = \{M \in \mathcal{L}(\mathcal{M}) \mid \emptyset \overset{mr}{\Rightarrow} M\}$. Given a model M that conforms to a metamodel $\mathcal{M}$, i.e., $M \in \mathcal{L}(\mathcal{M})$, let $M \vdash mr$ mean that M is syntactically defined by mr, i.e., that $M \in \mathcal{L}(mr)$. Furthermore, for meta-rules mr and mr', let

$mr \cdot mr' : \mathcal{L}(mr \cdot mr') = \{M' \in \mathcal{L}(\mathcal{M}) \mid \emptyset \stackrel{mr}{\Rightarrow} M \stackrel{mr'}{\Rightarrow} M'\}$ denote their composition. Finally, let mr^* denote an arbitrary composition of mr, i.e., $mr \cdot \ldots \cdot mr$. We now use this notation to define VTGG rules in the following.

$r = (L_C, R_C)$ is a *class rule*[2] iff $L_C = \emptyset, R_C \vdash cr_R$, where:

$$cr_R := mr_1 \cdot mr_2^* \cdot mr_3 \tag{1}$$

$r = (L_A, R_A)$ is an *association rule* iff $L_A \vdash ar_L, R_A \vdash ar_R$, where:

$$ar_L := cr_R \cdot cr_R, \quad ar_R := ar_L \cdot mr_4 \cdot mr_2^* \cdot mr_3^* \tag{2}$$

The dashed arrow in mr_4 is used to demand that s and s' must be connected by some path in the view model for mr_4 to be applicable.

$r = (L_{IC}, R_{IC})$ is an idle *class rule* iff $L_{IC} \vdash icr_L, R_{IC} \vdash icr_R$, where:

$$icr_L := cr_R, \quad icr_R := icr_L \cdot mr_2^* \cdot mr_3^* \tag{3}$$

$r = (L_{IA}, R_{IA})$ is an *idle association rule* iff $L_{IA} \vdash iar_L, R_{IA} \vdash iar_R$, where:

$$iar_L := ar_R, \quad iar_R := iar_L \cdot mr_2^* \cdot mr_3^* \tag{4}$$

A $VTGG = (\mathcal{M}_S \leftarrow \mathcal{M}_C \rightarrow \mathcal{M}_V, \mathcal{R})$ is a TGG with the following restrictions:

1. Every rule $r \in \mathcal{R}$ is either a class rule, an association rule, or is idle.
2. There is exactly one class rule for every non-abstract view class.
3. There is exactly one association rule for every association in the view metamodel and the context required by the association rule must be guaranteed by the class rules of the source and target classes of the association. Formally, with $r_A = (L_A, R_A)$ an association rule as defined above, and $\uplus$ denoting the disjoint union of graphs:

$$\forall (L_A, R_A) \in \mathcal{R}, \exists (L_C, R_C) \in \mathcal{R}, \exists (L_C', R_C') \in \mathcal{R} : L_A \subseteq R_C \uplus R_C' \tag{5}$$

4. The context required by every idle class rule must be guaranteed by the corresponding class rule:

$$\forall (L_{IC}, R_{IC}) \in \mathcal{R}, \exists (L_C, R_C) \in \mathcal{R} : L_{IC} \subseteq R_C \tag{6}$$

5. The context required by every idle association rule must be guaranteed by the corresponding association rule:

$$\forall (L_{IA}, R_{IA}) \in \mathcal{R}, \exists (L_A, R_A) \in \mathcal{R} : L_{IA} \subseteq R_A \tag{7}$$

6. When actually applying association and idle rules in a transformation sequence, only the context guaranteed by (5), (6) and (7) can be used.

Example: After defining the set of VTGG restrictions, we can consider our running example and check if the restrictions hold. The rules depicted in Fig. 3 are indeed class rules as they can be constructed according to (1). For instance, for $r_1 = (L_{r_1}, R_{r_1})$, $L_{r_1} = \emptyset$ and $R_{r_1} \vdash mr_1 \cdot mr_2 \cdot mr_2 \vdash cr_R$. Similarly, the rules depicted in Fig. 4 are association rules as they can be constructed according to (2). For instance, for $r_6 = (L_{r_6}, R_{r_6})$, $L_{r_6} \vdash (mr_1 \cdot mr_2) \cdot mr_1 \vdash cr_R \cdot cr_R \vdash ar_L$ and $R_{r_6} \vdash ar_L \cdot mr_4 \cdot mr_3 \vdash ar_R$. Furthermore, $L_{r_6} \subseteq R_{r_3} \uplus R_{r_2}$ as required

---

[2] Note that $L_C \subseteq R_C$ must hold as a class rule is a rule.

by (5). Finally, the rules in Fig. 5 are idle as they can be constructed according to (3) and (4). For instance, for $r_9 = (L_{r_9}, R_{r_9})$, $L_{r_9} \vdash cr_R \vdash icr_L$ and $R_{r_9} \vdash icr_R \cdot mr_2 \vdash icr_R$. Furthermore, $L_{r_9} \subseteq R_{r_1}$ as required by (6).

VTGGs Are Correct: To show correctness for VTGGs, we have to prove that incremental view updates (view to source) via BT_{VTGG}, denoting the optimized incremental backward transformation for VTGGs, are consistent with the VTGG. For a given model triple $M = M_S \leftarrow M_C \rightarrow M_V \in \mathcal{L}(VTGG)$ and a change to the view $\delta_V \in \Delta_V$, we do this constructively by stating how the following cases (corresponding to the four types of supported changes) must be handled:

(1) Object Creation: As there must exist exactly one class rule r_V for every class V in the view metamodel, creating an object o_V of type V in the view corresponds to applying r_V to create o_V and the corresponding source structure as defined in the rule. As the given model triple M is in $\mathcal{L}(VTGG)$, there exists a sequence of VTGG rule applications $r_1, r_2, \ldots, r_k$ that can be used to create M. As the class rule r_V, according to (1), is of the form $(\emptyset, R_V)$ it is independent of all other rules and can be applied to extend the sequence to $M' = r_1, r_2, \ldots, r_k, r_V$. The resulting model triple M' is, therefore, in $\mathcal{L}(VTGG)$ and is consistent.

(2) Link Creation: As there must exist exactly one association rule r_A for every association A in the view metamodel, creating a link l_A of type A in the view model between two objects o_V and $o_{V'}$ of type V and V', respectively, corresponds to applying the association rule r_A. As o_V and $o_{V'}$ already exist in the view, they can only have been created by applying the corresponding class rules r_V and $r_{V'}$, respectively. As the VTGG restriction (2) guarantees that the required context (which *must* be used!) for applying r_A is implied by the applications of r_V and $r_{V'}$, the sequence of rule applications $M = r_1, \ldots, r_V, \ldots, r_{V'}, \ldots, r_k$ is extended to $M' = r_1, \ldots, r_V, \ldots, r_{V'}, \ldots, r_k, r_A$, implying correctness. Note that r_A is only allowed to depend on r_V and $r_{V'}$.

(3) Link Deletion: To correctly propagate deletion of a link l_A in the view model, the *scope of influence* of the change must be determined. In the case of link deletion, only idle association rule applications r_{IA} can depend on source elements created by the corresponding association rule r_A according to (4). As no other rule applications can depend on idle association rule applications, the latter can be safely reverted by deleting all created elements in the source. After reverting all dependent idle association rule applications, the link deletion can be propagated by reverting the application of the association rule r_A, deleting the link in the view and the corresponding source structure. The remaining sequence of rule applications is valid (a possible sequence of VTGG rule applications).

(4) Object Deletion: The scope of influence of deleting an object in the view comprises all association rule applications that created incident links to the deleted object and all idle class rule applications that require the deleted object as context. To delete an object in the view, therefore, all incident links must be deleted and appropriately propagated to the source model according to *Link*

Deletion, then all dependent idle class rule applications are reverted, before finally reverting the class rule application used to create the object to be deleted. As all dependent rule applications are thus reverted, the remaining sequence of rule applications is valid and propagation of object deletion is correct.

VTGGs Are Complete: The four cases distinguished above also define Δ_T, the set of supported changes to the view. As the arguments for correctness describe constructively how the allowed changes are to be propagated for an arbitrary model triple, it follows that *every* allowed change can be propagated successfully in this manner. BT_{VTGG} is, therefore, complete.

VTGGs Are Efficient: BT_{VTGG} is efficient, as the VTGG restrictions guarantee a local scope of influence (defined above for correctness of BT_{VTGG}). Propagating changes, therefore, depends only on elements in the scope of influence of the change, which is, by construction, independent of the size of the models.

5   Runtime Measurements

Our runtime results, depicted in Fig. 8, were obtained by measuring the time required to create and add a UIPart to randomly generated view models of increasing size (1000 – 30,000 elements). The VTGG rules for our running example were used to generate a TGG batch transformation (blue curve), a TGG-based synchronizer (red curve), and a VTGG-based implementation, all with the same model transformation tool eMoflon (`www.emoflon.org`). The exact same update was executed 11 times (the median is shown in the plot) for each model size on a PC with an Intel(R) Core(TM)2 Duo 2.53GHz CPU, and 8GB RAM, running Windows 7 (64 Bit), Oracle JDK 1.7.007 and Eclipse 4.3.1. Although this is only one rather simple example with only a handful of rules, our results nonetheless

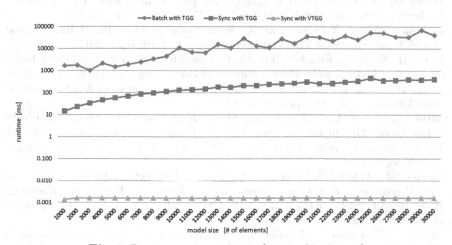

Fig. 8. Runtime measurements for running example

indicate that VTGGs have the potential of being magnitudes (μs as compared to ms for 30,000 elements) faster than the current standard TGG synchronization implemented according to [8]. Even more importantly, VTGGs are truly efficient in the sense of [8], meaning that the time required for synchronization is completely independent of the actual models size.

6   Conclusion and Future Work

In this paper we have formalized a view specification framework based on VTGGs. Motivated with a simplified but real-world application, we explained the necessary restrictions that enable an efficient implementation. Implementation details of our current VTGG implementation concerning, e.g., auxiliary data required to track rule dependencies and revert rule applications correctly and efficiently, detecting changes to the view via an appropriate notification framework, and the operationalization of attribute conditions in VTGG rules were out-of-scope for this paper and are currently being investigated and evaluated in detail. Possible extensions for VTGGs include: (i) reducing restrictions on class and association rules as a trade-off between expressiveness and formal guarantees, (ii) integrating ideas from [7] to support non-materialized views in cases where this is required, and (iii) extending our concept of views to other aspects such as methods.

References

1. Anjorin, A., Varró, G., Schürr, A.: Complex Attribute Manipulation in TGGs with Constraint-Based Programming Techniques. In: BX 2012. ECEASST, vol. 49, pp. 1–15. EASST (2012)
2. Bohannon, A., Foster, J., Pierce, B., Pilkiewicz, A., Schmitt, A.: Boomerang: Resourceful Lenses for String Data. ACM SIGPLAN Notices 43(1), 407–419 (2008)
3. Bohannon, A., Pierce, B.C., Vaughan, J.A.: Relational Lenses: A Language for Updatable Views. In: PODS 2006, pp. 338–347. ACM (2006)
4. Diskin, Z., Xiong, Y., Czarnecki, K.: From State- to Delta-Based Bidirectional Model Transformations: The Asymmetric Case. JOT 10, 1–25 (2011)
5. Ehrig, H., Ehrig, K., Ermel, C., Prange, U.: Consistent Integration of Models based on Views of Meta Models. Formal Aspects of Computing 22(3-4), 327–344 (2010)
6. Ehrig, H., Ehrig, K., Prange, U., Taentzer, G.: Fundamentals of Algebraic Graph Transformation, 1st edn. Springer (2006)
7. Jakob, J., Königs, A., Schürr, A.: Non-Materialized Model View Specification with Triple Graph Grammars. In: Corradini, A., Ehrig, H., Montanari, U., Ribeiro, L., Rozenberg, G. (eds.) ICGT 2006. LNCS, vol. 4178, pp. 321–335. Springer, Heidelberg (2006)
8. Lauder, M., Anjorin, A., Varró, G., Schürr, A.: Efficient Model Synchronization with Precedence Triple Graph Grammars. In: Ehrig, H., Engels, G., Kreowski, H.-J., Rozenberg, G. (eds.) ICGT 2012. LNCS, vol. 7562, pp. 401–415. Springer, Heidelberg (2012)
9. Nentwich, C., Capra, L., Emmerich, W., Finkelstein, A.: Xlinkit: A Consistency Checking and Smart Link Generation Service. ACM Transactions on Internet Technology 2(2), 151–185 (2002)

10. Nuseibeh, B., Kramer, J., Finkelstein, A.: ViewPoints: Meaningful Relationships are Difficult!. In: Clarke, L.A., Dillon, L., Tichy, F.W. (eds.) ICSE 2003, pp. 676–683. IEEE (2003)
11. Ranger, U., Gruber, K., Holze, M.: Defining Abstract Graph Views as Module Interfaces. In: Schürr, A., Nagl, M., Zündorf, A. (eds.) AGTIVE 2007. LNCS, vol. 5088, pp. 120–135. Springer, Heidelberg (2008)
12. Yokoyama, T., Axelsen, H., Glück, R.: Principles of a Reversible Programming Language. In: Ramírez, A., Bilardi, G., Gschwind, M. (eds.) CF 2008, pp. 43–54. ACM (2008)

Level-Agnostic Designation of Model Elements

Colin Atkinson and Ralph Gerbig

University of Mannheim, Germany
{atkinson,gerbig}@informatik.uni-mannheim.de

Abstract. A large proportion of the domain information conveyed in models is contained in the model element "designators" — the characterizing and identifying textual expressions appearing in the headers of model element visualizations. However, the notational support for representing such designators is usually non-uniform, incomplete and sensitive to the classification level at which a model element resides. Moreover, the relationship between the "names" in a model element's designator and the values of its linguistic and ontological attributes is often unclear. In the paper we present a simple but powerful Element Designation Notation (EDN) which allows the key information characterizing model elements to be expressed in a compact, uniform and level-agnostic way for the purposes of deep modeling. This not only simplifies and enriches the designation possibilities in traditional modeling scenarios, it paves the way for more expressive models of big data in which the location of data elements within the three key hierarchies — classification, containment and specialization — can be clearly and concisely expressed.

Keywords: Deep modeling, designation, level-agnostic modeling language, linguistic classification, ontological classification.

1 Introduction

The expressiveness of the textual information contained in the "headers" of model elements has a major impact on the overall quality of graphical models and their ability to convey domain information effectively. In general, the header of a model element is the dominant compartment that characterizes or "designates" it in a particular diagram. Often it is the only compartment appearing in a model element's visualization. The most common piece of information used to designate a model element is its local "name", but often other information is also included such as the element's type or Fully Qualified Name (FQN) — the local name prefixed by the element's location in the containment hierarchy.

Despite the importance of designation, the approaches used to designate model elements in today's visual modeling languages have three significant weaknesses. The first is their limited support for representing certain important kinds of characterizing information. More specifically, although today's modeling languages often allow a model element's type and/or FQN to be represented, none provides support for describing a model element's heritage (i.e. what it inherits from). The second weakness is that even when languages do provide support for

J. Cabot and J. Rubin (Eds.): ECMFA 2014, LNCS 8569, pp. 18–34, 2014.
© Springer International Publishing Switzerland 2014

expressing characterizing information beyond a model element's name, they do so in a non-uniform and level-dependent way. For example, the UML uses the ":" notation to label the type of a model element representing an "instance specification" but uses the guillemet notation to label the types of classes and meta classes (i.e. using stereotypes). The third weakness is that even though model element "names" are the most common and fundamental component of designators, it is often not clear exactly what the name of a model element actually is. For example, does the "name" of a model element given in its designator have to be the same as its linguistic name attribute, or can information from other "characterizing" attributes be used?

As long as models are fairly small and simple, these weaknesses do not cause a big problem because modelers are able to maintain a mental picture of the overall structure of a model and interpret each model element in terms of the memorized context. However, as soon as models start to become larger and more complex, and the information within them no longer fits within reasonably sized diagrams and/or packages, the lack of an effective designation approach significantly reduces a modeling language's ability to communicate information. This problem is evident when reading the UML 2.0 specification [13], for example, where it is notoriously difficult for modelers to keep a mental track of a meta model element's position in the inheritance and containment (i.e. package nesting) hierarchies, and thus of the cumulative set of properties it possesses. With the growing trend towards larger and more complex models in the context of big and linked data, the need to concisely and precisely characterize model elements will grow, and powerful designation notations will become increasingly important for the effective visualization of information.

In this paper we present a small notation, known as the Element Designation Notation (EDN), specially designed to support the presentation of designation information in the headers of model element visualizations. The notation is not limited to, or dependent on, one particular host modeling language, but deliberately aims to be compatible with the designation conventions of established mainstream languages such as UML, ORM [9] or ER Models [9]. Moreover, the notation is "level-agnostic" in that it is uniform across all ontological classification levels. In other words, the same notation is used to express classification, inheritance and containment information regardless of whether the model element represents an instance, a class or a meta class. This property is most advantageous when designating model elements in a level-agnostic modeling language such as the LML [3], but also simplifies designation in traditional languages such as the UML which squeeze multiple ontological levels into one linguistic level [5].

The remainder of this paper is structured as follows. In the next section we motivate the need for improved designation using extracts from the UML specification and introduce a small example to illustrate the UML's weaknesses. We then proceed in section 3 to describe our proposed designation approach in terms of the examples introduced previously. In the section following that, section 4, we show how the notation can be used in a deep modeling scenario. Finally we close with future work and conclusions in section 5.

2   Model Element Designation

Generally speaking, the designator appearing in the header compartment of a model element visualization serves to "name" the model element and distinguish it from others. However, these names are usually not just arbitrary unique strings. In the real world, the names used to designate objects often contain information characterizing their contextual relationship to other objects. For example, in most natural languages, human surnames often describe the nature of the work performed by the person, e.g. Smith (heritage) and in some languages it is common for surnames to describe where a person is from, e.g. "von Bremen" (containment). Moreover the convention of assigning given names and surnames to individuals essentially indicates that they are an instance of a particular kind of person e.g. "John Smith", (classification). For the same reason, the "names" used to designate model elements need to be able to convey rich contextual information characterizing elements based on their type, heritage and container. In this section we motivate the need for model element designation and show how it is currently supported in mainstream modeling languages. We use selected examples from the UML specification since this language currently provides the richest support for designation.

2.1   Identification

Figure 1 contains extracts from two figures in the UML specification which illustrate the basic identification role played by designators in the UML, and the issues surrounding their contents. The left hand side of Figure 1, (a), is a snippet of Figure 7.4 from the UML specification that shows the "Namespaces diagram of the kernel package", while the right hand side of Figure 1, (b), shows Figure 7.53 of the UML specification that illustrates how slots and values are represented in an instance specification. All the model elements in Figure 1 show the basic identification function of designators. The designators of the meta classes in Figure 1(a) basically contain just the "name" of the meta classes, while the designator of the instance specification in Figure 1(b) gives the object's name as well as its type.

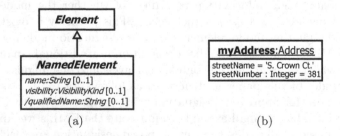

(a)   (b)

Fig. 1. Named element and instance specification example

The meta model fragment in Figure 1(a) was chosen because it shows that all instances of all meta classes that inherit from *NamedElement* (which includes classes and instance specifications) have a *name* attribute, which stores the "name" of a model element. This applies to M_2 classes as well as to M_1 classes since the MOF also has the same structure. A question that arises as a result is whether the value of the name string appearing in a model element's designator has to be the same as the value of its linguistic name attribute (i.e. the name attribute a model element possesses by being classified as a *NamedElement*). The obvious answer would be that they do have to be the same, but this significantly reduces a modeler's options when designing a model element's designator. In particular, it means that if the designator is to contain an identification string the model element's linguistic *name* attribute must have a value. If it does not, no identification information can be given in the designator. It also means that the designator cannot contain information from any of the ontological (i.e domain) attributes of the model element. For example, according to the UML specification it would not be possible to construct a designator for the instance specification in Figure 1(b) from its two ontological attributes (e.g. "381-S-Crown-Ct"), unless its name attribute had exactly this value, even though this would be a perfectly good identifier for the object.

2.2   Classification

The *myAdddress* instance specification in Figure 1(b) shows one of the main ways of defining classification information in UML designators — the usage of the ":" symbol to separate the name of the model element from its type. In fact, since it is often desirable to represent "any" instance of a type rather than one specifically named instance, the UML allows the name of an instance to be omitted and just the type to be given, prepended by ":". An instance with such a designator is said to be "anonymous". In the latest version of the UML it is even possible to omit both the instance name and the type of an instance specification and only designate it by the string ":".

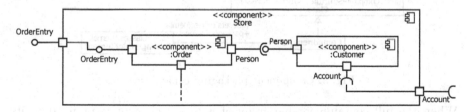

Fig. 2. Component types and instances example

Another notation for identifying the type of a model element in its header is shown in Figure 2 which is a snippet of Figure 8.2 from the UML specification. This uses the UML stereotype notation to "brand" a model element as being of a particular type. For example the model element *Store* is a class which is branded by the stereotype *component*, signifying that it is a component, as defined in the UML meta model. Essentially, the application of the stereotype classifies *Store* as being of type *Component*.

This example shows the redundancy and lack of uniformity in the UML approach for expressing classification information within model element designators — if a model element represents an instance specification at the lowest ontological level the "⁚" notation must be used, whereas if it represents a classifier at any other ontological level the stereotype notation must be used. This is not only confusing but adds complexity to the language. Figure 2 even contains model elements where two different notations are used in the same designator. The designators of the two model elements located within *Store* indicate that they are "anonymous" instances of the component types *Order* and *Customer* respectively, and that these in turn are instances of the type *Component*. This lack of a uniform notation for classification is what leads us to characterize the UML designation approach as being level-sensitive rather than level-agnostic.

2.3   Containment

Another important piece of characterizing information that can be included in a model element's designator is its containment — that is, the path of containers it is located (i.e. nested) within, up to the root container of the model. The UML's notation for representing containment in a model element's designator is shown in Figure 3 which is Figure 8.4 of the UML specification. The purpose of this figure is to illustrate the packaging capabilities of the meta class *Component* which it gains by virtue of inheriting from the meta class *Class*, located in the package *StructuredClasses*. This, in turn, is located in the package *CompositeStructures*, which in turn is located within the package *UML*. This gives it the ability to contain an unlimited number of *PackageableElements*. Since both of these classes reside in (are located in) other packages, their precise location within the containment hierarchy is given using the double colon notation "⁚⁚".

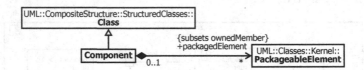

Fig. 3. Component packaging capabilities

When the full containment hierarchy of a model element is prefixed to its local name using this "⁚⁚" notation, the resulting string is referred to as the model element's Fully Qualified Name (FQN). These are frequently used in conjunction with the package "importing", "merging" and "combining" mechanisms which determine what model elements are included from other packages and how (i.e. whether they are copied or referenced, and whether or not they are visible to third parties). If a model element is included from another package without importing, merging or combining that package, the full, hierarchical name of the model element has to be shown in the designator.

2.4   Heritage

Since the properties of a class are determined by what it inherits from, as well as by what it is an instance of, a class's heritage is also an important piece of characterizing information. A powerful designation notation should therefore support the expression of such information. Unfortunately this is not possible in the UML or other existing modeling languages, with the result that diagrams are often more complex than necessary. This is illustrated by Figure 4 which shows a snippet of Figure 8.2 from the UML Specification. The main purpose of this figure is to show heritage information about the meta classes *Component* and *ComponentRealization* whose instances can "realize" instances of *Component*.

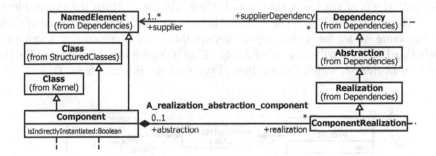

Fig. 4. Basic components package

Because the UML does not allow heritage information to be included in the designators of model elements the only way to do this is to include each superclass (direct or indirect) in the diagram and show explicit inheritance relationships between them. This not only clutters diagrams such as this one, it is also the basic reason why classes have to be visualized in packages where they do not belong simply to allow inheritance relationships to be displayed. This, in turn is one of the main reasons why the FQNs of classes have to be used when they are visualized "out of place". Related to this, Figure 4 illustrates another redundant, non-uniform practice often used to designate model elements in the UML — the use of the text "from PackageName" in parentheses under the class name to indicate where a class is "from". This is not official UML notation, but is commonly used, even in the UML specification. Note that in Figure 3 the class *UML::CompositeStructures::StructuredClasses::Class* is designated by its FQN but in Figure 4 it is designated using the "*(from StructuredClasses)*" notation.

2.5   Domain Example

Figure 5 shows an example of the use of the previously presented notations within a single model. The example contains two linguistic classification levels, labeled M_1 and M_2 according to the UML infrastructure conventions, but three ontological classification levels which are not explicitly labeled. The figure uses

UML instance specifications to squeeze the two bottom ontological classification levels into a single linguistic layer (M_1). In the top level of the figure the stereotype mechanism is used to define a domain meta class, Breed, with two attributes, *BreedName* and *FCINo*. Additionally a meta class *Product* is defined with the attribute *price*. In the level below resides an instance of *Breed* and *Product*, namely *Collie*, located in a package called *Breeds* which, in turn, is located in the *DogTaxonomy* package. In the UML designation notation, therefore, the fully qualified name of Collie is *DogTaxonomy::Breeds::Collie*. To characterize it as a *Breed* and a *Product* the stereotype notation "*«Breed, Product»*" is used. The model uses comments to assign the two meta attributes of *Collie*, *BreedName* and *FCINo*, the values *SheepDog* (a colloquial name for *Collie*) and *297* (the catalog number for *Collie*). *Collie* is also a subclass of *Dog*, which in turn is a subclass of *Animal*, which in turn is a subclass of *Thing*. At the bottom ontological level (within the same linguistic level — M_1), there is an anonymous instance of *Collie* with the same values for its corresponding attribute instances adding a value for *Collie*'s third meta attribute *price* of *12345*. This instance also has a value for the attribute, *DogName*, which its ontological type, *Collie*, inherits from *Dog*.

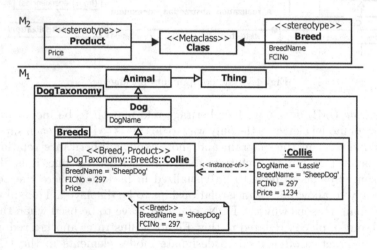

Fig. 5. Concrete example of the UML designation notation

This model highlights some of the weaknesses of the traditional UML notation mentioned above. In particular, it once again illustrates the different notations used to define the types of classes (e.g. the types of *Collie*) and instance specifications (e.g. the types of the anonymous instance of *Collie*), and highlights the motivation for including heritage information within designators as well as classification and containment information. For example, it is not possible to show in *Collie*'s designator that it is a subclass of *Dog*. Although not directly related to designation, the figure also highlights two fundamental weaknesses of "two-level" concrete syntaxes such as that of the UML — the artificial flatting of three ontological levels into two linguistic ones [5], and the lack of support for defining attributes, such as *BreedName*, that endure over more than one instantiation step. This forces modelers to redundantly redefine attributes for the sole purpose of passing them down to the next level.

3   The Element Designation Notation

The aim of the Element Designation Notation (EDN) proposed in this paper is to address the previously identified weaknesses and allow model elements to be designated in a uniform way across all ontological classification levels. In this section we first define the syntactic structure of the notation and then demonstrate the designation approach in the context of the examples introduced in the previous section. Wherever possible the concrete syntax used in the EDN is based on well-established notational conventions in existing modeling languages. The formalism used to describe the allowed syntactic structure of model element designators is syntax diagrams [6]. In this notation we use rounded rectangles for terminals and rectangles for non-terminals.

3.1   Basic Designator Structure

The designator of a model element consists of four basic parts, the heritage indicator (*heritage*), containment indicator (*containment*), identification indicator (*identification*) and classification indicator (*classification*) as shown in Definition 1. All of these parts are optional except the identification indicator. This is a mandatory part of a designator which defines the string by which the model element can be identified in constraints, transformations and domain-specific language (DSL) definitions etc. The identification indicator is therefore always the core part of a designator. It can optionally be highlighted using bold letters in long and complex designators.

Definition 1 (Designator Syntax)

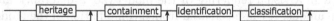

The two other parts closest to the identification indicator are the classification indicator and containment indicator. The classification indicator is placed as close as possible to the identification indicator, on its right hand side, separated by the well known colon notation popularized by the UML. The containment indicator, on the other hand, appears on the left hand side of the identification indicator using the well known dot notation popularized by programing languages such as Java. The heritage indicator appears furthest away from the identification indicator, at the very left of the designator. To indicate heritage the ">" notation is used as in Ruby [14] or in the EMF tree editor for meta models where it appears in the form "->". This ordering of the designator subsections is motivated by the fact that in popular programming languages like Java, fully qualified names are always specified by the containment information (i.e. package structure) followed by the identification indicator (i.e. class name).

A user can choose to display whole hierarchies by chaining the operators. If a user wants to reduce the complexity of a designator or is only interested in certain parts of a hierarchy (e.g. the root of the classification hierarchy) he can use the elision symbol in a designator. Elision is indicated by repeating the operator two times, which means that information is omitted between the left and right side of the designation operator. For simplicity, an elision symbol does not convey how much information is elided in an hierarchy. Also, in the case of inheritance and classification it is possible to indicate that more than one element exists at a particular point in the hierarchy by including those elements in a comma-separated list, optionally enclosed in square brackets. This allows multiple inheritance and multiple classification to be represented in designators.

EDN also allows designators to be nested recursively. A nested designator can appear wherever a simple identifier appears, surrounded by parentheses. They make it possible to provide more detailed information about the model elements participating in a designator. For example, the container of each model element participating in a heritage hierarchy can easily be shown in this way.

An example of a designator containing all four parts, based on the example in Figure 5, is *Animal>Dog>DogTaxonomy.Breeds.**Collie**:[Breed,Product]* (square brackets optional). This shows that Collie is located in the packages *DogTaxonomy* and *Breeds* and that it is a subclass of Dog which is a subclass of Animal. A comma separated list is used to indicate that *Collie* is classified by two types, namely *Breed* and *Product*. On the other hand, the designator *Thing>>**Collie*** can be employed to indicate that *Collie* is an indirect subclass of *Thing*. In *(M₁.Animal)>(DogTaxonomy.Dog)>Breeds.**Collie*** nested designators are used to display containment information for each element in the heritage hierarchy. The syntax used in these examples is elaborated in the following subsections.

3.2   Identification Indicator

The identification indicator of a model element is the component of the designator that identifies it in a visual rendering of the model (i.e. a diagram), and thus should ideally be unique. It can be created from a combination of the model element's ontological attributes or linguistic name attribute.

Definition 2 (Identifier Syntax)

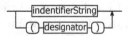

The syntactical form of an identification indicator is shown in Definition 2. The *identifierString* either starts with an alphabetic character or underscore followed by multiple alphabetic characters, digits and underscores, or can be an arbitrary string enclosed in quotation marks. Anonymous model elements are represented through the "~" symbol to indicate where the identifier would appear in complex designators. It is also possible to replace the identifier by a nested designator. This is not used in designators just showing the identifier of a single model element but can be helpful to more precisely describe an inheritance hierarchy by describing the containment of each superclass. Nested designator are surrounded by rounded brackets.

A search algorithm similar to the one employed in EMF [8] can be used to automatically determine the identifier of a model element. First the algorithm searches a model element for an expression which defines how the identifier for the model element is calculated. Second the algorithm searches for an ontological attribute called name, and if this is unsuccessful, for one called id. If no such attribute is found the algorithm searches for other attributes containing these two keywords (with the priority given to name). Finally, if still no identifier for a model element is found, the linguistic name of the model element is used as backup.

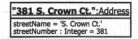

Fig. 6. Instance specification using EDN

The simplest example of a designator is a name such as *Collie* in Figure 5. An example of a designator using the nesting feature is *(M_1.Animal)>(DogTaxonomy .Dog)>Collie*. In this designator the identifiers of each model element of the inheritance hierarchy are enriched with containment information. An example of an identifier, *381 S. Crown Ct.*, composed of ontological attributes is shown in Figure 6 which is a variant of Figure 1(b). This identifier is composed from the ontological attributes *streetName* and *streetNumber*.

3.3 Classification Indicator

The exact grammar of the classification indicator in a designator is displayed in Definition 3. It shows the classification information for a model element using the familiar colon notation from the UML (:) followed by the identifier or a nested designator of the classifying model element. To use elision, the colon symbol is repeated twice (::). This collides with the UML notation for displaying containment, which must be taken into account when interpreting designators in the form proposed here. The model elements close to the root of the classification hierarchy are placed on the right and model elements close to the leaves are placed on the left. If an element has more than one classifier these can be shown in a comma-separated list optionally surrounded by rectangular brackets.

Definition 3 (Classification Indicator Syntax)

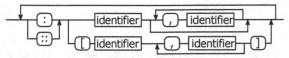

An example of a designator including classification information from the example in Figure 5 is *Collie:Breed,Product* indicating that *Collie* is classified by *Breed*

and *Product*. An example of single classification is **Dog**:*Class*. Another example is ∼:*Collie:Breed,Product* showing the whole classification hierarchy of the anonymous instance of *Collie*. One can observe here that only one notation was chosen to display classification crossing multiple ontological levels instead of two (i.e. stereotype notation and colon notation). To show the elements at the top of the classification hierarchy only ∼::*[Breed,Product]* is needed.

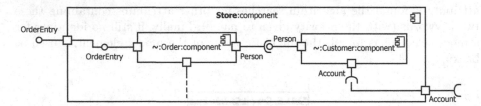

Fig. 7. Component types and instances using EDN

The classification information in Figure 2 is represented in Figure 7 as follows — ∼:Order:component and ∼:Customer:component. This corresponds exactly to the information shown in the header for the instance of *Order* in Figure 2. Using the nesting capability of EDN it would also be possible to, for example, directly represent the container of *Order* — (Store:Component).∼:Order: Component.

3.4   Containment Indicator

A containment indicator displays a model element's location in the containment tree which can be composed of various model elements including classification levels. The syntax is shown in Definition 4. The model element that is closest to the containment root is placed on the left and the model element which is closest to the containment tree leaves is placed on the right. The visual metaphor for representing containment is a dot (.) motivated by the notation used in many programming languages such as Java or C#. One of the motivations for not using the UML's double-colon notation is that this would collide with the notation used for elided classification. To elide an unspecified number of containers in a containment indicator, the dot notation is repeated twice (..). In contrast to heritage and classification, it is not possible to display two containers at a given point in the containment hierarchy, because the containment hierarchy is always a tree, and model elements can only have one container.

Definition 4 (Containment Indicator Syntax)

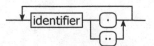

An example in the context of Figure 5 is *DogTaxonomy*.**Dog** stating that *Dog* is located in *DogTaxonomy*. An example of a more complex containment indicator is M_1.*DogTaxonomy*.*Breeds*.**Collie**. If only the containment root is of interest the

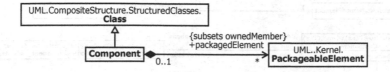

Fig. 8. Basic components package using EDN

designator could be $M_1..$*Collie*. It would also be possible to show the root and immediate container in the following way $M_1..$*Breeds.Collie*.

Using this notation for the containment of the model element *Class* in Figure 3 would result in a designator of the form shown in Figure 8. The UML's double colon notation that collides with the EDN's elided classification notation is transformed into the dot notation (*UML.CompositeStructures.StructuredClasses.Class*). In the case of *PackageableElement* the elision notation is used to indicate that it is contained in the *Kernel* package which itself is indirectly contained in the *UML* package.

3.5 Heritage Indicator

The heritage indicator expresses information about a model element's inheritance hierarchy (i.e. about its direct and indirect superclasses). The heritage indicator syntax is shown in Definition 5. Model elements at the root of the inheritance hierarchy are located on the left hand side of a heritage indicator whereas model elements which are close to the leaves are located on the right hand side. Building on a proposal first put forward in [4] we use the "greater than" symbol (>) to show that the model element on the right is a subclass of the model element on the left. Elision is supported by repeating the heritage symbol twice (>>). This notation is similar to that used in other languages such as Ruby. EMF's tree based meta model editor also uses a similar notation to indicate heritage — "->". Multiple supertypes at the same heritage level are displayed as a comma-separated list, optionally surrounded by square brackets.

Definition 5 (Heritage Indicator Syntax)

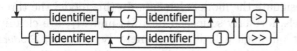

Applying the heritage indicator to show the direct supertype of *Collie* in Figure 5 results in *Dog>Collie*. The whole inheritance hierarchy can be shown by *Thing>Animal>Dog>Collie*, whereas the first and last supertypes in the hierarchy can be shown by *Thing>>Dog>Collie*.

The ability to represent heritage information in model element designators allows relationships between model elements in different packages to be shown in a greatly simplified way. For example, it would be possible to avoid the need to include the *Class* model element in Figure 3 by designating the Component model element in the following way — (UML.CompositeStructures.StructuredClasses.

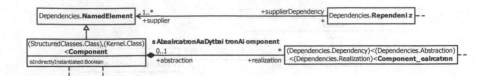

Fig. 9. Component types and instances

Class)>**Component**. Similarly, superclasses of *Component* and *ComponentRealization* in Figure 4 can be avoided by changing their designators to the ones shown in Figure 9 — (StructuredClass.Class),(Kernel.Class)>**Component** and (Dependencies.Dependency)>(Dependencies.Abstraction)>(Dependencies.Realization)>**ComponentRealization**, respectively. If the goal of the diagram is to show that *ComponentRealization* is the descendent of one particular model element, such as *Dependency*, for example, the intermediate model elements can be omitted using the elision notation — (Dependencies.Dependency)>..>**ComponentRealization**.

4 Level-Agnostic Designation Example

Up to this point all the examples of EDN statements have been in the context of the UML modeling framework which squeezes multiple ontological levels into two linguistic levels (the M_2 and M_1 levels of the UML infrastructure). However, as mentioned above, the real power of the EDN becomes evident when it is used in deep (i.e. multi-level) models where ontological classification levels are strictly separated from linguistic ones, and multiple ontological classification levels can be modeled. In this section we present an example of how the EDN could be used to designate model elements in a deep version of the domain example shown in section 2. The host language that we use to visualize this example is the Level-agnostic Modeling Language [3], but the approach is compatible with any deep modeling language such as Nivel [1], Metadepth [11], DPF [10], Cross-layer modeler [7] or OMME [15].

Figure 10 shows a deep (multi-level) version of the example from Figure 5, in which the EDN is used to designate the model elements. In this model the three ontological classification levels, formerly squeezed into M_2 and M_1, are cleanly represented in three distinct ontological levels. The meta types *Class*, *Product* and *Breed* are at the most abstract level — O_0. The stereotype definitions are translated into specializations in which the stereotypes *Product* and *Breed* are transformed into subtypes of *Class*.

The middle level, O_1, contains the class level of the UML example without the instance specifications. Thus, *Animal*, *Dog* and *Collie* are located at this level. The UML packages have been translated into clabject's (*DogTaxonomy*, *Breeds*) containing other clabjects. Classification is no longer indicated by using the stereotype guillemet notation but using the EDN designation syntax for classification. Additionally no extra notation is needed to assign values to meta attributes defined in a meta model extension in contrast to the UML version

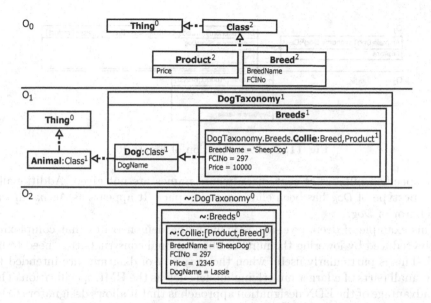

Fig. 10. Deep model using advanced EDN

where comments are used to assign values to classifying stereotypes. Another difference to the UML version is that containment information is presented using the EDN's dot notation. The instance specification, the anonymous instance of *Collie*, now appears at the lowest ontological level, disentangling the classification information which was originally squeezed into one level, (M_1), but should naturally occupy two levels. Here, again, the uniform designation syntax is used to indicate classification across two levels (i.e. *~:Collie:[Breed,Product]*). Also the name of the instance is not underlined since the notation is uniform across all classification levels (i.e. is level-agnostic). Comparing the UML version against the LML version with EDN designators, it can be observed that: 1. classification is clearly expressed across multiple classification levels, 2. attributes are handled uniformly regardless of whether they originate from a stereotype, meta class or class and 3. classification designation is expressed in a uniform way regardless of whether a classifier is a meta class, meta model extension or a class.

The example in Figure 10 can be further refined to highlight certain properties of the model. Figure 11 shows a version which might be useful in a specification focusing only on *Collie*. This figure leaves out the meta level O_0 since all information conveyed in it is present in O_1. The designator of *Collie* shows that it is an instance of *Breed* and *Product* which are themselves subclasses of *Class*. The attribute of *Collie* defined by the classifiers of the instance are present in its attributes compartment. The packages have been omitted to save space. They are indicated by the designators of *Dog*, *Collie* and the anonymous instance of *Collie*. *Dog* is contained by *DogTaxonomy* and *Collie* is contained by *Breeds* which is contained by *DogTaxonomy*. The anonymous instance of *Collie* is nested within

Fig. 11. Shortened version of Figure 10

an unspecified number of containers, whose names are not given. Additionally the supertype of *Dog* has been elided to save space. It appears as *Animal* in the designator of *Dog*.

This example of deep, level-agnostic modeling demonstrates that complexity can be reduced by lowering the number of notational constructs that need to be used. This is particularly useful when the majority of diagrams are intended to show small parts of a larger underlying model such as the UML specification. The key advantage of the EDN designation approach is that it allows designators to be scaled to best fit the problem in hand. In some situations the exact containment, classification or heritage of a model element is not important or relevant. In general it is possible to include the optimal amount of designation information needed reducing the information overload of modelers.

5   Conclusion

In this paper we have presented a simple yet powerful approach for constructing information-rich designators for model elements in any host modeling language. A comparison of a model expressed in the UML to a model expressed in LML using EDN reveals several advantatges of the appraoch including: 1. full compatibility with established conventions, i.e. all information conveyable in UML designators can be shown in a familiar notation, 2. complete level-agnosticness with respect to ontological classification levels, 3. the ability to support heritage information as well as containment and classification information and 4. support for fine control of precisely what information is shown about a model element's location in the containment, inheritance and classification hierarchies (i.e. full list of parents, elided list of parents, etc.). Of these features, items 2 , 3 and 4 are new to the state-of-the-art and to our knowledge are not currently supported in any other language.

While the enhanced simplicity and symmetry will be helpful in all kinds of models, the enhanced expressiveness is likely to be of most use to advanced modelers especially when working with large scale models. One of the big obstacles to the use of visual modeling languages is that graphical diagrams quickly become cluttered and complex as the amount of information they convey grows, especially when it comes to information that is typically conveyed using edges (e.g. inheritance). By providing a more powerful and concise way of capturing this kind of information in model element designators, models can convey the same information in a much simpler, less cluttered and visually clearer form.

Although this work focuses on graphical languages we are confident that textual languages can also benefit from the form of designation presented in this paper. For instance the Human-Usable Textual Notation (HUTN) [12] or textual multi-level modeling frameworks such as MetaDepth could be enriched with the designation approach suggested here. The approach can also be used to enhance DSLs created with a multi-level modeling environment such as Melanee [2]. In such a scenario designation could be employed to enrich naming in graphical and textual DSLs. Designation can also be used to identify model elements in constraint and transformation languages.

The designation approach described in this paper is implemented in our deep modeling tool Melanee. Each model element's designation is controllable via a small Designation Query Language. We are currently working on improving this query language and build a console which can be used to dynamically query model elements for designation information. We are also planning to build the designation syntax into the transformation capabilities provided with Melanee and the deep OCL dialect which is currently under development.

Acknowledgments. We are grateful to Thomas Kühne for contributing towards the work described in this paper through his co-authorship of [4] which first suggested the idea of a level-agnostic designation notation that includes heritage information.

References

1. Asikainen, T., Männistö, T.: Nivel: A metamodelling language with a formal semantics. Software & Systems Modeling 8 (2009)
2. Atkinson, C., Gerbig, R.: Melanie: Multi-level modeling and ontology engineering environment. In: Proceedings of the 2nd International Master Class on Model-Driven Engineering: Modeling Wizards. ACM, New York (2012)
3. Atkinson, C., Kennel, B., Goß, B.: The level-agnostic modeling language. In: Malloy, B., Staab, S., van den Brand, M. (eds.) SLE 2010. LNCS, vol. 6563, pp. 266–275. Springer, Heidelberg (2011)
4. Atkinson, C., Anshelevich, E.: Strict profiles: Why and how. In: Evans, A., Caskurlu, B., Selic, B. (eds.) UML 2000. LNCS, vol. 1939, pp. 309–322. Springer, Heidelberg (2000)
5. Atkinson, C., Kühne, T.: Reducing accidental complexity in domain models. Software & Systems Modeling 7(3) (2008)
6. Braz, L.M.: Visual syntax diagrams for programming language statements. SIGDOC Asterisk J. Comput. Doc. 14(4), 23–27 (1990)
7. Demuth, A., Lopez-Herrejon, R.E., Egyed, A.: Cross-layer modeler: A tool for flexible multilevel modeling with consistency checking. In: Proceedings of the 19th ACM SIGSOFT Symposium and the 13th European Conference on Foundations of Software Engineering, ESEC/FSE 2011. ACM, New York (2011)
8. Eclipse Foundation: Bug 39618 - Improve label feature search algorithm (2003), https://bugs.eclipse.org/bugs/show_bug.cgi?id=39618

9. Halpin, T., Morgan, T.: Information Modeling and Relational Databases. The Morgan Kaufmann Series in Data Management Systems. Elsevier Science (2008)
10. Lamo, Y., Wang, X., Mantz, F., Bech, O., Sandven, A., Rutle, A.: Dpf workbench: A multi-level language workbench for mde. In: Proceedings of the Estonian Academy of Sciences (2013)
11. de Lara, J., Guerra, E.: Deep meta-modelling with metadepth. In: Vitek, J. (ed.) TOOLS 2010. LNCS, vol. 6141, pp. 1–20. Springer, Heidelberg (2010)
12. OMG: Human-usable textual notation (hutn) specification (2010), http://www.omg.org/spec/UML/2.4.1
13. OMG: Uml superstructure 2.4.1 (2011), http://www.omg.org/spec/HUTN/1.0
14. Rubylearning.com: Inheritance (2013), http://rubylearning.com/satishtalim/ruby_inheritance.htm
15. Volz, B., Jablonski, S.: Towards an open meta modeling environment. In: 10th Workshop on Domain-Specific Modeling. ACM, New York (2010)

Towards Scalable Querying
of Large-Scale Models

Konstantinos Barmpis and Dimitrios S. Kolovos

Department of Computer Science, University of York,
Heslington, York, YO10 5DD, UK
{kb,dkolovos}@cs.york.ac.uk

Abstract. Hawk is a modular and scalable framework that supports monitoring and indexing large collections of models stored in diverse version control repositories. Due to the aggregate size of indexed models, providing a reliable, usable, and fast mechanism for querying Hawk's index is essential. This paper presents the integration of Hawk with an existing model querying language, discusses the efficiency challenges faced, and presents an approach based on the use of derived features and indexes as a means of improving the performance of particular classes of queries. The paper also reports on the evaluation of a prototype that implements the proposed approach against the Grabats benchmark query, focusing on the observed efficiency benefits in terms of query execution time. It also compares the size and resource use of the model index against one created without using such optimizations.

Keywords: Scalability, model querying, model-driven engineering.

1 Introduction

The popularity and adoption of MDE in industry has increased substantially in the past decade as it provides several benefits compared to traditional software engineering practices, such as improved productivity and reuse [1], which allow for systems to be built faster and cheaper. However, certain limitations of supporting tools such as poor scalability which prevent wider use of MDE in industry [2,3] will need to be overcome. Scalability issues arise when large models (of the order of millions of model elements) are used in MDE processes.

When referring to scalability issues in MDE they can be split into the following categories [4]:

1. Model persistence: storage of large models; ability to access and update such models with low memory footprint and fast execution time.
2. Model querying and transformation: ability to perform intensive and complex queries and transformations on large models with fast execution time.
3. Collaborative work: multiple developers being able to query, modify and version control large-scale shared models in a non-invasive manner.

This paper contributes to the study of scalable techniques for large-scale model persistence and querying by presenting the use of derived attributes to substantially improve the efficiency of certain types of model queries, and reporting on

J. Cabot and J. Rubin (Eds.): ECMFA 2014, LNCS 8569, pp. 35–50, 2014.

the results obtained by exploring the integration of the Hawk [5] and Epsilon [6] frameworks that have been used to implement this. This paper builds upon [5] by discussing the implementation of the query layer the tool provides. In this work we assume that the reader is familiar with the organization of 3-level metamodeling architectures such as MOF/EMF.

The remainder of the paper is organized as follows. Section 2, introduces model version control, Hawk and model indexing. Section 3 presents Hawk's query layer and discusses how it can be optimized by use of derived attributes in the store. Section 4 presents the prototype implementation of the integration of Hawk with the Epsilon platform for providing a general-purpose query layer. In Section 5 this prototype integration is evaluated using variations of the Grabats benchmark, in order to test its performance. Finally, Section 6 discusses the application of these results and identifies interesting directions for further work in this area.

2   Background

This section briefly introduces version control in the context of MDE, provides an overview of Hawk and discusses querying, providing an overview of the various forms available today that have motivated the work presented here.

2.1   Model Version Control

To tackle the challenge of collaborative development and version control of large models, model-specific repositories and version control systems (such as CDO[1] and ModelCVS) have been proposed. The main advantages of such systems is that they provide support for synchronous collaboration, on-demand loading and locking of model fragments, and global server-side queries on models. On the downside, such repositories are typically proprietary, re-implement similar functionality (user management, model fragment locking/unlocking, check-in/out), and lack in features such as branching and tagging. Moreover, such repositories need to be administered (e.g. backed up) separately, and there is limited tool support for them outside the environment for which they were initially developed for (e.g. integration with other IDEs, continuous integration systems, and other 3rd-party model measurement and analysis tools). Finally, they arguably lack in robustness compared to file-based version control systems such as Subversion and Git.

As such, switching from a file-based to a model-specific version control system can require a significant leap of faith, which can become even more challenging if the models in question are of significant business value. On the other hand, in order to perform meaningful queries on models stored in a file-based version control system (e.g. to identify cross-references between model files or to search for model elements with particular properties across the entire repository), these models need to be first checked out in the developer's workspace and loaded into memory. This can be tedious, or even impossible, for large-scale models.

---

[1] http://www.eclipse.org/emf/cdo

2.2   Hawk

The limitations identified on both sides of the spectrum have motivated us to design and implement a framework (Hawk) that enables developers to perform queries on models stored in established file-based version control systems, without needing to maintain a complete copy of them in their local workspace. To achieve this, Hawk acts as a middle-man that creates and maintains indexes of models stored in remote file-based version control repositories; a *model index*[2] is a persisted form of a collection of (potentially interconnected) models, and its aim is to provide support for efficient querying of these models at a model element granularity. As discussed in [5], in our view, this provides an orthogonal approach for addressing the scalability concern that does not interfere with the current state of practice.

This section briefly describes the architecture, design, and prototype implementation of Hawk to provide context for how it is used for indexing large models and consequently to efficiently query such model indexes.

System Architecture and Design. Hawk aims at delivering a system capable of working with diverse file-based version control systems (VCS) and model persistence formats whilst providing a comprehensive API through which modeling and model management tools can query it. It needs to be scalable so that it can accommodate large sets of models, and non-invasive (the VCS repositories should not need to be modified or configured).

Hawk comprises components which monitor a set of version control systems, parse and index relevant models stored in them. For details on supported version control systems, model formats, index persistence back-ends as well as additional components of Hawk readers can refer to [5].

Overview of a Hawk Model Index. Based on results obtained through extensive benchmarking [4], we have decided to use a NoSQL graph database (Neo4J[3]) for persisting model indexes. An example of such an index, containing a simple library metamodel and a model that conforms to it, is illustrated in Figure 1. In general, a model index typically contains the following entities:

- **Repository Nodes.** These represent a VCS repository and contain its URL and last revision. They are linked with relationships to the *Files* they contain.
- **File Nodes.** These represent files in a repository and contain information on the file such as the path, current revision and type. They are linked with relationships to the *Elements* or *Metamodels* they contain.
- **Metamodel Nodes.** These represent metamodels and contain their names and their unique namespace URIs (in EMF, these would be *EPackages*[4]). They are linked with relationships to the (metamodel) *Types* they contain.

---

[2] This should not to be confused with a *database index* provided by many SQL and NoSQL databases.

[3] http://neo4j.org/

[4] We choose to draw parallels with concepts from EMF as they are well-understood and unambiguous.

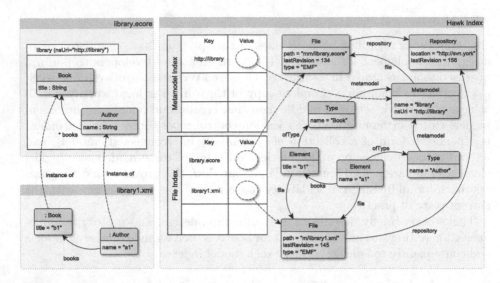

Fig. 1. High-level overview of the contents of a library model index (persisted in a NoSQL graph database)

- **Type Nodes.** These represent metamodel types (*EClass*es in EMF terminology) and contain their name. They are linked with relationships to their (model) *Element* instances.
- **Element Nodes.** These represent model elements (*EObject*s in EMF terminology) and can contain their attributes (as properties) and their references (to other model elements) as relationships to them.
- **Indexes.** Metamodel nodes and File nodes are indexed[5] in the store, so that their nodes can be efficiently accessed for querying (commonly used as starting points for complex graph traversal queries).

It is worth noting that a model index such as the one presented above may end up being a fully copy of the actual models found on the relevant version control system but it does not have to be. In principle, if some contents of the model are not deemed useful they can be omitted in order to gain an improvement in injection and possibly query time.

2.3   Querying of Model Indexes

To be of practical value, a model indexing framework such as Hawk needs to be able to provide correct and efficient responses to queries made on its indexes. There are two principal ways of querying a model index:

Native Querying. The most straightforward, and often the most performant, way of querying an index is using the native API of its persistence back-end. In a model stored in a database the API provided by the tool providing the driver

---

[5] http://components.neo4j.org/neo4j-lucene-index/snapshot/

used to persist said model would be used with a relevant query language (such as SQL statements if a relational database is used or Cypher if a Neo4J NoSQL database is used), or using direct API calls in a programing language such as Java. Nevertheless, it also demonstrates certain shortcomings which should be considered:

- *Query Conciseness.* Native queries can be particularly verbose and, consequently, difficult to write, understand and maintain. An example of this can be found in Section 6.1 of [4].
- *Query Abstraction Level.* Native queries are bound to the specific technology used; they have to be engineered for that technology and cannot be used for a different back-end without substantial alteration in most cases.

Back-End Independent Navigation and Querying. An alternative way to access and query models is through higher-level query languages that are independent of the persistence mechanism. Examples of such languages include the Object Constraint Language (OCL), the Epsilon Object Language (EOL) [7] (from the Epsilon [8] platform) and the Atlas Transformation Language (ATL), which abstract over concrete model representation and persistence technologies using intermediate layers such as the *OCL pivot metamodel* [9] and *Epsilon Model Connectivity* [6] layer.

In terms of execution, queries expressed in such high-level languages can be executed on an in-memory representation of the model, or translated into queries expressed in persistence-level query languages such as SQL and XQuery[6], at compile-time or at run-time. Full translation is only feasible in cases where the high-level and the lower-level query languages are isomorphic in terms of capabilities. This is not always the case: for example, EOL supports dynamic dispatch which is not supported in SQL. Even when full compile-time translation is not feasible, partial translation at run-time has been shown to deliver significant performance improvements as seen in [10].

3   Scalable Model Index Querying

This section will use the library example seen in Figure 1 as a running example and will discuss how derived attributes can be used to improve the performance of queries made on Hawk model indexes. The principal aim of this work is to present how using such derived attributes can greatly improve performance of relevant queries made on such model indexes and to provide incentive for building a complete framework for supporting them in Hawk.

3.1   Querying a Model Index

Regardless of the use of native or back-end independent querying, in order to respond to a query (from now on referred to as the *library query*) requesting the authors that have more than N books in the example index, the following steps would have to occur:

---

[6] http://journal.ub.tu-berlin.de/eceasst/article/viewFile/108/103

1. The starting point of the query would have to be found. In this case, the collection of all instances of *Author* in the model would have to be retrieved.
2. For each author node, the number of the "books" relationships of the node identified in step 2 would need to be counted and compared against *N*.

Step 1 is easy to perform in Hawk as an index of *Metamodels* is kept which can be used to rapidly provide a starting point for a query which requires elements of a specific type (such as *Author* instances for example). If a query uses the whole model index as a starting point then there is no optimization to be performed as the entire model index would have to be traversed in order to find the Node representing the *Author* type. Step 2 where we can begin optimizing to improve the execution time of queries which have to iterate (possibly on multiple levels) to find a result.

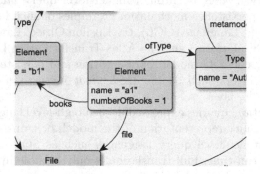

Fig. 2. Pre-computing the number of books of each author

An effective way to increase query efficiency is to pre-compute and cache – at indexing time – information that can be used to speed up particular queries of interest. Using the library example, we can store the total number of books of each author under a new, derived, 'numberOfBooks' attribute attached to each author, as shown in Figure 2. By pre-computing and caching this information, the query above can be rewritten so that it does not have to iterate though all the books of each author, but instead it can directly compare *N* against the value of its (derived) 'numberOfBooks' property.

3.2   Adding Derived Attributes

Our aim in this work is to explore the impact that such derived attributes can have on the performance of queries on large model indexes. As such, we have opted for a minimal approach for defining derived attributes and their derivation logic. In our current prototype, we need to create a derived attribute on the relevant *EClass* (i.e. a derived integer attribute 'numberOfBooks' on the *EClass Author*) and annotate it as 'HawkDerivedFeature'. As illustrated in Figure 3, the derivation logic is specified using an OCL-like (EOL in our prototype) expression in the details of the annotation. Such attributes are currently created manually

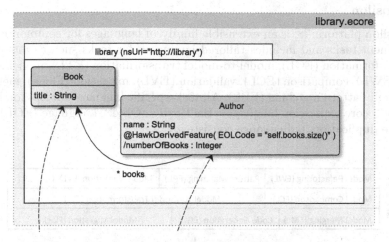

Fig. 3. Defining the *numberOfBooks* derived attribute

by the user and if they cannot be resolved a simple error value is produced in the index.

Since our focus is only on evaluating the performance improvements delivered, several interesting engineering problems that would have to be addressed by a usable system have been intentionally ignored:

- How to enable the declaration of derived attributes when using an immutable metamodel (e.g. UML);
- How to efficiently handle non-parsable expressions (on the expression language level) or expressions failing on a model element basis (but parsable);
- How to allow parsers from other expression languages to be easily integrated with the framework;
- How to efficiently deal with metamodel evolution, specifically how to handle types of changes such as only evolving the annotations, evolving some of the metamodel elements themselves but retaining the same annotations, evolving both the metamodel elements and the annotations at the same time.

The following section discusses how we evaluate the derived attribute value computation expressions and how we then use the computed values to enhance the performance of queries in our prototype.

4 Implementation

Before discussing the derived attribute computation and caching process, this section introduces Epsilon and its Model Connectivity Layer (EMC). It then discusses implementation details of Hawk's query layer integration with Epsilon.

4.1 Epsilon

The Epsilon platform [8] is an extensible family of languages for common model management tasks and includes tailored languages for tasks such as model-to-text transformation (EGL), model-to-model transformation (ETL), model refactoring (EWL), comparison (ECL), validation (EVL), migration (Flock), merging (EML) and pattern matching (EPL). All task-specific languages in Epsilon build on top of a core expression language – the Epsilon Object Language (EOL) – to eliminate duplication and enhance consistency.

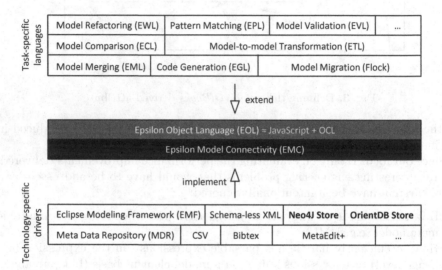

Fig. 4. The Epsilon Model Connectivity Layer

As seen in Figure 4, EOL – and as such all languages that build on top of it – is not bound to a particular metamodeling architecture or model persistence technology. Instead, an intermediate layer – the Epsilon Model Connectivity layer – was introduced to allow for seamless integration of any modeling back-end.

The Epsilon Model Connectivity Layer (EMC). This layer of Epsilon uses a driver-based approach where integration with a particular modeling technology is achieved by implementing a *driver* that conforms to a Java interface (*IModel*) provided by EMC. For a more detailed discussion on EMC and the *IModel* interface, the reader can refer to Chapter 3 of [6].

4.2 Querying a Hawk Model Index Using the Epsilon Object Language

Below, we summarize the implementation of the important methods needed by an EMC driver to enable integration with Epsilon, as well as that of the derived attributes used by Hawk's driver to improve its query performance.

Table 1. Interesting methods in the IModel interface

Method	Return Type	Description
allContents()	Collection<?>	Returns a collection containing all of the nodes contained in the index in the form of *NeoId-Wrappers*
hasType(String type)	boolean	Returns whether the type *type* exists in the index by trying to find it through the *Metamodel* index of the store.
getAllOfType(String type)	Collection<?>	Returns a collection containing all of the objects of type *type* in the index by first invoking hasType(type) and, if successful, finding the type using the *Metamodel* index and then creating a collection of *NeoIdWrappers* containing every element which has an *ofType* relationship to *type*.
getTypeOf(Object instance)	Object	Returns the type node of the element *instance* in the index by directly accessing the node *instance* (as this method is always passed a *NeoId-Wrapper* as the *instance*) and navigating its *ofType* relationship to get the type node. The returned object is a *NeoIdWrapper*.
isOfType(Object instance, String type)	boolean	Returns whether the node *instance* in this model is of type *type* by first invoking hasType(type) and, if successful, invoking getTypeOf(instance) and performing a String comparison on the resulting names.
knowsAboutProperty(Object instance, String property)	boolean	Returns whether the element *instance* in this index can have the structural feature *property* by first invoking getTypeOf(instance) and then invoking the EMF method *getEStructuralFeature(type, property)*.

IModel Interface Method Implementations. In order to use Epsilon's EOL to query model indexes stored in Hawk, an implementation of the IModel interface is required. In Table 1 we present a description of various methods of interest in the IModel interface and a summary of their implementation details in Hawk. Note that any model element loaded into memory is of Java class *NeoIdWrapper*. This is a lightweight object which contains only the location of the relevant model element in the store (its 'id' value for example in a Neo4J NoSQL Graph database) as well as a reference to the Epsilon model it is part of; this object can be used to load the element's attributes and relationships on demand.

Derived Attribute Value Computation. As discussed above, in the current prototype, we use EOL expressions to describe the derived attributes to be computed. For example, to derive the feature 'numberOfBooks' on an *Author* node, we use the 'self.books.size()' expression, as shown in Figure 3. The keyword 'self' denotes the element itself and since in this case the element is an *Author* instance (as the code was in an *EAnnotation* placed on the *EClass Author*) it will successfully evaluate the expression, returning the value *1* in this case. Such EOL expressions are actually executed, after the model insertion has been completed, using Hawk's EMC driver to query the database. Empirical data on the impact this has on total insertion time can be found in Section 5.

Reverse Reference Navigation. In the spirit of EMF's eContainer() method which allows an *EObject* to get access to its container object, Hawk provides a mechanism for reverse-navigating a containment reference in order to access the container. This feature is embedded into the parser by means of prefixing the relevant reference with "revRefNav_". For example, say one has an object 'A' with a containment reference called 'contain' to an object 'B'. Then, by typing "B.revRefNav_contain" in EOL, we get as a result object A.

5   Evaluation

In this section, the Grabats metamodel and models are used to perform various performance tests on the query layer of Hawk.

5.1   The Grabats 2009 Case Study

For evaluating query execution performance in Hawk we use large-scale models extracted by reverse engineering existing Java code. The updated version of the JDTAST metamodel used in the *SharenGo Java Legacy Reverse-Engineering* MoDisco use case[7], presented in the Grabats 2009 contest [11] described below, as well as the five models provided in the contest, are used for this purpose.

In this metamodel, there are *TypeDeclarations* that are used to define Java classes and interfaces, *MethodDeclarations* that are used to define Java methods (in classes or interfaces, for example) and *Modifiers* that are used to define Java modifiers (like static or synchronized) for Java classes or Java methods. Figures of the relevant subset of the JDTAST metamodel are found in works like [4,12].

The Grabats 2009 contest comprised several tasks, including the case study used in this paper for benchmarking different model querying and pattern detection technologies. More specifically, task 1 of this case study is performed, using all of the case studies' models, set0 – set4 (which represent progressively larger models, from one with 70447 model elements (set0) to one with 4961779 model elements (set4)), all of which conform to the JDTAST metamodel.

These models are injected into Hawk for the insertion benchmark and then queried using the Grabats 2009 task 1 query (from now on referred to as the

---
[7] http://www.eclipse.org/gmt/MoDisco/useCases/JavaLegacyRE/

Grabats query) [13]. This query requests all instances of *TypeDeclaration* elements which declare at least one *MethodDeclaration* that has static and public modifiers and has the declared type being its returning type.

In the following sections we use this case study as a running example to illustrate the Hawk implementation and evaluate the results of using this JDTAST metamodel (and models).

5.2   Execution Environment

Performance figures that have been measured on a PC with Intel(R) Core(TM) i5-2300 CPU @ 2.80GHz, with 8GB of physical memory, and running the Windows 7 (64 bits) operating system are presented. The Java Virtual Machine (JVM) version 1.7.0_45-b18 has been restarted for each measure as well as for each repetition of each measure. In each case, 6GB of RAM has been allocated to the JVM (which includes any virtual memory used by the embedded Neo4J database server running the tests). **Results are in seconds and Megabytes, where appropriate**.

5.3   Model Insertion

Tables 2 and 3 show the results for the insertion of the various Grabats XMI models into Neo4J using three variants of the metamodel (derivation strategies):

Table 2. Model Insertion, Size Results

Model	Size (in Mb)		
	Original	DerivedMethodDeclaration	DerivedTypeDeclaration
Set0	20.474	20.542	20.533
Set1	61.193	61.388	61.226
Set2	534.448	547.339	535.156
Set3	1184.09	1219.15	1186.28
Set4	1279.42	1317.68	1281.88

- **Original.** This is the unaltered version of the JDTAST metamodel provided by the Grabats contest.
- **DerivedMethodDeclaration.** This version of the JDTAST metamodel includes three *EAnnotation* attributes (named *isPublic, isStatic* and *isSameReturnType*) in the *MethodDeclaration* class which contain the EOL code to derive (as a boolean) whether:
  - The current instance of this *MethodDeclaration* (self) has as return type the *TypeDeclaration* it is contained in. The EOL code reads as follows:

```
self.returnType.isTypeOf(SimpleType) and self.
   revRefNav_bodyDeclarations.isTypeOf(TypeDeclaration) and
   self.returnType.name.fullyQualifiedName == self.
   revRefNav_bodyDeclarations.name.fullyQualifiedName
```

– The current instance of this *MethodDeclaration* (self) is public. The EOL code reads as follows:

```
self.modifiers.exists(mod:Modifier|mod.public=="true"))
```

– The current instance of this *MethodDeclaration* (self) is static. The EOL code reads as follows:

```
self.modifiers.exists(mod:Modifier|mod.static=="true"))
```

Where the attribute *revRefNav_bodyDeclarations* allows reverse-navigation of the containment reference (*bodyDeclarations*) and retrieves the instance of the containing class (this is necessary as the JDTAST metamodel does not specify an opposite reference to the containment *bodyDeclarations*).

– **DerivedTypeDeclaration.** This version of the JDTAST metamodel includes a single *EAnnotation* attribute (named *isGrabats*) in the *TypeDeclaration* class which contains the EOL code to derive (as a boolean) whether the this instance (self) fulfills the Grabats query requirements. The EOL code reads as follows:

```
self.bodyDeclarations.exists(md:MethodDeclaration|md.modifiers
   .exists(mod:Modifier|mod.public=="true") and md.modifiers.
   exists(mod:Modifier|mod.static=="true") and md.returnType.
   isTypeOf(SimpleType) and md.returnType.name.
   fullyQualifiedName == self.name.fullyQualifiedName)
```

From table 2 we note that the increase in size when deriving attributes is very small (0.288% – 2.99%) so the only performance concern would be the increase in insertion time. In table 3 the numbers in brackets represent the time taken for the derivation of the attributes to be computed (which happens after the full model insertion). From table 3 we calculate the insertion time increases (using: $\frac{derivationtime}{totaltime - derivationtime} \times 100\%$) and present them in table 4. Table 4 demonstrates how there is a substantial (but reasonable) increase in insertion time for both derivation strategies presented. What is interesting is that even though DerivedTypeDeclaration computes a much heavier expression, due to the fact that it is performed sparsely, it requires comparable (and even slightly lower) insertion time to the DerivedMethodDeclaration strategy.

These results demonstrate that even though it is reasonable to add derived attributes even for quite complex derivations, careful consideration is needed so only important attributes are derived, otherwise it can result in unacceptable insertion times.

Table 3. Model Insertion, Execution time Results

Model	Execution Time (in seconds)		
	Original	DerivedMethodDeclaration	DerivedTypeDeclaration
Set0	16	16 (0.12)	16 (0.10)
Set1	34	36 (1.46)	37 (1.16)
Set2	553	658 (73)	625 (19)
Set3	2287	2650 (404)	2486 (347)
Set4	2502	2947 (493)	2893 (477)

Table 4. Model Insertion, Execution time Increase Percentage

Model	Execution Time Increase (in %)	
	DerivedMethodDeclaration	DerivedTypeDeclaration
Set0	0.756	0.629
Set1	4.23	3.237
Set2	12.48	3.135
Set3	17.99	16.22
Set4	20.09	19.74

5.4 Query Execution Time

Table 5 shows the results for performing the first Grabats 2009 [11,13] query on the various persisted models. As previously mentioned, the Grabats query finds all occurrences of *TypeDeclaration* elements that declare at least one public static method with the declared type as its returning type. For these tests three queries have been created in EOL (Q1 – Q3):

- *Q1* reads:

```
TypeDeclaration.all.collect(
  td|td.bodyDeclarations.select(
    md:MethodDeclaration|md.modifiers.exists(mod:Modifier|mod.
      public=="true")
    and md.modifiers.exists(mod:Modifier|mod.static=="true")
    and md.returnType.isTypeOf(SimpleType)
    and md.returnType.name.fullyQualifiedName == td.name.
      fullyQualifiedName ) )
```

This query (Q1) is the basic Grabats query using the original metamodel to insert the relevant models into Hawk. As such it only uses attributes found in the unaltered JDTAST metamodel.

- *Q2* reads:

```
TypeDeclaration.all.collect(
  td|td.bodyDeclarations.select(
    md:MethodDeclaration|md.isPublic == "true"
    and md.isStatic == "true"
    and md.isSameReturnType == "true" ) )
```

This query (Q2) contains the annotations described above for the Derived-MethodDeclaration insertion. As it uses attributes found in the unaltered JDTAST metamodel as well as the derived attributes 'isPublic', 'isStatic' and 'isSameReturnType'.

- *Q3* reads:

```
TypeDeclaration.all.select( td|td.isGrabats == "true" )
```

This query (Q3) contains the annotations described above for the Derived-TypeDeclaration insertion. As it uses attributes found in the unaltered JD-TAST metamodel as well as the derived attribute 'isGrabats'.

Table 5. Grabats Query Execution Time Results

Model	Execution Time (in seconds)				
	Original	DerivedMethodDeclaration		DerivedTypeDeclaration	
	Q1	Q1	Q2	Q1	Q3
Set0	0.391	0.391	0.281	0.391	0.172
Set1	0.797	0.794	0.651	0.750	0.516
Set2	5.398	5.583	3.893	5.521	1.890
Set3	11.358	14.979	8.427	13.916	3.543
Set4	13.333	15.962	9.198	15.363	3.776

Query Q1 is run on all three types of inserted models as it does not contain any new constructs. Q2 is run on models which have used the DerivedMethod-Declaration annotations as it contains constructs using features derived by virtue of that annotated metamodel. Q3 is similarly run on models which have used the DerivedTypeDeclaration annotations.

It should be noted that the querying of the original models (using the original query – Q1) in Epsilon, which was presented in [4] has slightly worst execution times as it uses an older version of the EMC driver implemented for Hawk (and also ran Java 1.6).

The first interesting thing to note here is that running Q1 on the models with derived attributes is slightly less performant on the larger models (set2 – set4) than running it on the unaltered model. This is to be expected as the driver has to navigate through a larger database in these cases (as it is augmented with the derived attributes). As such, any operation which requires iteration on attributes of an object will possibly be slower than originally. Running Q1 on DerivedMethodDeclaration is slightly slower than Q1 on DerivedTypeDeclaration as DerivedTypeDeclaration only introduces one new attribute (isGrabats) for each *TypeDeclaration* while DerivedMethodDeclaration introduces three new attributes for each *MethodDeclaration* (and there are more *MethodDeclaration* instances than *TypeDeclaration* ones).

Looking at Q2, we see that it offers a significant performance increase to the original tests with mean improvement of 26.23% and maximum improvement of 31.01% (on the largest model, set4). Similarly for Q3 we note an even larger improvement in performance with mean 59.35% and maximum 71.68% (again, on the largest model, set4).

These results support the idea that for both small and large model sizes the targeted use of derived attributes can greatly benefit the resulting queries. What's more, these results seem to indicate that the larger the model size the more effective using derived attributes is in improving performance. Taking the larger models (set2 – set4) we note that the improvement percentage stays roughly the same or even tends to increase with the size of the model.

6   Conclusions and Further Work

From the empirical data collected we can conclude that using derived attributes in Hawk greatly improves the performance of queries performed that make use of them. There seems to be a steady (almost entirely positively correlated) relationship between the percentage increase in the performance gain (in terms of execution time) on queries performed and model size. Nevertheless there are two compromises to be made when considering the use of such attributes. The first is that the insertion time of models containing derived attributes is slower than the original models due to the overhead of deriving them. The second is that using several broad derived attributes, while less performant than using one single targeted derived attribute (while taking the same if not more time to insert), enables their possible use for different queries on the model while the targeted attribute can only be used in a much narrower scope. Finally, we note that general queries performed on models using derived attributes seem to be slightly less performant than ones using the original model; as such, derived attributes should only be used when there is reasonable confidence that they will be required (for example when needing to perform a known heavyweight transformation or query on the model).

Obtaining these encouraging results motivates us for implementing a fully engineered solution of using derived attributes in Hawk, while taking into account the concerns mentioned at the end of Section 3.1, in the future. Firstly, restricting the types of expressions allowed for derived attributes to be computed, so that model evolution can be performed in reasonable time, is planned. Next, a way to persist the expressions for derived attributes outside the metamodel, when the metamodel is immutable for example, will be looked at. Finally, use of embedded indexes found in Graph NoSQL databases in order to index specific attributes of interest, with the goal of further increasing query performance when such attributes are required for much of the computation of the query, will be investigated.

Acknowledgements. This research was part supported by the EPSRC, through the Large-Scale Complex IT Systems project (EP/F001096/1) and by the EU, through the MONDO FP7 STREP project (#611125).

References

1. Mohagheghi, P., Fernandez, M.A., Martell, J.A., Fritzsche, M., Gilani, W.: MDE Adoption in Industry: Challenges and Success Criteria. In: Chaudron, M.R.V. (ed.) MODELS 2008 Workshops. LNCS, vol. 5421, pp. 54–59. Springer, Heidelberg (2009)
2. Kolovos, D.S., Paige, R.F., Polack, F.A.: Scalability: The Holy Grail of Model Driven Engineering. In: Proc. Workshop on Challenges in MDE, Collocated with MoDELS 2008, Toulouse, France (2008)
3. Mougenot, A., Darrasse, A., Blanc, X., Soria, M.: Uniform Random Generation of Huge Metamodel Instances. In: Paige, R.F., Hartman, A., Rensink, A. (eds.) ECMDA-FA 2009. LNCS, vol. 5562, pp. 130–145. Springer, Heidelberg (2009)
4. Barmpis, K., Kolovos, D.: Evaluation of contemporary graph databases for efficient persistence of large-scale models. Journal of Object Technology (to appear, 2014)
5. Barmpis, K., Kolovos, D.: Hawk: Towards a scalable model indexing architecture. In: Proceedings of the Workshop on Scalability in Model Driven Engineering, Big-MDE 2013, pp. 6:1–6:9. ACM, New York (2013)
6. Kolovos, D.S., Rose, L., Garcia, A.D., Paige, R.F.: The Epsilon Book (2008), http://www.eclipse.org/epsilon/doc/book/
7. Kolovos, D.S., Paige, R.F., Polack, F.A.C.: The Epsilon Object Language. In: Rensink, A., Warmer, J. (eds.) ECMDA-FA 2006. LNCS, vol. 4066, pp. 128–142. Springer, Heidelberg (2006)
8. Paige, R.F., Kolovos, D.S., Rose, L.M., Drivalos, N., Polack, F.A.: The Design of a Conceptual Framework and Technical Infrastructure for Model Management Language Engineering. In: Proc. 14th IEEE International Conf. on Engineering of Complex Computer Systems, Potsdam, Germany (2009)
9. Willink, E.: Aligning OCL with UML. In: Proceedings of the Workshop on OCL and Textual Modelling. Electronic Communications of the EASST (2011)
10. Kolovos, D.S., Wei, R., Barmpis, K.: An approach for efficient querying of large relational datasets with ocl-based languages. In: XM 2013–Extreme Modeling Workshop, p. 48 (2013)
11. Grabats2009: 5th Int. Workshop on Graph-Based Tools (2012), http://is.tm.tue.nl/staff/pvgorp/events/grabats2009/
12. Pagán, J.E., Cuadrado, J.S., Molina, J.G.: A repository for scalable model management. Software & Systems Modeling, 1–21 (2013)
13. Sottet, J.S., Jouault, F.: Program comprehension. In: Proc. 5th Int. Workshop on Graph-Based Tools (2009)

OCLR: A More Expressive, Pattern-Based Temporal Extension of OCL

Wei Dou, Domenico Bianculli, and Lionel Briand

SnT Centre - University of Luxembourg, Luxembourg, Luxembourg
{wei.dou,domenico.bianculli,lionel.briand}@uni.lu

Abstract. Modern enterprise information systems often require to specify their functional and non-functional (e.g., Quality of Service) requirements using expressions that contain temporal constraints. Specification approaches based on temporal logics demand a certain knowledge of mathematical logic, which is difficult to find among practitioners; moreover, tool support for temporal logics is limited. On the other hand, a standard language such as the Object Constraint Language (OCL), which benefits from the availability of several industrial-strength tools, does not support temporal expressions.

In this paper we propose *OCLR*, an extension of OCL with support for temporal constraints based on well-known property specification patterns. With respect to previous extensions, we add support for referring to a specific occurrence of an event as well as for indicating a time distance between events and/or from scope boundaries. The proposed extension defines a new syntax, very close to natural language, paving the way for a rapid adoption by practitioners. We show the application of the language in a case study in the domain of eGovernment, developed in collaboration with a public service partner.

1 Introduction

Complex software systems, such as modern enterprise information systems, call for the definition of requirements specifications that include both functional and non-functional aspects (such as QoS, Quality of Service). In both cases, the specifications might characterize (quantitative) aspects of the system that involve temporal constraints. Examples of these constraints are bounds on the sequence and/or number of occurrences of system events, possibly conjuncted with constraints on the temporal distance of events.

These types of specifications have been catalogued in various collections of property specification patterns, to help analysts and developers in expressing typical, recurrent properties of a system, using a generalized yet structured and precise form. The majority of property specification patterns have emerged in the context of concurrent, real-time critical systems [7,13,10], though there have been recent proposals of specification patterns for specific domains, like service-based applications [1]. In all cases, the patterns have been formalized in terms of some temporal logic, either the classic ones like LTL and CTL or a more specialized version like SOLOIST [2]. One problem in using a specification language

J. Cabot and J. Rubin (Eds.): ECMFA 2014, LNCS 8569, pp. 51–66, 2014.

based on a temporal logic is that it requires a strong theoretical background, which is rarely found in practitioners. Moreover, tool support for the verification of properties expressed in temporal logic is prototypal and limited, at least if considered in the context of applying this kind of formal method at a scalable, industrial-grade level.

One of the specification languages that has found a significant consensus and adoption in industry is the Object Constraint Language (OCL) [11], used to specify constraints on models, and now a standard in the context of model-driven engineering practice. However, OCL does not support the specification of temporal requirements. There have been several research proposals to extend OCL with temporal constructs. Nevertheless, in the scope of a collaboration with a public service partner active in the domain of eGovernment, we found that the available temporal extensions of OCL do not meet the expressiveness requirements as determined in our field study, based on realistic specifications extracted from a collection of eGovernment business process descriptions.

In this paper we propose a new language, called *OCLR*, to fill the expressiveness gap that we found on the field. *OCLR* is an extension of OCL that supports temporal constraints based on some of the well-known property specification patterns. More specifically, we advance the state of the art by introducing support for referring to a specific occurrence of an event in scope boundaries as well as for indicating a time distance between events and/or from scope boundaries. Our language extends OCL in a minimal fashion while maximizing the expressiveness of temporal properties; moreover, the syntax is very close to natural language, to encourage practitioners to use it. To show the feasibility of using *OCLR* in realistic scenarios, we include a case study in the context of an eGovernment application developed by our public service partner.

In the future, our intent is to adopt *OCLR* in the context of a larger project on model-driven run-time verification[1] of business processes. Since in this project we plan to leverage existing industrial-strength OCL tools, such as constraint verification engines, we decided to minimize, by design, the differences between the models underlying *OCLR* and OCL. We believe that making *OCLR* a *minimal* extension of OCL will make the translation[2] of *OCLR* expressions into regular OCL ones much easier than performing the same translation starting from expressions written in a language much more distant from OCL, such as a temporal logic.

The rest of this paper is structured as follows. In Sect. 2 We discuss the motivations for which and the context in which this work has been developed. Section 3 introduces *OCLR*, its syntax and the (informal) semantics[3]. In Sect. 4 we show the application of *OCLR* in a case study in the domain of eGovernment. We survey related work in Sect. 5. Section 6 concludes the paper, providing directions for future work.

---

[1] In fact *OCLR* stands for "OCL for Run-time verification".

[2] The translation from *OCLR* to OCL is out of the scope of this paper.

[3] The complete definition of the formal semantics of *OCLR* is available in [6].

2   Motivations

This work has been developed as part of an ongoing collaboration with CTIE (Centre des technologies de l'information de l'Etat), the Luxembourg national center for information technology. The main role of CTIE is to lead the development of electronic government (eGovernment) initiatives within Luxembourg, with the ultimate goal of delivering digital public services to citizens and enterprises, as well as improving the processes followed by the public administration.

The business processes designed for public administrations are usually highly complex and require the interaction of different stakeholders. In particular, they act as the "glue" to orchestrate different information systems, possibly by many different organizations, in an effort to foster cooperation of various administrations. Given the complexity and the many interactions foreseen for eGovernment business processes, designing effective and efficient processes to drive e-service delivery is one of the most challenging tasks for public administrations. For these reasons, their development is gradually moving towards model-driven techniques. This is the case for CTIE, which has developed in-house a model-driven methodology for designing eGovernment business processes.

Usually these processes are designed as compositions of services provided by different organizations, administrations, or third-party suppliers. A service integrator has to monitor the execution of the third-party services it uses to check whether they fulfill their obligations (both in terms of functional and non-functional properties), so that the business process itself can meet its requirements. Furthermore, it is also important to verify at run time whether the business process execution complies with the constraints specified during the modeling phase, to detect when a failure occurs and to possibly determine corrective actions. In this context, we are involved in a project on model-driven, run-time verification of (eGovernment) business processes.

One of the first steps of this project consisted in identifying the type of constraints to check at run time. We analyzed several applications developed by CTIE and scrutinized the requirements specifications associated with all use cases and business process descriptions. We were able to recast the majority of specifications written in natural language using the system of property specification patterns (and scopes) proposed by Dwyer et al. [7]. However, in some cases the original definitions proposed in [7] had to be extended to match the system specifications. For example, the definitions of property specification scopes, used to refer to the extent of a program execution over which a pattern must hold, had to be extended to support references to a specific occurrence of an event (not only the first one as in [7]), as in the requirement "event A shall occur before the *second* occurrence of event X". Another variant of this type of scope boundary that we found is the one with requirements on the distance between events, such as "event A shall occur *five time units before the second* occurrence of event X". In some cases, the requirements specifications had to be expressed in terms of some real-time specification patterns [13,10], which quantitatively define distance among events and durations of events.

Based on the results of this phase, we pondered over the definition of a high-level specification language for expressing this type of constraints. The intrinsic temporal nature of the requirements specifications we found, including also real-time constraints, could have suggested to follow the direction of building on some temporal logic. However, specification languages based on temporal logic require a certain mathematical knowledge that is not easy and common to find among practitioners, such as business analysts or software engineers. Moreover, the array of tools available for the verification of temporal logic is limited, especially if one considers the additional requirement of applying them in realistic industrial contexts. Based on these limitations, given the model-driven engineering practice already in place at our public service partner, we decided to define our specification language as *an extension* of OCL. In this way, we can build on a language that is standardized, is known among practitioners, and has a wide set of well-established, industrial-strength tools, like constraints verification engines.

3   OCLR

The design of *OCLR* is based on Dwyer et al.'s property specification patterns system [7]. This system defines five scopes (*globally, before, after, between-and*, and *after-until*) and eight patterns (*universality, absence, existence, bounded existence, precedence, response, precedence chain*, and *response chain*).

In the definition of *OCLR* we decided to support all these scopes and patterns, with the following extensions:

- The possibility, in the definition of a scope boundary, to refer to a specific occurrence of an event, as in "before the second occurrence of event X...". In the original definition of the pattern systems, boundaries of scopes refer implicitly to the first occurrence of an event.
- The possibility to indicate a time distance with respect to a scope boundary, as in "at least (at most) two time units before the n-th occurrence of event X...".
- Support for expressing time distance between events occurrences, to express properties like a bounded response, such as "event B should occur in response to event A within 2 time units".

These design choices have been motivated by the type of properties that we have found while analyzing the requirement specifications of our public service partner, as well as by the lack of support for them in the current temporal extensions of OCL (see Sect. 5).

OCLR has been inspired by the design of Temporal OCL [12], another pattern-based temporal extension of OCL. As we will discuss in more detail in Sect. 5, Temporal OCL lacks the language features described above. Nevertheless, we borrow from it the notion of *event*, i.e., a predicate that specifies a set of instants within the time line; the specific types of events supported in the language are described in the following subsection.

3.1 Syntax

The syntax of *OCLR* (also inspired by the one of Temporal OCL [12]) is shown in Fig. 1: non-terminals are enclosed in angle brackets, terminals are enclosed in single quotes, and underlined italic words are non-terminals defined in the OCL grammar [11]. An ⟨*OCLR block*⟩ comprises a set of conjuncted ⟨*TemporalClauses*⟩ beginning with the keyword 'temporal'. Each temporal clause contains a temporal expression that consists of a ⟨*scope*⟩ and a ⟨*pattern*⟩; the scope specifies the time slot(s) during which the property described by the pattern should hold.

⟨*OCLRBlock*⟩	::=	'temporal' ⟨*TemporalClause*⟩+
⟨*TemporalClause*⟩	::=	[⟨*simpleNameCS*⟩] ':' [⟨*Quantif*⟩] ⟨*TemporalExp*⟩
⟨*Quantif*⟩	::=	'let' ⟨*VariableDeclarationCS*⟩ 'in'
⟨*TemporalExp*⟩	::=	⟨*Scope*⟩ ⟨*Pattern*⟩
⟨*Scope*⟩	::=	'globally'
	|	'before' ⟨*Boundary1*⟩
	|	'after' ⟨*Boundary1*⟩
	|	'between' ⟨*Boundary2*⟩ 'and' ⟨*Boundary2*⟩
	|	'after' ⟨*Boundary2*⟩ 'until' ⟨*Boundary2*⟩
⟨*Pattern*⟩	::=	'always' ⟨*Event*⟩
	|	'eventually' ⟨*RepeatableEventExp*⟩
	|	'never' ['exactly' ⟨*IntegerLiteralExpCS*⟩] ⟨*Event*⟩
	|	⟨*EventChainExp*⟩ 'preceding' [⟨*TimeDistanceExp*⟩] ⟨*EventChainExp*⟩
	|	⟨*EventChainExp*⟩ 'responding' [⟨*TimeDistanceExp*⟩] ⟨*EventChainExp*⟩
⟨*Boundary1*⟩	::=	[⟨*IntegerLiteratureExpCS*⟩] ⟨*SimpleEvent*⟩ [⟨*TimeDistanceExp*⟩]
⟨*Boundary2*⟩	::=	[⟨*IntegerLiteratureExpCS*⟩] ⟨*SimpleEvent*⟩ ['at least' *IntegerLiteratureExpCS* 'tu']
⟨*EventChainExp*⟩	::=	⟨*Event*⟩ (',' ['#' ⟨*TimeDistanceExp*⟩] ⟨*Event*⟩)*
⟨*TimeDistanceExp*⟩	::=	⟨*ComparingOp*⟩ ⟨*IntegerLiteratureExpCS*⟩ 'tu'
⟨*RepeatableEventExp*⟩	::=	[⟨*ComparingOp*⟩ ⟨*IntegerLiteratureExpCS*⟩] ⟨*Event*⟩
⟨*ComparingOp*⟩	::=	'at least' | 'at most' | 'exactly'
⟨*Event*⟩	::=	(⟨*SimpleEvent*⟩ | ⟨*ComplexEvent*⟩) ['|' *Event*]
⟨*ComplexEvent*⟩	::=	'isCalled' '(' 'anyOp' [',' 'pre:' ⟨*OCLExpressionCS*⟩] [',' 'post:' ⟨*OCLExpressionCS*⟩] ')' ['\' ⟨*Event*⟩]
⟨*SimpleEvent*⟩	::=	⟨*SimpleCallEvent*⟩ | ⟨*SimpleChangeEvent*⟩
⟨*SimpleChangeEvent*⟩	::=	'becomesTrue' '(' ⟨*OCLExpressionCS*⟩ ')'
⟨*SimpleCallEvent*⟩	::=	'isCalled' '(' ⟨*OperationCallExpCS*⟩ [',' 'pre:' ⟨*OCLExpressionCS*⟩] [',' 'post:' ⟨*OCLExpressionCS*⟩] ')'

Fig. 1. Grammar of OCLR

The definitions of ⟨*Event*⟩s that can be used in a temporal expression are adapted from [12]. The keyword 'isCalled' represents a *call event*, which corresponds to a call to an operation. Under the hypothesis of atomicity of operations, we merge into a single call event, the events corresponding to the call, the start, and the end of an operation. A call event has three parameters: the called operation; the precondition (optional, in the form of an OCL expression) that acts as guard over the system pre-state and the operation parameters for the actual call execution; the postcondition (optional, in the form of an OCL expression) that acts as guard over the system post-state and the return value of the call invocation. Notice that a call event is raised only if the operation is invoked *and* both the precondition and the postcondition are satisfied. The keyword 'anyOp' is used if no operation is specified; in this case the call event becomes a state change event, from the state determined by the precondition to the state determined by the postcondition. The keyword 'becomesTrue' denotes a state change event parameterized with the OCL expression provided as parameter: it corresponds to the state in which the input expression becomes true (which implies that in the previous state it evaluated to false). We also support the disjunction '|' and the exclusion '\' operations on events.

3.2 *OCLR* at Work

We now present some examples of properties that can be expressed with *OCLR*, in order to provide the reader with a high-level, intuitive understanding of the language. We consider the history trace shown in Fig. 2 and for each property indicate whether it is violated or not by the trace. First, we define the properties in English:

1. "Event C shall happen 8 time units after the second occurrence of event X." (satisfied)
2. "Event A shall happen within 30 time units after the first occurrence of event X." (satisfied)
3. "Event C shall eventually happen after at least 3 time units since the first occurrence of event X; and it shall happen before event Y if the latter happens." (violated)
4. "After the second occurrence of event X, event C shall eventually happen exactly twice." (satisfied)
5. "Event C shall happen at least once between every first occurrence of event X and the next event Y; the time interval between event X and the first occurrence of event C shall be at least 5 time units." (violated)

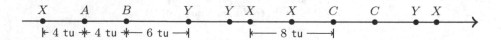

Fig. 2. Sample events traces

6. "Event B shall happen at least 3 time units before the first occurrence of event Y." (satisfied)
7. "Before the first occurrence of event Y, once event X occurs, event A shall happen followed by event B; the time interval between X and A shall be at least 3 time units." (satisfied)

The corresponding *OCLR* expressions are shown below:

1. temporal: after 2 X exactly 8 tu eventually C
2. temporal: after X at most 30 tu eventually A
3. temporal: after 1 X at least 3 tu until Y eventually C
4. temporal: after 2 X eventually exactly 2 C
5. temporal: between X at least 5 tu and Y eventually at least 1 C
6. temporal: before Y at least 3 tu eventually B
7. temporal: before Y A, B responding at least 3 tu X

3.3 Informal Semantics

In this section we present the informal semantics of the scopes and the patterns supported in *OCLR* expressions; they correspond to non-terminals $\langle Scope \rangle$ and $\langle Pattern \rangle$, respectively. The full definition of the formal semantics is available in the extended version of this paper [6].

Scopes. For the description of scopes, we refer to the trace of events depicted in Fig. 3. We use symbols X and Y as shorthands for events that can be derived from the non-terminal $\langle SimpleEvent \rangle$.

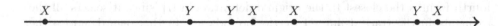

Fig. 3. A sample trace for the description of scopes

Before. This scope identifies a portion of a trace up to a certain boundary. The general template for this scope in *OCLR* is "before [m] X [$\langle ComparingOp \rangle$ n tu]", where elements between brackets are optional, 'm' and 'n' are integers derived from the non-terminal $\langle IntegerLiteratureExpCS \rangle$, and 'tu' stands for "time unit(s)". This template can be expanded in four forms: 1) "before X", 2) "before X $\langle ComparingOp \rangle$ n tu", 3) "before m X", 4) "before m X $\langle ComparingOp \rangle$ n tu". The first two forms are convenient shorthands for the third and fourth ones, respectively, with m = 1. The form "before m X" selects the portion of the trace up to the m-th occurrence of event X; see, for example, the top row in Fig. 4, where the interval from the origin of the trace up to the third occurrence of X is highlighted with a thick line. The form "before m X $\langle ComparingOp \rangle$ n tu" has three variants, depending on the possible expansions of non-terminal $\langle ComparingOp \rangle$:

- "before m X at least n tu" identifies the scope from the origin of the trace up to n time units before the m-th occurrence of X;
- "before m X at most n tu" identifies the scope starting at n time units before the m-th occurrence of X and bounded to the right by the m-th occurrence of X;
- "before m X exactly n tu" pinpoints the time instant at n time units before the m-th occurrence of X.

Examples of these three variants of scopes are shown with thick segments in Fig. 4, with m = 3 and with n = 2.

After. This scope identifies a portion of a trace starting from a certain boundary. It has a dual semantics with respect to the *before* scope. We provide an intuition of its semantics using Fig. 5, where the possible variants of this scope are represented as thick segments.

Between-And. This scope identifies portion(s) of a trace delimited by two boundaries. The general template for this scope in *OCLR* is "between [m1] X [at least n1 tu] and [m2] Y [at least n2 tu]", where elements between brackets are optional, 'm1', 'm2', 'n1', 'n2' are integers derived from the non-terminal ⟨*IntegerLiteratureExpCS*⟩, and 'tu' stands for "time unit(s)". This template can be expanded in four forms:

- "between m_1 X [at least n_1 tu] and m_2 Y [at least n_2 tu]";
- "between X [at least n_1 tu] and m_2 Y [at least n_2 tu]";
- "between m_1 X [at least n_1 tu] and Y [at least n_2 tu]";
- "between X [at least n_1 tu] and Y [at least n_2 tu]".

The first form is the most general: it selects the single segment of the trace delimited by the m_1-th occurrence of event X and the m_2-th occurrence of event Y happening after the m_1-th occurrence of X. The second and third forms are shorthands for the first one, with m1 = 1 and m2 = 1, respectively. The fourth form is the closest to the original definition in [7], since it selects all the segments in the trace delimited by the boundaries. In this regard, notice the difference with respect to the expression "between 1 X and 1 Y", which selects the segment delimited by the first occurrence of X and the first occurrence of Y after X. In all forms it is possible to use the expression at least n tu when defining boundaries, with the same meaning described for the scope *before*. Four examples of the *Between-and* scope are shown in Fig. 6.

After-Until. This scope is similar to *Between-and*, with the difference that each identified segment extends to the right in case the event defined by the second boundary does not occur; this peculiarity can be noticed in the first two rows of Fig. 7, and compared with those in Fig. 6.

Globally. This scope corresponds to the entire trace shown in Fig. 3.

Note that all scopes but those using the 'exactly' keyword do not include the events occurring at the boundaries of the scope itself.

Patterns. *OCLR* supports the eight patterns defined in [7].

Universality. It states that a certain event should *always* happen within the given scope.

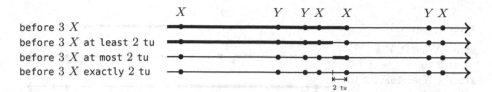

Fig. 4. Scope: before

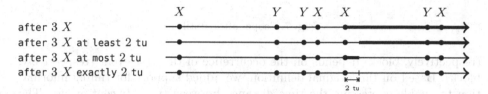

Fig. 5. Scope: after

Existence. It indicates that the given scope contains some occurrence(s) of a certain event. This pattern comes in four forms:

- "eventually *A*" means that the event *A* happens at least once;
- "eventually at least m *A*" means that *A* happens at least *m* times;
- "eventually at most m *A*" means that *A* happens at most *m* times;
- "eventually exactly m *A*" means that *A* happens exactly *m* times.

The last three forms are variants of the *bounded existence* pattern, a subclass of the *existence* one.

Absence. It states that a certain event *never* occurs in the given scope. It is also possible to specify that a specific number of occurrences of the same event should not happen, as in "never exactly 2 *X*", which says that *X* should never occur exactly twice.

Precedence. This pattern (also available in the variant called *precedence chain*) indicates the precondition relationship between a pair of events (respectively, the two blocks of a chain) in which the occurrence of the second event

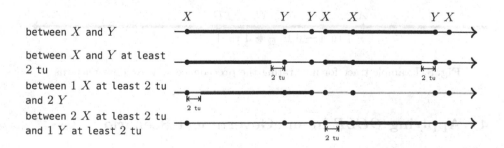

Fig. 6. Scope: between-and

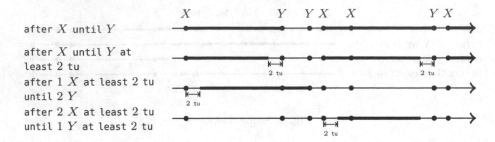

Fig. 7. Scope: after-until

(respectively, block) depends on the occurrence of the first event (respectively, block). Based on this original definition, we added support for timing information to enable expressing the time distance between two adjacent events. The semantics can be explained using the following example and the event trace in Fig. 8; the expression "A `preceding at most 10 tu` B, `#at least 5 tu` C" indicates that the event A is the precondition of the block "B followed by C", that the time distance between A and B is at most 10 time units, and the time distance (expressed using the # operator) between events B and C is at least 5 time units. Here, A (at the left of 'preceding') represents the first block of the chain, while the expression "B, `#at least 5 tu` C" represents the second block (at the right of 'preceding').

Response. This pattern (also available in the variant called *response chain*) specifies the cause-effect relationship between a pair of events (respectively, the two blocks of a chain) in which the occurrence of the first event (respectively, first block) leads to the occurrence of the second event (respectively, second block). The property "C, D `responding at most 10 tu` A, `#at least 5 tu` B" specifies that two successive events A and B stimulate the sequential occurrence of C and D, and the time interval between A and B should be at least 5 time units; the time interval between B (second element of the first block) and C (first element of the second block) should be at most 10 time units. This property is violated by the example in Fig. 8, because the time distance between A and B is only 4 time units.

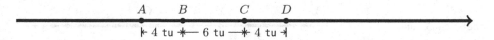

Fig. 8. Example trace for illustrating the precedence and response patterns

4   Applying *OCLR* in an eGovernment Scenario

In this section we present a case study where we show the use of *OCLR* in the context of an eGovernment application developed by our public service partner.

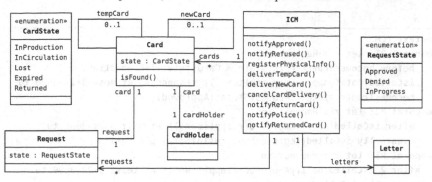

Fig. 9. Conceptual model of the ICM process

We illustrate some properties (selected from the 47 we analyzed) of a business process model related to three use cases. The goal is to investigate whether *OCLR* can precisely capture all temporal and timed properties of a real eGovernment system. The case study description has been sanitized for the purpose of not disclosing confidential information and also to obtain a model at the minimum level of detail required to illustrate and express the properties.

The scenario describes the *Identity Card Management (ICM)* business process, which is in charge of issuing and managing the ID cards of the diplomatic personnel of the country. A sanitized version of the conceptual model corresponding to this scenario is shown in Fig. 9. The *ICM* business process deals with the card requests, the production of the cards, and the returns of the cards once expired. The *ICM* process also keeps track of the state of a card (`CardState`), which can be, for example, `InCirculation` or `Expired`. A card `Request` can be in different states, such as `Approved`, `Denied`, and `InProgress`. Once a request for a card is submitted to the *ICM* system, it is evaluated and then either approved or denied. After the approval, the *ICM* system asks the production system to issue a physical card. The card will then be delivered to the applicant. The *ICM* also deals with events such as the damage, loss, or expiration of cards.

Sample Properties. We now list the requirements specifications associated with three uses cases of the *ICM* system, and show how the corresponding properties can be expressed in *OCLR*.

Card Request. The following requirements are associated with the use case related to the card request:

R1 Once a card request is approved, the applicant is notified within three days; this notification has to occur before the production of the card is started.

R2 The applicant has to show up within five days from the notification to get her personal data collected.

R3 If the applicant does not show up within five days after the second notification, the request will be denied and the applicant notified about the refusal.

```
1  context ICM
2  temporal R1: let r : Request in
3     before becomesTrue(r.card.state = CardState::InProduction)
4     isCalled(notifyApproved(r.applicant)) responding at most 3*24*3600 tu
5     becomesTrue(r.state = RequestState::Approved)
6  temporal R2: let r : Request in
7     after isCalled(notifyApproved(r.applicant)) at most 5*24*3600 tu
8     eventually isCalled(registerPhysicalInfo(r.applicant))
9  temporal R3: let r : Request in
10    after 2 isCalled(notifyApproved(r.applicant)) at least 5*24*3600 tu
11    eventually isCalled(notifyRefused(r.applicant))
```

Property R1 is expressed in lines 2–5. The *before* scope is delimited by the event that corresponds to a change in the state of the card (`c.state=CardState::InProduction`). The *response* pattern is bounded (time units are expressed in seconds) and requires the notification to the applicant (`notifyApproved`) to happen in response to a change in the state of the request (`r.state=RequestCard::Approved`). Property R2 (lines 6–8) combines an *after* scope with an *existence* pattern. A similar structure is used in R3 (lines 9–11), where the *after* scope uses the second occurrence of `notifyApproved` as the boundary.

Card Loss. The following requirements are associated with the use case related to the loss of a card:

L1 If a card is reported as lost to the *ICM* and has not been found yet, a temporary card will be sent to the card holder within 1 day.

L2 If the card has not been found yet, a new card will be delivered to the holder within five days after the report of the loss.

L3 After the card loss is reported, if the card is found, within at most three days the delivery of the new card will be canceled and a notification to return the temporary card will be sent.

```
1  context ICM
2  temporal L1: let c: Card in
3    after becomeTrue(c.state = CardState::Lost) at most 24*3600 tu
4    eventually isCalled(deliverTempCard(c.tempCard,
5                     pre: c.state=CardState::Lost))
6  temporal L2: let c : Card in
7    after becomeTrue(c.state = CardState::Lost) at most 5*24*3600 tu
8    eventually isCalled(deliverNewCard(c.newCard),
9                     pre: c.state=CardState::Lost)
10 temporal L3: let c: Card in
11   after becomeTrue(c.state = CardState::Lost)
12   isCalled(c.isFound(), pre: c.state=CardState::Lost)
13   preceding at most 3*24*3600 tu
14   isCalled(cancelCardDelivery(c.newCard),
15           pre: c.newCard.state <> CardState::InCirculation),
16   isCalled(notifyReturnCard(c.cardHolder))
```

Both properties L1 and L2 use an *after* scope combined with an *existence* pattern. Notice that in both cases the additional condition "card not found yet" is expressed as a precondition of the operation which is the argument of isCalled in the *existence* pattern (deliverTempCard and deliverNewCard). Property L3 combines an *after* scope with a *precedence chain* pattern, where the first block corresponds to finding the card (isFound) and the second block is the chain of cancelCardDelivery and notifyReturnCard.

Card Expiration. The following requirements are associated with the use case related to the expiration of a card:

E1 Once a card expires, the holder is notified to return the card at most twice.
E2 After five days from the second notification to the holder about the expiration of the card, if the card has not been returned yet, the police is notified.
E3 Once a card is returned, the holder will receive a confirmation within one day.

```
1  context ICM
2  temporal E1: let c:Card in
3    after becomesTrue(c.state = CardState::Expired)
4    until becomesTrue(c.state = CardState::Returned)
5    eventually at most 2 isCalled(notifyReturnCard(c.cardHolder),
6                    pre:c.state <> CardState::Returned)
7  temporal E2: let c:Card in
8    after 2 isCalled(notifyReturnCard(c.cardHolder),
9                pre: c.state <> CardState::Returned)
10   exactly 5*24*3600 tu
11   eventually isCalled(notifyPolice(c.cardHolder),
12               pre: c.state <> CardState::Returned)
13 temporal E3: let c:Card in
14   globally isCalled(notifyCardReturned(c.cardHolder),
15               pre: c.state = CardState::Returned)
16   responding at most 24*3600 tu
17   becomesTrue(c.state = CardState::Returned)
```

Property E1 uses an *after-until* scope, delimited by the events corresponding to the expiration of the card (c.state=CardState::Expired) and the return of the card (c.state=CardState::Returned). A *bounded existence* pattern is used to specify the maximum amount of notifications (notifyReturnCard) that can happen. In property E2 we use an *after* scope combined with the keyword 'exactly' to pinpoint the exact time instant in which the police is notified (notifyPolice). Property E3 states an invariant of the system (using the *globally* scope) for the *response* pattern correlating the return of the card (c.state=CardState::Returned) to the notification to the holder (notifyCardReturned).

5 Related Work

There have been several proposals for extending OCL with support for temporal constraints. In the rest of this section we summarize them and discuss their differences and limitations with respect to *OCLR*.

One of the first proposals is OCL/RT [4], which extends OCL with the notion of timestamped events (based on the original UML abstract meta-class Event) and two temporal modalities, "always" and "sometimes". Events are associated with instances of classifiers and, by means of a special satisfaction operator, it is possible to evaluate an expression at the time instant when a certain event occurred. The OCL/RT extension allows for expressing real-time deadline and timeout constraints but requires to reason explicitly at the lowest-level of abstraction, in terms of time instants.

Cabot et al. [3] extend UML to use UML/OCL as a temporal conceptual modeling language, introducing the concepts of *durability* and *frequency* for the definition of temporal features of UML classifiers and associations. They define temporal operations in OCL through which it is possible to refer to any past state of the system. These operations are mapped into standard OCL by relying on the mapping of the temporally-extended conceptual schema into a conventional UML one, which explicitly instantiates the concepts of time interval and instant. However, the temporal operations are geared to express temporal integrity constraints on the model, rather than temporal properties correlating events of the system.

The majority of the proposals regarding temporal extensions of OCL are realized by extending the language with temporal operators/modalities borrowed from standard temporal logic, such as "always", "until", "eventually", "next". A preliminary work in this direction appeared in [5]. Lavazza et al. [14] define the Object Temporal Logic (OTL), which allows users to write temporal constraints on Real-time UML (UML-RT) models. In particular, it supports the concepts *Time*, *Duration* and *Interval* to specify the time distance between events. Nevertheless, the language is modeled after the TRIO temporal logic [15], and the properties are written using a low level of abstraction. Ziemann and Gogolla [18] proposes TOCL, an extension of OCL with elements of a linear temporal logic, to specify constraints on the temporal evolution of the system states. Being based on linear temporal logic, TOCL does not support real-time constraints. The work on Flake and Mueller [8] goes in a similar direction, proposing an extension of OCL that allows for the specification of past- and future-oriented time-bounded constraints. They do not support event-based specifications; moreover, the proposed mapping into Clocked LTL does not allow to rely on standard OCL tools. Kuester-Filipe and Anderson propose a liveness template for future-oriented time-bounded constraints, as those than can be captured with a *response* or *existence* pattern. This template is defined in terms of the real-time temporal logic of knowledge, interpreted over timed automata, to allow for formal reasoning. The expressiveness of this extension is very limited, since it supports only one template. Soden and Eichler [17] propose Linear Temporal OCL (LT-OCL) for languages defined over MOF meta-models in conjunction with operational semantics. LT-OCL contains the standard modalities of Linear Temporal Logic. The interpretation of LT-OCL formulae is defined in the context of a MOF meta-model and its dynamic behavior specified by action semantics using the M3Actions framework.

The approaches that are most similar to *OCLR* are those that extend OCL with support for Dwyer et al.'s property specification patterns [7]. Flake and Mueller [9] propose a state-oriented temporal extension of OCL for user-defined classes that have an associated Statechart. The pattern-based temporal expressions refer to configurations of Statecharts. With respect to *OCLR*, they do not support the specification in terms of events. Moreover, the expressions corresponding to the patterns are not first-class entities of the language, hence they are more verbose and less close to natural language. Robinson [16] presents a temporal extension of OCL called OCL_{TM}, developed in the context of a framework for monitoring of requirements expressed using a goal model. OCL_{TM} includes all the operators corresponding to standard LTL modalities, and supports Dwyer et al.'s patterns and timeouts in patterns. In this regard, it is very close to the expressiveness of *OCLR*, though it supports neither the reference to a specific occurrence of an event in scope boundaries nor the association of time shifts to boundaries (as *OCLR* does with the keywords 'at least', 'at most', 'exactly'). Kanso and Taha [12] introduce Temporal OCL, a pattern-based temporal extension of OCL. As discussed in Sect. 3, *OCLR* borrows some language entities from Temporal OCL. Although the support for temporal patterns is very similar between the two languages, Temporal OCL does not allow references to specific event occurrences in scope boundaries and it lacks support for timing information, such as the distance between events and the distance from a scope boundary.

6 Conclusion and Future Work

A broad class of requirements for modern complex software systems involves temporal constraints, possibly enriched with timing information. Current approaches for specifying requirements either lack the expressiveness (as in the case of OCL) required for this new class of properties or require mathematical expertise (e.g., temporal logic). In this paper we presented *OCLR*, a novel temporal extension of OCL based on common property specification patterns, and extended with support for referring to a specific occurrence of an event in scope boundaries, and for specifying the distance between events and/or from boundaries of the scope of a pattern. We presented the semantics of the language and its application to a case study in the domain of eGovernment.

This work has been developed as part of a broader collaboration with our public service partner CTIE, the Luxembourg state center for information technology, in the context of a project on model-based run-time verification of eGovernment business processes. We are currently working on defining the mapping between *OCLR* and OCL, in order to take advantage of the industrial-strength tools available to check OCL constraints. Our next steps will focus on defining a model-based run-time verification technique for properties written with *OCLR*, and integrating it in the business process run-time platform of our partner. We also plan to conduct an empirical study to assess the improvements provided by *OCLR* when adopted as specification language in the development life cycle of our partner, and also to improve the language, integrating feedback from practitioners and adding support for other specification patterns [1].

Acknowledgments. This work has been supported by the National Research Fund, Luxembourg (FNR/P10/03). We would like to thank the members of the Prometa team at CTIE, in particular Lionel Antunes, Ludwig Balmer, Henri Meyer, Manuel Rouard, for their help with the analysis of the case study.

References

1. Bianculli, D., Ghezzi, C., Pautasso, C., Senti, P.: Specification patterns from research to industry: A case study in service-based applications. In: Proc. ICSE 2012, pp. 968–976. IEEE (2012)
2. Bianculli, D., Ghezzi, C., San Pietro, P.: The tale of SOLOIST: A specification language for service compositions interactions. In: Păsăreanu, C.S., Salaün, G. (eds.) FACS 2012. LNCS, vol. 7684, pp. 55–72. Springer, Heidelberg (2013)
3. Cabot, J., Olivé, À., Teniente, E.: Representing temporal information in UML. In: Stevens, P., Whittle, J., Booch, G. (eds.) UML 2003. LNCS, vol. 2863, pp. 44–59. Springer, Heidelberg (2003)
4. Cengarle, M.V., Knapp, A.: Towards OCL/RT. In: Eriksson, L.-H., Lindsay, P.A. (eds.) FME 2002. LNCS, vol. 2391, pp. 390–409. Springer, Heidelberg (2002)
5. Conrad, S., Turowski, K.: Temporal OCL: Meeting specification demands for business components. In: Unified Modeling Language: System Analysis, Design, and Development Issues, pp. 151–165. IGI Global (2001)
6. Dou, W., Bianculli, D., Briand, L.: OCLR: a more expressive, pattern-based temporal extension of OCL. Tech. Rep. TR-SnT-2014-2, SnT Centre - University of Luxembourg (February 2014), http://hdl.handle.net/10993/15339
7. Dwyer, M.B., Avrunin, G.S., Corbett, J.C.: Patterns in property specifications for finite-state verification. In: Proc. ICSE 1999, pp. 411–420. IEEE (1999)
8. Flake, S., Mueller, W.: Past- and future-oriented time-bounded temporal properties with OCL. In: Proc. SEFM 2004, pp. 154–163. IEEE (2004)
9. Flake, S., Müller, W.: Expressing property specification patterns with OCL. In: Software Engineering Research and Practice, pp. 595–603. CSREA Press (2003)
10. Gruhn, V., Laue, R.: Patterns for timed property specifications. Electron. Notes Theor. Comput. Sci. 153(2), 117–133 (2006)
11. Object Constraint Language (2012), http://www.omg.org/spec/OCL/ISO/19507/
12. Kanso, B., Taha, S.: Temporal constraint support for OCL. In: Czarnecki, K., Hedin, G. (eds.) SLE 2012. LNCS, vol. 7745, pp. 83–103. Springer, Heidelberg (2013)
13. Konrad, S., Cheng, B.H.C.: Real-time specification patterns. In: Proc. ICSE 2005, pp. 372–381. ACM (2005)
14. Lavazza, L., Morasca, S., Morzenti, A.: A dual language approach extension to UML for the development of time-critical component-based systems. Electron. Notes Theor. Comput. Sci. 82(6), 121–132 (2003)
15. Morzenti, A., Mandrioli, D., Ghezzi, C.: A model parametric real-time logic. ACM Trans. Program. Lang. Syst. 14, 521–573 (1992)
16. Robinson, W.N.: Extended OCL for goal monitoring. ECEASST 9 (2008)
17. Soden, M., Eichler, H.: Temporal extensions of OCL revisited. In: Paige, R.F., Hartman, A., Rensink, A. (eds.) ECMDA-FA 2009. LNCS, vol. 5562, pp. 190–205. Springer, Heidelberg (2009)
18. Ziemann, P., Gogolla, M.: OCL extended with temporal logic. In: Broy, M., Zamulin, A.V. (eds.) PSI 2003. LNCS, vol. 2890, pp. 351–357. Springer, Heidelberg (2004)

Interpretation of Linguistic Architecture

Ralf Lämmel and Andrei Varanovich

Software Languages Team
University of Koblenz-Landau, Germany
http://softlang.wikidot.com/

Abstract. The megamodeling language *MegaL* is designed to model the linguistic architecture of software systems: the relationships between software artifacts (e.g., files), software languages (e.g., programming languages), and software technologies (e.g., code generators) used in a system. The present paper delivers a form of interpretation for such megamodels: resolution of megamodel elements to resources (e.g., system artifacts) and evaluation of relationships, subject to designated programs (such as pluggable 'tools' for checking). Interpretation reduces concerns about the adequacy and meaning of megamodels, as it helps to apply the megamodels to actual systems. We leverage *Linked Data* principles for surfacing resolved megamodels by linking, for example, artifacts to *GitHub* repositories or concepts to *DBpedia* resources. We provide an executable specification (i.e., semantics) of interpreted megamodels and we discuss an implementation in terms of an object-oriented framework with dynamically loaded plugins.

Keywords: megamodel, interpretation, technological space, software language, software technology, ontology, *Linked Data*.

1   Introduction

The notion of megamodeling has seen much recent interest specifically in the MDE community with diverse application areas such as model management [2], software architecture [12], and models at runtime [18]. Different definitions of 'megamodel' are in use, see, for example, [4] for a more recent proposal. Usually, it is assumed that a megamodel is a model whose model elements are again models by themselves while the term 'model' is interpreted in a broad sense to include metamodels, conformant models, and transformation models.

In our recent work [7], we have introduced a megamodeling approach that it is not tailored to MDE; it is, in fact, meant to be applicable to arbitrary technological spaces [16]. To this end, we have introduced the megamodeling language *MegaL* for modeling the linguistic architecture of software systems, i.e., a system's architecture in terms of relationships between conceptual entities such as languages and technologies as well as actual entities ('artifacts') such as files. Until now, *MegaL* models lacked a proper interpretation which should define how to link megamodel nodes to actual resources (such as system artifacts or documentation) and edges to functionality for checking relationships.

J. Cabot and J. Rubin (Eds.): ECMFA 2014, LNCS 8569, pp. 67–82, 2014.

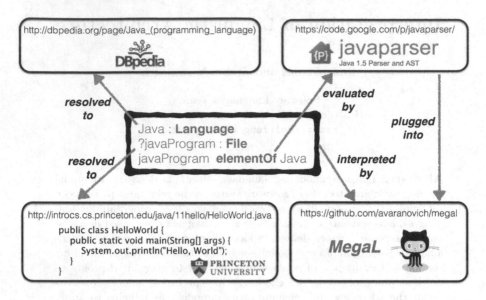

Fig. 1. Interpretation of a megamodel

The present paper[1] fills in the notion of interpretation of megamodels. In this manner, we provide a general facility to apply megamodels to actual systems and to validate the claims that are made by megamodels.

Consider Figure 1 for an illustration. The megamodel in the center of the figure declares a language Entity 'Java', a file entity parameter 'javaProgram', and a relationship between these entities such that the latter is an element of the former. Thus, the megamodel essentially describes a trivial Java-based system. The *MegaL* model can be interpreted as indicated in the figure, subject to a configuration and suitable plugins not shown here in detail. The interpretation entails these aspects:

⋄ The language 'Java' is resolved in terms of the corresponding resource (page) according to the ontology provided by *DBpedia*.
⋄ The parameter 'javaProgram' is resolved to the on-line version of a 'hello world' program on a web server at the *Princeton University*.
⋄ The 'elementOf' relationship is evaluated by the Java parser of the *javaparser* project hosted on *Google Code*.

Characteristics of the Approach. We begin with characteristics of the basic *MegaL* approach, essentially inherited from [7].

⋄ *Extra models on top of systems*: A megamodel is seen as an abstraction over an existing system, added 'after the fact', as opposed to forming a part of a system or expressing its composition, as in the case of model management.

---

[1] The paper's website: http://softlang.uni-koblenz.de/megal-interpretation/

◇ *Flexibility in terms of technological spaces*: Software technologies and systems may involve different technological spaces (such as grammarware or Javaware) without preference for a specific one such as MDE.

◇ *Decreased relevance of metamodels*: Metamodels or metamodel-like artifacts (e.g., schemas) are often unavailable or of limited relevance outside cleanroom MDE. That is, we often refer to languages instead of metamodels, i.e., to conceptual entities rather than artifacts.

We continue with characteristics of interpretation. These are the **contributions** of the present paper.

◇ *Resource-based resolution of entities*: The entities in a megamodel may be resolved to resources that can be addressed with URIs, thereby enabling transparent reuse of existing ontologies (e.g., *DBpedia*) and repositories (e.g., *GitHub* repos). We leverage *Linked Data* principles.

◇ *Flexibility in terms of ontologies*: There does not exist a comprehensive ontology for software engineering. Thus, different ontologies, subject to a plugin infrastructure, may be combined to assign meaning to the entity types and the conceptual entities in a megamodel.

◇ *Tool-based interpretation of relationships*: Relationships may be interpreted by designated programs ('tools'), e.g., a program implementing the membership test for a given language. This is supported by a plugin infrastructure, without favoring any particular semantics formalism.

◇ *Traceability recovery*: The actual semantics of transformation relationships is often inaccessible, as it is buried in software technologies. Thus, it may be preferable to construct a simplified and accessible variant of the actual semantics which provides insight due to its simplicity and through recovered traceability links for the involved artifacts.

Road-Map of This Paper. §2 describes *MegaL* without interpretation; it also develops a relatively simple, illustrative megamodel, which will serve as the running example of the paper. §3 develops the central notion of megamodel interpretation including its implementation as an object-oriented framework. §4 provides an executable specification (semantics) of interpreted megamodels. §5 discusses related work. §6 concludes the paper.

2 Megamodeling with *MegaL*

This section describes the language elements of *MegaL*. We develop a relatively simple, illustrative megamodel, which will serve as the running example of the paper. All original aspects of interpretation are deferred to the next two sections.

2.1 *MegaL* Entities

All *entities* in a megamodel must get assigned an *entity type*. These types are also defined in *MegaL*. Entity types are declared as subtypes of the root entity type *Entity* or subtypes thereof. In this manner, a classification hierarchy (i.e., a taxonomy or ontology of entity types) is described. Here are some reusable entity types, as declared in actual *MegaL* syntax:

Set < *Entity* // *Sets such as languages; see below*
Language < *Set* // *Languages as sets, e.g., sets of strings*
Technology < *Entity* // *Technologies in the sense of conceptual entities*
Artifact < *Entity* // *Artifacts as entities with a physical manifestation*
File < *Artifact* // *Files as a common kind of artifact*
Function < *Set* // *A function such as the meaning of a program*
FunctionApplication < *Entity* // *A particular application of a function*

Entity types are exercised in entity declarations as those of Figure 1:

Java : *Language* // *Entity Java is of type Language*
?javaProgram : *File* // *Entity (parameter) javaProgram is of type File*

We defer the discussion of the exact difference between entities and entity parameters (see the prefix '?') until we deal with resolution in §3.

2.2   *MegaL* Relationships

All relationships between entities are instances of appropriate relationship types. Again, these types are defined in *MegaL*. Here are some reusable relationship types, as declared in actual *MegaL* syntax:

elementOf < *Entity* * *Set* // *Membership in the set–theoretic sense*
conformsTo < *Artifact* * *Artifact* // *Conformance in the sense of metamodeling*
defines < *Artifact* * *Entity* // *Such as a grammar defining a language*
domainOf < *Set* * *Function* // *The domain of a function*
rangeOf < *Set* * *Function* // *The range of a function*
inputOf < *Entity* * *FunctionApplication* // *The input of a function application*
outputOf < *Entity* * *FunctionApplication* // *The output of a function application*
partOf < *Entity* * *Entity* // *A physical or conceptual containment relationship*

Relationship types are exercised in declarations as this one of Figure 1:

javaProgram elementOf Java

2.3   An Illustrative Megamodel

Let us capture key aspects of ANTLR usage in a software system. ANTLR[2] is (among other things) a parser generator that targets, for example, Java. Thus, ANTLR can be used to generate Java code for a parser for some language from a grammar given in ANTLR's grammar notation.

Entities. We declare the essential entities of ANTLR usage for parser generation:

ANTLR : *Technology* // *The technology as a conceptual entity*
Java : *Language* // *The language targeted by the parser generator*
ANTLR.Notation : *Language* // *The language of parser specifications*
ANTLR.Generator : *Function* (*ANTLR.Notation* → *Java*)
?aLanguage : *Language* // *Some language being modeled with ANTLR*

---

[2] http://www.antlr.org/

*?aGrammar : **File** // Some grammar defining the language at hand*
*?aParser : **File** // The generated parser for the language at hand*
*?anInput : **File** // Some sample input for the parser at hand*

We leverage a notation for compound entities; see the names *ANTLR.Notation* and *ANTLR.Generator*. That is, ANTLR's notation for grammars is a conceptual constituent of the ANTLR technology as such. ANTLR's generation semantics is also such a constituent. The dot notation implies part-of relationships as follows:

*ANTLR.Notation **partOf** ANTLR // Notation is conceptual part of technology*
*ANTLR.Generator **partOf** ANTLR // Generator semantics as well*

We also leverage special notation for function entities; see the declaration of *ANTLR.Generator*. The arrow notation is desugared as follows:

*ANTLR.Notation **domainOf** ANTLR.Generator*
*Java **rangeOf** ANTLR.Generator*

Relationships. The previously declared entities engage in relationships as follows:

*aGrammar **elementOf** ANTLR.Notation // The grammar is given in ANTLR notation*
*aGrammar **defines** aLanguage // The grammar defines some language*
*aParser **elementOf** Java // Java is used for the generated parser*
ANTLR.Generator(aGrammar) ↦ aParser // Generate parser from grammar
*anInput **elementOf** aLanguage // Wanted! An element of the language*
*anInput **conformsTo** aGrammar // Conform also to the grammar*

The declaration of the '↦' relationship is actually a shorthand. We need a designated entity for the function application. Thus, desugaring yields this:

*ANTLR.GeneratorApp1 : **FunctionApplication***
*ANTLR.GeneratorApp1 **elementOf** ANTLR.Generator*
*aGrammar **inputOf** ANTLR.GeneratorApp1*
*aParser **outputOf** ANTLR.GeneratorApp1*

3   Interpretation of Megamodels

Interpretation entails resolution of megamodel entities and evaluation of megamodel relationships. Resolution of entity parameters commences in a 'pointwise' manner in that the parameters are mapped to specific URIs. Resolution of entities (as opposed to parameters) commences in a schematic manner, subject to 'resolvers' (i.e., programs) for mapping entity names to URIs. Evaluation relies on 'evaluators' (again, programs) for checking the relevant relationships and possibly producing traceability evidence. Pointwise mappings, resolvers, and evaluators are identified in a configuration that goes with a megamodel.

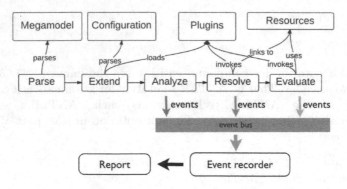

Fig. 2. *MegaL* processing pipeline

3.1 Megamodel Processing

The *MegaL* processor is a Java-based object-oriented framework. Given a megamodel and a configuration, the *MegaL* processor performs the steps summarized in Figure 2.

That is, the megamodel is parsed into an abstract syntax tree based on a suitable object model. In the next step, the configuration file is processed and the corresponding plugins are dynamically loaded and associated with the appropriate AST nodes for entity and relationship types. In the next step, the megamodel and the plugins are analyzed for well-formedness and mutual compliance; see §4 for a precise, formal account. Eventually, resolvers and evaluators are invoked. Resolution determines entity URIs and pings them for availability. Evaluation applies evaluators to the resources (the underlying content) of entities.

Along this pipeline, events are triggered and reported, making the process fully transparent. Any resolution and evaluation problems would also be reported along the way. For instance, the resolution of the 'Java' entity of Figure 1 is reported as follows:

> Looking up entity type *Language*.
< Looked up entity type *Language* successfully.
> Linking entity *Java*.
  ◇ URI located via configuration.
< Linked entity *Java* successfully.

Ideally, all entities of a megamodel should be resolved (successfully) and relationships should be evaluated (successfully). However, this is not always feasible. That is, one may be missing resolvers or evaluators for some of the exercised entities and relationships. In this sense, interpretation may be incomplete, but this would be evident from the event report generated by megamodel processing.

3.2 Configuration of the Interpretation

Configuration relies on a simple JSON-based DSL with language elements for URI mapping and registration of mapping resolvers as well as evaluators.

```
{
  "links" : [ {
    "name": "javaProgram",
    "resource" : "http://introcs.cs.princeton.edu/java/11hello/HelloWorld.java"
  } ],
  "resolvers" : [ { "plugin" : "megal.resolvers.dbpedia" } ],
  "evaluators" : [ {
    "plugin" : "megal.evaluators.FileElementOfLanguage"
    "checkers" : [ { "plugin" : "megal.checkers.languages.Java" } ]
  } ]
}
```

Fig. 3. The configuration for the megamodel in Figure 1

Figure 3 shows the configuration for the introductory Java example. In the 'links' section, the parameter 'javaProgram' is resolved in a pointwise manner so that it links to the 'hello world' program on Princeton University's web server. In the 'resolvers' section, we register a *DBpedia* resolver which is prepared to resolve entity names of the language type to resource URIs on *DBpedia*. In particular, this resolver handles the 'Java' entity of the megamodel. In the 'evaluators' section, we register an evaluator '....FileElementOfLanguage', which can evaluate 'elementOf' relationships when the left operand is a file resource and the right operand is a language. The 'elementOf' plugin relies on second-level plugins, 'checkers', for individual languages. In the configuration file, we register indeed a checker (i.e., a membership test) for 'Java'. This checker is a wrapper around the Java parser of the javaparser project. In the *MegaL* project, we aim at collecting all such plugins as consolidated and reusable interpretations of well-defined resources identified through *Linked Data* principles.

3.3   Application to the Running Example

Let us consider the interpretation of the megamodel for ANTLR, as introduced in §2.3. To begin with, we should pick some software system which exercises ANTLR. Clearly, there is no shortage of such systems. As it happens, the *MegaL* implementation itself also uses ANTLR. Thus, let us apply the *MegaL* model for ANTLR to *MegaL*'s parser.

Entity Parameters. They are resolved as follows:

aLanguage The language at hand is fixed to be *MegaL*. A link is needed. We choose to link to the language's *GitHub* project.[3]

aGrammar The grammar at hand is the ANTLR-based parser specification of *MegaL*. Thus, we need to link to a specific file *.../MegaL.g4* in said repository.

aParser The parser at hand is a Java source-code file *.../MegaLParser.java* that was generated by ANTLR—again, a file in said repository.

anInput Any *MegaL* source could be linked here. We choose to link to *MegaL*'s prelude with the predefined types, as discuss in §2—again, a file in said repository.

---
[3] https://github.com/avaranovich/megal/

Entities. They are resolved as follows:

Java A *DBpedia* resolver is used as explained in §3.2.

ANTLR The *DBpedia* resolver may not be used here because we rely on the fact that *ANTLR* is a compound entity with constituents, as listed below. In the 101companies project [6], software technologies, languages, and concepts are organized in an ontological manner. There is a suitable composition-aware '101companies' resolver for technologies, which links *ANTLR* to a resource.[4]

ANTLR.Notation Use the same resolver as for *ANTLR*.

ANTLR.Generator Use the same resolver as for *ANTLR*.

ANTLR.GeneratorApp1 An application is a pair of the input and output entities. Thus, an application entity is resolved, at a basic level, once input and output are resolved. A more advanced resolution entails the identification of a system artifact's fragment that expresses the application. More specifically, the application of ANTLR's generator could be pinpointed in a build script.

Relationships. They are evaluated as follows:

elementOf The evaluator *....FileElementOfLanguage* of §3.2 is enriched by additional second-level plugins (i.e., 'checkers') to serve *aLanguage* (thus, *MegaL*) and *ANTLR.Notation*—in addition to just *Java* previously.

conformsTo Another evaluator *....FileConformsToFile* is needed. It is the language of the right operand which defines the applicable conformance semantics. The result of a conformance test can be richer than just a Boolean value; it may be a set of traceability links between the operands; see §3.4.

defines An evaluator *....Triangle* is used which simply checks that a megamodel with the relationship '*x defines y*' also contains the relationships '*z elementOf y*' and '*z conformsTo x*'. This is Favre's triangle [5].

'↦' In fact, we evaluate *ANTLR.GeneratorApp1 elementOf ANTLR.Generator* after desugaring. That is, we need to check that *aParser* is the output generated by *ANTLR.Generator* from *aGrammar*. There are several options for checking function applications. As suggested earlier, we may pinpoint the actual application, e.g., in a build script. We could also pinpoint traces of the application, e.g., the Java comment included by ANTLR into the generated source file. We could also apply the function (i.e., run the generator) and compare the result with the existing output artifact. Ultimately, we may analyze input and output and establish problem-specific traceability links based on our understanding of the mapping, thereby also sharing our understanding with others. This is illustrated below.

3.4 Traceability Recovery

Traceability links may be recovered, for example, for conformance relationships and function application relationships (i.e., 'transformations'). This is illustrated for the application of *ANTLR.Generator*. The input, *aGrammar*, is essentially a list of ANTLR rules with unique nonterminals on the left-hand sides. The output, *aParser*, is essentially a Java file exercising certain code patterns. In particular, for each nonterminal n, there is a corresponding method that implements the rule:

```
public final nContext n() throws RecognitionException { ... }
```

```
// Get methods of interest
val methods = aParser.getMembers()
    .filter(x => x.isInstanceOf[MethodDeclaration])
    .filter(x => ((x.getThrows().map(y => y.getName()).
        contains("RecognitionException"))))
// Get grammar rules
val rules = aGrammar.rules
// Check 1:1 correspondence of names including the same order
val isAlligned = methods.zip(rules).forall(x => x._1.getName().equals(x._2))
```

Fig. 4. Scala-based traceability check for ANTLR's generator

Thus, a suitable approach to traceability recovery is to retrieve nonterminals from the grammar and all relevant methods from the generated Java source and to check for a 1-1 correspondence; see Figure 4 for illustration. For brevity, we show simplified evaluator code that only checks for correspondence, while the actual evaluator collects traceability links (i.e., pairs of URIs) of the following form:

⟨ "http://.../MegaLParser.java/class/MegaLParser/method/megamodel/1" ,
"http://.../MegaL.g4/grammar/megal/rule/megamodel/1" ⟩

The URIs describe the relevant fragments in a language-parametric manner. That is, the URIs start with the actual resource URI for the underlying artifact. The rest of the URI, which is underlined for clarity, describes the access path to the relevant fragment. To this end, syntactical categories of the artifact's language (see 'class' and 'method' versus 'rule') and names of abstractions (see 'megamodel') are used. (We note that 'megamodel' is the first nonterminal, in fact, the startsymbol of the grammar for *MegaL*.)

4   Executable Specification of *MegaL*

The following specification of *MegaL* clarifies the meaning of entity resolution and relationship evaluation. The specification assumes an abstract *MegaL* syntax— without convenience notation for functions and function applications and without consideration of compound entities. The specification does also not cover traceability recovery (§3.4).

4.1   Specification Style

The specification is a deductive system, as commonplace for type systems and operational semantics. The specification is executable—directly as a logic program in Prolog.[5] *MegaL* is not a regular programming language. Thus, it requires some

---

[4] http://101companies.org/resources/technologies/ANTLR

[5] The specification is available from the paper's website. Basic logic programming is used, except for higher-order predicates [17] for list processing: *map* (for applying a predicate to the elements of a list), *filter* (for returning the elements that satisfy a predicate), and *zip* (for building a list of pairs from two lists).

insight to identify counterparts for what is usually referred to as static versus dynamic semantics.

We assume that interpreted megamodels consist of two parts: the actual megamodel and (the description of) the interpretation—the latter as an abstraction of the configuration, resolvers, and evaluators used in the actual implementation of §3. Given a megamodel MM and an interpretation $Interp$, the informal process of Figure 2 is formally described as follows:

$process(MM, Interp) \Longrightarrow$
   $megamodel(MM)$, % Inductive syntax definition of megamodels
   $okMegamodel(MM)$, % Well–formedness relation for megamodels
   $interp(Interp)$, % Inductive syntax definition of interpretations
   $okInterp(Interp)$, % (Trivial) well–formedness of interpretations
   $correct(MM, Interp)$, % Correctness of interpretation w.r.t megamodel
   $complete(MM, Interp)$, % Completeness of interpretation w.r.t. megamodel
   $evaluate(MM, Interp)$. % Evaluation of relationships

We discuss the contributing judgments in turn.

4.2 Abstract Syntax of Megamodels

A megamodel is a list of *declarations*. There are declarations for entity-types (*etdecls*), relationship types (*rtdecls*), entities (*edecls*), entity parameters (*pdecls*), and relationships (*rdecls*). The declared names are atoms ('ids') and so are all the references to the names. Thus:

$megamodel(MM) \Longrightarrow map(decl, MM)$.
$decl(\textbf{etdecl}(SubT, SuperT)) \Longrightarrow atom(SubT), atom(SuperT)$.
$decl(\textbf{rtdecl}(R, T_1, T_2)) \Longrightarrow atom(R), atom(T_1), atom(T_2)$.
$decl(\textbf{edecl}(E, T)) \Longrightarrow atom(E), atom(T)$.
$decl(\textbf{pdecl}(E, T)) \Longrightarrow atom(E), atom(T)$.
$decl(\textbf{rdecl}(R, E_1, E_2)) \Longrightarrow atom(R), atom(E_1), atom(E_2)$.

4.3 Well-Formedness of Megamodels

Well-formedness is defined as a family of relations, as usual, on the syntactical domains. Well-formedness ensures that all referenced names of entity types, relationship types, and entities (or parameters) are actually declared. (This is part of what we call 'Analyze' in Figure 2.) We omit most of these routine definitions; a more insightful detail is well-formedness of relationship declarations:

$okRDecl(MM, \textbf{rdecl}(R, E_1, E_2)) \Longrightarrow$
   $member(\textbf{rtdecl}(R, Tl_1, Tr_1), MM)$, % RType exists
   $getEntityType(MM, E_1, Tl_2)$, % Type of left entity
   $getEntityType(MM, E_2, Tr_2)$, % Type of right entity
   $subtypeOf(MM, Tl_2, Tl_1)$, % Left type Ok
   $subtypeOf(MM, Tr_2, Tr_1)$. % Right type Ok

That is, any declared relationship between two entities E_1 and E_2 must be based on a relationship-type declaration for the same relationship symbol R with entity types Tl_1 and Tr_1 such that the actual entity types Tl_2 and Tr_2 are subtypes of the declared types Tl_1 and Tr_1. Subtyping is defined in terms of the type hierarchy defined by entity-type declarations. This is subtyping like in a single-inheritance OO programming language.

4.4   Abstract Syntax of Interpretations

We invent a representation of interpretations (say, definitions) of parameters (*pdefs*), entity types (*etdefs*), and relationship types (*rtdefs*). In this manner, we abstract from the plugins of the OO framework and the configuration as discussed in §3. Thus:

interp(Interp) $\Longrightarrow$ *map(def, Interp).*
*def(**pdef**(E, U))* $\Longrightarrow$ *atom(E), uri(U).*
*def(**etdef**(T, F))* $\Longrightarrow$ *atom(T), function(F, [atom], [uri]).*
*def(**rtdef**(R, T_1, T_2, P))* $\Longrightarrow$ *atom(R), atom(T_1), atom(T_2), predicate(P, [uri, uri]).*

That is, a parameter definition (*pdef*) associates an entity parameter E with a URI U; an entity-type definition (*etdef*) associates an entity type T with a function F mapping entity names to URIs; a relationship-type definition (*rtdef*) associates a relationship type $\langle R, T_1, T_2 \rangle$ with a predicate P on entity URIs. Thus, *etdef*s and *rtdef*s model resolvers and evaluators, respectively. We view the aforementioned predicates and functions here as being defined by their extension, i.e., a suitable set of tuples. Thus:

predicate(Tuples, Types) $\Longrightarrow$ *set(Tuples), map(tuple(Types), Tuples).*
function(Tuples, Domain, Range) $\Longrightarrow$ *... % likewise for functions*
tuple(Types, Tuple) $\Longrightarrow$ *zip(Types, Tuple, TT), map(apply, TT).*

In the actual implementation, resolvers and evaluators are of course programs that may retrieve resources via the URIs over the internet.

4.5   Correctness and Completeness

We present correctness and completeness as two aspects of well-formedness of the megamodel-interpretation couple. (We do not discuss well-formedness of interpretations by themselves, as there are only a few trivial constraints.)

   Correctness means that an interpretation does not provide any definitions that are not possibly needed by the associated megamodel. Provision of superficial definitions may be acceptable, though, in practice.

   Completeness means that an interpretation suffices to resolve all entities or parameters and to evaluate all relationships for a given megamodel. As discussed, in practice, we do not necessarily require completeness, as we may be unable to resolve certain entities or to evaluate certain relationships, at a given point. However, ambiguities regarding resolution or interpretation should be reported.

   Correctness and completeness are again specified as families of relations. For example, here is the judgment for establishing correctness of relationship-type definitions w.r.t. a megamodel.

*correctRTDef(MM, **rtdef**(R, Tl_1, Tr_1, _))* $\Longrightarrow$
   okT(MM, Tl_1), % Left entity type exists

okT(MM, Tr_1), % Right entity type exists
member($rtdecl(R, Tl_2, Tr_2)$, MM), % Relationship type exists
subtypeOf(MM, Tl_1, Tl_2), % Definition vs. declaration (left)
subtypeOf(MM, Tr_1, Tr_2). % Definition vs. declaration (right)

That is, for each relationship-type definition of the interpretation, we can find a corresponding declaration of the megamodel which uses the same or more general entity types.

Let us also consider the counterpart from the family of relations for completeness, i.e., the relation for establishing that a given relationship can be evaluated unambiguously by a definition. This judgement is involved—it is comparable to resolution of names in a non-trivial programming language.

% Relationship—type definition unambiguous
completeDecl(MM, Interp, $rdecl(R, El, Er)$) $\Longrightarrow$
getRTDef(MM, Interp, R, El, Er, _).

% Determine suitable relationship—type definition
getRTDef(MM, Interp, R, El, Er, RTDef) $\Longrightarrow$
getEntityType(MM, El, Tl), % Look up left entity type
getEntityType(MM, Er, Tr), % Look up right entity type
filter(applicableRTDef(MM, R, Tl, Tr), Interp, RTDefs),
reduceRTDefs(MM, RTDefs, RTDef).

% Applicability of a relationship—type definition
applicableRTDef(MM, R, Tl_1, Tr_1, $rtdef(R, Tl_2, Tr_2)$) $\Longrightarrow$
subtypeOf(MM, Tl_1, Tl_2),
subtypeOf(MM, Tr_1, Tr_2).

% Eliminate more general relationship—type definition
reduceRTDefs(_, [RTDef], RTDef). % One rtdef left
reduceRTDefs(MM, $RTDefs_1$, RTDef) $\Longrightarrow$
member($RTDef_1, RTDefs_1$), % Pick some rtdef
member($RTDef_2, RTDefs_1$), % Pick some rtdef
$RTDef_1 \neq RTDef_2$, % Two different rtdefs
$RTDef_1 = rtdef(R, Tl_1, Tr_1, _)$,
$RTDef_2 = rtdef(R, Tl_2, Tr_2, _)$,
subtypeOf(MM, Tl_1, Tl_2),
subtypeOf(MM, Tr_1, Tr_2),
delete($RTDefs_1, RTDef_2, RTDefs_2$), % Remove the more general rtdef
reduceRTDefs(MM, $RTDefs_2$, RTDef).

This approach is similar to instance resolution in Haskell [11], the one for multi-parameter type classes with overlapping instances specifically [19]. That is, definitions ('instances' in Haskell terms) are not proactively rejected by themselves—just because they are overlapping in some sense. Instead, any given relationship is considered as to whether it can be associated uniquely with a definition that is more specific than all other applicable definitions.

4.6   Evaluation of Relationships

Evaluation is straightforward at this stage, as all preconditions have been established. That is, entities or parameters thereof can be replaced by URIs and relationships can be evaluated on the URIs for the arguments. Thus:

*evaluateDecl(MM, Config, **rdecl**(R, El, Er))* ⟹
  *getRTDef(MM, Config, R, El, Er, **rtdef**(_, _, _, P)),*
  getEUri(MM, Config, El, Ul),
  getEUri(MM, Config, Er, Ur),
  applyPredicate(P, [Ul, Ur]).

% Get URI for entity via definition
getEUri(MM, Config, E, U) ⟹
  getEntityType(MM, E, T), % Look up entity type
  *member(**etdef**(T, F), Config), % Look up definition*
  applyFunction(F, [E], [U]). % 'Resolve'

% Application of extension−based predicates and functions
applyPredicate(Tuples, X) ⟹ *member(X, Tuples).*
applyFunction(Tuples, Arg, Res) ⟹ *append(Arg, Res, X), member(X, Tuples).*

Soundness (i.e., alignment between 'type system' and 'semantics') follows trivially in this approach—as the completeness judgment immediately ensures that all instances of entity resolution and relationship evaluation can be attempted. Thus, the only remaining option for *evaluateDecl* to fail is that a resolution was not successful or a specific relationship failed.

5   Related Work

We compare *MegaL* with several approaches to megamodeling. The Atlas MegaModel Management approach (AM3) conveys the idea of modeling in the large, establishing and using general relationships, such as conformance, and metadata on basic macroscopic entities (mainly models and metamodels) [2]. Based on the assumption that all managed artifacts are models conforming to precise metamodels, a solution for typing megamodeling artifacts is proposed in [20]. Model typing is based on the conformance relationship; metamodels are used as types. *MegaL* is clearly not restricted to modeling resources and does not require an existence of metamodels. Also, *MegaL*'s approach to megamodel interpretation provides an open, heterogenous type system.

A formal, graph-oriented view on megamodels is considered in [4]; entities are vertices and relations are edges between them. It is argued, that the semantics of relations are hidden in the type name and are not presented in the megamodel. To fill this gap, the authors zoom into nodes and edges and disassemble them into more elementary building blocks. In the case of *MegaL*, such a formal analysis of the relationships is less relevant, as it is not directly applicable to actual software projects and technologies. Instead, as shown in §3.4, we leverage tool-based relationship evaluators with optional traceability recovery. *MegaL* is also influenced by existing megamodeling patterns and idioms, discovered in theoretical work [8,5,4].

In a comprehensive survey [21] of traceability in MDE, the authors conclude, that traceability practices are still emerging, specifically in the MDE context. *MegaL*'s interpreted megamodels may associate entities in relationships with traceability links, as it was shown in §3.4. This approach is again heterogenous in terms of the technological spaces; it assumes a language-parametric approach to fragment location. Traceability is also used in megamodeling for models at runtime [18], where high-level relationships between models are derived from observable low-level traceability between model elements.

A type system and a type inference algorithm for declarative languages with constraints for MDE are presented in [13]. Elsewhere [1], OCL [10] constraints and ATL rules [14] are used to implement consistency and conformance checking.

Megamodels of metamodels and model transformations are organized into an architectural framework [9], which promotes re-usability of architectural elements and realizes architectural descriptions [12]. We plan to re-implement such descriptions in *MegaL*, thereby providing evidence of its usefulness as an architecture description language.

MegaL relies on the resources to be exposed via HTTP and uniquely identifiable: Such resources can be directly exposed via web servers and web-accessible source control systems. Another promising direction is to apply *Linked Data* [3] principles, which allows attaching rich metadata. *MegaL* already applies such principles, e.g., in the sense of the *DBpedia* and 101companies resolvers. *Linked Data* principles are also leveraged in [15] in a related manner for the purpose of exposing facts about artifacts in software repositories.

6   Conclusion

We have equipped the megamodeling notion for the linguistic architecture of software systems with a language mechanism for resolving entities, capturing traceability between them, and evaluating relationships. Our approach is not tailored to MDE. We applied the approach to a megamodeling scenario that indeed involves elements of Javaware and grammarware. We formalized the key ideas of interpreted *MegaL* models in a deductive system and described an open-source implementation. Without this enhancement, megamodeling does not provide enough validated insight into actual systems.

The types of megamodeling relationships with the underlying entity types represent patterns of the linguistic architecture of software systems. *MegaL* has already been applied to some typical scenarios of technology usage, as they are demonstrated by software systems in the 101companies chrestomathy [6], thereby capturing important entity and relationship types. It remains to develop a comprehensive megamodeling ontology in a systematic and transparent manner.

Additional topics for future work include these: i) raise the level of abstraction for traceability recovery by establishing a language-independent DSL layer standardizing fact extraction and link composition; ii) support of the evolution of entities and linked resources by including timestamp and version information; iii) search-based instantiation of megamodels for a given software system; iv) 'megamodeling in the large' support in the sense of refinement and composition expressiveness; v) 'megamodeling as a service' to simplify the setup of the interpreter with its diverse plugins providing support for different technological spaces and relying on different platforms.

References

1. Bézivin, J., Jouault, F.: Using ATL for Checking Models. ENTCS 152, 69–81 (2006)
2. Bézivin, J., Jouault, F., Rosenthal, P., Valduriez, P.: Modeling in the Large and Modeling in the Small. In: Aßmann, U., Akşit, M., Rensink, A. (eds.) MDAFA 2003. LNCS, vol. 3599, pp. 33–46. Springer, Heidelberg (2005)
3. Bizer, C., Heath, T., Berners-Lee, T.: Linked data - the story so far. Int. J. Semantic Web Inf. Syst. 5(3), 1–22 (2009)
4. Diskin, Z., Kokaly, S., Maibaum, T.: Mapping-aware megamodeling: Design patterns and laws. In: Erwig, M., Paige, R.F., Van Wyk, E. (eds.) SLE 2013. LNCS, vol. 8225, pp. 322–343. Springer, Heidelberg (2013)
5. Favre, J.-M.: Foundations of meta-pyramids: Languages vs. metamodels – Episode II: Story of thotus the baboon. In: Language Engineering for Model-Driven Software Development, number 04101 in Dagstuhl Seminar Proceedings (2005)
6. Favre, J.-M., Lämmel, R., Schmorleiz, T., Varanovich, A.: 101companies: A Community Project on Software Technologies and Software Languages. In: Furia, C.A., Nanz, S. (eds.) TOOLS 2012. LNCS, vol. 7304, pp. 58–74. Springer, Heidelberg (2012)
7. Favre, J.-M., Lämmel, R., Varanovich, A.: Modeling the Linguistic Architecture of Software Products. In: France, R.B., Kazmeier, J., Breu, R., Atkinson, C. (eds.) MODELS 2012. LNCS, vol. 7590, pp. 151–167. Springer, Heidelberg (2012)
8. Favre, J.-M., Guyen, T.N.: Towards a Megamodel to Model Software Evolution through Transformations. ENTCS 127(3) (2004); Proc. of the SETra Workshop
9. Favre, L., Martinez, L.: Formalizing mda components. In: Morisio, M. (ed.) ICSR 2006. LNCS, vol. 4039, pp. 326–339. Springer, Heidelberg (2006)
10. O.M. Group: Object Constraint Language Object Constraint Language, OMG Available Specification, Version 2.0 (2006)
11. Hall, C.V., Hammond, K., Jones, S.L.P., Wadler, P.: Type Classes in Haskell. TOPLAS 18(2), 109–138 (1996)
12. Hilliard, R., Malavolta, I., Muccini, H., Pelliccione, P.: Realizing Architecture Frameworks Through Megamodelling Techniques. In: Proc. of ASE 2010, pp. 305–308. ACM (2010)
13. Jackson, E.K., Schulte, W., Bjørner, N.: Detecting Specification Errors in Declarative Languages with Constraints. In: France, R.B., Kazmeier, J., Breu, R., Atkinson, C. (eds.) MODELS 2012. LNCS, vol. 7590, pp. 399–414. Springer, Heidelberg (2012)
14. Jouault, F., Kurtev, I.: Transforming Models with ATL. In: Bruel, J.-M. (ed.) MoD-ELS 2005. LNCS, vol. 3844, pp. 128–138. Springer, Heidelberg (2006)
15. Keivanloo, I., Forbes, C., Hmood, A., Erfani, M., Neal, C., Peristerakis, G., Rilling, J.: A linked data platform for mining software repositories. In: Proc. of MSR 2012, pp. 32–35. IEEE (2012)

16. Kurtev, I., Bézivin, J., Akşit, M.: Technological Spaces: An Initial Appraisal. In: Proc. of CoopIS, DOA 2002, Industrial Track (2002)
17. Naish, L., Sterling, L.: Stepwise enhancement and higher-order programming in prolog. Journal of Functional and Logic Programming 2000(4) (2000)
18. Seibel, A., Neumann, S., Giese, H.: Dynamic hierarchical mega models: Comprehensive traceability and its efficient maintenance. Software & Systems Modeling 9(4), 493–528 (2010)
19. Sulzmann, M., Schrijvers, T., Stuckey, P.J.: Principal Type Inference for GHC-Style Multi-parameter Type Classes. In: Kobayashi, N. (ed.) APLAS 2006. LNCS, vol. 4279, pp. 26–43. Springer, Heidelberg (2006)
20. Vignaga, A., Jouault, F., Bastarrica, M., Brunelière, H.: Typing Artifacts in Megamodeling. Software and Systems Modeling, 1–15 (2011)
21. Winkler, S., von Pilgrim, J.: A survey of traceability in requirements engineering and model-driven development. Software and System Modeling 9(4), 529–565 (2010)

Alloy4SPV: A Formal Framework for Software Process Verification

Yoann Laurent[1], Reda Bendraou[1], Souheib Baarir[1,2],
and Marie-Pierre Gervais[1,2]

[1] Sorbonne Universites, UPMC Univ Paris 06, UMR 7606, LIP6, F-75005, Paris,
France
[2] Universite Paris Ouest Nanterre La Défense, F-92001, Nanterre, France
{yoann.laurent,souheib.baarir,reda.bendraou,marie-pierre.gervais}@lip6.fr

Abstract. In this paper we present a framework for software process verification called ALLOY4SPV which uses a subset of UML2 Activity Diagrams as a process modeling language. In order to achieve software process verification, we i) define a formal model of our process modeling language using first-order logic, ii) we give it a formal semantics based on the fUML standard, and iii) we implement this formalization using the Alloy language [1]. In order to ease its adoption by process modelers, our framework comes with a graphical tool and a ready to use and customizable set of software process properties. We categorize these properties into two categories, syntactical and behavioral. We extend the set of behavioral properties we identified from the literature with two new categories that we defined, namely, organizational properties which relate to resource management and planning during process execution and business properties which are project/process specific properties.

1 Introduction

In the current state of practice, process model defects are discovered too late, usually at realization time, after the process has proved to be inefficient or having some behavioral issues such as deadlocks, unreachable activities, inefficient use of resources and timing problems. This could have been avoided with adequate process verification tools that would have formally verified the process model before its deployment in real projects. By process verification we mean determining in advance that the process model exhibits a certain desirable behavior.

In the field of business processes many approaches have been proposed for process verification [2,3,4,5,6,7]. These approaches address mainly the verification of some well-known *behavioral properties* that must be guaranteed by all process's executions. The literature addresses essentially what it is called *soundness properties* [7]. These properties guarantee the absence of deadlocks, unreachable activities, and other anomalies that can be detected without domain knowledge.

Software processes are concerned with additional and critical constraints related to their human-oriented nature. They imply many creative tasks that rely on many factors such as time, human agents and resource management. The

J. Cabot and J. Rubin (Eds.): ECMFA 2014, LNCS 8569, pp. 83–100, 2014.

success of a software process depends then also on the preservation of many best practices and organizational constraints. We call these constraints *organizational properties* and we consider them as a subcategory of *behavioral properties* since a state space exploration is required to guarantee their preservation for all possible process's executions. Examples of such properties are to make sure, for instance, that the process or an activity will terminate before a given deadline whatever the execution path, make sure that there will be enough agents to perform the activities of the process, etc.

Another point with current process verification approaches is about the formalism and tools they rely on for performing the verification. Whatever the process modeling language, a formal semantics is given to the language by mapping its constructs to either variants of automata [2,8], Petri Nets [9,10,7,6,5] or process algebra [3,4]. However this means that we are relying on the semantics and concepts of the targeted formal language in terms of expressiveness, e.g. Petri Nets, instead of the modeling language itself. Even if Petri Nets (with their different variants) can represent anything defined in terms of an algorithm, this does not imply that the modeling effort is acceptable. Van der Aalst's paper [11] gives concrete examples of some *Workflow Patterns* that need very complex Petri Nets extensions and tricks to represent them while this is expressed very naturally in UML Activity diagrams (AD) [12].

The approach we promote in this paper through our framework ALLOY4SPV is different in the sense that we define the formal semantics of the process modeling language using Alloy instead of relying on the semantics of any of the above-mentioned formal languages. Alloy is a declarative modeling language based on first-order logic and relational calculus for expressing complex structural and behavioral constraints [1]. Alloy's logic is quite generic and does not commit to a particular specification style [13]. We believe that this is more natural and allows to preserve the expressiveness of the process modeling language.

As a software process modeling language (SPML), ALLOY4SPV uses UML2 Activity Diagrams (AD) which have been given recently a precise execution semantics through the new OMG's fUML standard (Foundational UML) [14]. The choice of UML AD is motivated by the fact that AD are part of a standard widely used in the industry, it has been identified as a good SPML candidate [15,16], a good tooling support is provided, and it supports most of the workflow patterns as identified by [17]. However, it is worth noticing that our approach is applicable to other languages such as the BMPN which is more used in the business process community.

Finally, ALLOY4SPV comes with a graphical tool that includes a ready to use and configurable set of process properties in order to ease its adoption by process modelers. Our main goal is to gather under the same umbrella a graphical tool for software process modeling, execution and verification which supports all kinds of properties and most of all which preserves the semantics of the process modeling language. We hope that this would encourage a larger adoption of the process verification discipline and thus, a better management of software projects costs and quality.

The next section starts by introducing the set of properties we identified for software process verification. Section 3 and 4 give the different steps we followed for building ALLOY4SPV. An evaluation of our framework is given in Section 5. Related work is given in Section 6. Conclusion and some promising perspectives are sketched in Section 7.

2 Properties for Software Process Verification

In this section we present a categorization of the different properties that can be expressed on software process models. It represents the outcome of a literature review in the business process domain and in software methods and practices.

Over the last decade, many kinds of process properties have been studied [7,5]. They mainly fall into two categories: *syntactical properties* and *behavioral properties*. They are used respectively either to enforce some structural constraints, viewed as invariants, that cannot be expressed with the process modeling language itself or to determine in advance whether a process model exhibits certain (un)desirable behaviors. Even if syntactical errors seem quite obvious to detect by process modelers and enforced by process editors, some constraints may escape the modeler's attention which leads to incorrect process models. This has been confirmed by the study in [18], where 34 process models among 600 of the SAP company process referential were incorrect after analysis.

While the verification of *syntactical properties* is well supported by many approaches [19], they neither guarantee the soundness of process models nor that organizational constraints will be respected. To this aim, in the following we introduce *behavioral properties*. We will give the definition of soundness and focus on the two subcategories of behavioral properties that we introduce, namely *organizational* and *business properties*.

2.1 Behavioral Properties

They express constraints that must be guaranteed by all possible executions of the process. The literature addresses essentially a subcategory of such properties called *soundness properties*. As introduced in [7], soundness tends to check three desirable properties: (i) a started process can always complete (*option to complete*); (ii) it should not have any other activity running when the process ends (*proper completion*); and (iii) the process should not contain activities that will never be executed (*no dead transition*). For instance, to answer the question "will the process terminate?" on the process from Figure 1, a property is expressed to check that whatever the process execution, at the

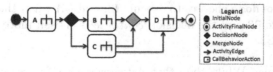

Fig. 1. Example of deadlock in a UML AD due to the control flow

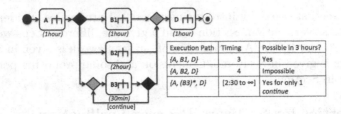

Fig. 2. Example of a UML AD with duration associated to actions

end, the `ActivityFinalNode` is executed. Here, a counter-example is exhibited: $\{Initial, A, Decision, B, Merge\}$, when the `DecisionNode` chooses to execute action B, then action D can never be executed (since action C is not) leading to a deadlock situation.

In the literature, we also find references that relate to soundness focusing on data-flow analysis rather than on control-flow [5]. The goal is to validate the workflow against different data problems such as *missing data*, i.e., when a data element needs to be accessed, but either it has never been created or it has been deleted without having been created again, *inconsistent data*, i.e., if an activity is using this data while another one is writing to it or is destroying it in parallel, and so on.

Existing approaches for process verification focus either on control-flow or data-flow, and only few of them ensure both [20]. However, as stated in the introduction, none of them takes into account the particularity of software processes. They treat the process as a simple workflow without covering the range of properties related to the *organizational* or *business constraints* which can highly influence the execution of the process. We introduce these kinds of properties through two new subcategories.

Organizational Properties. They cover organizational constraints about the time to perform the activities of the process, and different kinds of resources (agents, equipment...) problems like *missing resource*, i.e., when an activity requires a resource which may not be available and *inefficient resource use*, i.e., when the resource is inefficiently utilized during the process execution. The goal is to answer questions like: "is it possible to finish the process *on time* whatever the path taken?" "Is the agent always busy?" "Would the process be at activity X before a given deadline?" All these questions are important since they directly influence the decisions taken by the project manager. Figure 2 shows a process on which each activity is associated with a duration and a table displaying the 3 execution paths. Assuming that the process manager plans to do the process in 3 hours, there is 2 cases on which the process will not finish on time: (i) when the `DecisionNode` chooses to execute B2 and (ii) when the `DecisionNode` chooses to execute B3 and the decision *continue* is chosen more than once after the execution of B3.

Business Properties. While the other categories specify properties that must hold for all processes, business properties represent specific properties tailored

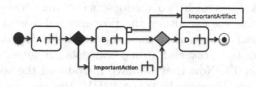

Fig. 3. Example of a correct UML AD

to a given process. They play an important role since a process could be syntactically correct and valid against some soundness properties but still violates some business constraints. Therefore, business properties can be used to highlight the importance of a given activity in the process, the fact that one activity should be executed, before, after or between other activities, and so on. Figure 3 shows a simple process considered correct against all the properties from the precedent categories (i.e., syntactical, soundness, organizational). However, ImportantAction activity is considered critical in the sense that the process modeler wants it to be executed at least one time during the process enactment. "Is ImportantAction executed whatever the choice made during the process execution?" On this example, it is not always the case since the execution path $\{Initial, A, Decision, B, Merge, D, Final\}$ finishes the process without executing ImportantAction. Another question here could be: "is ImportantArtefact (i.e., the goal of the process) always available at the end of the process? " The other execution path $\{Initial, A, Decision, ImportantAction, Merge, D, Final\}$ shows that it exists a path on which the artefact is not created.

Table 1 summarizes the set of properties we identified. Due to space restrictions we cannot detail all of them. Some of them were already introduced to illustrate the examples while others will be used in Section 5. It is worth noting

Table 1. Overview of the software properties we identified

CATEGORY	DEFINITION
(1) Syntactical	
SynWorkflow	Syntactical errors on the workflow of the process *(e.g. the source and target of an edge are different)*
SynOrganizational	Syntactical errors on the organizational part of the process *(e.g. the same agent cannot be assigned more than one time to the same activity)*
(2) Soundness	
OptionToComplete	A started process can always complete
ProperCompletion	No other activity should be running when the process terminates
NoDeadTransition	All the activities must be reachable
Soundness with data	
MissingData	The data are always present when they need to be accessed *(e.g. no data missing to start an activity)*
UselessData	The data created are always used *(e.g. no data created but never used before the process ends)*
InconsistentData	The data can never be in an inconsistent state *(e.g. no data modified by multiple activities in parallel)*
(3) Organizational	
InTime	There is enough time to perform the activities *(e.g. the process will terminate before X hours/days)*
MissingResource	No missing resource to start an activity *(e.g. there are enough agents to do the process)*
InefficientResourceUse	No resources that are inefficiently used *(e.g. the agents have always activity to do)*
(4) Business	
ExistenceActivity	A is executed more/less/(between) X (and Y) times
ExistenceTimeActivity	A is executed before/after/(between) X (and Y) time unit
ExistenceTimeData	ArtefactA is available before/after/(between) X (and Y) time unit
ExistenceTimeResource	ResourceA is used before/after/(between) X (and Y) time unit
Relation	A is executed before/after/in-parallel/in-exclusion/(between) B (and C)
RelationData	ArtefactA is available before/after/in-exclusion of ArtefactB
RelationActivityData	ArtefactA is available before/after/in-parallel/in-exclusion/(between) the execution of B (and C)
...	...
LogicBased	e.g. Existence(A) implies Existence(B) else Existence(C)
	e.g. Existence(A) implies (ExistenceData(ArtefactA) and ExistenceData(ArtefactB))
...	

that the properties distinguish two versions: *weak* and *strong*. The *strong* one ensures that whatever the execution, the property holds while the *weak* one is more permissible and ensures that the property holds for at least one execution. An example of the *weak* and *strong* concepts are given in the case study presented in Section 5.1. Now that we have introduced the set of properties to be integrated into our framework ALLOY4SPV, the next section presents the required steps for the formal software process verification.

3   Formal Verification of Software Processes

The classical approach to achieve the verification of a model (a process model in our case) with respect to a given property, consists beforehand in defining the two entities formally. Then, these entities are submitted to a so-called *model-checker* tool, which will answer to the question of (un)satisfaction of the property by the process model.

In a previous work, we proposed a first-order formalization of fUML for process verification [21]. We have formally reduced the representation of a software process to a vertex-labeled graph. Each graph's node corresponds to a UML Activity node according to its type (i.e. Control, Executable or Object Node). Each graph's arc corresponds to a UML Activity edge (i.e. Control or Object Flow). The execution semantics of this formalism is based on the notions of *states, enabling* and *firing* of transitions, similar to those used in the Colored Petri Nets [22]. Figure 4 shows an excerpt of the UML class diagram handled by our formalization. The formalization addresses a subset of fUML encompassing only the concepts required for process modeling as identified in [15]. To be able to reason about each dimension of the process, the formalization covers both *control* and *data-flow* of the process through the use of the AD notations, and takes into account the associated organizational data such as *resources* and *timing* constraints.

3.1   Alloy: A Language and Tool for Relational Models

Using our formalization [21], the next step is to choose an implementation language. Alloy [1] was chosen for this purpose. Alloy is a formal language, which has

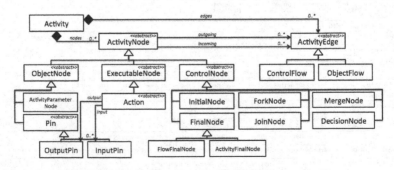

Fig. 4. Excerpt of the fUML Activity meta-model handled by our formalization

been applied to modelling of systems in a wide range of application domains. It is supported by the `Alloy Analyzer`, a tool, which allows fully automated analysis through SAT solving. Hereunder, we highlight the valuable points that motivated our choice for Alloy:

- It supports a wide variety of properties such as invariants, user-defined assertions, LTL [13] and CTL formulas with fairness constraints [23].
- It is expressive enough to represent a UML-based model associated with OCL constraints [24].
- Alloy's logic is quite generic and does not enforce the user to a particular specification style for modeling and verifying reactive systems.
- It allows one to choose the on-the-shelf SAT-solvers (MiniSat, ZChaff,...).
- It owns a graphical tool as well as an API to integrate seamlessly the verification into a process environment.

The Alloy language provides a set of concepts allowing to specify elements and constraints using the notions of *signatures*, *relations*, *facts* and *predicates*. A signature (`sig`) defines a set of idioms and relationships between them. They are similar to type declarations in an object-oriented language, and represent the basic entities. Facts (`fact`) are statements that specify constraints about idioms and relationships. These statements must always hold; they are close to the concept of invariants in other specification languages. Predicates (`pred`), as opposed to facts, define constraints which can evaluate to true or false. Alloy provides two commands to run the `Alloy Analyzer`: `run` and `check`. Command `run` instructs the analyzer to search for an instance satisfying a given formula, and `check` attempts to contradict a formula by searching for a counter-example.

4   Alloy4SPV: A Framework for Software Process Verification

This section presents our framework based on the concepts presented so far. We present the high-level overview of our approach and introduce how to represent the different concepts of the software process using the Alloy language in order to enable their automatic verification. Then, we introduce the tool built on top of our framework.

4.1   High-level Overview

ALLOY4SPV is the name of our framework enabling software process verification. This framework is based on our fUML formalization and is implemented using different Alloy modules. Figure 5 shows an overview of the workflow to achieve the process verification using ALLOY4SPV within a Process-centered Software Engineering Environments (PSEE). It takes a `Process Model` in the form of UML2 AD as input. The `Properties View` allows the process modelers to select and express properties through a graphical interface. The `Process View` displays the results about the verification.

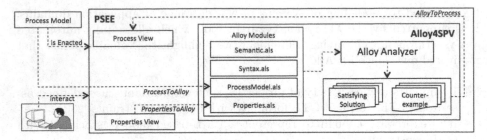

Fig. 5. High-level overview of ALLOY4SPV

ALLOY4SPV is composed of four modules, i.e., `Semantic.als`, `Syntax.als`, `ProcessModel.als` and `Properties.als`. In the following, we detail the content of these static and dynamic ALLOY4SPV modules required by the `Alloy Analyzer` to check a process model. The goal here is to give an overview of the way ALLOY4SPV is implemented using the Alloy language rather than giving an exhaustive definition.

4.2 Static Modules

`Syntax.als` represents the syntax of the software process modeling language (SPML). It contains signatures and relations that represent meta-classes and attributes from a subset of the UML AD meta-model (see Figure 4). Listing of Figure 6 shows a sample focusing on the `ActivityEdge`. The signatures follow the hierarchy of the UML AD metamodel.

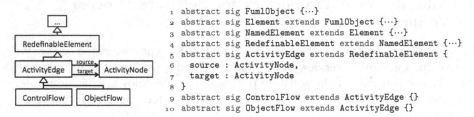

```
1  abstract sig FumlObject {...}
2  abstract sig Element extends FumlObject {...}
3  abstract sig NamedElement extends Element {...}
4  abstract sig RedefinableElement extends NamedElement {...}
5  abstract sig ActivityEdge extends RedefinableElement {
6    source : ActivityNode,
7    target : ActivityNode
8  }
9  abstract sig ControlFlow extends ActivityEdge {}
10 abstract sig ObjectFlow extends ActivityEdge {}
```

Fig. 6. Focus on `ActivityEdge` from `Syntax.als`

`Semantic.als` corresponds to the behavioral part of the SPML. It represents the notions of *states, enabling* and *firing* of transitions defined in the formalization. Since Alloy does not commit to a particular specification style, there is no standard way to model and verify reactive systems. However, several patterns have been proposed to address this issue. We adopt the traces pattern [1] to model the sequences of executions of an abstract machine. This pattern imposes a total ordering over the `State` signature and forces that every pair of consecutive states satisfy the given predicate. Listing 1.1 shows a simplified excerpt of this module. The `State` signature represents the configuration on which the process is at a given time of its execution. Therefore, a set of `States` represent a complete execution.

```
1   open util/ordering[State]
2   // a State carries the execution information (e·g·, tokens, offers, timing and so on)·
3   sig State {
4       heldTokens : ActivityNode →one Int,
5       offers : ActivityEdge →one Int,
6       localClock : ExecutableNode →one Int,
7       globalClock : Int,
8       running : Status
9   }
10  // traces pattern, the regular way to model reactive systems using Alloy
11  fact traces {
12      // constrains all the State to abide from the transition predicate
13      all s: State - last | let s' = s·next | {
14          s·running = Running implies {
15              transition[s,s'] // use ''enabling'' and ''firing'' predicates, defined in
                        the formalization
16          } else {
17              endLoop[s,s']
18  } } }
```

Listing 1.1. Excerpt of `Semantic.als`

4.3   Dynamic Modules

`ProcessModel.als` represents the instance of the process to analyze. Listing of Figure 7 shows a basic process represented using signatures declared in `Syntax.als`. This module is generated from the `Process Model` using a simple model transformation routine, the `ProcessToAlloy` routine, we developed using Java Emitter template (JET); it is basically the Alloy representation of the input `Process Model` [24].

```
1   // Process - Workflow
2   one sig Initial extends InitialNode {} {···}
3   one sig Code extends CallBehaviorAction {} {···}
4   one sig Final extends ActivityFinalNode {} {···}
5   one sig InitialToA extends ControlFlow {} {
6       source = Initial
7       target = Code }
8   one sig AToFinal extends ControlFlow {} {
9       source = Code
10      target = Final }
11  // Process - Organizational
12  one sig Coder extends Role {}
13  one sig John extends Agent {}
14  fun role : Agent →set Role { John →Coder }
15  fun reqRole : ExecutableNode →set Role { Code →Coder }
16  fun reqNbAgent : ExecutableNode →Int { Code →1 }
17  fun reqTiming : ExecutableNode →Int { Code →1 }
```

Fig. 7. `ProcessModel.als` represented in the ALLOY4SPV framework

`Properties.als` contains the commands to run the **Alloy Analyzer** over a given set of properties to be checked. Listing 1.2 shows an example of `Properties.als` generated using the `PropertiesToAlloy` routine. The `checkFinal` predicate states that there is some `State` on which the `Final` node is active. Then, the `check` command tries to contradict this predicate by finding a model execution on which there is no `State` with this last property. If the `Alloy Analyzer` finds a counter-example, this means that the `Process Model` is subject to a deadlock. The problems given to the `Alloy Analyzer` are solved within a user-specified scope that bounds the size of the domains making it finite and reducible to a boolean formula to be checked by the SAT solver. All the scope of the Alloy signatures are straightforwardly determined by the input process model, e.g. 3 `ActivityNodes` on the process imply a scope of 3 for the `ActivityNode` signature. The only exception concerns the scope of the `State` signature, i.e. the trace length on which the process is analyzed, which is determined using *incremental-scoping* technique.

```
1 pred checkFinal {some s : State | s.getTokens[Final] = 1}
2 check {checkFinal} for 0 but 5 State, 5 FumlObject, 1 Role, 1 Agent
```

Listing 1.2. Example of verification from `Properties.als`

4.4   Analysis of the Results

When satisfying solutions and/or counter-examples are computed by the `Alloy Analyzer`, the results are displayed back to the `Process View` using the `AlloyToProcess` routine. This routine analyzes the results returned by the `Alloy Analyzer` (e.g., extracting the path leading to the deadlock) and displays it on the `Process View`. Figure 8 shows a model found by the `Alloy Analyzer`. In this figure, the model is an instance satisfying the `checkFinal` predicate (`run` command) on the (simple) process from Figure 7. The simple and double stroke circle represent respectively the `ActivityFinalNode` and the `InitialNode`. The hexagons correspond to the `ActivityEdge` while the `ActivityNode` corresponds to the yellow inversed house. Thus, the `AlloyToProcess` routine simply consists in looking through the set of relations of the found model.

4.5   Graphical Tool Associated to Alloy4SPV

On top of ALLOY4SPV, we have developed a prototype currently provided as an Eclipse EMF plugin. It comes with a library of predefined properties ready to be checked and also allows to add some common *business properties* through

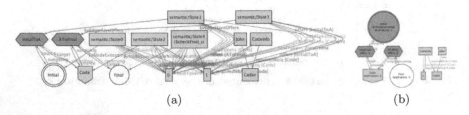

(a)   (b)

Fig. 8. (a) Model satisfying the `checkFinal` predicate found by the `Alloy Analyzer`, (b) projected over the first `State` signature

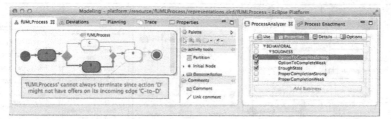

Fig. 9. Process Analyzer using the ALLOY4SPV framework

a graphical interface. The user only has to check in the interface the desired properties, and fill the parameter if required (e.g., maximum time to terminate the process). The *business properties* can be added through pre-defined templates, e.g. select the ActionA which must always be executed before ActionB. Figure 9 shows a screenshot of our tooling for process modeling and enactment emphasizing the process view and its analyzer. The prototype relies on Obeo UML Designer for modeling and displaying graphically the process. When the verification is performed, the path leading to the counter-example (if any) is highlighted in green for "run" properties, and in red for "check" properties. Moreover, CommentNodes are directly inserted into the model displaying the errors which must be corrected on the model. It is worth noting that the prototype does not require any formal background by the process agent. Everything is automated through the use of the graphical interface to ease tool's adoption.

5   Evaluation

This section presents the evaluation of ALLOY4SPV, by checking some of the properties on a sample of the OpenUP process [25] and on randomly generated processes [26].

5.1   OpenUP Case Study

We use the software process model illustrated in Figure 10 as a motivating example. It is the DevelopSolutionIncrement activity from the OpenUP process [25] represented using UML2 AD. In OpenUP, when a requirement needs to be developed in an iteration, a new DevelopSolutionIncrement activity is assigned to a developer and a tester. The responsability of the developer is to create a design and an implementation for that requirement while the tester writes and runs developer tests against the implementation to make sure that it works as designed. This activity contains 15 ActivityNode and 18 ActivityEdge. Note that ObjectNodes are excluded for sake of readability.

In the following, some properties from each category of Table 1 are presented. The goal here is to show how the properties are expressed with ALLOY4SPV rather than presenting every single one exhaustively.

(1) **Syntactical Properties:** Testing that each edge has a different source and target is expressed such as:

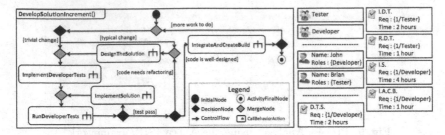

Fig. 10. DevelopSolutionIncrement activity from OpenUP

```
1  pred edgeDifferentTargetSource {
2      all n : ActivityEdge | { not n·source = n·target }
3  }
4  check {edgeDifferentTargetSource} for ···
```

(2) Soundness Properties: The *option-to-complete* property is expressed by declaring that at the end, there must be some State in which the Final node is active:

```
1  pred OptionToComplete {
2      some s : State | s·hasTokens[Final]
3  }
4  run {OptionToComplete} for ···
5  check {OptionToComplete} for ···
```

The run command asks the Alloy Analyzer to find a model on which the process terminates. If a result is found, it means that there is at least an execution on which the process terminates (*weak option-to-complete*). The check command ensures the *strong option-to-complete* by checking for a counter-example on which the execution will not lead to the Final node. It is worth noting that the OptionToComplete property will always find a counter-example due to the loops inside the workflow. This is because no *fairness* constraints is applied. We eliminate this problem by adding a fact constraint inside the Semantic.als module that forces *fairness* (i.e., the same outgoing edge cannot be taken infinitely often).

(3) Organizational Properties: To check that it is possible to finish the process in less than x hours, the OptionToComplete predicate is augmented such that the execution time value at the last State is below a given value:

```
1  pred finalAndTiming[t:Int] {
2      OptionToComplete and last·globalClock < t
3  }
4  run {finalAndTiming[5]} for ···
```

To check that, at any time during the process execution, there are enough agents to perform the running activities (assuming that all agents are identical) is expressed such as:

```
1  pred enoughAgent {
2      all s:State | #{ node : ExecutableNode | s·hasTokens[node] } < = #Agent
3  }
4  check {enoughAgent} for ···
```

Table 2. Metrics from the Alloy Analyser executed on the `DevelopSolutionIncrement` activity

PROPERTY	VARS	CLAUSES	CNF GEN.	SAT SOLVING	MODEL FOUND?
check edgeDifferentTargetSource	7k	20k	1s	9ms	no
run OptionToComplete	663k	1842k	57s	2s	yes
check OptionToComplete	658k	1840k	56s	15s	no
check enoughAgent	664k	1848k	51s	48s	no
check enoughAgentFor[Developer]	664k	1845k	45s	38s	no
check after[I.S., R.D.T.]	664k	1843k	49s	16s	no
run finalAndTiming[5]	1470k	4612k	125s	23s	yes

In this case, the `enoughAgent` predicate states that at each `State` of the process execution, the number of executing activities is less or equal to the total number of performers.

There is also the possibility to have a finer grained property which takes into account different roles (e.g., coder, designer...) of the agents. The first `check` verifies only for the `Developer` role while the latter verifies all the roles of the process:

```
1 pred enoughAgentFor[r : Role] {
2     all s:State | #{ node : ExecutableNode | s·hasTokens[node] and r in node·reqRole}
        < = #{ a : Agent | a·role = r}
3 }
4 check {enoughAgentFor[Developer]} for ···
5 check {all r:Role | enoughAgentFor[r]} for ···
```

(4) Business Properties: The process modeler may want to check that when the `ImplementSolution` activity is performed, the developed solution is always tested with the `RunDeveloperTests` activity afterward. To express this business property, the process modeler does not have to manipulate the Alloy language but just to select the two actions `ImplementalSolution` and `RunDeveloperTests` and apply the *after* constraint through the ALLOY4SPV graphical interface. Thus, the property checks that anytime the `ImplementSolution` is executed, there is some `State` in the future (`s.^next` is the transitive closure of `next` and corresponds to all the following `State` of s such as `s.next+s.next.next+s.next...`) on which `RunDeveloperTests` is executed:

```
1 pred after[a,b:ExecutableNode] { // defined in the Semantics·als module
2     all s:State | s·hasTokens[a] implies
3         some ss : s·^next | ss·hasTokens[b]
4 }
5 check {after[ImplementSolution, RunDeveloperTests]} for ···
```

In order to perform the verification of the aforementioned properties with respect to the part of the OpenUP process in Figure 10, `Alloy Analyzer` reduces the verification to a SAT problem. It is presented to a SAT solver (MiniSat among others) in a Conjunctive Normal Form (CNF) format. A CNF is a conjunction of clauses. Each clause represents a disjunction of variables. A satisfying assignement to a SAT problem consists of a boolean affectation to the variables such that all clauses are satisfied. Usually, the complexity of a SAT problem is measured by the numbers of clauses and variables.

All analyses were performed on a MacBook Air 2011 with Intel Core i5 processor and 4GB of RAM with Mavericks as OS. Table 2 summarizes the obtained results where column 1 represents the analyzed property. Columns 2 and 3 represent, respectively, the number of generated variables and clauses. Columns 4 and 5 represent, respectively, the time to generate the CNF and to solve the SAT problem. Finally, column 6 indicates if a model is found (i.e. satisfiability for a run command, and counter-example for a check command).

Besides, these results highlight the effectiveness of our tool w.r.t. a concrete example [25]. Actually, even if the whole generated SAT problems present a relatively high complexity (almost 2 million clauses and over 600 thousand variables), the solving time is less than one minute for untimed properties. The timed-related properties (run finalAndTiming[5]) have a similar ratio in terms of clauses and variables but require more time due to the presence of extra states introduced by the clocks to handle the time elapsing. The full details with examples of the ALLOY4SPV modules can be found on our website[1].

5.2   Randomly Generated Processes

One of the challenges we face to validate our approach is the inability to find realistic data and models. The small set of samples and "toy" models publically available in the literature is insufficient to conduct a serious empirical study to validate works around software process analysis and verification. Moreover, due to privacy reasons, partner companies are reluctant to share their models representing the result of years of best practices and the capitalization of developers and project managers know-how which took time to design.

This problem led us to develop our own process generator [26]. We used it to randomly generate processes ranging from 10 to 100 UML elements. These processes have only control-flow nodes without loops and contain sequential routing (ControlFlow edges), action to perform (OpaqueAction), parallel routing (ForkNode), synchronizer (JoinNode), conditional routing (DecisionNode) and merging structure (MergeNode). Even if our processes are artificial, they present a high-level of realism. The model generator reproduces how a modeler could have developed a process in a real situation. It generates the process through a sequence of Change Patterns [27]. Each process is then checked w.r.t. the OptionToComplete property and only models without counter-examples are kept (only the largest verification time is of interest).

Figure 11 shows the solving-times to check this property. These results show that the solving times are reasonable w.r.t. the complexity of the generated models (in terms of number of UML elements). Actually, the generated SAT problem of the model with 100 UML elements contains almost 18 billion clauses and 8 million variables and is resolved in 31 minutes which highlights the fact that our SAT problems belong to a relatively easy-to-solve SAT category. Once again, this emphasizes the effectiveness of our approach.

---

[1] http://pagesperso-systeme.lip6.fr/Yoann.Laurent/

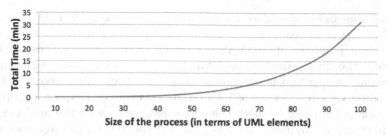

Fig. 11. Total time to check the `OptionToComplete` property depending on the process size

6   Related Work

There is an extensive literature on verifying process models. Since a lot of the work has been done in the business process community, we do not restrict ourselves to the verification of *software* processes. Generally, the verification is based on mapping the process model into mathematical formalisms used to model systems such as automata, Petri Nets or process algebra.

Many approaches have origins in the Petri Nets formalism, either because the modeling language is based on it (e.g., Workflow Nets [9]) or through a mapping to it [10]. In [9], Van der Aalst et al. introduce the Workflow Nets, a particular class of Petri Nets dedicated to the modeling of workflow with an augmented graphical notation (e.g., AND-splits, AND-joins and so on). In [6] a large number of industrial business processes have been successfully checked on the soundness properties using the LoLa model checker. In [10], the process modeled in UML AD is mapped to Colored Petri Nets [22] in order to enable automatic verification. Due to the fact that Petri Nets enjoy an easily understandable and graphical notation as well as a plethora of mature tools enabling efficient analysis, they have been widely applied in the process analysis field. However, even if the verification of Petri Nets based process is efficient to check properties such as reachability, liveness and boundness, they fail when the system needs to handle a wide variety of data. The use of data on the system multiplies the number of places and introduces some state space explosion problems making the analysis difficult (sometimes impossible). Moreover, these approaches focus only on the soundness properties.

Other approaches use process algebra [3,4], a strict and well-established theory that support the automatic verification of properties of systems behavior as well as Petri Nets. In [3], the authors show how the Communicating Sequential Processes (CSP) algebra can be applied to model complex workflow systems. They use the FDR (Failures-Divergences Refinement) model-checker to automatically check behavioural properties. Liu et al. [4] transforms models expressed in Business Process Execution Language (BPEL) into π-calculus. They also capture compliance rules in the graphical Business Property Specification Language (BPSS) and automatically translate them into temporal logic. This approach is able to handle the verification of both *soundness* and *business properties*. However, process algebra such as π-calculus is limited in the ability to support most of the workflow patterns [17] used in processes.

Further approaches are based on domain-specific language. Eshuis et al. [2] check UML AD in the context of workflow modeling by translating the activity into the input language of NuSMV, a symbolic model checker. The work was done before the finalisation of the UML 2.0 specification, thus the semantics used remains unclear and many assumptions have been made about it. Guelfi et al. [8] propose a translation of UML AD into Promela (Process or Protocol Meta Language) in order to check behavioral properties with the model-checker SPIN. However, no implementation is provided and the set of properties which may be checked are not precise.

In the case of UML AD verification, all these formalisms have been investigated: (1) process algebra using π-calculus [28] and CSP (Communicating Sequential Processes) [29], (2) automaton using NuSMV formalism [2] and Promela (Process or Protocol Meta Language) [8], and (3) Petri Nets formalism through transformation [10]. However, only the work of Abdelhalim et al. [29] is based on the fUML semantics, but lacks by focusing the verification only on deadlocks.

To sum up, most of the approaches focus on verifying control-flow related properties and only a few treat the data on the process. Despite the numerous approaches to check behavioral properties on a process, none of them proposes to check the *organizational properties*. To our knowledge, no approach proposes to check syntactical and all the behavioral properties in a unified way as promoted by ALLOY4SPV.

7   Conclusion and Future Work

While verification is a critical and an important endeavor in software development, it still remains the Achilles heel of software processes and a main source of their low adoption. Indeed, with the increasing complexity and size of processes, process modelers need adequate tooling support to simulate and to verify their processes before their use in real projects. Some critical processes may reach more than 250 activities, with very complex workflows, dependencies, loops, synchronizations, and without an automated and exhaustive verification, possible sources of inconsistencies and problems may persist. The formalization on which ALLOY4SPV is based is able to deal with control- and data-flow, resources, and timing aspects of the process in a unified way. Therefore, ALLOY4SPV and its associated interface is able to verify automatically a wide range of properties without the user's intervention and allows one to verify some *business properties*. Currently, the tool is under evaluation within the European MERgE project, whose main goal is to develop and demonstrate innovative concepts and design tools addressing both "safety" and "security" concerns in development processes.

The case study and the tool proved the feasibility of our approach, however some improvements to our approach are already under realization. Even if our evaluation shows relatively good performance, we believe that there is still room for improvement. Many optimization techniques can be explored: (1) using *slicing technique*, i.e. partially generates the `Semantic.als` to cope only with the need of the properties; (2) using graph reduction techniques to reduce the size of the process [30];

and (3) treat the properties related to time in a more efficient way based on the expertise of well-known approaches such as timed automata [31].

Acknowledgments. The authors' work is funded by the MERgE project (ITEA 2 Call 6 11011).

References

1. Jackson, D.: Software Abstractions: logic, language and analysis. Mit Pr. (2011)
2. Eshuis, R.: Symbolic model checking of uml activity diagrams. TOSEM 15(1), 1–38 (2006)
3. Wong, P.Y.H., Gibbons, J.: A process-algebraic approach to workflow specification and refinement. In: Lumpe, M., Vanderperren, W. (eds.) SC 2007. LNCS, vol. 4829, pp. 51–65. Springer, Heidelberg (2007)
4. Liu, Y., Muller, S., Xu, K.: A static compliance-checking framework for business process models. IBM Systems Journal 46(2), 335–361 (2007)
5. Trčka, N., van der Aalst, W.M.P., Sidorova, N.: Data-flow anti-patterns: Discovering data-flow errors in workflows. In: van Eck, P., Gordijn, J., Wieringa, R. (eds.) CAiSE 2009. LNCS, vol. 5565, pp. 425–439. Springer, Heidelberg (2009)
6. Fahland, D., Favre, C., Jobstmann, B., Koehler, J., Lohmann, N., Völzer, H., Wolf, K.: Instantaneous soundness checking of industrial business process models. In: Dayal, U., Eder, J., Koehler, J., Reijers, H.A. (eds.) BPM 2009. LNCS, vol. 5701, pp. 278–293. Springer, Heidelberg (2009)
7. van der Aalst, W., Van Hee, K., ter Hofstede, A., Sidorova, N., Verbeek, H., Voorhoeve, M., Wynn, M.: Soundness of workflow nets: Classification, decidability, and analysis. Formal Aspects of Computing 23(3), 333–363 (2011)
8. Guelfi, N., Mammar, A.: A formal semantics of timed activity diagrams and its promela translation. In: IEEE 12th Asia-Pacific Software Engineering Conference, APSEC 2005, p. 8 (2005)
9. van der Aalst, W.M.: The application of petri nets to workflow management. Journal of Circuits, Systems, and Computers 8(01), 21–66 (1998)
10. Jung, H.T., Joo, S.H.: Transformation of an activity model into a colored petri net model. In: IEEE TISC, pp. 32–37 (2010)
11. Ter Hofstede, A.: Workflow patterns: On the expressive power of (petri-net-based) workflow languages. In: of DAIMI, University of Aarhus, Citeseer (2002)
12. Wohed, P., van der Aalst, W.M.P., Dumas, M., ter Hofstede, A.H.M., Russell, N.: Pattern-based analysis of the control-flow perspective of uml activity diagrams. In: Delcambre, L.M.L., Kop, C., Mayr, H.C., Mylopoulos, J., Pastor, Ó. (eds.) ER 2005. LNCS, vol. 3716, pp. 63–78. Springer, Heidelberg (2005)
13. Cunha, A.: Bounded model checking of temporal formulas with alloy. arXiv preprint arXiv:1207.2746 (2012)
14. OMG: Semantics of a foundational subset for executable uml models (fuml) version 1.0 (2011), http://www.omg.org/spec/FUML/
15. Bendraou, R., Gervais, M.-P., Blanc, X.: Uml4spm: A uml2. 0-based metamodel for software process modelling. In: Briand, L.C., Williams, C. (eds.) MoDELS 2005. LNCS, vol. 3713, pp. 17–38. Springer, Heidelberg (2005)
16. Bendraou, R., Jézéquel, J., Gervais, M., Blanc, X.: A comparison of six uml-based languages for software process modeling. IEEE Transactions on Software Engineering 36(5), 662–675 (2010)

17. van Der Aalst, W.M., Ter Hofstede, A.H., Kiepuszewski, B., Barros, A.P.: Workflow patterns. Distributed and Parallel Databases 14(1), 5–51 (2003)
18. Mendling, J., Moser, M., Neumann, G., Verbeek, H.M.W., van Dongen, B.F., van der Aalst, W.M.P.: Faulty epcs in the sap reference model. In: Dustdar, S., Fiadeiro, J.L., Sheth, A.P. (eds.) BPM 2006. LNCS, vol. 4102, pp. 451–457. Springer, Heidelberg (2006)
19. Hsueh, N., Shen, W., Yang, Z., Yang, D.: Applying uml and software simulation for process definition, verification, and validation. Information and Software Technology 50(9), 897–911 (2008)
20. Trcka, N., van der Aalst, W., Sidorova, N.: Analyzing control-flow and data-flow in workflow processes in a unified way. Computer Science Report (08-31) (2008)
21. Laurent, Y., Bendraou, R., Baarir, S., Gervais, M.-P.: Formalization of fUML: An Application to Process Verification. In: Jarke, M., Mylopoulos, J., Quix, C., Rolland, C., Manolopoulos, Y., Mouratidis, H., Horkoff, J. (eds.) CAiSE 2014. LNCS, vol. 8484, pp. 347–363. Springer, Heidelberg (2014)
22. Jensen, K.: Coloured petri nets. Petri nets: Central models and their properties, 248–299 (1987)
23. Vakili, A., Day, N.: Temporal logic model checking in alloy. Abstract State Machines, Alloy, B, VDM, and Z, 150–163 (2012)
24. Anastasakis, K., Bordbar, B., Georg, G., Ray, I.: Uml2alloy: A challenging model transformation. In: Engels, G., Opdyke, B., Schmidt, D.C., Weil, F. (eds.) MODELS 2007. LNCS, vol. 4735, pp. 436–450. Springer, Heidelberg (2007)
25. Eclipse: Openup, http://epf.eclipse.org/wikis/openup/
26. Laurent, Y., Bendraou, R., Gervais, M.P.: Generation of Process using Multi-Objective Genetic Algorithm. In: Proceedings of the 2013 International Conference on Software and Systems Process. ACM (2013) (to be published)
27. Weber, B., Reichert, M., Rinderle-Ma, S.: Change patterns and change support features–enhancing flexibility in process-aware information systems. Data & Knowledge Engineering 66(3), 438–466 (2008)
28. Dong, Y., ShenSheng, Z.: Using π-calculus to formalize uml activity diagram for business process modeling. In: IEEE ECBS, pp. 47–54 (2003)
29. Abdelhalim, I., Sharp, J., Schneider, S., Treharne, H.: Formal verification of tokeneer behaviours modelled in fuml using csp. In: Dong, J.S., Zhu, H. (eds.) ICFEM 2010. LNCS, vol. 6447, pp. 371–387. Springer, Heidelberg (2010)
30. Sadiq, W., Orlowska, M.E.: Analyzing process models using graph reduction techniques. Information Systems 25(2), 117–134 (2000)
31. Alur, R., Dill, D.L.: A theory of timed automata. Theoretical Computer Science 126(2), 183–235 (1994)

Sensor Data Visualisation: A Composition-Based Approach to Support Domain Variability

Ivan Logre, Sébastien Mosser, Philippe Collet, and Michel Riveill

Université Nice – Sophia Antipolis
CNRS, I3S, UMR 7271
06900 Sophia Antipolis, France
{logre,mosser,collet,riveill}@i3s.unice.fr

Abstract. In the context of the *Internet of Things*, sensors are surrounding our environment. These small pieces of electronics are inserted in everyday life's elements (*e.g.*, cars, doors, radiators, smartphones) and continuously collect information about their environment. One of the biggest challenges is to support the development of accurate monitoring dashboard to visualise such data. The *one-size-fits-all* paradigm does not apply in this context, as user's roles are variable and impact the way data should be visualised: a building manager does not need to work on the same data as classical users. This paper presents an approach based on model composition techniques to support the development of such monitoring dashboards, taking into account the domain variability. This variability is supported at both implementation and modelling levels. The results are validated on a case study named SMARTCAMPUS, involving sensors deployed in a real academic campus.

Keywords: Variability, Data visualisation, Sensors, Model composition.

1 Introduction

Sensors are everywhere. The *Internet of Things* (IoT) paradigm relies on a world of interconnected objects, able to communicate between each others and collect data about their context. Day after day cars, smartphones and buildings collect information about our living environment, generating zettabytes of sensed data. The Gartner group predicts up to 26 billions of things connected to the Internet by 2020. Intechno Consulting estimates that this market will generate up to 180 billions of euros worldwide. Being able to exploit and interpret these data means to keep control of this mass of information. Considering data obtained from sensors, there is a need to ease the design of monitoring dashboards as raw data remain useless for a user [1]. Aggregating the correlated data into accurate visualisation interfaces allows humans to interpret them, transforming raw values into meaningful information.

Such dashboards support users while interpreting these data, allowing one to take decisions based on the sensed data. The main challenge to tackle is then to support the intrinsic variability of this domain. This variability is twofold

J. Cabot and J. Rubin (Eds.): ECMFA 2014, LNCS 8569, pp. 101–116, 2014.

and thus triggers two concurrent challenges: *(i)* each user wants to use a dashboard dedicated to her very own needs, and *(ii)* visualisation libraries used at runtime provide different visualisation widgets to be used to implement such dashboards. In this context, model-driven engineering approaches can support the first challenge by capturing concepts used by the dashboard designers and providing appropriate tool support. To tackle the second challenge, *Software Product Lines* (SPLs) are defined as "*a set of software-intensive systems that share a common, managed set of features and that are developed from a common set of core assets in a prescribed way*" [2]. SPL engineering is based on the idea that the reusable artefacts encapsulate common and variable aspects of a family of software systems [3,2]. As a consequence, SPLs provide a way to model widget variability, relying on strong logical foundations and configuration support.

The contribution of this paper is to describe a tool-supported approach enabling the mass customisation of dashboards. The approach relies on a dedicated meta-model that captures the concepts used to design a dashboard. The variability of the different visualisation libraries is captured using feature models, expressed according to the concepts defined in the meta-model. The tool support implements the link between the meta-model and the feature models, supporting users while designing dashboards and ensuring code generation to reach runtime environments.

We describe in SEC. 2 the SMARTCAMPUS project, which relies on sensors deployment in a real academic campus. This project serves both as motivation and application for our work. SEC. 3 describes the PTAH meta-model, used to support a user while designing a monitoring dashboard. SEC. 4 describes the method used to capture the variability of a given visualisation library, and how visualisation libraries are composed. SEC. 5 describes the benefits of the approach based on a scenario extracted from the SMARTCAMPUS use case. Finally, SEC. 6 discusses related work, and SEC. 7 concludes this paper by exposing some perspectives for further researches.

2   Motivations and Running Example

This section describes the SMARTCAMPUS project as a motivating example for our contribution. It illustrates the two main challenges this paper addresses: *(i)* how one can design a monitoring dashboard at the right level of abstraction and *(ii)* how such a dashboard can be realised with respect to the existing libraries at the implementation level.

2.1   The SmartCampus Project

The University of Nice-Sophia Antipolis is exploiting a new campus named SophiaTech[1], located in the Sophia Antipolis technology park. The ultimate goal of this project is to consider sensors deployed in buildings as an open platform to let final users (*i.e.*, students, professors, administrative staff) build their

---

[1] http://campus.sophiatech.fr/en/index.php

own innovative services on top of the collected (open) data. This SMARTCAMPUS project was started in September 2013 and involves a team of 18 persons. The development effort is focused on data visualisation, data collection and scalability issues. We consider here this project has a use case in order to bring actual visualisation needs from a real world problem.

The objective of the project is to develop a *middleware* acting as a mediation layer between sensors deployed in buildings and developers who want to develop innovative services based on these data. The functional analysis phase (ended in December 2013) relied on a survey and users interviews to identify prototypical scenarios to be used as relevant validation test cases. As a result, the following three scenarios were identified:

- *Parking lot occupation.* The campus contains five different parking lots, with different occupation rates. Final users complained about the difficulty to find an available parking place. With respect to environmental constraints, the occupation rate of each lot is aggregated based on data collected from sonar sensors (located on arbour overhanging the cars) and counters based on infra-red rays located at the entry and exit portals of each lot. But if users only want to know where to park their car on the morning, the estate department of the University aims at aggregating statistics to analyse the occupation rates of each parking and take decisions based on these data.
- *Crowd monitoring.* The food court of the campus is currently under-sized, leading to long queues during rush hours. Students have identified the need to estimate the waiting time in the cafeteria and the restaurant. The implementation of such a crowd monitoring system is possible with a simple image processing algorithm analysing the video stream of a webcam. Based on the very same technological stack, additional counters can be deployed to measure people traffic in different places, *e.g.*, library, main corridors.
- *Heating regulation.* The heating system of the campus suffered from regulation issues when initially started. As a consequence, data collected from temperature sensors deployed in the buildings had to be aggregated and visualised in dashboard, of which an example is depicted in FIG. 1, as a support for the technical team fixing the steam stream throughput in the different pipes. These sensors can now be used to assess the temperature in the buildings, identifying open doors or windows during winter and optimising the heating effort distribution in the building by comparing the occupancy and temperature of rooms.

2.2   Challenges

The implementation of these use cases in the SMARTCAMPUS context triggers two major issues: *(i)* there were almost as many dashboards needed as interviewed users and *(ii)* at the implementation level, developing such dashboards is error-prone and time-consuming.

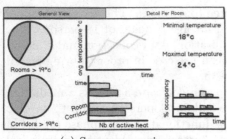 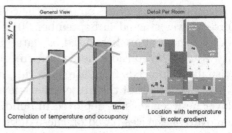

(a) Sensors overview   (b) Zoom on a specific floor

Fig. 1. Mockup of an heating regulation dashboard, designed by campus' users

Designing Multiple Dashboards (C_1). Based on the interviews conducted during the analysis phase, we identified the tremendous variability of monitoring dashboards. Actually, SMARTCAMPUS is a prototypical example of an open-data platform: the availability of data about the environment empowers the end users, allowing each one to design a dashboard based on her very own needs. Unfortunately, if tools used to mockup dashboards are usable by end-users (*e.g.*, Balsamiq[2], see FIG. 1), they cannot be used to generate executable dashboards. Moreover the implementation of such dashboards requires technological skills (*e.g.*, web programming knowledge) that slowed down or even stopped the development effort. Users also experiment a gap between the expression of their functional needs and the organisation of the corresponding data and visualisations into a well-formed dashboard. As a consequence, the first challenge is to support the mass customisation of monitoring dashboards, at the appropriate level of abstraction.

Handling the Technological Variability (C_2). The implementation of such dashboards is a complex task. Even if we have restricted the technological stack to web-based interface (it is one of the assumptions made by the SMARTCAM-PUS Description of Work document), many widget libraries can be used to implement these dashboards, *e.g.*, AmCharts[3], Highcharts[4], D3.js[5]. These libraries are heterogeneous, and offer different widgets with their own specificities. For example, *(i)* AmChart offers 58 different widgets, *(ii)* Highchart offers 54 widgets and 13 additional widgets dedicated to large datasets (named Highstock), and *(iii)* D3.js offers 133 widgets. The effervescence around the big data and open data paradigms fosters the frequent publication of new tools and widget libraries to support data visualisation. Moreover, even if we consider a single library, the evolution of the widget referential must be handled. For example, the D3.js library is based on a community of users, and new widgets are frequently added to the library by external contributors. This proliferation of visualisation

---

[2] http://balsamiq.com
[3] http://www.amcharts.com
[4] http://www.highcharts.com
[5] http://d3js.org

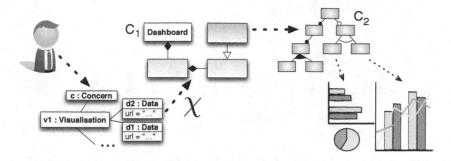

Fig. 2. Global overview of the approach

solutions has become an obstacle to efficient choices during the design of monitoring dashboards, thus our second challenge is to handle the variability of the offered amount of solutions.

The contribution of this paper is to address these two challenges, as depicted in FIG. 2. The user interacts with a model to describe what she wanted to visualise (C_1), and variability models are exploited to support the selection of concrete widgets among the existing ones, including code generation (C_2).

3 Supporting Dashboard Design Variability (C_1)

This section describes a meta-model that tackles the first challenge identified in SEC. 2: "How one can design a monitoring dashboard according to her very own needs?". To address this challenge, the key idea is to tame the complexity of dashboard design using a dedicated meta-model. This meta-model allows a user to focus on the way she wants to compose her data, and does not require implementation knowledge. It focuses on the different visualisation concerns one can apply to a given datasets, and is not bound to any concrete library implementation. Thus, at this level of abstraction, the user is completely free to work. The binding with existing visualisation libraries, as well as the introduction of new libraries with respect to this meta-model corresponds to C_2 (see SEC. 4).

Restricting the domain to its essence, a designers works according to three dimensions while designing a dashboard: *(i)* the data involved in the dashboard according to her monitoring needs (*i.e.*, "What am I visualising"), *(ii)* the different visualisation concerns applied to these data (*i.e.*, "How do I visualise it?") and finally *(iii)* the spatial and temporal layout of the dashboard (*i.e.*, "Where and when do I visualise it?").

We consider here a prototypical example extracted from the SMARTCAMPUS analysis: heat regulation in corridors. For a given corridor, one wants to exploit a temperature sensor to identify issues in the regulation of the heated air streams. Nevertheless, the temperature is impacted by the presence of people: a group of people chatting in the hallway increases the air temperature, and people exiting or entering the hallway through the external doors lower it. Thus, one needs to correlate the data collected from the air temperature sensor and the presence

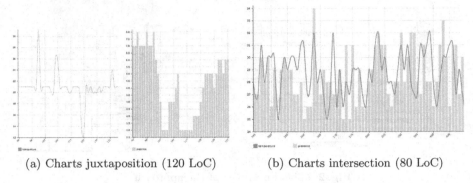

(a) Charts juxtaposition (120 LoC)   (b) Charts intersection (80 LoC)

Fig. 3. Two alternative dashboards realising part of the "heat regulation" use case

counter one to properly analyse the data. This can be done in multiple ways with respect to the user habits, as depicted in FIG. 3 using the AmCharts library. These two datasets can be visualised as charts displayed side by side (FIG. 3a), or the two datasets can be composed in the same chart (FIG. 3b). Considering that working at the implementation level is not acceptable for the SMARTCAMPUS users (due to a lack of programming knowledge), a dedicated meta-model is provided to focus on the level of abstraction expected by the users. This meta-model is named PTAH[6] and depicted in FIG. 3. We describe the concept it defines according to the three dimensions identified at the beginning of this section.

"What am I visualising?". At this level, the user focuses on the data sets she wants to visualise. Based on the state of practice in the IoT domain, we consider in PTAH that data collected from a given sensor are available as a resource published at a dedicated URL, following the REST paradigm. The `DataSet` concept allows one to refer to such an URL while modelling a dashboard. Metadata about the collected information are defined by the `Field` concept: a user expresses that the *temperature* `DataSet` is indexed by a `Field` named t_{temp} typed as a `Date`, and contains a value (another `Field`) named *temp* typed as a `Numerical` value. If the underlying data format supports meta-data definition (*e.g.*, the SensorML standard published by the OGC [4]), it is possible to automatically infer from the dataset description the different `Field`s it contains. Even if it does not happen in this example due to its simplicity, a user often needs to adapt the data she wants to visualise, *e.g.*, selecting only an excerpt or intersecting a given dataset with another one. To support this task, and considering that the definition of datasets in PTAH is very close to relational algebra, we reified in the meta-model the six classical operators available in database querying systems: *(i)* projection, *(ii)* selection, *(iii)* renaming, *(iv)* set difference, *(v)* set union, and *(vi)* Cartesian product. Considering a mobile sensor (*e.g.*, a smartphone) collecting both geographical location and Wi-Fi signal strength [5] in the campus according to time, one can rely on the previous "classical" relation operators to compose these data in order to bind the signal strength to a given

---

[6] The Egyptian god of craftsmen and creation.

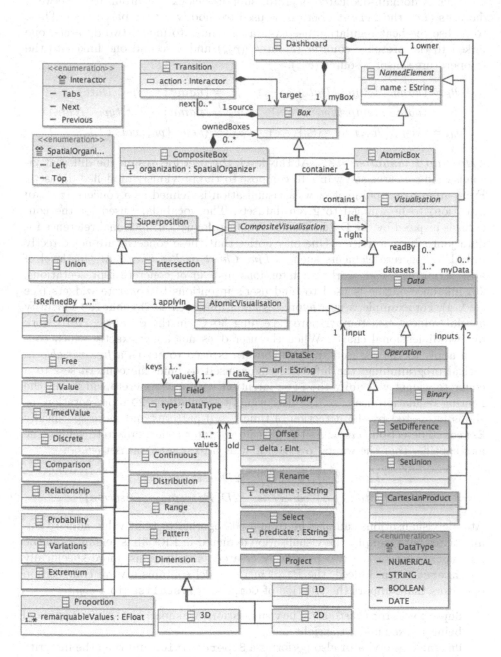

Fig. 4. Excerpt of the PTAH meta-model, supporting dashboard design

location. A domain-dedicated operator supports clock synchronisation between datasets (*i.e.*, the `Offset` operator is used to modify a time-based key). Thus, to realise the heat regulation use case, a user have to model two datasets: one linked to the presence counter resource, (p_{ds}) and a second one linked to the temperature sensor resource (θ_{ds}).

$$\theta_k = (name : t, type : Date) \qquad p_k = (name : t, type : Date)$$
$$\theta_v = (name : temp, type : Num) \qquad p_v = (name : count, type : Num)$$
$$\theta_{ds} = (key : \{\theta_k\}, vals : \{\theta_v\}, \dots) \qquad p_{ds} = (key : \{p_k\}, vals : \{p_v\}, \dots)$$

"How do I visualise it?". At this level, the user focuses on the different visualisation concerns she wants to compose to the previously modelled datasets. From an abstract point of view, a visualisation is defined as a concern (*i.e.*, an intention) to be applied to given datasets. The vocabulary used for the concerns is inspired by the Data Visualisation Catalogue[7], a functional reference for data journalism activities. One may notice that these concerns are not directly linked to concrete elements such as *Line Chart* or *Pie Chart*. At this level of abstraction, the user works on intentions instead of concrete representations. An inference engine is used to bind user's intentions to concrete widgets (see SEC. 4). For example, a user expresses intentions such as `Threshold` to identify special values (*e.g.*, temperature exceeding 30°C) in the datasets, `2D` to work on two-dimensional charts. When the user does not know exactly which concern apply to the datasets, a `Free` concern is used to act as a *free variable* in logical programming: the inference engine used to bind the concern sets to a concrete widget will unify the `Free` intention with any concrete widget. In the heating regulation use case, the user wants to visualise a `2D` representation, as she is interested by the detection of time-based patterns and more specifically `Extremum` detection (vis_θ). As the presence counter collects discrete values, she also specifies that she wants to visualise it as a `Discrete` dataset (vis_p).

$$vis_\theta = (data : \{\theta_{ds}\}, concerns : \{2D, Extremum\})$$
$$vis_p = (data : \{p_{ds}\}, concerns : \{2D, Extremum, Discrete\})$$

Atomic visualisations can also be composed together to built value-added visualisations. For example, the visualisation depicted in FIG. 3b is semantically the `Superposition` of the two previously created visualisations, more specifically an `Intersection`. Indeed, the PTAH meta-model contains several composition operators that support the creation of `CompositeVisualisation`, *e.g.*,:

- `Superposition` (*abstract*). The visualisations are superposed, the left operand being stacked under the right one.
- `Union`. This operator also performs a `Superposition` and keep the integrity of the datasets to visualise both entirely.
- `Intersection`. This operator performs a `Superposition` and process the datasets to only keep data within common time range.

---

[7] http://datavizcatalogue.com/

"Where and when do I visualise it?". Finally, the different visualisation must be composed together from a layout point of view. The PTAH meta-model allows a user to compose visualisation spatially as Boxes (*where*, [6]), and to arrange several Boxes together in a sequence of execution (*when*). Thus, the dashboard depicted in FIG. 3a contains two Boxes (one for each visualisation), composed in a CompositeBox that uses the Left spatial organiser. The dashboard depicted in FIG. 3b contains only one box, bound to the intersection of the two previously created visualisations.

$$\text{FIG. 3a} = Box_C(Left, \{Box(vis_\theta), Box(vis_p)\})$$
$$\text{FIG. 3b} = Box(vis_\theta \cap vis_p)$$

Complex dashboards like the one depicted in FIG. 1 requires Transition from one box to another one. For example, in the heating regulation use case, a tab system is used to switch from the global overview dashboard to the floor-based one. This is supported in PTAH through the definition of Transition that holds a given Interactor, *e.g.*, Next (replacing the current element by the targeted one), Tabs (supporting the user while going back and forth).

4   Handling the Technological Variability (C_2)

The PTAH meta-model was designed as flexible as possible: the concepts defined in this meta-model are intrinsically freed from technical concerns such as concrete widget implementations. As a consequence, there is no immediate link between the meta-classes and concrete widgets. Thus, if one wants to generate concrete visualisation code from a PTAH model, each concept from PTAH must be associated to an implementation pattern that supports it. The challenge addressed here is twofold: *(i)* there is a tremendous number of available visualisation libraries and *(ii)* the relationship between concrete widgets and PTAH concepts is not a simple one-to-one mapping.

Actually, when the user builds a visualisation in PTAH, she is following a kind of configuration process to obtain a visualisation product, just like in SPLs. Considering a variability model of a given domain, one can configure a product of the SPL by selecting needed features [7]. The general idea is that the reusable artefacts encapsulate common and variable aspects of a family of software systems in a manner that facilitates planned and systematic reuse. In our case each Concern concept defined in PTAH is clearly a feature, and each concrete product satisfies (or not) such features. Thus, it is possible to rely on variability modelling techniques and existing configuration tools (formally based on propositional logic and SAT-solving algorithms) to support the realisation of a PTAH model at the concrete level.

The main difficulty is now to build the associated variability model. To support this task, we used a tool-assisted methodology that relies on Feature Models (FMs) [8,9] to model variability, and a merging operator (denoted as μ), depicted in FIG. 5 on these feature models [10]. The key idea of this methodology is to

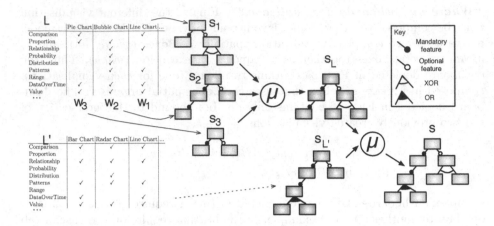

Fig. 5. Merge process used to build the variability model

focus on the different products available, *i.e.*, each widget provided by a given library L, and to characterise it using the terms of the targeted meta-model, ensuring by construction the consistency of features with the selected elements in the meta-model. As a result, we obtain a variability matrix describing each concrete widget $\{w_1, \ldots, w_n\} \in L$ using PTAH concepts. Each widget descriptor w_i is considered as an asset and is associated to a FM s_i that can only derive a single product: w_i. This technique is directly inspired from the construction of feature models from product descriptions [11]. The set of FMs $\{s_1, \ldots, s_n\}$ is then merged using the μ operator, which implements a "merge with strict union" [10]. Being automatic, this operation facilitates the addition or edition of a widget description.. Formally, this operator ensures that given two FMs s and s', the result of $\mu(s, s')$ can be used to derive the products modelled by s and the ones modelled by s', without any additions or restrictions. As a consequence, the result of $\mu(s_1, \mu(s_2, ...)) = s_L$ implements, together with the widget descriptors, the product line that exactly models all the widgets available in L. To introduce a new library L' in the product line, the same process is applied to produce $s_{L'}$, and the resulting product line is eventually obtained as $s = \mu(s_L, s_{L'})$.

We consider here the AmCharts visualisation library. According to its demonstration web page, it defines 58 concrete widgets[8]. Each widget was analysed according to the PTAH concepts, and an excerpt of the resulting comparison matrix is represented in TAB. 1. Based on this matrix exported as a CSV file, each column is translated into a tool-ready representation of each descriptor, using the Familiar language [12] (see FIG. 6).

The resulting feature model, based on a simplified version of the AmCharts that only contains 12 widgets is depicted as a feature diagram in FIG. 7 (31 additional constraints not shown). This model is then exploited to support the user while defining models conforms to the PTAH meta-model. For example, the

---

[8] http://www.amcharts.com/demos/

Table 1. Excerpt of the AmChart variability matrix

Feature \ Product	Pie	Bubble	Line	...
Comparison	✓		✓	
Proportion	✓	✓		
Relationship		✓	✓	
Probability		✓		
Distribution		✓		
Patterns		✓	✓	
Extremum		✓	✓	

Feature \ Product	Pie	Bubble	Line	...
Range				
Discrete	✓	✓		
Value	✓	✓	✓	
Variations		✓	✓	
TimedValue		✓	✓	
Dimension(s)	1D	3D	2D	

```
fm1 = FM(widget:Name Comparison Proportion Value Discrete Dimension;
              Name:"Pie Chart"; Dimension:1D;)
//...
fm10 = FM(widget:Name Comparison Relationship Patterns DataOverTime Value
Discrete Variations Dimension; Name:"Step Chart"; Dimension:2D;)
// ...
amCharts = merge sunion fm_*
```

Fig. 6. Excerpt of the Familiar code used to model the AmChart library

visualisation vis_θ refers to the features 2D and **Extremum**. While configuring the AmCharts feature model with the selection of these two features, the configuration engine results in four potential candidates to realise this intention: *Line chart, Smoothed Line, Bar chart* or a *Column chart*, i.e., 33% of the initial product set. Considering that the second visualisation vis_p refers in addition to the feature **Discrete**, leading to cut the widget dedicated to continuous data and resulting to only offer a *Bar chart* or a *Column chart*, i.e., 13% of the initial widget set. This example illustrates the reduction of possibilities induced by the use of a feature model related to the PTAH meta model.

5   Validation

The validation of the contribution described in this paper relies on a prototype implemented in Java. It provides a semi-automated support for the presented approach, according to the following steps: *(i)* the user expresses a dashboard composition using the PTAH meta-model, *(ii)* the tool search for an equivalent solution handled by a library, interacting with the user to select concrete widgets and finally the tool *(iii)* automatically generate the corresponding and executable code in HTML/CSS and JavaScript.

The following example illustrates the benefits of our contribution in comparison with the required manual manipulations needed while using the solutions provided by the state of practice. Considering a fixed number of data set (here three different temperature sensors), the user want to prototype several dashboards in order to chose the final one she is going to use to monitor her system. We consider here only the AmCharts library, and more specifically only two types of widgets among the 58 available in this library: *(i) Line charts* and *(ii)*

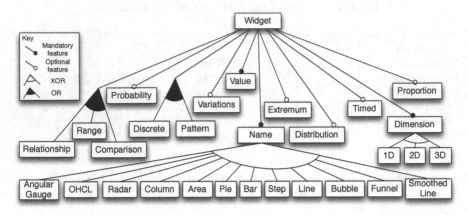

Fig. 7. Feature diagram generated by Familiar tool

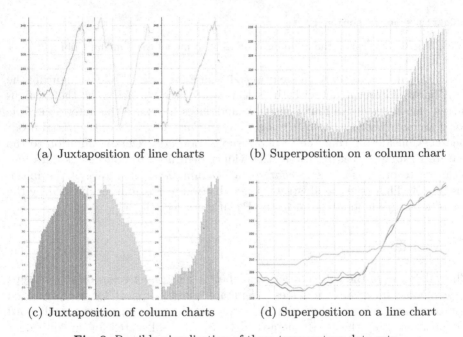

(a) Juxtaposition of line charts   (b) Superposition on a column chart

(c) Juxtaposition of column charts   (d) Superposition on a line chart

Fig. 8. Possible visualisation of three temperature data sets

Column charts. We represent in FIG. 8 four different prototype associated to these three datasets.

We describe in TAB. 2 the cost of transforming one dashboard into another one, in terms of code instructions. It illustrate the time-consuming aspect of a prototyping process, even on this limited scenario. For example, in order to prototype the figure FIG. 8a, giving that the code of FIG. 8b is already available, one needs to remove 54,84% of the existing instructions and add 134,41% of new

Table 2. Cost of changing a given visualisation choice at the implementation level

Evolution From	To	LoC impact dels	adds	Evolution From	To	LoC impact dels	adds
	FIG. 8c	11%	11%		FIG. 8c	55%	134%
FIG. 8a	FIG. 8b	75%	31%	FIG. 8b	FIG. 8a	55%	134%
	FIG. 8d	75%	31%		FIG. 8d	18%	18%
	FIG. 8a	11%	11%		FIG. 8c	55%	134%
FIG. 8c	FIG. 8b	75%	31%	FIG. 8d	FIG. 8a	55%	134%
	FIG. 8d	75%	31%		FIG. 8b	18%	18%

code. Even between two representations that looks close to each other (*e.g.*, FIG. 8a and FIG. 8c), up to 11% of the code needs to be changed.

The concrete dashboards depicted in FIG. 8 can be classified into two categories: *(i)* visualising three graphs at a time (FIG. 8a and FIG. 8c) or *(ii)* comparing the three datasets on the very same graph (FIG. 8b and FIG. 8d). Inside each categories, the main difference between the two dashboards is the discrete representation of the data sets, leading to a line-based representation (continuous) or a column-based one (discrete). Thus, at the PTAH level, the only difference between these elements are the layout and the visualisation concerns applied to each data sets, which corresponds exactly to the semantics expected at the user level. Then, one can represent and generate these different visualizations with a 14 elements model for FIG. 8a and FIG. 8c, and a 12 elements model for FIG. 8b and FIG. 8d.[9]

6   Related Work

The *Interaction Flow Modeling Language* (IFML, [13]) is a standard of the OMG dedicated to model and generate front-end applications and human computer interactions. IFML's purpose is to model front-end of applications composed of several layers, supporting the compositions required in such domain and the links with other layers of the application. In comparison, PTAH is dedicated to the design of monitoring dashboards thus our approach focuses on sensor data visualisations and related specific compositions. Both approaches are complementary, as our composition model can reify the IFML concept of *ViewComponent* in order to handle this specific type of visualisation, and we could use IFML expressiveness in terms of events and user actions to define dashboard transitions. The *CAMELEON Reference Framework* (CRF, [14]) offers a methodology for human-computer interfaces design and generation. Our meta-model can be seen as a specialised implementation of the abstract visualisation layer described in CRF, allowing one to design complex data visualisations that are not yet supported by UsiComp [15] (reference implementation of the CRF). Indeed, the support in UsiXML is currently more focused on form-based interfaces, which

---

[9] details available at http://www.i3s.unice.fr/~logre/ECMFA14.html

are not completely adapted to sensor data visualisation. The concept of mashups as "composed applications" has reach the user interfaces domain [16]. This way of composing *User Interfaces* (UIs) suffers from a lack of globalisation of their composition process, mainly focused on spatial arrangement and connection between data and widgets, where the PTAH meta-model brings useful concepts to handle the goal through visualisation concerns. Work on spatial composition in mashups is nonetheless an inspiration for further work. *COntext sensitive Multi-target widgETs* (COMETs, [17]) model abstract interactors that can be composed to design UIs. The effort has been placed on the context adaptation of those form interface elements. Such an approach complements ours, handling the context awareness part as we focus on the proper design of resulting interfaces and the link with real world solutions, provided that COMETs could represent composite widgets.

Software product lines engineering techniques [2,3] have been used in many domains, but only a few works considered them in the context of UIs. Blouin *et al.* use aspect-oriented techniques coupled with feature selections based on the context change at runtime so that dynamic adaptations of UIs can be realised [18]. Variability modeling and SPL techniques are also used to cover the whole development of Rich Internet Applications, including UIs components [19]. However, it only captures the UI relations to the rest of the web architectures, not the fine-grained selection of widgets. As for the construction of the feature models from the widgets description, the followed approach is directly inspired from Acher *et al.* work where the authors automatically extract a feature model from tabular data describing wiki engines [11]. This approach seems the best suited to our needs as other extraction techniques deal with different software artifacts such as source code [20], some models [21], or feature combinations [22]. Besides, the merge operation on feature models that we use in our approach is itself based on the results of She et. al. on reverse engineering feature models [23].

7   Conclusions and Perspectives

In this paper, we described a tool-supported approach used to tame the complexity of monitoring dashboard design. Based on a set of concrete scenarios extracted from a real deployment of sensors in an academic campus, we proposed a meta-model to support the design of monitoring dashboard, so that one can specify the *what, how, when* and *where* with no implementation knowledge.As the meta-model has been defined to meet business requirements of dashboard designers, it seems reusable for sensor data visualization in other contexts.We also proposed a variability model to facilitate the configuration of user-specific dashboard product from the obtained dashboard model. Then, code generation mechanisms are used to obtain a concrete dashboard executed at runtime, based on user's intention expressed at the model level.

In order to complete this work, we aim at using goal models, such as task trees employed in the Human-Computer Interaction community, as an entry point to define the scenario the user wants to perform. From this representation of her intention, we plan to extract constraints and guidance about the design of a model, conforming to our meta-model and adapted to her goals. This upstream work seems necessary before choosing the final concrete syntax of PTAH and integrating all parts in a tool, on which we plan to perform an empirical validation of the construction time using our approach.As perspectives, we also plan to use feature models to represent the variability of possible customisation of each widget, extracting this knowledge from the library API, and allowing the user to choose a configuration from those models. These parameter requirements will impact the design of the composition model, implying a bottom-up approach in contrary to the contribution of this paper, which can be seen as top-down. In conclusion, we aim at dealing at the same time with both capacities, leading us to define bidirectional links between our models, and thus providing a better support for tailored visualisation dashboard development.

Acknowledgements. Authors want to thanks Simon Urli for his expertise with Familiar and the SMARTCAMPUS team: Romain Alexandre, Mireille Blay-Fornarino, Cecile Camilieri, Adrien Casanova, Cyril Cecchinel, Joel Colinet, Thomas Di'Meco, Fabien Foerster, Mathieu Jimenez, Laura Martellotto, Jean Oudot, Jérome Rancati, Marie-Catherine Turchini and Guillaume Zanotti.

References

1. Few, S.: Information Dashboard Design. O'Reilly (2006)
2. Pohl, K., Böckle, G., van der Linden, F.J.: Software Product Line Engineering: Foundations, Principles and Techniques. Springer (2005)
3. Clements, P., Northrop, L.M.: Software Product Lines: Practices and Patterns. Addison-Wesley Professional (2001)
4. Botts, M., Robin, A.: OpenGIS Sensor Model Language (SensorML) Implementation Specification. Technical report, OGC (July 2007)
5. Haderer, N., Rouvoy, R., Seinturier, L.: Dynamic Deployment of Sensing Experiments in the Wild Using Smartphones. In: Dowling, J., Taïani, F. (eds.) DAIS 2013. LNCS, vol. 7891, pp. 43–56. Springer, Heidelberg (2013)
6. Brel, C., Pinna-Déry, A.M., Faron-Zucker, C., Renevier, P., Riveill, M.: Onto-Compo: An Ontology-Based Interactive System To Compose Applications. In: Seventh International Conference on Web Information Systems and Technologies(WEBIST 2011), pp. 322–327. Springer (May 2011)
7. Svahnberg, M., van Gurp, J., Bosch, J.: A taxonomy of variability realization techniques: Research articles. Softw. Pract. Exper. 35(8), 705–754 (2005)
8. Kang, K., Kim, S., Lee, J., Kim, K., Shin, E., Huh, M.: Form: A feature-oriented reuse method with domain-specific reference architectures. Annals of Software Engineering 5(1), 143–168 (1998)
9. Batory, D.: Feature models, grammars, and propositional formulas. In: Obbink, H., Pohl, K. (eds.) SPLC 2005. LNCS, vol. 3714, pp. 7–20. Springer, Heidelberg (2005)
10. Acher, M., Collet, P., Lahire, P., France, R.: Composing feature models. In: van den Brand, M., Gašević, D., Gray, J. (eds.) SLE 2009. LNCS, vol. 5969, pp. 62–81. Springer, Heidelberg (2010)

11. Acher, M., Cleve, A., Perrouin, G., Heymans, P., Vanbeneden, C., Collet, P., Lahire, P.: On extracting feature models from product descriptions. In: Eisenecker, U.W., Apel, S., Gnesi, S. (eds.) VaMoS, pp. 45–54. ACM (2012)
12. Acher, M., Collet, P., Lahire, P., France, R.B.: Familiar: A domain-specific language for large scale management of feature models. Sci. Comput. Program. 78(6), 657–681 (2013)
13. Rossi, G.: Web modeling languages strike back. IEEE Internet Computing 17(4), 4–6 (2013)
14. Calvary, G., Coutaz, J., Thevenin, D., Limbourg, Q., Bouillon, L., Vanderdonckt, J.: A unifying reference framework for multi-target user interfaces. Interacting with Computers 15(3), 289–308 (2003)
15. García Frey, A., Ceret, E., Dupuy-Chessa, S., Calvary, G., Gabillon, Y.: Usicomp: An extensible model-driven composer. In: EICS, pp. 263–268 (2012)
16. Wilson, S., Daniel, F., Jugel, U., Soi, S.: Orchestrated user interface mashups using w3c widgets. In: Harth, A., Koch, N. (eds.) ICWE 2011. LNCS, vol. 7059, pp. 49–61. Springer, Heidelberg (2012)
17. Demeure, A., Calvary, G., Coninx, K.: Comet(s), a software architecture style and an interactors toolkit for plastic user interfaces. In: Graham, T.C.N. (ed.) DSV-IS 2008. LNCS, vol. 5136, pp. 225–237. Springer, Heidelberg (2008)
18. Blouin, A., Morin, B., Beaudoux, O., Nain, G., Albers, P., Jézéquel, J.M.: Combining aspect-oriented modeling with property-based reasoning to improve user interface adaptation. In: Proceedings of the 3rd ACM SIGCHI Symposium on Engineering Interactive Computing Systems, EICS 2011, pp. 85–94. ACM, New York (2011)
19. Meliá, S., Gómez, J., Pérez, S., Díaz, O.: Architectural and technological variability in rich internet applications. IEEE Internet Computing 14(3), 24–32 (2010)
20. Xue, Y.: Reengineering legacy software products into software product line based on automatic variability analysis. In: Proceedings of the 33rd International Conference on Software Engineering, ICSE 2011, pp. 1114–1117. ACM, New York (2011)
21. Zhang, X., Haugen, Ø., Møller-Pedersen, B.: Model comparison to synthesize a model-driven software product line. In: de Almeida, E.S., Kishi, T., Schwanninger, C., John, I., Schmid, K. (eds.) IEEE SPLC, pp. 90–99 (2011)
22. Haslinger, E.N., Lopez-Herrejon, R.E., Egyed, A.: On extracting feature models from sets of valid feature combinations. In: Cortellessa, V., Varró, D. (eds.) FASE 2013 (ETAPS 2013). LNCS, vol. 7793, pp. 53–67. Springer, Heidelberg (2013)
23. She, S., Lotufo, R., Berger, T., Wasowski, A., Czarnecki, K.: Reverse engineering feature models. In: Taylor, R.N., Gall, H., Medvidovic, N. (eds.) ICSE, pp. 461–470. ACM (2011)

Identifying and Visualising Commonality and Variability in Model Variants

Jabier Martinez[1,2], Tewfik Ziadi[2], Jacques Klein[1], and Yves le Traon[1]

[1] SnT, University of Luxembourg
Luxembourg, Luxembourg
{jabier.martinez,jacques.klein,yves.letraon}@uni.lu
[2] LIP6, Université Pierre et Marie Curie
Paris, France
tewfik.ziadi@lip6.fr

Abstract. Models, as any other software artifact, evolve over time during the development life-cycle. Different *versions* of the same model are thus existing at different times. Model comparison of different versions has received a lot of attention in recent years. However, existing techniques focus on comparing only two model versions at the same time to identify model differences. Independently of model versioning context, another dimension of variation, called *variation in space*, appears in models. Contrary to *variation in time*, variation in space means that a set of model *variants* exists and should be maintained. Comparing all these model variants to identify common and variable elements becomes thus a major challenge. Current approaches for model variants comparison lack of flexibility and appropriate visualisation paradigm. The contribution of this paper is the Model Variants Comparison approach (MoVaC). This approach compares a set of model variants and identifies both commonality and variability in the form of what is referred to as *features*. Each feature consists in a set of atomic model-elements. MoVaC also visualizes the identified features using a graphical representation where common and variable features are explicitly presented to users. We validate the approach on two use cases demonstrating the flexibility of MoVaC to be applied to any kind of EMF-based model variants.

1 Introduction

One of major challenges in model-driven engineering is model comparison and it has received a lot of attention in recent years. Indeed, models, as any other software artifact, evolve over time during the development life-cycle. Different *versions* of the same model are thus existing at different times. Moreover, since different models may be capturing different viewpoints of a system, model comparison is becoming particularly relevant in industrial contexts where different developers work on the same model [7]. In addition, model comparison is an enabler for complex operations such as merging, model compositions and model transformations.

J. Cabot and J. Rubin (Eds.): ECMFA 2014, LNCS 8569, pp. 117–131, 2014.

The first generation of comparison techniques mainly focused on a single kind of models such as UML models [1,10,13]. However, in recent years, and motivated by the success of the Eclipse Modeling Framework (EMF) [4], generic approaches have been proposed to compare any kind of EMF-based models. EMF Compare [3] and EMF DiffMerge [5] are examples of such platforms.

All these generic approaches are limited to a comparison between two versions only. This limitation can be explained because, historically these approaches have been inspired by classical software version control systems [8] where the main issue is to manage *variation in time*. Two program versions are thus analysed to identify differences and eventually merge them. However, with the emergence of software product lines engineering [16], another dimension of variation, called *variation in space*, appears in models. Contrary to variation in time, variation in space means that a set of model *variants* exists and that all these variants should be maintained. Model variants cohabit and evolve at the same time, each of them addressing some new specific requirement of the system, some dedicated features or functionality. Thus the models life-cycle is no longer linear, but it is a tree with parallel variant branches. The problem is that no instrument exists to capture this tree-like evolution of model variants. Comparing all these model variants to identify common and variable elements become thus a major challenge as the interest is to be able to compare more than two models. The objective of this comparison is to eventually refactor these model variants to adopt a software product line approach.

Another observation in existing model comparison platforms is that they only focus on the identification of differences between two model versions but the common part is not explicitly identified in the result of the models comparison. For instance, when we use EMF Compare to compare two model versions, the displayed result only highlights the differences. Common elements can be obtained implicitly by manipulating the result calculated by EMF Compare [3] or the comparison result of EMF DiffMerge. However, this information is not presented explicitly. This also can be justified by the fact that control version systems only aim identifying differences to apply merge. In variation in space it is of high relevance to present explicitly the commonality of the set of model variants as this represents the core that is shared by all model variants.

This paper proposes a new approach for model comparison that can be applied to a set of models variants instead of binary comparison of two models. The approach is called **Mo**del **V**ariants **C**omparison (MoVaC). Beyond offering a systematic and semantically well founded comparison method, another interest is to contribute a generic approach that can be applied for any EMF based models and also to provide a visualisation paradigm of the obtained result.

The rest of paper is organized as follows: Section 2 discusses related work while Section 3 presents an illustrative example. Section 4 presents our approach and applies it on the example. Section 5 presents the validation of the approach and Section 6 concludes this work and presents some perspectives.

2   Related Work

Stephan et al. [19] and *Kolovos et al.* [14] present complete surveys on model comparison and a classification of existing approaches. They showed that several definitions for model comparison exist. In this paper, we consider model comparison as presented by *Brun et.al.* [3]. In this context, model comparison is decomposed in two main steps:

- *Calculation*: In this first step, a procedure, a method or an algorithm is proposed to compare models.
- *Representation and Visualisation*: The outcome of the calculation can be represented in some form and a visualisation is displayed to users.

Existing comparison approaches differ by the way they consider these two steps. The approaches for managing model versions, such as EMF Compare [3] and EMF DiffMerge [5], implement the two steps. EMF Compare uses various statistics and metrics to calculate the match score in the calculation step and the result of the comparison is presented by means of models. EMF DiffMerge is based on customizable Match and Diff policies. However, and as mentioned above, the main observation concerning these approaches is that they only compare two model versions at the same time. If we consider the variation in space dimension where a set of model variants coexist at the same time, these approaches do not allow comparing all these model variants together. EMF Compare and EMF DiffMerge also lack in explicitly highlighting commonality.

Independently from model versioning, the problem of comparing model variants is well known in Software Product Line Re-engineering [9] where the main issue is to analyse a set of model variants to identify commonality and variability. Some of the approaches in this area are related to a specific kind of artifacts and therefore are not generic. *Ryssel et al* [18] compare model variants that are represented as function-blocks. *Ziadi et al.* [21] propose an approach to analyse the source code through the use of UML class diagrams of a set of software variants and identify commonality and variability between them. These approaches are not generic and they do not provide a visualisation paradigm.

Rubin et al. [17], study the problem of model variants comparison mainly in the context of UML models (UML statecharts). They compare a set of UML statecharts with the goal to refactor them as a product line. The authors use XMI principles to represent model variants. They thus justify that their approach can be applied for any kind of meta-models. However, no visualisation paradigm is provided. Indeed, they are focusing on merging input product variants into a generic model and not on highlighting commonality and variability between model variants.

Existing approaches in the context of Software Product Line Re-engineering compare a set of model variants at the same time. However, they only consider the Calculation step. The Representation and Visualisation step is not considered. This is because their main objective concerns refactoring model variants into a product line model without including a domain expert in the process.

We claim that the domain expert must take part in the analysis of the mined commonality and variability information for product line adoption.

In this paper we propose the MoVaC approach that allows comparing a set of model variants at the same time to identify commonality and variability between them. Beyond offering a meta-model independent calculation step, our approach provides a graphical visualisation of the comparison result using the concepts of Features. The approach will be presented in Sect. 4.

3   Illustrative Example

As a concrete example, we use throughout this paper a set of UML model variants representing a set of banking systems [21]. Each model variant represents a simple banking application. The variation between these model variants is related to: limit on the account, consortium entity, and to the currency exchange, which are only present in some variants. Figure 1 illustrates the eight model variants that we consider for comparison. The differences between these model variants concern the presence, or absence, of some classes, attributes and/or operations. The first `Product1Bank` UML model represents a full model. It contains all model elements to support limit on account, consortium entity, and currency exchange. On the contrary, in the `Product2Bank` model, the `Account` class is defined without the limit and currency attributes. We also note the absence of `Converter` and `Consortium` classes. The `Product3Bank` model is defined with information related to currency exchange and consortium but without all elements related to the limit capacity.

In next section, we apply our comparison approach on these model variants to identify commonality and variabilities.

4   Model Variants Comparison Approach

MoVaC[1] is a meta-model independent approach which compares a set of model variants to identify the commonality and the variability between them. To achieve this comparison, our approach follows the general framework of model comparison presented in Sect. 2. It thus consists in two main steps: The *Calculation* and *Representation and Visualisation* steps. Next subsections present each step.

4.1   Step 1: Calculation

As mentioned above, the calculation step in model comparison approaches consists in defining an algorithm that identifies commonality and variability between the model variants. The main idea of MoVaC is to divide each model variant into a Set of Atomic Model-Elements (SoAMEs). Model comparison between a set of model variants is then defined as an equivalence relation between their SoAMEs.

---

[1] The source-code of MoVaC could be found at
https://bitbucket.org/jabi/but4reuse

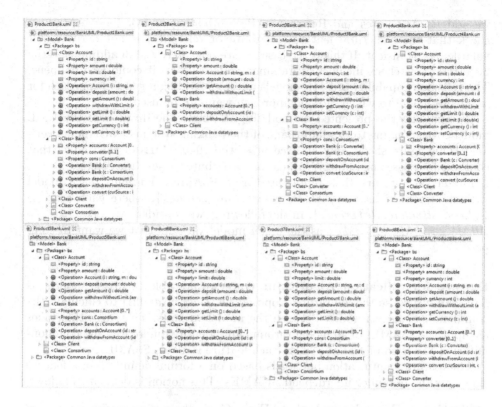

Fig. 1. Eight UML model variants for the banking systems

This step starts by dividing each model variant into a SoAMEs. Each Atomic Model-Element(AME) represents a model element in the model variant. Then, we propose to reuse the algorithm proposed in [21] to identify commonality and differences in what is called features. The following sections presents SoAMEs and summarise the comparison algorithm.

Dividing a Model on a Set of Atomic Model-Elements: As shown by *Blanc et al.* [2] models are artifacts that can be expressed as a sequence of *elementary construction operations* and we have used a similar approach. By using the Meta Object Facility (MOF) concepts [15] we are able to divide any model compliant with the MOF specification. The AMEs in our approach are:

- *Class*: It consists of a "parent" Class and the class "object" itself.
- *Attribute*: It consists of an "owner" Class, an "attribute identifier" and a "value".
- *Reference*: It consists of an "owner" Class, a "reference identifier" and a set of "referenced" Classes.

We implemented this division of models using a pre-order tree traversal of the model by following the containment references. After adding each Class we add its Attributes and References. Before adding any of these AMEs we check that the structural feature (attribute or reference) is not derived, nor volatile, nor transient. If this is the case we are not interested in adding it to the SoAMEs. This check includes containment references as it could also happens. The reflexion capability of EMF models allows providing a generic approach for any meta-model to which MoVaC approach wants to be used.

By applying the presented method, Fig. 2 shows the division of the UML model corresponding to `Product1Bank` of the banking systems UML model variants. This figure shows only an excerpt of the 1049 AMEs of this model that contains 67 classes including UML classes, attributes, operations etc.

Model variants are thus represented as a SoAMEs. Formally, each model variant is defined as a set $M_i = \{ame_1, ame_2, ..ame_n\}$, where each $ame_i \in \{Class, Attribute, Reference\}$. In the following, we consider $AllMVs = \{M_1, M_2, ..M_N\}$ as the set of model variants that we want to compare.

Feature Identification Algorithm: Once we are able to divide models as SoAMEs, we reuse the algorithm proposed by *Ziadi et al.* [21] to calculate the commonality and variability between the model variants. This algorithm takes as input the SoAMEs of all model variants and identify differences and commonalities in the form of *features* where each feature is also a SoAMEs.

The feature identification process is based on a formal definition of a feature that uses the notion of interdependent AMEs. This notion is defined as follows.

Definition 1 (Interdependent AMEs). *Given the set of model variants that we want to compare AllMVs, two AMEs (of models of AllMVs) ame₁ and ame₂ are interdependent if and only if they belong to exactly the same products of AllMVs. In other words, ame₁ and ame₂ are interdependent if the two following conditions are fulfilled.*

1. $\exists M \in AllMVs \ ame_1 \in M \wedge ame_2 \in M$.
2. $\forall M \in AllMVs \ ame_1 \in M \Leftrightarrow ame_2 \in M$.

Since interdependence is an equivalence relation on the set of AMEs of *AllMVs*, it leads us to the following definition of a feature.

Definition 2 (Feature). *Given AllMVs a set of products, a feature of AllMVs is an equivalence class of the interdependence relation of the AMEs of AllMVs.*

The application of the feature identification algorithm to the SoAMEs of the banking models provides the features depicted by Fig. 3. In order to ease the reading we only present representative AMEs from the full SoAME of each feature. The `Feature 0` gathers all the AMEs that are present in all the product variants. We have the `bs` package with the `Bank`, `Account` and `Client` classes as well as the shared package of the used data-types. The `Feature 1` concerns the limit information. This feature contains the Attribute AME related to the `withdrawWithoutLimit` operation in the `Account` class. A domain expert could

Fig. 2. Excerpt of a Bank UML model atomic elements

be able to analyse this and conclude that this is the case when the Bank has withdraw without limit. On the other hand, `Feature 4` presents the other possible case when the Bank has withdraw with limit. This way in `Feature 4` we have the Attribute AME related to the `withdrawWithLimit` operation. It also contains primitives to create the `limit` field, its getter and the method defining limit checking. `Feature 2` consists in the `Consortium` class and the given property and constructor operation of the `Bank` class. `Feature 3` includes all the needed classes and operations to manage currency exchange.

Comparing Atomic Model-Elements: The feature identification algorithm presented in previous section requires the definition of equals operator between AMEs. This section clarifies how this comparison between AMEs is performed. We rely mainly on existing techniques of model comparison that are highly extensible. These techniques enable to define when elements are equals or not for a given specific purpose and to deal with meta-model peculiarities. MoVaC

Fig. 3. Bank UML Models features

specifies a default comparison of AMEs that can be easily customized through extension points. More precisely, using the classification by *Kolovos et al.* [14] MoVaC default model comparison behaviour is static identity-based matching but MoVaC implementation provides standard Eclipse extension mechanisms to contribute signature based-matching if required.

We have implemented the equals boolean methods for each of the AMEs. We extensively used EMF DiffMerge that enables to compare two Model Scopes using Match and Diff policies.

- *Class*: Two *Class* AMEs are equals if we isolate each of the "objects" in a scope that contains only these elements and the Diff Policy returns no difference in the comparison. The Diff policy ignores all the attributes and references. This way it will not return that an `EObject` is different if they have different attributes or references. To check the "equals" for attributes and references we rely on the Attribute and References AMEs. The Match policy used by default consists in retrieving the ID attribute of the element and, if not defined, it tries to infer it checking different serialization mechanisms as XMI ids etc.
- *Attribute*: In EMF each defined attribute in the meta-model has an identifier (for example Operation_Name for the attribute Name of the Operation meta-object). Two *Attribute* AMEs will be the same if they deal with the same attribute identifier and if the owner objects of the attribute are the

same. Finally, the Diff policy is in charge of deciding whether the values of the attributes should be considered equals for this attribute identifier. The default implementation of the Diff policy just performs an equals operation on the values.

- *Reference*: As well as with Attributes, two *Reference* AMEs are equals if they share the same reference identifier and if the owner objects are the same. Then we check that the referenced classes are the same. If it is an ordered reference the objects must appear in the same positions. If not ordered then it is only needed that all the elements are present in the other Reference AME.

4.2 Step 2: Representation and Visualization

The visualization eases to show the different features and their presence and relative position in the set of model variants. By selecting the eight models that integrate the Banking systems UML Model variants we apply the MoVaC approach and we obtain the visualization presented on Fig. 4. Each bar represents one of the model variants and the stripes on each of the bars are the SoAMEs as computed by the division algorithm. This way the length of the bar represents the number of AMEs and consequently we will have bars with different lengths. As we can see the height of `Product1Bank` is greater than the height of `Product2Bank` as their SoAMEs sizes are 1049 and 567 respectively.

The MoVaC approach displays the list of identified features. Figure 4 shows the feature list previously mentioned for the Banking systems. Each feature has an assigned color. The stripes (AMEs) of the Model variants are colorized with the color of the feature that the AME belongs to. As illustrated in the Fig. 4, a specific feature could consist of AMEs that are scattered through the bar. This is because MoVaC displays AMEs of each model variant in the order that these AMEs are constructed in the first Calculation step. For example if we look at `Feature 2` of `Product5Bank` it has two parts. The first part will correspond to the Property and Operations related to Consortium in the Bank class while the second part will correspond to the Consortium UML class itself. The separation between the two parts are AMEs from other features. This helps locating and understanding the distribution of AMEs in model variants.

For the implementation of the visualisation we used the extensible visualiser of the Eclipse project AspectJ Development Tools [6]. It was originally used for visualising cross-cutting concerns in different modules. This visualisation method was already used for source code clone visualisation [20].

Apart from the main visualization presented here, other functionalities of this visualization are:

- *Filtering*: Using the checkboxes on the Feature list we can select which features we want to visualize. Also by selecting one of the bars we have the option to automatically show only the features that this bar contains.
- *Analyze features*: The visualization has functionality to show the content of each Feature. That means that we can have the text representation of all the atomic elements that compose each of the Features.

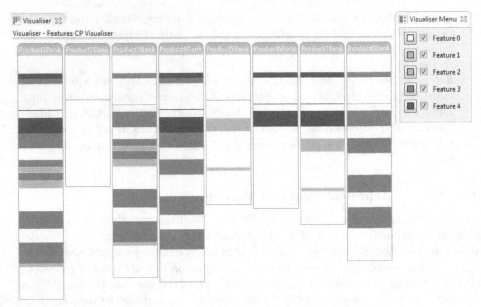

Fig. 4. Bank UML Model variants comparison

- *Analyze atomic elements*: By clicking on a stripe of any bar we get the text representation of the selected atomic element.
- *Export*: It is possible to export the relation of Models and Features in a separated file that could be opened in a spreadsheet application for further processing or visualisation. Table 1 presents this relation between existing Banking systems and the Features.

Table 1. Relation of existing Bank models and identified features

	P1Bank	P2Bank	P3Bank	P4Bank	P5Bank	P6Bank	P7Bank	P8Bank
Feature 0	X	X	X	X	X	X	X	X
Feature 1		X	X		X			X
Feature 2	X		X		X		X	
Feature 3	X		X	X				X
Feature 4	X			X		X	X	

5   Evaluation and Discussion

5.1   Case Studies

In the last section, we applied our approach on the illustrative example concerning the Banking UML model variants. For the evaluation purposes, we present here a second case study. This example concerns Vending Machine variants represented as statecharts. These vending machines statechart variants were introduced in previous work [11]. The statecharts models are not UML based, the

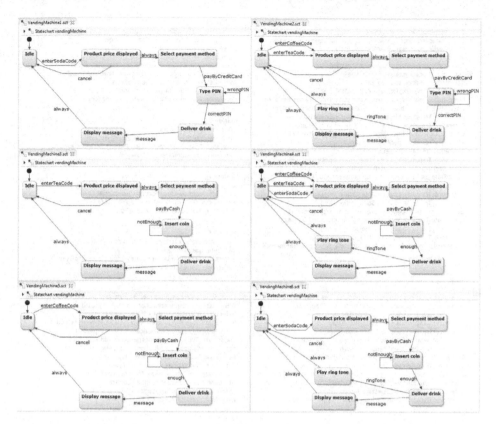

Fig. 5. Six SCT Vending machines model variants

meta-model used is the Yakindu Statechart Tools meta-model [12]. Figure 5 shows the six analysed variants. The objective of these Vending Machines is to provide different kinds of drinks. For example, VendingMachine1 provides only Soda while VendingMachine4 provides all types of drinks. There could be also support for different payment methods for the customers. VendingMachine1 only provides credit card payment while VendingMachine1 only accepts cash. Some of the Vending machines, see VendingMachine2 and VendingMachine3, alert the customer that the drink is ready through a ring tone. Apart from that, other states and transitions are common such as the Idle, Select payment method, Deliver drink and Display message states.

We applied the MoVaC approach to the six model variants for the Vending Machine. Figure 6 illustrates the obtained features. Feature 0 gathers the SoAMEs shared by all the model variants. We have for example the main region and the mentioned states Idle, Product price displayed, Select payment method, Deliver drink and Display message. Feature 3, Feature 4 and Feature 5 contain respectively the SoAMEs related to the state transitions of entering the code of Soda, Coffee or Tea. Feature 1 corresponds to the cash payment method while

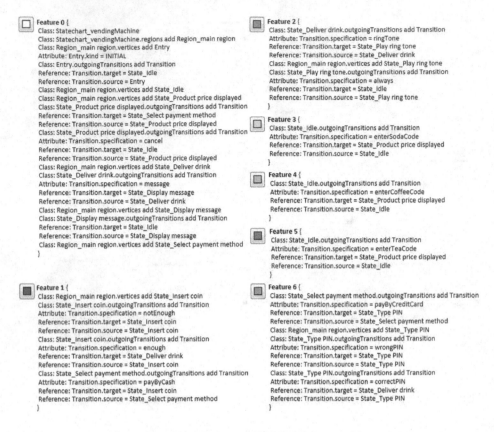

Fig. 6. Vending Machine SCT Model variants features

Feature 6 corresponds to the credit card payment method. Finally, `Feature 2` contains the states and transitions regarding the ring tone alert.

The visualisation of the obtained features is presented on Fig. 7. Table 2 illustrates the relation between Features and model variants.

5.2 Evaluation

In this section the MoVaC approach is assessed considering the following research questions:

- *RQ1: Soundness of the comparison.* Is the approach able to identify correctly the commonality and variability of a set of models?
- *RQ2: Flexibility.* Is the approach applicable to various modelling meta-models?

Soundness of the Comparison (RQ1). The first research question amounts to evaluate correctness of the commonality and variability identified and visualised with our approach. As mentioned above, the case studies that we used

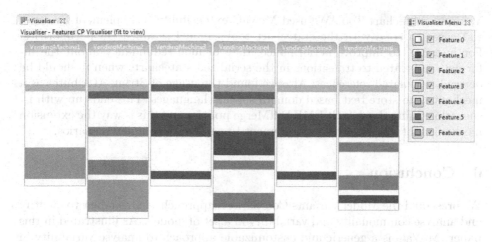

Fig. 7. Vending Machine SCT Model variants comparison

Table 2. Relation of existing Vending machine models and identified features

	SCT 1	SCT 2	SCT 3	SCT 4	SCT 5	SCT 6
Feature 0	X	X	X	X	X	X
Feature 1			X	X	X	X
Feature 2		X		X		X
Feature 3	X			X		X
Feature 4		X		X	X	
Feature 5		X	X	X		
Feature 6	X	X				

in this paper are inspired from papers [21](for the Banking UML model variants), and [11](for the vending machines). In addition to the model variants, these papers also present the actual commonality and variability in terms of features. We thus manually compared the obtained features with those initially presented in these papers. The evaluation shows that that we get a full matching between commonality and variability identified by our approach and those initially presented in the mentioned papers.

Flexibility (RQ2). We validate our approach on two case studies that are based on two different meta-models. The MoVaC approach successfully presents to the user commonality and variability of model variants in terms of features. This shows that it is a generic approach and that it can be used for any EMF based meta-model. However, and as presented in Sect. 4.1, our approach depends on the AME's comparison method. In our implementation of the MoVaC approach we used EMF DiffMerge default policies but we are aware that current complex modeling tools require this AMEs comparison method to be extended to other policies. It is the case for SCT model variants that are based on the

Yakindu Statechart Tool. We used MoVaC extensibility to implement two special cases to cope with the statechart tool's model serialization peculiarities. For instance, to improve performance, they include redundancy about the informations related to transitions in the serialized statecharts when it should be derived/calculated references. Also we found the usage of String Attributes as a mechanism to store text based domain specific languages. This ends up with issues while using the default EMF DiffMerge policies and this is way the extension mechanism of MoVaC was a requirement to cope with complex scenarios.

6   Conclusion

We presented the Model Variants Comparison approach as an enabler to identify and analyse commonality and variability in a set of models. As illustrated in this paper, MoVaC is a generic and customizable approach to analyse variability in space among different variants. MoVaC also implements the visualisation step where commonality and variability between model variants are presented to users in the form of what is referred to as features. We validated our approach on two case studies. As further work we aim to apply it in an industrial scenario dealing with huge model variants.

Acknowledgements. The present work is supported by the Fonds National de la Recherche (FNR), Luxembourg, under the project MODEL C12/IS/3977071.

References

1. Alanen, M., Porres, I.: Difference and union of models. In: Stevens, P., Whittle, J., Booch, G. (eds.) UML 2003. LNCS, vol. 2863, pp. 2–17. Springer, Heidelberg (2003)
2. Blanc, X., Mounier, I., Mougenot, A., Mens, T.: Detecting model inconsistency through operation-based model construction. In: ICSE, pp. 511–520 (2008)
3. Brun, C., Pierantonio, A.: Model differences in the eclipse modeling framework. UPGRADE, The European Journal for the Informatics Professional 9(2), 29–34 (2008)
4. Eclipse: Eclipse modeling framework project (2014), http://www.eclipse.org/modeling/emf
5. Eclipse: Emf diff/merge: a diff/merge component for models (2014), http://eclipse.org/diffmerge/
6. Eclipse: The visualiser, ajdt: Aspectj development tools (2014), http://www.eclipse.org/ajdt/visualiser/
7. Engel, K.-D., Paige, R.F., Kolovos, D.S.: Using a model merging language for reconciling model versions. In: Rensink, A., Warmer, J. (eds.) ECMDA-FA 2006. LNCS, vol. 4066, pp. 143–157. Springer, Heidelberg (2006)
8. Estublier, J.: Software configuration management: A roadmap. In: Finkelstein, A. (ed.) ICSE - Future of SE Track, pp. 279–289. ACM (2000)
9. Fenske, W., Thüm, T., Saake, G.: A taxonomy of software product line reengineering. In: Collet, P., Wasowski, A., Weyer, T. (eds.) VaMoS, p. 4. ACM (2014)

10. Girschick, M., Darmstadt, T.: Difference detection and visualization in uml class diagrams. Tech. rep. (2006)
11. Istoan, P., Biri, N., Klein, J.: Issues in model-driven behavioural product derivation. In: VaMoS, pp. 69–78 (2011)
12. itemis: Yakindu statechart tool (2014), http://statecharts.org
13. Kelter, U., Wehren, J., Niere, J.: A generic difference algorithm for uml models. In: Liggesmeyer, P., Pohl, K., Goedicke, M. (eds.) Software Engineering. LNI, vol. 64, pp. 105–116. GI (2005)
14. Kolovos, D.S., Di Ruscio, D., Pierantonio, A., Paige, R.F.: Different models for model matching: An analysis of approaches to support model differencing. In: Proceedings of the 2009 ICSE Workshop on Comparison and Versioning of Software Models, CVSM 2009, pp. 1–6. IEEE Computer Society, Washington, DC (2009), http://dx.doi.org/10.1109/CVSM.2009.5071714
15. OMG: Meta object facility (mof) core specification (2006), http://www.omg.org/spec/MOF/2.0/
16. Pohl, K., Böckle, G., van der Linden, F.: Software Product Line Engineering: Foundations, Principles and Techniques (2005)
17. Rubin, J., Chechik, M.: Combining related products into product lines. In: de Lara, J., Zisman, A. (eds.) FASE. LNCS, vol. 7212, pp. 285–300. Springer, Heidelberg (2012)
18. Ryssel, U., Ploennigs, J., Kabitzsch, K.: Automatic variation-point identification in function-block-based models. In: GPCE, pp. 23–32 (2010)
19. Stephan, M., Cordy, J.R.: A survey of model comparison approaches and applications. In: Hammoudi, S., Pires, L.F., Filipe, J., das Neves, R.C. (eds.) MODELSWARD, pp. 265–277. SciTePress (2013)
20. Tairas, R., Gray, J., Baxter, I.: Visualization of clone detection results. In: Proceedings of the 2006 OOPSLA Workshop on Eclipse Technology EXchange, Eclipse 2006, pp. 50–54. ACM, New York (2006)
21. Ziadi, T., Frias, L., da Silva, M.A.A., Ziane, M.: Feature identification from the source code of product variants. In: CSMR, pp. 417–422 (2012)

Modular DSLs for Flexible Analysis: An e-Motions Reimplementation of Palladio

Antonio Moreno-Delgado[1], Francisco Durán[1], Steffen Zschaler[2], and Javier Troya[3]

[1] University of Málaga
{amoreno,duran}@lcc.uma.es
[2] King's College London
szschaler@acm.org
[3] Vienna University of Technology
troya@big.tuwien.ac.at

Abstract. We address some of the limitations for extending and validating MDE-based implementations of NFP analysis tools by presenting a modular, model-based partial reimplementation of one well-known analysis framework, namely the Palladio Architecture Simulator. We specify the key DSLs from Palladio in the e-Motions system, describing the basic simulation semantics as a set of graph transformation rules. Different properties to be analysed are then encoded as separate, parametrised DSLs, independent of the definition of Palladio. These can then be composed with the base Palladio DSL to generate specific simulation environments. Models created in the Palladio IDE can be fed directly into this simulation environment for analysis. We demonstrate two main benefits of our approach: 1) The semantics of the simulation and the non-functional properties to be analysed are made explicit in the respective DSL specifications, and 2) because of the compositional definition, we can add definitions of new non-functional properties and their analyses.

1 Introduction

It has been generally recognised that the non-functional properties (NFPs)—for example, performance or reliability—of a system are central to the success of a software development project. The later in the process an error in NFPs is discovered, the more costly will it be to repair. There is, therefore, a need for early predictive analysis of NFPs.

Model-driven engineering (MDE) advocates the use of models as the primary artefacts in software development. It has been recognised that this provides opportunities for very early analysis of NFPs based on early design models. These models can often be transformed into analysis models (e.g., in the form of Petri nets or queuing networks) that can be analysed or simulated by standard tooling [1,2,3,7,8,9].

Typically, in these approaches a design model is translated into an analysis model which is then evaluated by a dedicated analysis tool. Alternatively,

J. Cabot and J. Rubin (Eds.): ECMFA 2014, LNCS 8569, pp. 132–147, 2014.
© Springer International Publishing Switzerland 2014

the design model is translated into a simulation of the system to be built. In both cases, however, the semantics of the non-functional property to be analysed and of the analysis technique are only represented implicitly as encoded in the transformations or analysis tools. This causes two problems:

1. *Validation of analysis.* As there is no explicit specification of the analysis nor a high-level representation of the NFPs to be analysed, it is difficult for users to be sure that they are analysing the correct property of their system (see, e.g., [12] for a discussion of some of the subtleties that might need to be considered). Conversely, it is also very difficult for tool providers to validate the correctness of their tooling, which has a direct impact on the correctness of their predictions.
2. *Maintainability and extensibility of analyses.* The tool implementations, especially in the transformations producing simulations, often tangle code concerned with different NFPs. For example, the transformations used in the Palladio Architecture Simulator [9] tangle code for performance and reliability simulations. This makes the code very difficult to maintain and, in particular, extend to support new NFPs.

In previous work [6,10,17], we have explored the modular definition of non-functional properties as parametrised domain specific languages (DSLs) in the e-Motions framework [11]. In the present paper, we demonstrate how these ideas can be integrated with predictive analysis of architectural software models by providing a modular reimplementation of a substantive part of the Palladio Architecture Simulator [9]. In particular, we have re-implemented the Palladio Component Model [3], its workload model, and parts of its stochastic expressions model. However, instead of implementing transformations to analysis models or simulators as done in Palladio, we have explicitly modelled the simulations as graph transformations in the e-Motions framework. Each NFP to be analysed is then modelled as an independent, parametrised DSL ready to be composed with the base Palladio model. This addresses the above two problems in the following ways:

1. There is an explicit specification of both the simulation mechanism and the NFPs to be analysed. These models can be inspected and reasoned about separately giving more assurance of correctness of the simulation results.
2. Modular definition of NFPs as separate, parametrized DSLs allows its reuse, but also makes it easy to define additional NFPs to be analysed. For a particular analysis problem, the relevant NFP DSLs can then be selected from a library and composed as required. Our previous work in [5] provides guarantees for preservation of semantics under composition, that is, the consideration of additional NFPs (satisfying certain restrictions) do not change the behaviour of the system being modeled.

While our approach may not be as performant for large models as the native Palladio implementation, its modular and model-based nature mean that new analyses can be prototyped very effectively. These might then still be translated into native implementations tightly integrated with Palladio where efficiency of analysis is a concern over full validation of analysis. We present in this paper the specification of the NFPs response time and throughput, but new types of analysis could be easily added. One such analysis that could be easily prototyped in our approach is support for dynamic systems — this possibility has already been explored in [17]. In e-Motions, this effectively amounts to a number of additional rewrite rules for the base model.

The remainder of this paper is structured as follows. Section 2 provides some background on the two MDE frameworks our work relies on, namely Palladio and e-Motions. Section 3 explains how the Palladio DSL has been defined in the e-Motions system. Section 4 describes the way observers are defined and how they are woven with the Palladio system to enrich the definition of its behavior for the observation of NFPs. Section 5 illustrates our approach on a concrete example and compares the results obtained by Palladio and by its e-Motions counterpart. We wrap up with some conclusions and future work in Section 6.

2   Preliminaries

Our work is based on two MDE frameworks: We use Palladio [9], and in particular the Palladio Component Model (PCM) [3], to allow modelling of component-based systems and their performance-relevant properties; and we use e-Motions to implement simulations of these systems' performance properties (as well as of other non-functional properties). In this section, we provide some background on both frameworks to ground the discussion that will follow.

2.1   Palladio

The Palladio Architecture Simulator [9] is a predictive software analysis tool developed by the group around Ralf Reussner at KIT in Karlsruhe, Germany. It consists of a number of metamodels, foremost the Palladio Component Model (PCM) [3], that allow the high-level modelling of component-based architectures and their properties relevant for performance and reliability analysis. Instances of these metamodels are then transformed in preparation for analysis. Palladio supports two kinds of predictive analyses: 1) by transformation into a program that runs a simulation of the architecture's behaviour and 2) by transforming to a formalism more amenable to analysis—for example, Queuing Petri Nets [14]. In both cases, the semantics of the models, and in particular of the non-functional properties being analysed, is encapsulated in the transformations. This makes it very difficult to understand and validate these semantics. This is particularly problematic as more non-functional properties are supported: the current transformations support performance and reliability, but already are quite complex. Palladio consists of over 4 million lines of code written in 12 languages.[1]

Fig. 1 shows a very simple example of a component specification in Palladio. It shows a so-called resource-demanding service-effect specification (RDSEFF)

---

[1] Based on data obtained from http://www.ohloh.net/p/palladio on Feb. 4, 2014.

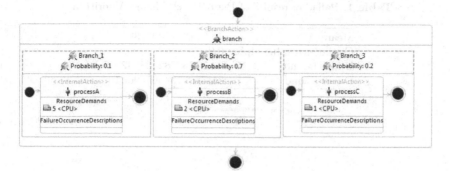

Fig. 1. Component model

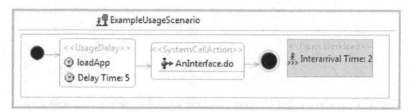

Fig. 2. Usage model

describing the key performance-relevant elements of a component's behaviour. In particular, Fig. 1 shows that the control flow in our component may branch into either of three flows, with different CPU demands for each flow. Each branch is associated with a particular branch probability to indicate the likelihood of a particular branch being taken. This is the kind of information required to perform execution-time analysis on the component's behaviour as is standard in software performance engineering (see, e.g., [13]). In addition, we could model failure information to support reliability analysis.

Fig. 1 is only half the story. We also need to provide information about how the component is used to be able to provide useful predictions of performance. In Fig. 2, we see an example usage model specifying a particular workload for our component. This part of the model uses standard workload terminology to specify an open workload with an inter-arrival time of 2 time units. When a request arrives, there is a delay of 5 units loading the application, after which a call to our component is executed. With these models we now have enough information to run a first basic simulation of our system.

The Palladio Simulator offers the results of the analysis of performance and reliability of the system being analysed in different formats. For example, for the above model, it gives the mean response time and confidence intervals in Table 1. The chart in Fig. 3 represents the cumulative distribution function of the system's response time. Since the CPU resource gets saturated, the response time keeps increasing along time. For 1,000 runs, tasks take up to 90 time units.

Table 1. Palladio: results of Plain Batch Means Algorithm

Mean value:	41.97139713971397
Confidence value alpha:	0.9
Upper bound:	52.17187782288832
Lower bound:	31.770916456539624

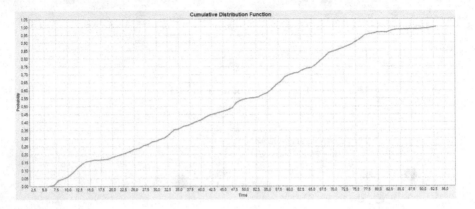

Fig. 3. Cumulative distribution function of the system's response time

2.2 The e-Motions System

e-Motions [11] is a graphical framework that supports the specification, simulation, and formal analysis of real-time systems. It provides a way to graphically specify the dynamic behaviour of DSLs using their concrete syntax, making this task very intuitive. The abstract syntax of a DSL is specified as an Ecore meta-model, which defines all relevant concepts—and their relations—in the language. Its concrete syntax is given by a GCS (Graphical Concrete Syntax) model, which attaches an image to each language concept. Then, its behaviour is specified with (graphical) in-place model transformations.

e-Motions provides a model of time, supporting features like duration, periodicity, etc., and mechanisms to state action properties. From a DSL definition e-Motions generates an executable Maude [4] specification which can be used for simulation and analysis. Other tools in the Maude formal environment, as its model checker or its reachability analysis tool, can also be used on this specification.

In-place transformations are defined by rules, each of which represents a possible *action* of the system. These rules are of the form [NAC]* × LHS → RHS, where LHS (left-hand side), RHS (right-hand side) and NAC (negative application conditions) are model patterns that represent certain (sub-)states of the system. The LHS and NAC patterns express the conditions for the rule to be applied, whereas the RHS represents the effect of the corresponding action. A LHS may also have positive conditions, which are expressed, as any expression in the RHS, using OCL. Thus, a rule can be applied, i.e., triggered, if a match of the

LHS is found in the model, its conditions are satisfied, and none of its NAC patterns occurs. If several matches are found, one of them is non-deterministically chosen and applied, giving place to a new model where the matching objects are substituted by the appropriate instantiation of its RHS pattern. The transformation of the model proceeds by applying the rules on sub-models of it in a non-deterministic order, until no further transformation rule is applicable.

In e-Motions, there are two types of rules to specify time-dependent behaviour, namely, *atomic* and *ongoing* rules. Atomic rules represent atomic actions with a duration, which is specified by an interval of time. Atomic rules with duration zero are called *instantaneous* rules. Ongoing rules represent actions that progress continuously over time while the rule's preconditions (LHS and not NACs) hold. Both atomic and ongoing rules can be scheduled, or be given an execution interval.

3   Palladio into e-Motions

The PCM is a DSL [3], and therefore we may define it in e-Motions. As for any DSL, the definition of the PCM includes its abstract syntax, its concrete syntax and its behavior.

Since the Palladio system has been developed following MDE principles, and specifically it is implemented using the Eclipse Modeling Framework (EMF), its metamodel may be directly used as abstract syntax definition of Palladio in e-Motions. Palladio models consist of several views, namely UsageModel, System, etc., corresponding to the different developer roles. These models are conformant to metamodels Core PCM, StoEx, Units, ... used by the different Eclipse plug-ins in the PCM Bench.[2]

The concrete syntax is provided by a GCS model in which each concept in the abstract syntax of the DSL being defined is linked to an image. Since these images are used to graphically represent Palladio models in e-Motions, we have used the same images that the PCM Bench uses to represent these concepts. This way, we maintain the PCM's look in the e-Motions definition.

The PCM Bench supports the design of the models corresponding to the different views that each developer role has to fill. However, these models define the architecture of a system. Transformations of PCM models into queueing network models or stochastic process algebra provide the necessary predictive analysis for the PCM models. Thus, the semantics of the properties to be analysed as well as of the analysis methods themselves are implicitly encoded in the transformations and support tooling.

In e-Motions, we describe how systems evolve by describing all possible changes of the models by corresponding visual rewrite rules, that is, time-aware in-place transformation rules. Since the PCM metamodel only specifies those concepts relevant for the PCM language and the models obtained from the PCM Bench cannot

---

[2] The metamodel provided to e-Motions must have a single package in a single file. Since the PCM metamodel is defined in several packages in several files, we have developed a higher-order transformation to prepare the input models.

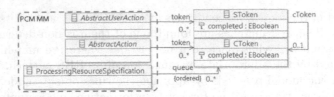

Fig. 4. Token metamodel

be directly simulated or analyzed, we have conservatively enriched the PCM metamodel with new concepts to handle the control flow. We call this new metamodel Palladio*. Specifically, Palladio* has an additional metamodel `Token`, which includes two classes `SToken` and `CToken`. The former is specified at the system model (`UsageModel`) level, and the latter at the component model (`RDSEFF`) level. Both `SToken` and `CToken` classes have a *Bool* attribute `completed`, which states whether an action with this token is accomplished. References—with cardinality *— to classes `SToken` and `CToken` have been added to `AbstractUserAction` and `AbstractAction`, respectively. An ordered reference `queue` from `ProcessingResourceSpecification` to `CToken`, with multiplicity *, is used as a queue in which actions wait until resources of the corresponding type are available. Fig. 4 shows the `Token` metamodel and the references from classes of PCM to `SToken` and `CToken`.

We may visualize that the execution of a Palladio model has a token "moving around" such model. An action with a token has the control of execution — the `completed` attribute of a `Token` object becomes `true` once the action is completed, then it can be moved to its successor action. In fact, there might be several concurrent executions, since new tasks may keep arriving to the system, depending on its work load. The execution of each of these tasks proceeds independently, as far as the required resources are available — modelled by the rule in Fig. 6.

Since the extension of the metamodel has been done in a conservative way, every model conforming to the Palladio metamodel is also conforming to the Palladio* metamodel. As we will see in Section 5, this will allow us to take models generated in the PCM bench directly into e-Motions, and use them to perform simulations in the e-Motions definition of Palladio.

In Palladio, an open workload specifies system usage intensity with an inter-arrival time, i.e., the time between two user arrivals at the system, as a random variable with some probability distribution. It models an infinite stream of users arriving at a system, which execute their scenario, and then leave the system. Fig. 5(a) shows the `OpenWorkloadSpec` rule, which specifies the behaviour of a `UsageScenario usSc` with an `OpenWorkload ow`. When the rule is triggered, a new system token is added to the first action of the system, i.e., the `start` action. Moreover, the rule is fired every `owRate`, which is a local variable whose value is given by `ow`'s random variable.

A `ScenarioBehaviour`, which is included in a `UsageScenario`, is composed of a set of actions, which can be `Start`, `Stop`, `EntryLevelSystemCall`, `Branch`, and

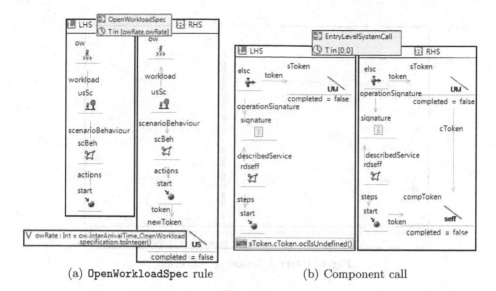

(a) `OpenWorkloadSpec` rule   (b) Component call

Fig. 5. New request rule specification

Loop. These actions are modelled in e-Motions, since they are used to describe the behaviour of system components. Components are independently specified in Palladio, and can be instantiated from a `ScenarioBehaviour` by `Signatures`. The `EntryLevelSystemCall` action represents the invocation of a component.

The rule in Fig. 5(b) shows our definition of an `EntryLevelSystemCall` in e-Motions. If a (sub)-state matches its LHS, the `SToken` object associated to the `EntryLevelSystemCall` action remains in this action, while a new `CToken` is created and linked to the `start` action of the invoked component (effectively building up a call stack). As the rule's header shows, this rule is instantaneous (it takes zero time).

The rule in Fig. 6 shows the behaviour of an `InternalAction`, which represents the execution of an internal activity by a component service, possibly using some resources, like HDD or CPU. In Palladio, these executions present a high-level abstraction, and the resource demands are expressed as a single stochastic expression. The duration of the action depends on the parameters of the demanded resources. Resources are limited by the available number of resources of that type (`PRS.numberOfReplicas`). Tokens are served following an FCFS strategy by using a queue associated to each resource type. Only the first `PRS.numberOfReplicas` tokens in the queue `PRS.queue` get to be executed. Once an internal action is executed, its token is removed from the queue (`PRS.queue->excluding(t)`).

The complete e-Motions definition of the Palladio DSL is available at `http://atenea.lcc.uma.es/Palladio`.

Once the whole DSL has been defined, and given a model as initial state, it may be simulated by applying the rules describing its behaviour. This model

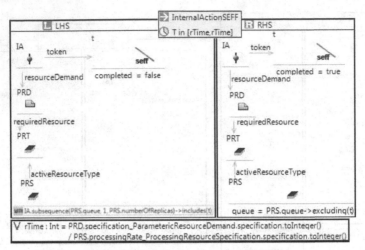

Fig. 6. Internal Action specification

does not collect information on NFPs, and therefore is not ready for performance analysis. We enrich them later, as explained in the following section.

4   NFPs by Observation

In previous work, we have proposed an approach for the specification and monitoring of non-functional properties using *observers* [15,16]. They are objects with which we extend the e-Motions definition of systems for the analysis of NFPs by simulation, such as mean and max cycle times, busy and idle cycles of operation units, throughput, mean-time between failures, etc. We also explored in [6,17] how to define observers generically and independently from any system, so that they can afterwards be woven and merged with different systems. Given systems described as DSLs and generic DSLs defining the different observers, we can use these composition mechanisms to combine them. The result is that we can use the combined enriched system DSL to monitor NFPs of our systems.

We proved in [5] that, given very natural requirements on the observers and the instantiating mappings, the system thus obtained was a conservative enrichment of the original system, in the sense that the observers added *do not change the behaviour of the system.*

Given an e-Motions definition of Palladio as the one presented in Section 3, we can then enrich it with the definition of the observers we wish, which can be selected from a library of generically specified observers. Specifically, we can select both those observers that monitor non-functional properties available in the Palladio Simulator as well as those that monitor other properties. The NFPs chosen can then be analysed by simulation.

4.1   Generic Observers

We present in the first place a generic DSL for monitoring the *response time*, which is a property included in the analysis made by Palladio. Response time can be defined as the time that elapses since a request arrives to a system until it is served. Hence, the same generic notion allows us to measure the response time of information packets being delivered through a network, the number of cars being manufactured in a production line, the number of passengers checking-in in an airport, etcetera. Given the description of a system, in order to measure response time, we basically need to register the time at which requests appear in the system, and the time at which they are completed. With this data and a simple calculation, we can easily get the response time.

A generic DSL achieving this is shown in Fig. 7. Its abstract syntax (the metamodel in Fig. 7(a)) contains three generic and two concrete classes – generic classes are shown with a shaded background. System, Serve and Request are parameter classes to be instantiated by specific classes, as explained in Section 4.2. The System class represents the whole system, which is composed of a set of Servers. These, in turn, can have Requests to be processed. The class RespTimeOb represents the observer for measuring the response time mean. Its three attributes represent the number of requests already processed (counter), the accumulated time by them (tAcc), and the current average response time (respT). Note that there is yet another observer in this metamodel, TimeStampOb, used to store the times of incoming Requests.

The behaviour of this DSL is defined by the in-place transformation rules in Fig. 7, in which parametric concepts have no concrete syntax, they are depicted as boxes with a shaded background. Observer objects have a concrete syntax, that will also be used to depict them in the woven rules (see below). Rule CreateRespTOb deals with the creation of the response time observer. Its LHS includes a condition that avoids the creation of new observer objects if there is one, ensuring that only one of these observers is created per instantiated object. We see in its RHS that the observer is associated to the system. Rule RequestArrives generates a time stamp observer whenever a new Request appears. The observer gets associated to the Request and keeps the time at which it appears in the system — note the presence of the system class Clock, which provides the current time. Finally, rule CompletedRequest computes the response time every time a Request is consumed — the Request and its associated observer have disappeared in the RHS. Attribute counter of RespTimeOb keeps the number of completed Requests, while tAcc contains the addition of cycle times of all Requests, i.e., the time they have spent in the system. Finally, attribute respT uses the former two attributes to calculate the response time of the System.

Fig. 8 shows a DSL for the *throughput* observer. Throughput can be defined as the average rate of requests processed by a system. Given the description of a system, in order to measure this property, we basically need to be able to count the number of processed requests, and calculate its quotient with time. The abstract syntax (metamodel in Fig. 8(a)) contains the same parametric

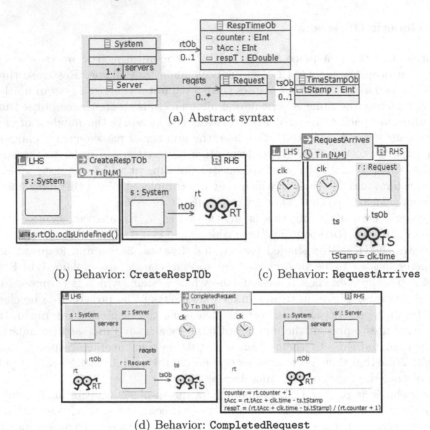

(a) Abstract syntax

(b) Behavior: `CreateRespTOb`   (c) Behavior: `RequestArrives`

(d) Behavior: `CompletedRequest`

Fig. 7. Response Time observer DSL definition

classes as the one for response time and the `ThroughputOb` class that represents the observer. The `counter` attribute stores the number of `Requests` that are completed, while `thp` is used to keep the actual throughput.

Its behaviour is also defined by three transformation rules. The `CreateThpOb` rule creates the observer, as the corresponding rule for the response time observer. Rule `UpdateCounter` increases the `counter` attribute of the observer every time a `Request` is served. Finally, we have an ongoing rule where the value of throughput is computed, which keeps the value `thp` updated as time evolves.

4.2 Adding Observers to System Specifications

In order to introduce observers in our specifications in e-Motions, we need to weave both the metamodel and the behaviour specifications of a specific system and the generic observer DSL. In other words, the parametric components of the observers DSLs get instantiated with specific components. This is done by defining a correspondences model [6,10]. For example, for weaving the metamodel of

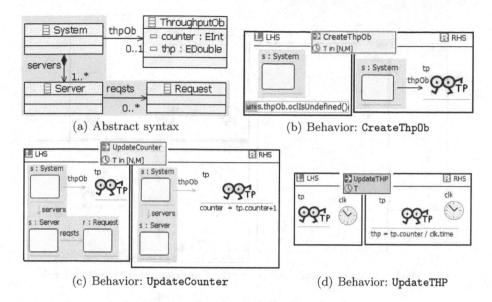

(a) Abstract syntax   (b) Behavior: `CreateThpOb`

(c) Behavior: `UpdateCounter`   (d) Behavior: `UpdateTHP`

Fig. 8. Throughput observer DSL definition

response time (Fig. 7(a)) with the metamodel of our Palladio implementation in
e-Motions, the `System` class is mapped to the `ScenarioBehaviour` class, `Server`
to `Start` and `Request` to `SToken`. The weaving of metamodels is quite straightforward, and we do not show the resulting metamodel due to space limitations.
Let us focus here on the weaving of rules.

Regarding rules, we basically need to map each rule in the source DSL to a rule
in the target one. The mapping defined for the metamodel does most of the rest.
Rule `RequestArrives` (Fig. 7(c)) is woven with the `OpenWorkloadSpec` rule of
our Palladio system (Fig. 5(a)), that represents the arrival of a new `SToken` into
the system. Rule `CreateRespTOb` of the observer DSL is woven with an identity
rule, triggering the creation of observer objects if they were not already created.
Finally, rule `CompletedRequest` (Fig. 7(d)) is woven with the `StopUsageModel`
rule, which models the elimination of a token upon its arrival to a `stop` action.

A similar mapping is provided for the throughput observer: rules `CreateThpOb`
and `UpdateTHP` are woven to the identity rule, as `CreateRespTOb`, and rule
`UpdateCounter` is mapped to `StopUsageModel`.

The result of weaving the response time and throughput observer DSLs and
the Palladio* DSL results in a DSL whose metamodel is the Palladio metamodel
enriched with the additional classes as indicated in the mappings, and the rules
defining its behaviour enriched with the observer objects. Figs. 9(a) and 9(b)
show the rules `OpenWorkLoad` (Fig. 5(a)) and `stop` as resulting from the weaving
process.

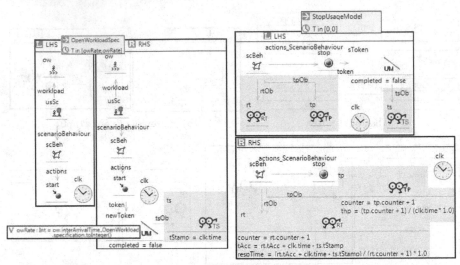

(a) Enriched `OpenWorkloadSpec` rule   (b) Ennriched `StopUsageModel` rule

Fig. 9. Woven rules

Using the same mechanisms these observers may be attached to other elements of the model. For instance, we can in this way measure the response time of each of the components in the system. Additional observers for other NFPs may be considered similarly.

5   Evaluation

Once the e-Motions definition of the Palladio DSL has been enriched with the desired observers, we may use it for analysing its performance by simulation. More specifically, since the Palladio* metamodel is a conservative enrichment, we may take models designed in the Palladio Bench and load them into e-Motions for simulation using the e-Motions definition of Palladio. The information in the observers can be accessed when the simulation has completed.

Following this procedure, we have simulated the Palladio model presented in Section 2 in the e-Motions definitions of Palladio, whose results are summarized in Table 2 (for a simulation of 1000 tasks). We can observe that the value obtained for response time is coherent with the one obtained in Palladio (cf. Table 1), since the e-Motions' value fits within the confidence interval returned by Palladio. Fig. 10 shows the cumulative distribution function for the simulation in e-Motions, while Fig. 11 shows the response time as a function of the time when a request entries the system, based on the e-Motions output. Since the queues get saturated, response times keep increasing.

Table 2. Case study's e-Motions results

Mean System Response Time	43.6626 seconds
Throughput	0.4804 seconds

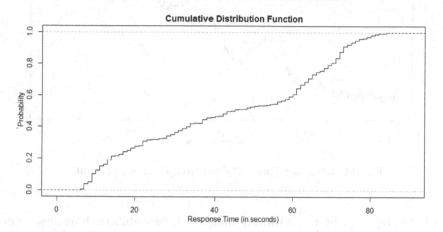

Fig. 10. Cumulative distribution function for the simulation in e-Motions.

6   Conclusions and Future Work

Non-functional properties of software, such as performance, reliability, or security, can determine success or failure of software systems. It is therefore important to be able to provide estimates of these properties as early as possible in the development process. Model-driven engineering has been viewed as a promising technology for addressing this problem because of its ability to transform early design models into analysis models. However, the semantics of the properties to be analysed as well as of the analysis methods themselves are typically encoded implicitly in the transformations and support tooling. Often, these encodings tangle semantics for multiple properties to be analysed. As a result, it becomes difficult a) to add new properties and analyses and b) to validate the transformation and analysis implementations themselves.

We have addressed this problem by presenting a modular, model-based partial reimplementation of one well-known analysis framework—the Palladio Architecture Simulator. We have specified key DSLs from Palladio in e-Motions, describing the basic simulation semantics as a set of graph-transformation rules. Different properties to be analysed have been encoded as separate, parametrised DSLs, independent of the definition of Palladio. We have then composed these DSLs with the base Palladio DSL to generate specific simulation environments. Models created in the Palladio IDE can be fed directly into our simulation environment for analysis.

We currently provide support for key Palladio features for the definition of usage models (start, stop, delay, and entry level system call) and component

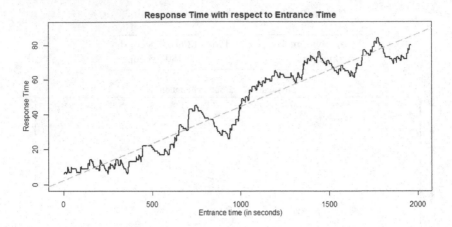

Fig. 11. Response Time obtained from e-Motions output

models (start, stop, branch with any number of probabilistic branches, internal action, and CPU specifications). Currently, we only have partial support of stochastic variables. Their full support is left as future work.

We have demonstrated two main benefits of our approach: 1) The semantics of the simulation and the non-functional properties to be analysed are made explicit in the respective DSL specifications, and 2) because of the compositional definition, it is easy to add definitions of new non-functional properties and their analyses. More importantly, our proposal provides a place were to experiment with new features and tailor solutions for specific problems at a very low development cost.

As future work, we plan to incorporate additional features to our definition of Palladio, as, e.g., full resource models, and failures and reliability analysis. Indeed, we foresee generic definitions of selectable features, such as resource handling and deployment strategies, etc. We also plan to experiment with other NFPs, such as reliability or security, and to use our flexible setting for the analysis of dynamic systems, where components and resources are dynamically added to or removed from the system under study. For instance, in [17], we showed how to maintain the value of cycle time around a specific goal. The dynamic system consisted of a production line where machines had two modes of processing parts: fast and slow. In this case, when the cycle time of parts was higher than the goal, the speed of the machines was increased. The opposite occurred when the parts were produced too fast. This self-adaptive behaviour was achieved by consulting the value of the cycle time observer during simulation.

Acknowledgments. We thank Samuel Kounev for his help in getting access to the Palladio internals. This work is partially funded by Project TIN2011-23795, by U. de Málaga, Campus de Excelencia Intl. Andalucía Tech, and by the EU under the ICT Policy Support Programme (grant no. 317859).

References

1. Balsamo, S., DiMarco, A., Inverardi, P., Simeoni, M.: Model-based performance prediction in software development: A survey. IEEE Transactions on Software Engineering 30(5), 295–310 (2004)
2. Becker, S., Grunske, L., Mirandola, R., Overhage, S.: Performance prediction of component-based systems: A survey from an engineering perspective. In: Reussner, R., Stafford, J.A., Ren, X.-M. (eds.) Architecting Systems. LNCS, vol. 3938, pp. 169–192. Springer, Heidelberg (2006)
3. Becker, S., Koziolek, H., Reussner, R.: Model-based performance prediction with the Palladio component model. In: Proc. 6th Int'l Workshop on Software and Performance (WOSP 2007). ACM (2007)
4. Clavel, M., Durán, F., Eker, S., Lincoln, P., Martí-Oliet, N., Meseguer, J., Talcott, C.: All About Maude - A High-Performance Logical Framework. LNCS, vol. 4350. Springer, Heidelberg (2007)
5. Durán, F., Orejas, F., Zschaler, S.: Behaviour protection in modular rule-based system specifications. In: Martí-Oliet, N., Palomino, M. (eds.) WADT 2012. LNCS, vol. 7841, pp. 24–49. Springer, Heidelberg (2013)
6. Durán, F., Zschaler, S., Troya, J.: On the reusable specification of non-functional properties in DSLs. In: Czarnecki, K., Hedin, G. (eds.) SLE 2012. LNCS, vol. 7745, pp. 332–351. Springer, Heidelberg (2013)
7. Fritzsche, M., Johannes, J., Zschaler, S., Zherebtsov, A., Terekhov, A.: Application of tracing techniques in model-driven performance engineering. In: 4th ECMDA Traceability Workshop (2008)
8. Grassi, V., Mirandola, R.: A model-driven approach to predictive non functional analysis of component-based systems. In: Proc. Workshop on Models for Non-Functional Aspects of Component-Based Software (2004)
9. Happe, J., Koziolek, H., Reussner, R.: Facilitating performance predictions using software components. IEEE Software 28(3), 27–33 (2011)
10. Moreno-Delgado, A., Troya, J., Durán, F., Vallecillo, A.: On the Modular Specification of NFPs: A Case Study. In: Proc. of XVIII JISBD, pp. 302–316 (2013)
11. Rivera, J.E., Durán, F., Vallecillo, A.: A graphical approach for modeling time-dependent behavior of DSLs. In: Proc. of VI./HCC 2009. IEEE (2009)
12. Röttger, S., Zschaler, S.: Tool support for refinement of non-functional specifications. Software and Systems Modeling Journal (SoSyM) 6(2), 185–204 (2007)
13. Smith, C.U., Williams, L.G.: Performance Solutions: A Practical Guide to Creating Responsive, Scalable Software. Object-Technology Series. Addison-Wesley (2002)
14. Spinner, S., Kounev, S., Meier, P.: Stochastic modeling and analysis using QPME: Queueing petri net modeling environment v2.0. In: Haddad, S., Pomello, L. (eds.) PETRI NETS 2012. LNCS, vol. 7347, pp. 388–397. Springer, Heidelberg (2012)
15. Troya, J., Rivera, J.E., Vallecillo, A.: Simulating Domain Specific Visual Models by Observation. In: Proc. of the 2010 Spring Simulation Multiconference, SpringSim 2010, pp. 128:1–128:8. ACM, New York (2010)
16. Troya, J., Vallecillo, A.: A domain specific visual language for modeling power-aware reliability in wireless sensor networks. In: Proc. of NFPinDSML 2012, pp. 3:1–3:6. ACM (2012)
17. Troya, J., Vallecillo, A., Durán, F., Zschaler, S.: Model-driven performance analysis of rule-based domain specific visual models. Information and Software Technology 55(1), 88–110 (2013)

Language-Independent Traceability with Lässig

Rolf-Helge Pfeiffer[1], Jan Reimann[2], and Andrzej Wąsowski[1]

[1] IT University of Copenhagen, Denmark
{ropf,wasowski}@itu.dk
[2] Technische Universität Dresden, Germany
jan.reimann@tu-dresden.de

Abstract. Typical programming languages, including model transformation languages, do not support traceability. Applications requiring inter-object traceability implement traceability support repeatedly for different domains. In this paper we introduce a solution for generic traceability which enables the generation of trace models for all programming languages compiling to Virtual Machine (VM) bytecode by leveraging automatically generated observer aspects.

We implement our solution in a tool called *Lässig* adding traceability support to all programming languages compiling to the Java Virtual Machine (JVM). We evaluate and discuss general feasibility, correctness, and the performance overhead of our solution by applying it to three model-to-model transformations.

Our generic traceability solution is capable of automatically establishing complete sets of trace links for transformation programs in various languages and at a minimum cost. Lässig is available as an open-source project for integration into modeling frameworks.

1 Introduction

Model-driven Software Development (MDSD) relies on use of models to design, construct and maintain software systems. Many models in this process are related by various semantic relations. For example, in generative setups, model transformations automatically convert models into other models.

Strict quality management processes usually require that a project can identify and retrieve these relations. This ability is known as *traceability* and the stored relations are known as *trace links*, which chronologically interrelate uniquely identifiable entities along a set of chained operations [15].

Co-evolution of related artifacts is a major challenge, especially for systems containing related models expressed in multiple languages [16]. If a model is modified, other related models need to be adapted accordingly. It is hard for developers to identify the affected artifacts. Trace links keep this information. Thus, automatic tracing of object relations via corresponding transformations, would allow us to dramatically improve tool support for co-evolution of multi-language software systems. In this paper we take a first step to support co-evolution of related artifacts by automatic tracing of object relations caused by transformations.

J. Cabot and J. Rubin (Eds.): ECMFA 2014, LNCS 8569, pp. 148–163, 2014.

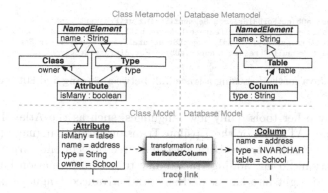

Fig. 1. Transformation of a class model attribute into a database model column

```
1  def Column create c: factory.createColumn() attribute2Column(Attribute a) {
2      if(!a.isMany) {
3          c.name = a.name
4          c.table = a.owner.class2Table()
5          c.type = a.type.name.toDbType()
6      }
7  }
```

Listing 1. A model transformation rule in Xtend transforming **Attributes** to **Columns** and causing a trace link between such instances

Strictly speaking, traceability concerns not only the links between models, but also relations between other artifacts, so for example between models and code, or between documentation and code. In this paper, we follow the unifying assumption of Bézivin that *everything is a model* [3], which includes code and documentation.

Consider an example transformation converting a class model into a database model; more precisely, the transformation of a class attribute to a database table column. Figure 1 shows the input and output languages of this transformation, while Listing 1 presents the transformation rule expressed in the popular Xtend language[1], which does not maintain explicit links between input and output.

A similar problem appears for transformations implemented in Java. Listing 2 shows an excerpt of **org.eclipse.emf.ecore.impl.EClassImpl** from the Eclipse Modeling Framework (EMF) [20], which locates **EObjects** based on fragments of unified resource identifiers. Here, no trace link is kept between the input instance of a **String** and the output instance of an **EObject**.

Trace links between objects are usually not maintained automatically by transformation programs, since traceability is not a first class concern in most languages used for implementing transformations. However, in the realm of object-orientation, where all development artifacts and their contents are objects, relations between development artifacts are described explicitly by transformation programs, but the traces between artifacts and their transformed contents cannot

---

[1] http://xtend-lang.org/

```
1   public EObject eObjectForURIFragmentSegment(String uriFragmentSegment) {
2     EObject result = eAllStructuralFeaturesData == null || eOperations != null && !
          eOperations.isEmpty() ? null : getEStructuralFeature(uriFragmentSegment);
3     return result != null ? result : super.eObjectForURIFragmentSegment(uriFragmentSegment);
4   }
```

Listing 2. A Java method causing a trace link between `String` and `EObject` instances

be utilized by other tools. Only few languages, such as the Atlas Transformation Language (ATL) [5] or the Epsilon Transformation Language (ETL) [12], automatically establish traces between the source objects and target objects of a transformation. So far, adding traceability to a transformation language has required deep insight into language design and advanced language implementation skills. It could not be done orthogonally, in a language independent manner, and clearly not by language users (as opposed to language designers and implementers). Today, if traceability support is required either the system needs to be implemented in a programming language with built-in traceability support or tracing has to be added to relevant methods or transformation rules. The former is not suitable for legacy systems, as it would require reimplementation. The latter misses the opportunity to reuse application independent functionality, and pollutes business logics with it.

To overcome the aforementioned problem we contribute the following: 1) A generic aspect-based model-driven solution to support traceability for all programming languages compiling to bytecode of a VM; 2) Lässig, a prototypical implementation[2] for programming languages compiling to JVM bytecode; 3) Identification of heuristics, which determine program structures creating trace links and discussion of extensions and alternative heuristics; 4) Evaluation of our solution by applying Lässig to three model transformations, each implemented in Xtend, Java, and Groovy.

The evaluation shows that the automatically established trace links are correct and complete. The obtained set of traces is similar to the one registered for ETL transformations, a language with dedicated traceability support. Finally, the additional runtime overhead for using the generic traceability approach is rather moderate. We hope that Lässig is of interest for tool builders and vendors allowing lightweight integration of traceability into modeling frameworks.

We proceed as follows. Section 2 presents the architecture of our generic traceability solution. We discuss the prototype implementation (Sect. 3), evaluate the idea (Sect. 4) and discuss the evaluation results (Sect. 5). Finally, we survey the related work (Sect. 6) and conclude with a sketch of future work (Sect. 7).

2   The Solution

2.1   Architecture

Previous work [8,24] argues to support traceability generically in existing transformation languages or frameworks by abstraction over particular transformation

---
[2] http://svn-st.inf.tu-dresden.de/websvn/wsvn/refactory/trunk/Lässig/

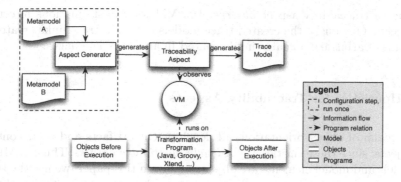

Fig. 2. Architecture for generic traceability

languages. With the help of such an abstraction trace links can be established generically for different transformation languages. We generalize this claim and argue that traceability can be generically added to arbitrary programming languages by relying on a common representation. Bytecode executed on VMs can serve as such a common denominator. Adding traceability to the common representation, uniformly integrates this orthogonal language feature to all programming languages compiling to the same VM.

Figure 2 illustrates the architecture of our solution for generic traceability. We use two metamodels to parametrize a code generator creating traceability code. The metamodels contain all classes for whose instances trace links should be established. In a model transformation scenario the metamodels are readily available as model transformations are specified on top of them.

We use aspect weaving to instrument the transformation code with the traceability code. Recall the transformation rule in Listing 1. The rule causes a trace link between an object `a` of type `Attribute` (the rule's argument) and an object `c` of type `Column` (return value) as properties of `a` are, with some modifications, assigned to properties of `c`. The concern of traceability could be introduced by inserting directives, such as `tracemodel.addLink(a,c)` to the end of every transformation rule.

Obviously, the concern of traceability is a cross-cutting concern [10,11,21] as it requires similar directives to be introduced in every transformation rule in any language in any domain that should support traceability. Such cross-cutting concerns are effectively handled by aspect-oriented programming, encapsulating recurring code in aspects. Aspects can be woven anywhere the concern is required, which is the reason for the aspect-oriented architecture of our solution. A traceability aspect is generated once, for each pairwise combination of metamodels. The traceability code within the aspects is conceptually similar to the previous example. The aspects and the aspect generation is detailed in Sect. 2.2.

Whenever programs transforming model elements of the types specified in the parametrization phase are executed on the VM, the traceability aspect is woven into the transformation's bytecode. There, trace links between transformed objects are automatically established and maintained in a trace model. We can say, that a traceability aspect *observes* the VM for transformations interrelating objects. Obviously, the created trace models maintain trace links created by programs of arbitrary domains implemented in arbitrary languages.

2.2   Heuristics for Traceability Aspects

In the realm of object-orientation, all development artifacts and their contents are objects, since these entities are *uniquely identifiable entities*. Thus, in MDSD, all models and model elements are objects again. In this paper, we use the terms *object* and *model element* synonymously. Our solution provides traceability at object level. Consequently, all *abstract* metaclasses in the parametrizing metamodels are not considered as traceable. Therefore, no traceability code is generated for them. Furthermore, our solution relies on the following two heuristics to automatically establish trace links when observing transformations.

(i) Related objects are an argument and a return value of a transformation (a method). Additionally, both objects are not `null` after method execution.
(ii) Related objects are both arguments of a transformation (a method) and at least one of them is modified during method execution.

The rationale for (i) is, that a method parametrized with an object and returning a non-null object likely reads the argument to return the corresponding result. Thereby, both objects are in relation and should be linked. The rationale for (ii) is similar. A method parametrized with two arguments, where after execution at least one argument is modified, likely reads one object to modify the other one. The simplicity of the two heuristics is their main power—it means that establishing trace links between objects can be done based on types of these objects and a simple check of input and output parameters of a method. It remains completely independent of the complexity of the transformation itself.

These heuristics are the basis for aspect generation. They are implemented in the traceability aspect generator (Fig. 2). A generated aspect contains four pointcuts for each combination of metaclasses in the parametrization metamodels. Recall the example of transforming a class' attributes to table columns (see Listing 1). Listing 3 illustrates the generated pointcut definitions for `Attribute` and `Column` types. The pointcuts `findMethodC` and `findMethodD` (lines 3 and 4), implement heuristic (i) where objects of types `Attribute` or `Column` are returned or are an argument respectively. For example, the pattern `execution(Attribute *(.. , Column, ..))` matches the execution of all methods with arbitrary name (`*`) returning an `Attribute` and a `Column` as argument. Pointcuts `findMethodA` and `findMethodB` (lines 1 and 2), implement heuristic (ii) where objects of `Attribute` and `Column` are both arguments. The pattern `execution(* *(.., Column, .., Attribute, ..))` matches the execution of all methods with arbitrary name and arbitrary return type (leading `*`) with two arguments of the respective types.

```
1  private pointcut findMethodA(Column t1, Attribute t2) : !within(Tracer) && execution(*
       *(.., Column, .., Attribute, ..)) && args(t1,t2,..);
2  private pointcut findMethodB(Attribute t1, Column t2) : !within(Tracer) && execution(*
       *(.., Attribute, .., Column, ..)) && args(t1,t2,..);
3  private pointcut findMethodC(Attribute t1) : !within(Tracer) && execution(Column *(..,
       Attribute, ..)) && args(t1,..);
4  private pointcut findMethodD(Column t1) : !within(Tracer) && execution(Attribute *(.. ,
       Column, ..)) && args(t1,..);
```

Listing 3. Generated traceability aspect for transformations between class models and relational schema

The aspect contains also advise blocks, which are not shown here, due to their size.[3] The advise blocks implement the checks of heuristics (i) and (ii) for non-null objects or for modified objects. Whenever the conditions of a heuristic hold in an executed transformation, a trace link is established.

Our experiments (Sect. 4) show that the two heuristics described above are quite powerful and generate correct trace models for our evaluation cases. In the design process we have considered two alternative heuristics, which we eventually discarded. We discuss them briefly below.

Transformation Rules with Multiple Arguments of the Same Type. As described, our solution establishes links for transformation rules with two arguments or with an argument and a return value which are combinations of two types (metaclasses). An extended heuristic would allow establishing trace links for transformation rules with either many arguments of the same type or with collections of types. Referring to the metaclasses used in Listing 3 the pointcuts realizing this heuristic could be implemented as shown in Listing 4. However, we do not to apply this heuristic as we consider such transformation rules "bad style" of programming. Transformations of collections should call transformations of single instances. The latter transformations are matched by heuristics (i) or (ii). A larger study applying Lässig to industrial model transformations could give an incentive to implement this heuristic.

Transformation Rules Containing Transformation Code. As discussed previously, our heuristics establish trace links based on execution of transformation rules, simply by inspecting the top activation frame on the call stack. A complex transformation encoded in a single rule results in a single trace link between the top most objects. Potentially, one could obtain more information, by inspecting the entire call stack, not just the top-most environment. An aspect observing temporally related accessor calls (get and set methods) of distinct objects within the control flow of a common transformation method could identify potential trace links between the accessed objects. However, such a heuristic would limit the generality of the solution, as not all JVM languages implement attribute access via accessor methods.

---

[3] http://svn-st.inf.tu-dresden.de/websvn/wsvn/refactory/trunk/Lässig/ dk.itu.sdg.aspect.tracemodel.generator/output/Tracer.aj shows the entire generated aspect.

```
1  private pointcut findMethod(Column t1, Attribute t2, Attribute t3, Attribute t4) : &&
       execution(* *(.., Column, .., Attribute, Attribute, Attribute, ..)) && args(t1,t2,t3,
       t4,..);
2
3  private pointcut findMethod(Collection t1, Attribute t2) : && execution(* *(.., Collection
       <Column>, .., Attribute, ..)) && args(t1,t2,..);
```

Listing 4. Generated traceability aspect for transformations between class models and relational schema

Note, our solution supports object-level granularity for trace links, where the level of granularity depends only on the method granularity a developer uses to implement transformations. The more methods implemented for different object metaclasses the more fine-grained the trace links. Attribute-level granularity is therefore supported if an *attribute* is a metaclass itself.

3   Lässig: An Implementation

We implement our solution in a tool called *Lässig* , which provides traceability support for all compiled programming languages executed on the Java Virtual Machine. Lässig is implemented as a set of Eclipse bundles: one bundle for the aspect generator, one bundle containing the traceability aspects, and one bundle containing the trace model itself. Lässig requires that the metamodels parametrizing the traceability aspect generator are available as EMF models. Such metamodels are most often readily available for model transformations. When adding traceability to programs in general, the metamodels need to be created. They should contain a metaclass for each traceable JVM type.

Lässig relies on Equinox Weaving[4] for aspect weaving. The traceability aspect resides in an OSGi bundle specifying which other bundles are observed, i.e., in which classes of other bundles the aspect is woven into. We use load-time weaving, which is triggered whenever the JVM loads a class for the first time.

When a transformation from an observed bundle is executed the woven traceability code is invoked and trace links are automatically recorded in an in-memory trace model. It can be used as a knowledge-base for tools supporting developers in coding and co-evolution, or it can be serialized and directly inspected by developers.

4   Evaluation

In order to evaluate the quality of generically established trace links of JVM programs we investigate the following research questions:

RQ1 What is the precision and recall of automatically established trace links with respect to the definition of *trace link* presented in Sect. 1?

---

[4] http://eclipse.org/equinox/weaving

RQ2 What is the precision and recall of automatically established trace links in comparison to those established by a transformation language with dedicated traceability support?

RQ3 What is the performance overhead, in terms of time, of the generic traceability solution applied to model transformations in different JVM languages?

Note that the precision and recall are always defined with respect to a reference set. To avoid bias, we compare recovered trace links to two different reference sets, instead of to idealized links. Thus, the precision and recall with respect to the reference sets are evaluated for answering **RQ1** and **RQ2**.

4.1   Experiment Setup

To evaluate our solution we rely on three model transformations as experiment subjects: (*i*) from tree models to graph models (tree2graph), (*ii*) from class models to relational schema (class2db), and (*iii*) from family models to person models (family2person). All three model transformations are well known canonical examples in the modeling community. We rely on independent specifications of these transformations from other projects. The specifications of tree2graph[5] and class2db[6] are taken from resources of the ETL community. The specification of family2person[7] is taken from the ATL transformation zoo.

These transformations are often used in teaching transformation languages, so they cover all major concepts used in transformations: rules transforming model elements, their properties, containment relations, and references. Thus, we believe that they are relevant evaluation subjects, with reasonable coverage of constructs.

We implement each of the transformations in three languages: Xtend, Groovy, and Java. Xtend is often used for model transformation implementations. It compiles to Java source code. Groovy is a dynamic programming language for the JVM. Each of them compiles to JVM bytecode. Xtend, Groovy, and Java are among the most popular languages used in practice for implementing model transformations. For this reason we believe they are interesting targets for evaluation of a language-independent traceability mechanism.

The transformation implementations in Xtend, Groovy, and Java follow a rule-based style. For each combination of metaclasses whose instances are transformed we implement a separate method (Groovy, Java) or rule (Xtend).

As input models we use a tree, family, and class model for the respective transformation. The models contain 6, 11, and 19 model elements respectively, see Table 1.

---

[5] http://www.eclipse.org/epsilon/examples/index.php?example=org.eclipse.epsilon. examples.tree2graph

[6] http://www.eclipse.org/epsilon/examples/index.php?example=org.eclipse.epsilon. examples.oo2db

[7] http://www.eclipse.org/atl/atlTransformations/#Families2Persons

Table 1. Number of trace links established for transformations in different languages

	Number of Trace Links			Model Sizes	
	Java	Groovy	Xtend	Input	Output
tree2graph	7	13	14	6	11
family2person	9	9	27	11	9
class2db	14	14	38	19	35

The experiment is conducted on a 2.9GHz Intel i7 Mac Book with 8GB of RAM, of which 4GB are assigned to the Java 6 virtual machine. We use AspectJ (1.7.2), Xtend (2.3.1), and Groovy (2.0.0).

4.2   Absolute Quality of Generic Traceability

RQ1. What is the precision and recall of automatically established trace links with respect to the definition of trace link *presented in Sect. 1?*

For each transformation we serialize a trace model after completion. To answer this question, we manually compare the input models and output models together with the automatically established trace models. Then, we investigate if the established trace links are correct (precision) with respect to the definition of *trace*, and if we missed some traces (recall). Correctness criteria are (*i*) that the linked objects exist in the input and output models, and (*ii*) that the associated transformation rules establishing a trace link exist and actually transform an object or parts of it into another object of the appropriate type.

Results. The numbers of established trace links are presented in Table 1. For example, for the tree2graph transformation Lässig establishes 7, 13, and 14 trace links for the Java, Groovy, and Xtend transformations respectively.

Recall the definition of a *trace link*. A trace links objects over a set of chained operations. Thus, a trace model for a language in which transformation rules are compiled to multiple methods in bytecode is incorrect if it does not contain multiple trace links for each method on bytecode level. In our experiment we found no incorrect links in this sense (100% precision and recall).

Discussion. The reason for the differing amount of established trace links for the three transformation languages is, that compilation of transformation rules to bytecode methods is language specific. For example, closures in Groovy methods (as in tree2graph) are compiled to separate unfolded methods in bytecode. Similarly, Xtend transformation rules creating model elements, are compiled to two consecutive methods. One for caching and one for the actual transformation.

We conclude that Lässig does not neglect trace links but establishes trace links correctly with respect to the programming language used.

Table 2. Number of conceptual trace links established for transformations in different languages compared to ETL trace links

	No. of Conceptual Trace Links				Model Sizes	
	ETL	Java	Groovy	Xtend	Input	Output
tree2graph	6	7	7	7	6	11
family2person	9	9	9	9	11	9
class2db	14	14	14	14	19	35

4.3 Relative Quality of Generic Traceability

RQ2. What is the precision and recall of automatically established trace links in comparison to those established by a transformation language with dedicated traceability support?

So far, we have established experimentally that trace links are correct with respect to our trace definition. Now, we investigate if the trace links are correct in comparison to those established by a language with first class traceability support. We implement and execute all three transformations in ETL. Since tree2graph and class2db were originally implemented in ETL we reuse these transformations. We manually convert family2person from ATL to ETL. Subsequently, we manually compare the ETL trace links with those established by Lässig. The trace link sets obtained with ETL serve as the baseline when investigating the research question.

Besides the correctness criteria explained in Sect. 4.2, the following criteria must be satisfied: The set of established trace links must not be smaller than the the one from ETL, i.e., there must be an injective mapping from the set of trace links generated by ETL to the set of trace links generated by Lässig.

Results. The results of this experiment are presented in Table 2. The first column contains the number of trace links established by ETL. For example, tree2graph in ETL results in 6 trace links. On the other hand Lässig establishes 7 trace links for Java, Groovy and Xtend respectively. Some languages produce more trace links than others for the same transformation due to the way they are compiled. To allow for a comparison we collapse multiple trace links from consecutively executed caching and transformation methods into *conceptual* trace links. Conceptual trace links relate to objects (disregarding JVM operations linking them) — so several links between the same objects are collapsed into a single one, if they only differ by consecutive operations on bytecode level causing the link, but all belong to the same transformation rule.

All links established by ETL are matched by links generated by Lässig (100% recall). In some cases Lässig establishes more trace links than a corresponding ETL transformation. For example the tree2graph transformation results in a precision of approximately 86%. For this transformation in Java, Groovy, and Xtend one false positive with respect to ETL is established respectively. For the other two transformations Lässig establishes a corresponding trace link for any ETL trace link. Thus, both precision and recall are 100% for these transformations.

Discussion. The disparity between the numbers of recovered traces by Lässig and ETL is caused by ETL implicitly transforming root model elements without an explicit transformation rule. For example, tree2graph in ETL consists of one transformation rule converting model elements of type `Tree` to model elements of type `Node`. The graph model's root element of type `Graph` is generated automatically without an explicit transformation rule. That is, ETL's trace model does not contain a trace link between two model elements of respective types `Tree` to `Graph`. On the other hand, all the Java, Groovy, and Xtend transformations consist of two transformation rules. One from model elements `Tree` to `Node` and one for model elements `Tree` to `Graph`.

Since our solution integrates traceability on bytecode level, Lässig's trace models for Xtend transformations are always larger than trace models from ETL transformations. For Java and Groovy they might be larger, depending on the chosen transformation rules and the chosen programming style. However, the larger trace models are still correct because they contain a corresponding trace link for each trace link in an ETL trace model.

4.4   Performance Overhead of Generic Traceability

RQ3. What is the performance overhead, in terms of time, of the generic traceability solution applied to model transformations in different JVM languages?

Introducing a new concern into a software system is always associated with a cost. To determine the performance overhead of generic traceability, we run a controlled experiment with two factors on the same experimental subjects as before: with Lässig enabled or disabled. For each factor, each transformation in Xtend, Groovy, and Java is run in five separate test suites. A *test suite* means that the transformation classes are reloaded in a new Eclipse instance because the first execution of a transformation is more costly due to weaving the traceability aspect (load-time weaving). After the initial transformation, it is re-run five times in each test suite. That is, each transformation is run 30 times in total, which allows for comparison of average runtimes.

Results. Table 3 provides an overview of results of time measures. For each of the three model transformations we provide the execution time in milliseconds. The speed ratio in the rightmost columns shows how much longer a transformation runs with traceability enabled compared to the same transformation without traceability. Effectively the cost of generic traceability (with respect to no traceability at all) ranges from 4% to 400%.

The only outlier in this experiment are the transformations implemented in Groovy. They are generally slower than those in Java and Xtend. Somewhat surprisingly, class2db in Groovy on the very first class load with enabled traceability is 2% faster than without traceability.

Discussion. It is obvious that all transformations take considerably longer on class load than in subsequent runs. Also obvious is that different languages are

Table 3. Average execution times of the model transformations

	Avg. Runtime [ms]			Speed Ratio		
	Java	Groovy	Xtend	Java	Groovy	Xtend
tree2graph						
with tracing on 1st class load	32.80	869.20	12.00	1.62	1.18	3.53
after 1st class load	0.16	1.36	0.56	2.00	1.31	2.33
without tracing on 1st class load	20.20	736.60	3.40			
after 1st class load	0.08	1.04	0.24			
family2person						
with tracing on 1st class load	62.60	602.20	59.00	4.89	1.51	5.18
after 1st class load	0.16	1.20	0.32	4.00	1.11	4.00
without tracing on 1st class load	12.80	399.60	11.40			
after 1st class load	0.04	1.08	0.08			
class2db						
with tracing on 1st class load	48.80	913.60	28.20	2.05	0.98	3.92
after 1st class load	0.92	3.84	1.64	1.35	1.04	2.93
without tracing on 1st class load	23.80	931.80	7.20			
after 1st class load	0.68	3.68	0.56			

more or less efficient in their JVM implementation. However, the large slow-downs can be observed in the time efficient implementations of Java and Xtend, where the average runtimes for each transformation with traceability enabled is always below two milliseconds. So, still with Lässig's traceability enabled, the transformations run fast. Performance of transformations is usually more important in high volume processing, and here it is beneficial that after the initial class loading, the performance usually improves.

For the measurement of Lässig's timing properties we may not have chosen a sufficiently large number of iterations, but we think that our results, after ignoring the outlier, give an indication of how much resources Lässig's traceability mechanism consumes on top of the plain transformations.

5   Threats to Validity

Threats to Internal Validity. First, the three subject model transformations might not be representative. They are all small, ranging from one rule in tree2graph to eight rules in class2db. However, other transformations, even if they consist of more rules, would not encode different transformation patterns. More importantly, Lässig's aspects consist of two Cartesian products of the sets of metaclasses from both metamodels A and B and creates four pointcuts for each metaclass tuple—one Cartesian product for $A \times B$ and one for $B \times A$. Thus, it is not relevant how complex the transformations are as Lässig only depends on matching metaclass tuples in the pointcuts. Thus, all executed transformation rules are traced independently of their complexity or their amount.

Second, the size and complexity of the chosen models and metamodels may be too small. However, even though the models may be small (six to 35 model elements), they contain all typical model structures, such as containment relations, references between model classes, etc. Again, the internal complexity of models and metamodels has no influence on the solution as the generated traceability code only relies on the Cartesian products of the metaclasses involved. Other structures in the transformed models are irrelevant for identification of executed transformation rules.

Third, when implementing the model transformations in Java, Groovy and Xtend we might be biased to implement method or rule signatures which are certainly matched by the pointcuts in the generated observing aspect. We tried to minimize this risk by converting the ETL and ATL transformations consistently to the other languages, just adjusting the syntax.

Lastly, the reliability for the performance overhead measurements could have been improved, first by larger input models as they result in longer runtimes per transformation decreasing the effects startup time delays caused by Just-In-Time compilations and the garbage collector. These effects could be further decreased by executing more iterations of each transformation. Running an extensive study for performance overhead of generic traceability will be addressed in future work.

Threats to External Validity. The choice of the experiment computer and the choice of concrete language versions, may produce particularly fast results when establishing the trace models. For reproducibility we will gladly share our experiment Eclipse setup if requested.

6   Related Work

As already mentioned, some model transformation languages provide built-in traceability support. For example, Tefkat [13] automatically generates a generic trace model for each transformation rule and traces can be customized within rules. Similarly, ETL [12] and ATL [25] automatically generate trace models via a post condition guarding a model transformation. Also QVT [14] has built-in traceability support. Similar to Lässig the three languages establish trace links between objects serving as arguments or as arguments and return values of transformation rules [1]. The main difference between Lässig and the previous languages is, that they implement traceability support for a particular language only. In contrast, Lässig is language independent. It applies the same traceability support to any JVM language as traceability is realized on bytecode level.

Currently, Lässig is applicable to languages compiling to Java bytecode. Interpreted languages cannot be supported generically as interpreters often obfuscate the relation between the program objects and JVM objects at the bytecode. Implementing interpreted languages via language workbenches, such as EMF-Text [2] or Xtext [6] and mapping them to Java is likely the least expensive manner to let Lässig provide traceability support to such languages.

Grammel et al. [9] categorize generation of trace models into two major groups. First, by utilizing the transformation program or second, independently of the transformation program. Clearly, Lässig utilizes the transformation program by observing its execution and establishing trace links as soon as objects of interest are modified. ETL's, ATL's, and QVT's traceability mechanisms fall into the same category. The second category is well researched as *model matching* [4,9,22,23] in the modeling community or as *schema matching* [17,19] in the database community. The former matches models and metamodels, in general object graphs, to each other and whenever a certain similarity measure between sub-graphs is fulfilled trace links are automatically created. The latter is similar to model-matching, although it often incorporates semantic analysis of the schemas in addition to their structural information.

Also other works [8,24] propose a solution for generic traceability support. Both solutions rely on a generic traceability interface abstracting from concrete transformation languages. In both solutions, this interface needs to be implemented repeatedly for any language which should support traceability, which is not required by Lässig.

Jouault [10] applies a model transformation to merge traceability rules into existing ATL transformation rules. This can be seen as an aspect-oriented programing-like technique for ATL, where ATL's metamodel is the join-point model for static weaving. This is similar to Lässig, which also requires a joinpoint model for aspect weaving. But thanks to relying purely on the JVM bytecode to provide the joinpoint model, Lässig is significantly more generic than Jouault's solution. Furthermore, Lässig automatically generates the traceability code out of metamodels. That is, Lässig provides traceability with no programming effort.

Fabro and Valduriez [7] utilize metamodels to generate model transformations semi-automatically. The goal is to relieve developers of manual implementation of recurring code patterns. Lässig can be considered a domain-specific refinement of the described solution, where the restriction to generation of traceability code allows for complete automation.

7   Future Work and Conclusion

We have introduced a solution for generic traceability for languages compiling to a VM. We provide Lässig, a prototype implementing our solution for all programming languages compiling to Java bytecode. We have demonstrated that Lässig is a practical and feasible solution. It automatically establishes correct and complete trace models.

Lässig has one limitation, the granularity of the trace model, i.e., the number of automatically established trace links depends on the quality of the observed transformation code. A transformation rule implementing a complex transformation of many objects of different types results in a trace model containing only a single trace link. We do not think that this limitation is very serious. First, implementing such a "bad style" transformation in, for example, ETL results in a similarly sparse trace model and second, such a sparse model still contains correct trace links maintaining more information than available without Lässig.

We demonstrate the capability of Lässig. We show that Lässig provides traceability at very low additional cost. It is neither necessary to manually implement traceability support for different domains in different languages nor is it necessary to learn aspect-oriented programming. Instead developers just parametrize a code generator with metamodels and thereby generate traceability aspects. We have experienced that Lässig generates 100% correct trace models. Currently, the only requirement is to follow good style of writing transformations, i.e., one method or transformation rule per combination of transformed metaclasses. Hence, transformation developers get traceability with very little effort. If they use EMF models there is no effort.

In the paper, we have used one step transformations to evaluate the tools. But Lässig can handle chains of transformations as well. If all the development artifacts are projected as models, it is possible to establish sequences of trace links that span larger parts of development process (end-to-end traceability), as long as all the steps are executed in a JVM.

In future we plan to evaluate Lässig in combination with code generators, i.e., model-to-text transformations. We assume that Lässig can be applied effectively since many generators use method signatures matching `pointcut findGenMethod (Type t1): execution(String *(.., Type, ..))&& args(t1,..)` pointcuts. Such a heuristics is likely to work with Xpand generator templates in Xtend. However verifying this requires extending Lässig to keep track of locations in the generated text file.

Furthermore, we investigate the feasibility of Lässig to foster co-refactoring capabilities of the generic model refactoring framework Refactory [18]. Lässig is used to determine traces from evolving to dependent models in case they relate to each other by transformation. Then Refactory can apply co-refactorings to dependent models.

Acknowledgements. We cordially thank Julia Schroeter and Claas Wilke for their helpful comments on an earlier version of this paper. This research has been co-funded by the European Regional Development Fund in the project #100135681/2804.

References

1. Aranega, V., Etien, A., Dekeyser, J.L.: Using an alternative trace for QVT. Electronic Communications of the EASST 42 (2011)
2. Aßmann, U., Bartho, A., Bürger, C., Cech, S., Demuth, B., Heidenreich, F., Johannes, J., Karol, S., Polowinski, J., Reimann, J., Schroeter, J., Seifert, M., Thiele, M., Wende, C., Wilke, C.: DropsBox: The Dresden Open Software Toolbox. Software & Systems Modeling 13(1), 133–169 (2014)
3. Bézivin, J.: On the unification power of models. Software & Systems Modeling 4, 171–188 (2005)
4. Castelo Branco, M., Troya, J., Czarnecki, K., Küster, J., Völzer, H.: Matching Business Process Workflows across Abstraction Levels. In: France, R.B., Kazmeier, J., Breu, R., Atkinson, C. (eds.) MODELS 2012. LNCS, vol. 7590, pp. 626–641. Springer, Heidelberg (2012)
5. Eclipse Foundation: ATLAS Transformation Language (April 2012), http://www.eclipse.org/m2m/atl
6. Eysholdt, M., Behrens, H.: Xtext: Implement your language faster than the quick and dirty way. In: Proceedings of the ACM International Conference on Object Oriented Programming Systems Languages and Applications (2010)

7. Fabro, M.D.D., Valduriez, P.: Towards the efficient development of model transformations using model weaving and matching transformations. Software & Systems Modeling 8, 305–324 (2009)
8. Grammel, B., Kastenholz, S.: A generic traceability framework for facet-based traceability data extraction in model-driven software development. In: Proceedings of the 6th ECMFA Traceability Workshop (2010)
9. Grammel, B., Kastenholz, S., Voigt, K.: Model Matching for Trace Link Generation in Model-Driven Software Development. In: France, R.B., Kazmeier, J., Breu, R., Atkinson, C. (eds.) MODELS 2012. LNCS, vol. 7590, pp. 609–625. Springer, Heidelberg (2012)
10. Jouault, F.: Loosely Coupled Traceability for ATL. In: Proceedings of the European Conference on Model Driven Architecture (ECMDA) Workshop on Traceability (2005)
11. Kiczales, G., Hilsdale, E., Hugunin, J., Kersten, M., Palm, J., Griswold, W.G.: An Overview of AspectJ. In: Lindskov Knudsen, J. (ed.) ECOOP 2001. LNCS, vol. 2072, pp. 327–354. Springer, Heidelberg (2001)
12. Kolovos, D.S., Paige, R.F., Polack, F.A.C.: The Epsilon Transformation Language. In: Vallecillo, A., Gray, J., Pierantonio, A. (eds.) ICMT 2008. LNCS, vol. 5063, pp. 46–60. Springer, Heidelberg (2008)
13. Lawley, M., Steel, J.: Practical Declarative Model Transformation with Tefkat. In: MODELS Satellite Events (2005)
14. Object Management Group: Meta Object Facility (MOF) 2.0 Query/View/Transformation Specification, V1.1 (January 2011), http://www.omg.org/spec/QVT/1.1/
15. Paige, R.F., Olsen, G., Kolovos, D., Zschaler, S., Power, C.: Building Model-Driven Engineering Traceability Classifications. In: 4th ECMDA Traceability Workshop (2008)
16. Pfeiffer, R.-H., Wąsowski, A.: Cross-Language Support Mechanisms Significantly Aid Software Development. In: France, R.B., Kazmeier, J., Breu, R., Atkinson, C. (eds.) MODELS 2012. LNCS, vol. 7590, pp. 168–184. Springer, Heidelberg (2012)
17. Rahm, E., Bernstein, P.A.: A survey of approaches to automatic schema matching. The VLDB Journal 10, 334–350 (2001)
18. Reimann, J., Seifert, M., Aßmann, U.: On the reuse and recommendation of model refactoring specifications. Software & Systems Modeling 12(3), 579–596 (2013)
19. Shvaiko, P., Euzenat, J.: A Survey of Schema-Based Matching Approaches. Data Semantics 4, 146–171 (2005)
20. Steinberg, D., Budinsky, F., Paternostro, M., Merks, E.: Eclipse Modeling Framework, 2nd edn. Pearson Education (2009)
21. Tarr, P., Ossher, H., Harrison, W., Sutton, Jr., S.M.: N degrees of separation: Multi-dimensional separation of concerns. In: Proceedings of the 21st International Conference on Software Engineering (1999)
22. Voigt, K.: Semi-automatic Matching of Heterogeneous Model-based Specifications. In: Engels, G., Luckey, M., Pretschner, A., Reussner, R. (eds.) Software Engineering (Workshops). LNI, vol. 160, GI (2010)
23. Voigt, K., Ivanov, P., Rummler, A.: MatchBox: Combined meta-model matching for semi-automatic mapping generation. In: Proceedings of the 2010 ACM Symposium on Applied Computing (2010)
24. Walderhaug, S., Johansen, U., Stav, E., Aagedal, J.: Towards a Generic Solution for Traceability in MDD. In: ECMDA Traceability Workshop, ECMDA-TW (2006)
25. Yie, A., Wagelaar, D.: Advanced traceability for ATL. In: 1st International Workshop on Model Transformation with ATL (2009)

A Family-Based Framework for i-DSML Adaptation

Samson Pierre, Eric Cariou, Olivier Le Goaer, and Franck Barbier

Université de Pau / LIUPPA, PauWare Research Group, BP 1155,
F-64013 PAU CEDEX, France
{firstname.name}@univ-pau.fr
http://www.pauware.com

Abstract. One of the main goals of Model-Driven Engineering (MDE) is the manipulation of models as software artifacts. Model execution is in particular a means to substitute models for code. Precisely, if models of a dedicated Domain-Specific Modeling Language (DSML) are interpreted through an execution engine, then this DSML is called interpreted-DSML (i-DSML for short). The possibility of extending i-DSML to adapt models directly during their execution, allows the building of adaptable i-DSML. In this article, we demonstrate that specializing adaptable i-DSML leads to the potential definition of accurate adaptation policies. Domain-specificities are the key factors to identify adaptations that really make sense. In effect, we introduce the concept of family as a mean to encapsulate adaptation operations that are attached to a particular domain. Families can be specialized with the special purpose of defining a hierarchy of adaptation contexts.

Keywords: Model execution, adaptation, i-DSML, models at runtime.

1   Introduction

The main goal of Model-Driven Engineering (MDE) is to cope with productive models to build software. This can be commonly achieved by generating the code of the software from the models. On another hand, it is also possible to directly execute a model. In this case, the software system is an execution engine implementing an execution semantics and interpreting a model. Such a model is written in an interpreted Domain-Specific Modeling Language or i-DSML for short [8]. With i-DSML, the ability to run a model prior to its implementation is a time-saving and henceforth cost-saving approach for at least two reasons: (a) it becomes possible to detect and fix problems in the early stages of the software development cycle and (b) ultimately the implementation stage may be skipped. One slogan associated to i-DSML could be *"what you model is what you get"* (WYMIWYG).

Meanwhile, software adaptation and self-adaptive software [15] have gained more and more interest. The runtime adaptation problem is commonly tackled as a two-stage adaptation loop (analyze–modify). In the MDE field, one of the most

J. Cabot and J. Rubin (Eds.): ECMFA 2014, LNCS 8569, pp. 164–179, 2014.

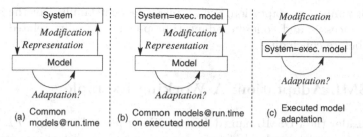

Fig. 1. Adaptation loops

prominent way to implement this loop is *models@run.time* [2], where models are embedded within the system during its execution and acting primarily as a reasoning support (case (a) in Fig. 1). The model is representing the current state of the system and the necessity of adaptation is checked through it. The required adaptation actions are then processed on the system. For adapting a model execution, these *models@run.time* principles can of course be applied (case (b) in Fig. 1). One can notice that in this particular case, there are two models at runtime. The first one is the executed model and the second one is the model representing its state in an adaptation purpose. As the content of the latter is based on the content of the former, this introduces a kind of redundancy between the two models which are hence containing similar or derived elements. In this case, why not directly integrating elements dedicated to the adaptation in the executed model? Even if it leads to complexify the model, it avoids the main disadvantage of *models@run.time* which is to maintain a consistent and causal connection between the system and the model for the model being a valid representation of the system at runtime. Now (case (c) in Fig. 1), the model is directly self-interrogating for managing its own adaptation. Such adaptable and executable models are written in an adaptable i-DSML [5, 6].

In this paper, we focus on the direct adaptation of an executed model (case (c) in Fig. 1) with the definition of adaptable i-DSML. To that extent, we propose an example about a homemade process modeling language. Through this example, we show that specializing the i-DSML leads to enabling automatic and relevant adaptation policies. Indeed, with general-purpose models (and without strong link to any particular business content), it is often difficult, even impossible, to define automatic adaptation actions. Adding new elements on the metamodel or restricting the space of possible models through additional constraints can unlock this situation. The concept of adaptation family is proposed for managing adaptable i-DSML specialization. A family is composed of a specialized metamodel and associated adaptation policies. Families may inherit from each other allowing the definition of hierarchies of families. Inheritance naturally offers the reuse, factorization and specialization of adaptation policies as for code in object-oriented programming.

The rest of this paper is organized as follows. The next section presents an i-DSML defining timed processes and shows that, in case of delay in the process execution, no adaptation action can be established. Sect. 3 defines the concept of families for managing adaptation. Sect. 4 presents some families for the i-DSML of timed processes and concrete adaptation policies. Finally, related work is discussed before concluding.

2   i-DSML Adaptation: A Working Example

Let us consider the i-DSML named *Process Description Language* (*PDL*), that is intended to model any kind of processes as an ordered list of activities. It is freely inspired from standard process languages like SPEM [13] or BPMN [1], which are typically coupled with workflow engines for their execution. Here, this is a simple version that supports parallel activities and includes time concerns. The metamodel and the execution semantics of such an i-DSML are described prior to an illustration of the latter in action is provided. Then, questions about its possible adaptations are raised.

2.1   Definition of the *PDL* Metamodel

Model execution and i-DSML have been widely studied, for instance in [3,4,6,8, 9,12]. All these works establish a consensus on model execution. Accordingly, in this section, the *PDL* i-DSML is described following the characterization of [6]. Fig. 2 defines its metamodel. A metamodel of an i-DSML first contains a static part. This part is simply a metamodel commonly defined for design purposes. Here, the goal of this static part is to define the elements which aim at forming the structure of a process. These elements are manifold and abstracted through the `ProcessElement` meta-element. The main concrete process element is a sequence containing a set of activities. Activities within a sequence are ordered as

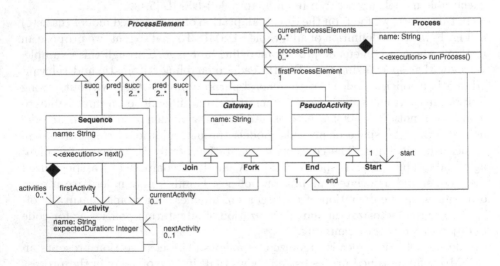

Fig. 2. Definition of the *PDL* i-DSML

each activity (except the last activity) has a next one. Each activity has an expected duration, which is the ideal time lapsing to complete the task. Sequence of activities can be parallelized through gateways. A fork aims at making several sequences parallel whereas a join is a synchronization point of several sequences. Finally, each process contains two pseudo-activities defining the beginning and the ending of the process.

Additionally, an i-DSML metamodel contains a dynamic part. Its goal is to be able to specify the current state of the model during its execution. Here, the dynamic part consists of two meta-associations in Fig. 2. The first one expresses for a process which process elements are currently active. The second one refers, for a sequence, to its current active activity, if any. The combination of the two gives the global state of the model under execution which is modified after each execution step.

The static and dynamic parts of the metamodel are augmented with OCL invariants expressing the well-formedness rules, for instance, there is no cycle between activities. Due to lack of place, they are not presented.

Finally, the metamodel of an i-DSML is associated with an execution semantics. Its goal is to express how the elements of the model are evolving during the execution. Concretely, the execution semantics only modifies the dynamic elements of the model and is implemented through a set of execution operations that can be attached to meta-elements. Here, the execution semantics is embedded within the runProcess() operation of Process and the next() operation of Sequence. For the sake of clarity, these special operations are prefixed by an <<execution>> conceptual stereotype. The runProcess() operation launches the process execution. Its first action consists in executing the start element of the process. Then, after the end of its execution, it executes its successor elements and so on, until reaching the last element of the process. Executing a sequence consists in executing its next() operation. If the sequence is just launched, it executes its first activity. Otherwise, it executes the next activity of the current one. Once an activity is finished, the next() operation is recalled and so on until reaching the end of the sequence. Executing a fork consists in executing each of its successor sequences. Executing a join consists in waiting for each of its predecessor sequences to be finished before executing its successor one.

2.2   A Software Development Process Defined Using *PDL*

As a familiar example, we choose to model a typical software development process (Fig. 3, top part). This process contains four sequences (represented as dashed rectangles): specification (Specify), implementation (Implement), documentation (Document) and distribution of the software (Distribute). The specification is the first task of the process whereas the distribution is the last one once everything else is finished. Between the two, the implementation and the documentation are realized in parallel. This is achieved through the fork named FID (*Fork for Implement and Document*) and the join JID (*Join for Implement and Document*). The specification contains two activities (represented by ellipses):

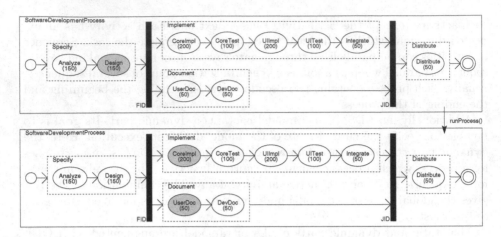

Fig. 3. A model conforming to the *PDL* i-DSML and its execution

analysis followed by design. The number beneath the activity name, here 150 for both, is the expected duration of the activity. The documentation contains user documentation and developer documentation activities. The implementation is the longest sequence: it begins with the core implementation, that is business logic and services implementation (CoreImpl) and its associated test activity (CoreTest). Next, the user interface is implemented (UIImpl) and tested (UITest). Finally, all implementations are integrated.

When the execution engine takes the model as input, the execution trace is formed by a collection of snapshots that correspond to every state of the model after an execution step. We start by the first activity of the first sequence (the Analyze activity). Then we continue with the next activity of this sequence (the Design activity). This situation is represented at the top of Fig. 3 where the current activity is filled with the gray color. After this, we encounter the fork, so, the first activity of each successor is activated (the CoreImpl and the UserDoc activities). This situation corresponds to the bottom of Fig. 3. Once each activity of these two sequences has been executed, we are able to cross the join. The last activity executed is then Distribute.

2.3   Toward the Adaptation of a Process

Still following the characterization of [6], an i-DSML is extended following two ways for becoming adaptable. First, the metamodel is extended with elements dedicated to the adaptation and second, an adaptation semantics is associated with the metamodel and implemented by the execution engine so that it is turned into an adaptation engine. The adaptation semantics aims at acting on the model for adapting it. This adaptation may have impacts on the whole model, including the modification, creation or deletion of static, dynamic or adaptation elements. Concretely, the adaptation semantics is implemented through two kinds of operations. The first kind is query operations returning a boolean and expressing if

an adaptation is required or not. They are called adaptation checks. The second
kind is adaptation actions that apply the adaptation on the model.

Concerning the *PDL* i-DSML, at first glance, a situation requiring adaptation
is when the process has been delayed. However, this necessitates to evaluating the laps between the expected duration and the real elapsed time. So, an
adaptation element has to be added on the metamodel: an `elapsedTime` attribute in the `Process` meta-element. This basic extension of the metamodel is
intuitively evident since having an elapsed time is a logical complement of an expected duration for an effective process execution. It is now easier to implement
a check operation that determines if we are late during the process execution.
It concretely requires comparing the expected durations of all already finished
activities to the real elapsed time.

Now the question is: "If we are late, what must we do?". The answer is:
"In the current definition of the i-DSML, we do not know!". Indeed, there is no
obvious adaptation action that can be processed without additional information.
We may imagine removing unnecessary activities in the rest of the process.
Which ones? An arbitrary erasure is clearly not a good idea. In the example, the
documentation and testing activities may be bypassed. We know that because
we have business knowledge on, in general, what a software development process
really is. Documentation is never at the core production of the subject software
and testing, in the worst case, can possibly be skipped if really required. The
problem is that the execution engine has no business vision and then, has not
this business knowledge. The engine agnostically processes the adaptation for
any kind of model, being a software development process or a cooking recipe.
Another idea would be to parallelize some activities to reduce the time of the
process execution. Typically, from a business knowledge viewpoint, we know that
the development of the business part can be potentially done in parallel with
the user interface development. Again, the engine does not have this business
knowledge.

As a conclusion, with the basic definition of the i-DSML (including a small
and evident extension), it is not possible to know how to adapt a *PDL* model.
In other words, it is not possible to define an adaptation semantics. The model
is too general. However, we foresee that with additional information, adaptation actions can be defined and make sense. The metamodel then needs to be
specialized to embed this additional information. More generally, the most specialized and constrained a metamodel is, the most automatic manipulation of
the model is possible. Besides, the most defining relevant adaptation semantics
is made possible. In the next section, we define the concept of family which is an
i-DSML specialization associated with a dedicated adaptation semantics. Then,
in Sect. 4, we define concrete adaptation families for the *PDL* i-DSML.

3   Family-Based Framework for i-DSML Adaptation

Assuming the fact that from a minimal i-DSML one can create various extensions, each providing a foundation for dedicated adaptations, it becomes highly

desirable to organize all these software pieces. That is why we propose in this paper the adaptation families and the specialization relationship between them.

3.1   Definition of a Family

Each metamodel of an i-DSML, with the definition of its meta-elements, leads to define a set of operations that make sense and are implementable based on these meta-elements and their associated constraints. These operations are those defining an execution or an adaptation semantics. Then, as these operations are tied with a given metamodel, we propose to logically group them under the form of a family. Here is the definition of a family:

Definition 1. *A family brings together a metamodel and a set of associated operations (execution operations, adaptation checks and adaptation actions). It provides guidance to a software designer that can glue together operations available in this context.*

Hence, a family is like a frame in which an engineer can dip into extant elements of solutions with confidence. Afterwards, she/he is responsible for their correct orchestration. A family is identified by an unique name referencing its metamodel and contains three kinds of elements:

1. Execution operations: operations that control the execution flow of the model.
2. Adaptation checks: boolean operations expressing if the current model is aligned with the execution environment or is respecting specific constraints. If not, adaptation must be undertaken.
3. Adaptation actions: operations that modify the content of the model in an adaptation purpose.

We call "attributes" all these elements within a family.

3.2   Family Specialization

The conclusion of the discussion of Sect. 2.3 was that specializing a metamodel is relevant for defining adaptation: the *PDL* i-DSML has first been extended and then, the discussion concluded on the necessity of extending it one step further to have the ability to define concrete adaptation semantics. As a consequence, we propose the specialization of families and thereby to build a hierarchy of families for defining adaptation semantics.

Specializing a family is based on specializing metamodels. Model typing and subtyping, that is specialization relationships between metamodels or metamodel parts, have been defined in [11,18,19]. The metamodel specialization we use in this paper is based on their definition. A metamodel defines a structure (a set of associated meta-elements) and is augmented with a set of invariants, typically written in OCL, for specifying the well-formedness rules. Following the UML profile spirit, a specialized metamodel strictly extends these two parts of a metamodel:

Definition 2. *A metamodel MM' is a specialization of a metamodel MM if MM' extends the structure and/or the invariants of MM. MM' is built by adding to MM, new meta-elements, new attributes in meta-elements, new operations in meta-elements and/or new associations between meta-elements without removing any existing elements of MM. MM' defines additional invariants without removing the existing ones of MM.*

The specialization of a family, that is the definition of a subfamily from a superfamily, is simply made by first specializing its metamodel. As this specialization is a strict extension and does not remove anything, all statements that are made about a superfamily also apply to all subfamilies. We lay down that subfamilies "inherit" execution operations, adaptation checks and adaptation actions from the superfamily. Anything that can be done (from an execution or adaptation viewpoint) with a model of the superfamily can also be done with a model of the subfamily.

Second, in addition to new elements (structural or invariants) in the metamodel, new attributes can be defined for a subfamily, that is, new execution operations, adaptation checks and adaptation actions. Concisely, a family specialization is defined as follows:

Definition 3. *A family F' is a specialization of a family F if the metamodel of F' is specializing the metamodel of F. F' inherits from all the attributes (execution operations, adaptation checks and adaptation actions) of F and can define additional ones.*

Multiple inheritance between metamodels and families is allowed. However conflicts are supposed to be avoided through a careful design.

As families can inherit from each other, it is then possible to define hierarchies of families. The root of a hierarchy is an i-DSML; dealing only with executable models without any adaptation concern. The root i-DSML family can be specialized to define either others i-DSML (without adaptation) or adaptable i-DSML (including adaptation). The more a family is placed at the bottom of the hierarchy, the more its metamodel is specialized and allows the definition of specific adaptation policies. Reaching a certain level of specialization, some adaptable i-DSML can even be based on specific business content as explained in the following subsection.

3.3   Domain versus Business Level Adaptation Policies

Another notion emerges from the previous ideas although it can be tricky to formalize it. Along with the generalization/specialization, a family may represent a set of business-neutral models or not. A business-neutral or domain-level scope expresses that an adaptation policy can be applied on any model conforming to the metamodel of the family, independently of its content (it is said to be "domain" because it is based only on the constructs of the *Domain-Specific Modeling Language*). Conversely, a business-level adaptation policy is based on specific business elements contained in the model. Domain-level families are generally placed on top of the hierarchy while business-level ones are placed in the bottom.

For example, constraining a process to have at least one fork is business-neutral and then situated at the domain level. Indeed, any process may potentially satisfy this fork constraint, regardless of its business content (a cooking recipe, a software development method, etc.), so that the associated adaptations can be reused across a large variety of models. Conversely, constraining a process to have an activity named "beat eggs" breaks the neutrality in the sense that it now presupposes that the process falls within the cooking domain. In that case, the adaptation written for such a family can be very accurate, but far from being reusable.

Technically speaking, the fringe between business-level and domain-level is somewhat fuzzy. However, we can say that if an adaptation semantics, within an adaptation check or an adaptation action, is based on literal values (such as the string value "beat eggs"), then the adaptation will be considered as business-level.

4   Putting *PDL* into the Framework

To give a better understanding of the ideas developed in the previous section, we reconsider the illustration of the *PDL* i-DSML from a family-based framework point of view. Fig. 4 defines a possible family hierarchy for our i-DSML. Each family is graphically described by a box with four compartments. They contain, from top to bottom: the name of the family that references the eponymous meta-model, the execution operations, the adaptation checks and the adaptation actions associated with the family. The hierarchy defines six families: one dedicated to execution only (*PDL*), one business-level family (*ManagedSkipAdaptPDL*) and four domain-level families. In order to distinguish these three kinds of family, an <<execution>>, <<business>> or <<domain>> conceptual stereotype has been placed above each family name. In this paper, we show only the metamodel of the family *DependSkipAdaptPDL* because, thanks to the inheritance, this meta-model contains all the elements defined in its superfamilies. It can then be used to describe the evolution of the metamodels along the hierarchy (excepting for the business-level family). This metamodel is represented on Fig. 5.

All specializations for the *PDL* i-DSML presented in the rest of this section are extending the structure of the metamodel. However, in many cases, restricting the possible models solely by addition of OCL invariants is sufficient to define adaptation policies. As an example, in [6], we study the adaptation of basic UML state machines in case of unexpected events. With a general state machine, no adaptation decision can be taken. However, imposing that a transition associated with each expected event is starting from each state of the state machine leads to be able to determine if an event is expected or not (there exists or not an associated transition). Moreover, imposing that a given event always targets the same state leads to be able to automatically know how to add a state and

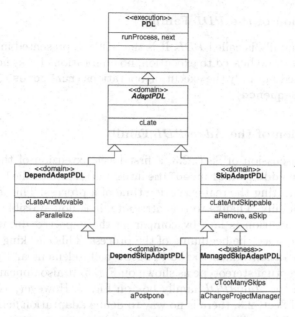

Fig. 4. Hierarchy of families for *PDL* adaptation

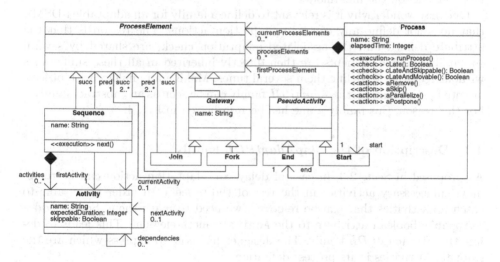

Fig. 5. The i-DSML corresponding to the *DependSkipAdaptPDL* family

transitions associated with the unknown event. These two restrictions are only defined through two OCL invariants without any modification of the metamodel, while they have a huge impact on the adaptation policies. Here lies the power of the concept of family.

4.1   Description of the *PDL* Family

The root of the family is called *PDL*. It is the i-DSML presented in Sect. 2.1. As this i-DSML is only dedicated to execution, no adaptation checks nor adaptation actions are defined but only the execution operations (`runProcess()` of `Process` and `next()` of `Sequence`).

4.2   Description of the *AdaptPDL* Family

Following the discussion of Sect. 2.3, a first basic extension of the *PDL* meta-model consists in adding an `elapsedTime` integer attribute to the `Process` meta-element and indicating the real execution time of a process. This leads to define the *AdaptPDL* family. Thanks to this attribute, it is now possible to determine if the process execution is late by comparing the expected duration with the real elapsed time since the beginning of the process. This checking is realized by the `cLate()` operation added to the `Process` meta-element and prefixed by a `<<check>>` conceptual stereotype as shown on Fig. 5. It also appears in the third compartment of the *AdaptPDL* family box on Fig. 4. However, as explained in the discussion of Sect. 2.3, there is no way to define adaptation actions with this metamodel yet. This will be done with the subsequent specializations adding new elements on the metamodel.

One may wonder why it is relevant to define a family for an adaptable i-DSML that does not define any concrete adaptation actions. The reason is that the attribute defined and the associated adaptation check, are shared by several subfamilies. These elements are then directly inherited in all these subfamilies without requiring to define them several times. Making an analogy with object-oriented programming, the *AdaptPDL* family can be seen as an "abstract family". For this reason, this family name has been italicized in Fig. 4.

4.3   Description of the *SkipAdaptPDL* Family

As proposed in Sect. 2.3, in case of delay, an adaptation action can be to remove unnecessary activities in the rest of the process. In order to be able to catch up activities that can be removed, we need to mark them. So, we add a `skippable` boolean attribute to the `Activity` meta-element. This leads to define the *SkipAdaptPDL* family. The designer has now to express which are the skippable activities in its process definition.

Thanks to this attribute, in addition to know that we are late with the `cLate()` adaptation check, it is now also possible to determine if a next activity is skippable. This checking is thus twofold and is realized by the `cLateAnd-Skippable()` adaptation check added to the `Process` meta-element as shown on Fig. 5. Two adaptation actions have been defined. The first one removes skippable activities (i.e., it modifies the static part of the i-DSML). This adaptation action is drastic and maybe the designer would appreciate a softer solution. Then, instead of statically removing skippable activities, we propose another adaptation action that only skips them (i.e., it modifies the dynamic part of the i-DSML, updating the current activity to the benefit of a next activity). These adaptation actions are respectively realized by the aRemove() and aSkip() operations added to the Process meta-element. They are prefixed by an <<action>> conceptual stereotype. As these operations are adaptation actions, they appear in the fourth compartment of the *SkipAdaptPDL* family box on Fig. 4.

As an example, in the Fig. 3, bottom hand side, the current activity is Design. If for the implementation sequence that follows this activity, the CoreTest and UITest are marked as skippable, once the CoreImpl activity finished and if we are late, the CoreTest activity will be skipped and the next executed activity will be UIImpl.

4.4 Description of the *DependAdaptPDL* Family

In Sect. 2.3, instead of removing unnecessary activities we suggest to parallelize some activities in order to decrease the time of the process. Obviously, we cannot select randomly activities that will be parallelized because an activity may depend on another. Consequently, this adaptation could be achieved only if we are aware of the dependencies between activities. In order to state these dependencies, we add a dependencies reference to the Activity meta-element. This leads to define the *DependAdaptPDL* family. From this reference, in addition to know that we are late with the cLate() adaptation check, it is now also possible to determine if a following activity is movable (taking into account its dependencies). This double checking is realized by the cLateAndMovable() adaptation check added to the Process meta-element as shown on Fig. 5. The corresponding adaptation action is to transform unique sequences into multiple sequences in parallel. This adaptation action is realized by the aParallelize() operation added to the Process meta-element as shown on Fig. 5.

Fig. 6 gives an example of this kind of adaptation. At the top, there is the model before adaptation. The dashed arrows represent the dependencies between activities. These dependencies have been defined by the designer. The number written between the parentheses after the process name indicates the elapsed time. We are currently late (350 instead of the expected 300) and some activities are movable (taking into account their dependencies). The bottom of Fig. 6 shows the corresponding model after adaptation. For example, for the implementation sequence, as CoreTest depends on CoreImpl, they must be part of the same sequence. This is the same for UITest and UIImpl. However, "Core" activities and "UI" activities have no dependencies between each other. This is why two subsequences have been created.

4.5 Description of the *DependSkipAdaptPDL* Family

Another interesting adaptation could be to postpone an activity (i.e., to move an activity toward the end of the process) in order to execute it only if we are not anymore late. It is acceptable to postpone an activity if it is skippable (because it will possibly not be done) but it cannot be postponed later than an activity which depends on it. Consequently, we need at the same time the notion of skippable

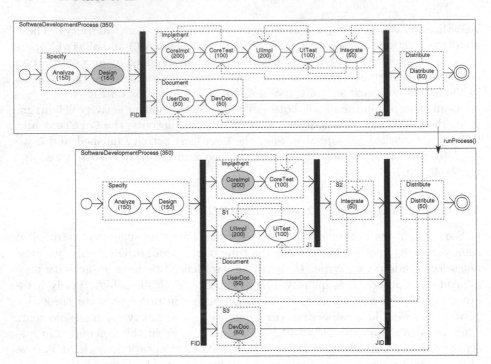

Fig. 6. The model before and after adaptation, conforming to the *DependAdaptPDL* family

activity and the idea of dependencies between these activities. In order to have these pieces of information at runtime, we build the *DependSkipAdaptPDL* family that inherits from two superfamilies: *SkipAdaptPDL* and *DependAdaptPDL*. It means that the elements available in the i-DSML are the ones corresponding to the i-DSML of these two families. In this way, a complex checking can be realized by combining the `cLateAndSkippable()` and `cLateAndMovable()` adaptation checks. The corresponding adaptation action is to shift an activity as far as possible toward the end of the process. This adaptation action is realized by the `aPostpone()` operation added to the `Process` meta-element as shown on Fig. 5. Thanks to multiple inheritance, we are able to write an adaptation rule that is based on the merging of two families.

So far, all the previous families were exclusively at a domain level. As explained in Sect. 3.3, it means that for processing the adaptation, there is no need to have information about what is representing the instance of the `Process` meta-element in terms of business. It could be for example a software development process or a cooking recipe, as well. To give a concrete example of business-level adaptation, the next subsection presents a business-level family.

4.6 Description of the *ManagedSkipAdaptPDL* Family

During the software development process, if we are really very late, a cause might be the project manager who is not skilled enough. Being very late may be defined by counting the skipped activities and specifying a maximum number of allowable skips. In this context, adaptation could be to fire the project manager and to hire a new one. This leads to define the *ManagedSkipAdaptPDL* family that is extending the *SkipAdaptPDL* family. This family defines a cTooManySkips() adaptation check that expresses if more than a given number (for instance three) of skips have already been done. The adaptation action aChangeProjectManager() of this family consists in creating a particular activity in the process: a *Change Project Manager* activity (this activity can be added in parallel of the existing activities of the process) which is immediately activated.

This family is at the business-level because we are aware that the instance of the Process meta-element will represent a project development with a manager. Such an activity will not make sense for all the processes defined with *PDL* i-DSML, such as a cooking recipe for example.

5   Related Work

In this article we highlighted some ideas coming from both the software architecture field and the MDE community in order to apply them to the recent concept of i-DSML.

Indeed, our inspiration is rooted in the works on architectural styles, a seminal research theme during the late 90s [10, 16, 17]. An architectural style defines a family of similar software architectures (e.g., client/server, pipe&filter, blackboard, etc.) and basically provides specific elements of design and rules to govern their arrangement. In [10] David Garlan highlighted a specialization relationship that may hold between styles (e.g., pipeline is a substyle of pipe&filter) so that some Architecture Description Languages (ADL) have supported this experimental feature, like ACME or ArchWare. Meanwhile, some authors have investigated how the concept of style could ease (self)-reconfiguration of systems at runtime [7, 14], based upon adaptation rules defined at the architecture-level and an adaptation loop very close to case (a) in Fig. 1, retrospectively speaking.

Likewise, Jim Steel *et al.* [18] proposed the model typing where, while conforming to a metamodel of course, a model may adhere to one or more types in the same way that an architecture described with an ADL may in addition satisfy to one or more styles. Logically, Clement Guy *et al.* [11] continued the works through the study of the subtyping relationship and more generally the influence of such a type-system at the model-level [19], but regardless to the adaptation issue.

6   Conclusion and Perspectives

In this paper, we have proposed a framework that enables the implementation of the direct adaptation of an executed model conforming to an adaptable i-DSML.

An adaptable i-DSML defines models that are directly executable and adaptable. The framework relies on the concept of family and aims at properly arranging a number of elements of several natures that all serve the definition of adaptable i-DSML. A family gathers a given metamodel of an i-DSML with operations dedicated to its execution and adaptation. We have showed, through an example, that specializing a metamodel of an i-DSML enables to define more relevant and accurate adaptation policies. For this reason, families can inherit from each other allowing us to defining hierarchies of families, from the most general to the most specific. The inheritance offers conceptually the same advantages as in object-oriented programming such as the reuse of existing adaptation policies, the factorization of the same policies through a common superfamily or the specialization of existing adaptation policies. A family can be defined at a domain or business level depending on the fact that they are based on a particular business content or not. We applied this approach on a concrete example of a process model where several families have been built thanks to the family specialization.

The engine executing and adapting a model must currently contain hard-coded adaptation rules. Indeed, the execution operations, adaptation checks and adaptation actions are orchestrated and weaved through the code of the developer within the execution engine. However, it can be useful to modify this orchestration during the execution of the model. If a family offers several adaptation actions, one can be more suitable than another, according to the current context. To achieve this in a suitable way, as a short-term perspective of this work, we plan to define an i-DSML dedicated to the orchestration of the available operations for a family. An orchestration model will be interpreted by the execution engine in addition to the executed model. Concretely, this model will define an adaptation semantics (combinations of adaptation checks and adaptation actions) and its weaving with the execution operations. In addition, we can reach meta-circularity if we turn the orchestration i-DSML into an adaptable i-DSML as explained in this article. This unified approach can succeed because this orchestration model ought to be modified during the execution. In other words, as raised in [6], the adaptation semantics can be adapted at runtime and thus leading to a true meta-adaptation.

References

1. Business Process Modeling Notation (BPMN) Version 1.2. Technical report (January 2009)
2. Blair, G.S., Bencomo, N., France, R.B.: Models@run.time. IEEE Computer 42(10), 22–27 (2009)
3. Breton, E., Bézivin, J.: Towards an understanding of model executability. In: Proceedings of the International Conference on Formal Ontology in Information Systems (FOIS 2001). ACM (2001)
4. Cariou, E., Ballagny, C., Feugas, A., Barbier, F.: Contracts for Model Execution Verification. In: France, R.B., Kuester, J.M., Bordbar, B., Paige, R.F. (eds.) ECMFA 2011. LNCS, vol. 6698, pp. 3–18. Springer, Heidelberg (2011)

5. Cariou, E., Le Goaer, O., Barbier, F.: Model Execution Adaptation? In: 7th International Workshop on Models@run.time (MRT 2012) at MoDELS 2012. ACM Digital Library (2012)
6. Cariou, E., Le Goaer, O., Barbier, F., Pierre, S.: Characterization of Adaptable Interpreted-DSML. In: Van Gorp, P., Ritter, T., Rose, L.M. (eds.) ECMFA 2013. LNCS, vol. 7949, pp. 37–53. Springer, Heidelberg (2013)
7. Cheng, S.-W., Garlan, D., Schmerl, B.R., Sousa, J.A.P., Spitnagel, B., Steenkiste, P.: Using Architectural Style As a Basis for System Self-repair. In: Proceedings of the IFIP 17th World Computer Congress - TC2 Stream 3rd IEEE/IFIP Conference on Software Architecture: System Design, Development and Maintenance, WICSA 3, pp. 45–59. Kluwer, B.V. (2002)
8. Clarke, P.J., Wu, Y., Allen, A.A., Hernandez, F., Allison, M., France, R.: Formal and Practical Aspects of Domain-Specific Languages: Recent Developments. In: Towards Dynamic Semantics for Synthesizing Interpreted DSMLs, ch. 9. IGI Global (2013)
9. Combemale, B., Crégut, X., Pantel, M.: A Design Pattern to Build Executable DSMLs and associated V&V tools. In: The 19th Asia-Pacific Software Engineering Conference (APSEC 2012). IEEE (2012)
10. Garlan, D., Allen, R., Ockerbloom, J.: Exploiting Style in Architectural Design Environments. SIGSOFT Softw. Eng. Notes 19(5), 175–188 (1994)
11. Guy, C., Combemale, B., Derrien, S., Steel, J.R.H., Jézéquel, J.-M.: On Model Subtyping. In: Vallecillo, A., Tolvanen, J.-P., Kindler, E., Störrle, H., Kolovos, D. (eds.) ECMFA 2012. LNCS, vol. 7349, pp. 400–415. Springer, Heidelberg (2012)
12. Lehmann, G., Blumendorf, M., Trollmann, F., Albayrak, S.: Meta-Modeling Runtime Models. In: Dingel, J., Solberg, A. (eds.) MODELS 2010 Workshops. LNCS, vol. 6627, pp. 209–223. Springer, Heidelberg (2011)
13. OMG. Software Process Engineering Metamodell SPEM 2.0 OMG Draft Adopted Specification. Technical report. OMG (2006)
14. Oreizy, P., Medvidovic, N., Taylor, R.N.: Runtime Software Adaptation: Framework, Approaches, and Styles. In: Companion of the 30th International Conference on Software Engineering (ICSE Companion 2008), pp. 899–910. ACM (2008)
15. Salehie, M., Tahvildari, L.: Self-adaptive software: Landscape and research challenges. ACM Trans. Auton. Adapt. Syst. 14, 14:1–14:42 (2009)
16. Shaw, M.: Comparing architectural design styles. IEEE Software 12(6), 27–41 (1995)
17. Shaw, M., Clements, P.: A Field Guide to Boxology: Preliminary Classification of Architectural Styles for Software Systems. In: The Twenty-First Annual International Computer Software and Applications Conference (COMPSAC 1997), pp. 6–13. IEEE Computer Society (1997)
18. Steel, J., Jézéquel, J.-M.: On model typing. Software and System Modeling 6(4), 401–413 (2007)
19. Sun, W., Combemale, B., Derrien, S., France, R.B.: Using Model Types to Support Contract-Aware Model Substitutability. In: Van Gorp, P., Ritter, T., Rose, L.M. (eds.) ECMFA 2013. LNCS, vol. 7949, pp. 118–133. Springer, Heidelberg (2013)

Normalizing Heterogeneous Service Description Models with Generated QVT Transformations*

Simon Schwichtenberg, Christian Gerth, Zille Huma, and Gregor Engels

s-lab - Software Quality Lab, University of Paderborn, Germany
{simon.schwichtenberg,gerth,zille.huma,engels}@upb.de

Abstract. Service-Oriented Architectures (SOAs) enable the reuse and substitution of software services to develop highly flexible software systems. To benefit from the growing plethora of available services, sophisticated service discovery approaches are needed that bring service requests and offers together. Such approaches rely on rich service descriptions, which specify also the behavior of provided/requested services, e.g., by pre- and postconditions of operations. As a base for the specification a data schema is used, which specifies the used data types and their relations. However, data schemas are typically heterogeneous wrt. their structure and terminology, since they are created individually in their diverse application contexts. As a consequence the behavioral models that are typed over the heterogeneous data schemas, cannot be compared directly. In this paper, we present an holistic approach to normalize rich service description models to enable behavior-aware service discovery. The approach consists of a matching algorithm that helps to resolve structural and terminological heterogeneity in data schemas by exploiting domain-specific background ontologies. The resulting data schema mappings are represented in terms of Query View Transformation (QVT) relations that even reflect complex n:m correspondences. By executing the transformation, behavioral models are automatically normalized, which is a prerequisite for a behavior-aware operation matching.

Keywords: SOA, Service Description, Ontologies, Behavioral Models, Matching.

1 Introduction

Due to their modularity, reusability, and flexibility, SOAs allow to realize software projects faster and may reduce development costs drastically. In such service-oriented scenarios, service providers offer services and service requesters request for services. The process to match service offers (SOs) with service requests (SRs) is called service discovery.

A service discovery that is performed manually is time-consuming and error-prone, since a user has to understand and compare all SOs and SRs individually. In addition, misinterpretations and misunderstandings of the services lead to

---

* This work was partially supported by the German Research Foundation (DFG) within the Collaborative Research Centre "On-The-Fly Computing" (SFB 901).

J. Cabot and J. Rubin (Eds.): ECMFA 2014, LNCS 8569, pp. 180–195, 2014.

inaccurate matching results. For this reason and to benefit from the plethora of existing services, an automatic service discovery is required that is based on comprehensive specifications of the services.

Existing service specification languages like Web Ontology Language for Web Services [15], Web Service Modeling Language [5], Semantic Annotations for WSDL and XML Schema [18], and the Rich Service Description Language [10,9] allow to create such comprehensive specifications. Typically, such a service specification includes a structural data schema and behavioral models, e.g., in form of visual contracts (VCs) [6]. VCs describe the behavior of SRs or SOs in terms of pre- and postconditions for their respective operations. The data schema specifies the used data types of the service and their relations. The behavioral models in turn are typed over the data schema. For the remainder, we assume that such a data schema is specified in terms of a Unified Modeling Language (UML) class model and describes the relevant concepts of a certain domain, e.g., tourism or banking. Consequently, complex data types are referred to as classes, primitive types as attributes, and instances of types as objects.

Since SOs and SRs are created independently, the structure and terminology of their class models are most likely heterogeneous, even if they specify services in the same domain of interest. As a consequence, the behavioral models typed over the class models cannot be compared directly and a behavior-aware operation matching of service requests and offers is not possible. The heterogeneity of the class models arises from different terminologies, granularity levels, and logical structuring. For example, two classes of the SR's and the SO's class models might have different but synonymous identifiers, since both denote the same concept. Analogously, homonyms must be addressed separately.

Matching classes and attributes is an important aspect to overcome the heterogeneity, e.g., to determine whether parameters and return values of provided and requested operations correspond to each other. Thereby, a single class does not necessarily have to correspond to a single other class. It is rather likely that sets of classes correspond to each other, resulting in complex 1:n, n:1, or even n:m mappings. However, complex mappings have received little attention in ontology matching approaches [19,16].

In this paper, we present an holistic approach to resolve the structural and terminological heterogeneity of rich service description models to enable a behavior-aware service discovery and composition. Our approach includes a class model matching algorithm that leverages domain-specific background ontologies, e.g., linguistic resources and the Semantic Web to establish semantic relations between similar classes across different models. From the obtained class model mappings, a QVT [1] script is generated automatically, whose particular relations reflect identified correspondences between classes of any cardinality. Using these QVT relations, we normalize behavioral models in rich service descriptions and make them directly comparable in order to enable a behavior-aware operation matching.

The remainder is structured as follows: In Sect. 2, we describe a scenario that illustrates the problem statement. Our approach for class model matching and

VC normalization is presented in Sect. 3 and Sect. 4. Tool support is introduced in Sect. 5. We discuss related work regarding class model and web service matching in Sect. 6. Finally, in Sect. 7 we conclude and give an outlook on future work.

2   Scenario

For the following, we assume that a service requester wants to create a service that allows its users to search and book hotel rooms. Therefore, the requester is interested in SOs of hotel chains that provide access to their room availability data or functionality to make bookings through a service interface. For that purpose, the requester specifies a SR, which is then compared with available SOs of hotel chains. We assume that SRs and SOs are specified using a service specification language, which consists at least of the following parts: (1) a UML class model specifying the data schema and (2) visual contracts, which specify pre- and postconditions for every requested and provided operation.

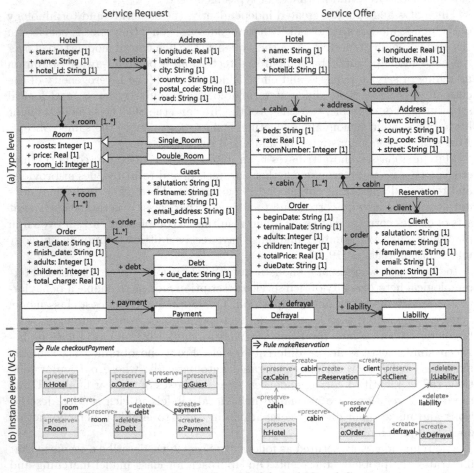

Fig. 1. Heterogeneous Class Models and Visual Contracts

Fig. 1 gives an example of such a SR and SO with their respective class models and two behavioral models in terms of visual contracts.

Obviously, both class models have some concepts in common. However, both use partially different terminologies for these concepts, e.g., the classes Debt and Liability. Further, classes do not necessarily correspond only to a single other class. For instance, Single_Room and Double_Room are specializations of Room in the SR, while there are no further specializations of Cabin in the SO. In addition, some attributes are widespread differently over several classes in both class models, resulting in complex 1:n, n:1, and n:m correspondences between classes. For instance, the attributes of Address in the SR are represented by Address and Coordinates in the SO.

The behavioral aspects of a service are described using VCs. A VC is a graph grammar rule, whose left-hand side (LHS) describes a precondition that must be fulfilled before a certain operation can be executed. The right-hand side (RHS) of the rule describes the effects of the operation execution. The graphs of the rule's LHS and RHS are instances of the SR or SO class model.

Fig. 1 (b) shows the VCs of the requested operation checkoutPayment and the provided operation makeReservation. The VC of checkoutPayment specifies the following behavior:

> After Guest g has paid the Debt d for his Order o of Hotel h's Room r, Debt d is deleted and a new Payment p is created instead.

This operation is similar to makeReservation that uses synonymous identifiers and additionally creates a Reservation after the payment. However, in order to match these models to decide whether the behavior of the operations is equivalent, the behavioral models need to be normalized. For that purpose, we propose the approach shown in Fig. 2.

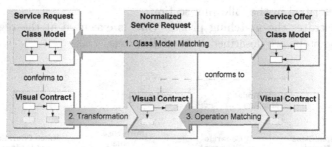

Fig. 2. Normalization Approach

Our approach consists of three steps: (1) First, we determine class and attribute mappings during *Class Model Matching* by considering background ontologies in order to overcome structural and terminological heterogeneity. (2) From the set of mappings, we generate a relational QVT script. By executing the Transformation, all VCs of the requester are retyped according to the class model of the SO. (3) After the normalization, the operations can be matched, e.g., by using the approach introduced in [10].

After the computation of a mapping between the class models of a SR and SO, we assume that the result is inspected by a user, since it may happen that manual intervention is required. For instance, in case of attributes with the same name but different types it is necessary to parse their values properly, e.g., by converting a float to an integer or by integrating an adapter. In such cases, the QVT script must be adjusted manually. To give an example: The registry might return a list of the ten best matching offers to the requester. The requester selects one of them and refines the QVT script if needed.

In the following sections, we describe the class model matching and the normalization in detail.

3   Class Model Matching

The following section introduces our approach for an automatic service discovery (SD). At first, the architecture and the process of the SD are defined. The rest of this section focuses on the class model matching and exemplifies the matching algorithm.

3.1   Automatic Service Discovery Process

In our approach, there are three parties that take part in the SD: service providers, service requesters, and a service registry. The registry is a central point to convey SRs to SOs. Providers publish specifications of their SOs at the service registry. Requesters inquiry the registry by SRs that are also specified as described in the previous section. The registry resolves the class model heterogeneity on-the-fly, retrieves matching SOs for the SR, and returns them to the requester. The requester can bind its SR to one of the proper SOs. The SD process is described in the following section.

Fig. 3 illustrates the matching process that is executed at the registry. The single process steps are described in the following.

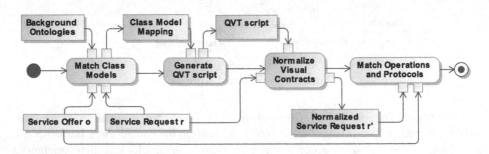

Fig. 3. Automatized Matching Process

Match Class Models: In the first step, the class models of all registered SOs and the currently inquired SR are matched. The class models are enriched with additional information from several background ontologies (BOs) to establish mappings between classes and attributes. The output of this step is a set of disjoint mappings that may have any kind of cardinality. Complex mappings enable a relation between n classes of the SO's class model and m classes of the SR's class model, with $n, m \leq 1$.

Generate QVT script: In the next step, a relational QVT script is generated from the set of mappings. Each QVT relation corresponds to a class mapping. If the classes of a particular mapping have attributes that were also mapped for their part, these attribute mappings are likewise considered in these relations. However, class and attribute mappings are considered in isolation, i.e. the mapped attributes do not necessarily have to be contained in classes of the same class mapping.

There are still some aspects of heterogeneity our class model matcher does not cover yet. In fact, more complex than 1:1 attribute mappings, association mappings, and correspondences between attributes and classes are not considered. Nevertheless, our class model matcher helps to resolve heterogeneity across class models, but we assume that the identified mappings are inspected by a user and adjusted if necessary before the script is executed to normalize visual contracts.

Normalize Visual Contracts: To normalize the requester's VCs, the QVT script is executed with these VCs as input. After the transformation, the SR's VCs conform to the class model of the SO. The normalization transforms the LHS and RHS of each VC separately and composes the results to a single normalized VC. It should be noticed, that it is also possible to normalize the VCs according to the class model of the SO, because relational QVT allows bidirectional transformations. As a useful by-product, the transformation can be used for a mediation service: Parameters of the SR as well as return values of the SO can be translated on-the-fly, when the SR and SO interact.

Match Operations and Protocols: Until now, only structural aspects of the SD have been addressed. On the contrary, operation matching takes the behavioral models of SRs and SOs into account. Our approach integrates the operation matching approach proposed by Huma et al. [10], which relies on VCs. The approach considers n-ary correspondences between operations. For example, a 1:1 operation mapping is established when the precondition of the requested operation covers at least the preserved and deleted objects of the provided operation and the postcondition of the provided operation covers at least the preserved and created objects of the requested operation. More complex matching strategies consider whole sequences of operations.

The approach of Huma et al. also comes with a protocol matching, which is out of scope in this paper. The following section concentrates on the service discovery step *Match Class Models*. The algorithm and its interplay with background ontologies is explained in detail.

3.2   Matching Algorithm

The following section exemplifies the class model matching algorithm which is a prerequisite for the normalization of the VCs. Fig. 4 shows the single steps of the algorithm that are explained in detail in the remainder.

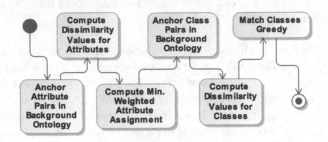

Fig. 4. Class Model Matching Algorithm

Anchor Attribute Pairs in Background Ontology: Class models of service descriptions are compact, because they focus on the implementation, abstract from irrelevant details, and ideally do not contain redundant information. Consequently, the information class models contain is typically not sufficient to establish semantic relations across different class models. Additional knowledge is required to establish these relations. In our approach, the class models are embedded in BOs (c.f. [3]), which model particular domains of interest more holistically than class models and hopefully builds bridges between the different class models.

Our approach is not limited to a certain ontology language or to a certain domain of interest. Rather any kind of ontologies can be used as long as they classify their concepts in a taxonomy. In particular, the algorithm can access common knowledge ontologies like the linguistic resource WordNet [14], the DBpedia ontology [13], and further Web Ontology Language (OWL) ontologies like Schema.org[1] or Umbel[2]. Furthermore, we included some domain-specific OWL ontologies with regard to the previously described scenario, e.g. OnTour[3] and the Travel Guide[4]. In order to support a certain ontology language, a respective programming interface must be implemented that returns the hypernyms for a given term. In addition, the ontologies can be imported into a database that maps terms to their hypernyms, which avoids to keep the whole ontology in memory and accelerates the anchoring step by leveraging database indexes.

During the anchoring, a BO is selected that contains two concepts with the same identifiers as the two attributes to be matched. This means a BO is selected for each individual attribute pair. The identifiers of the concepts and the attributes need not to be exactly the same: Different naming conventions like

---

[1] http://schema.org/

[2] http://umbel.org/

[3] http://e-tourism.deri.at/ont/

[4] https://sites.google.com/site/ontotravelguides

due_date and dueDate are also considered. For this purpose we use tokenization and elimation of stopwords like *of, the, a,* etc. [7]. Fig. 5 shows an anchoring of the attributes price and rate within the taxonomy of WordNet. By using different BOs for matching, it may happen that homonyms are misinterpreted if their semantics differs between the BOs. Although, in practice the number of homonyms shared between different domains of interest is minimal, homonyms may be inspected manually after the matching process.

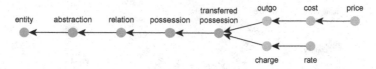

Fig. 5. Anchoring of rate and price in WordNet

Compute Dissimilarity Values for Attributes: It is a common technique to express the dissimilarity of two concepts as a number. The lower the value of the number, the less dissimilar the concepts are. The normalized dissimilarity is a function from a pair of model elements to a number that ranges over the unit interval of real numbers (c.f. [7]).

In the current step, all dissimilarity values for attributes are determined pairwise. Once two attributes have been anchored, their degree of dissimilarity is determined by the upward cotopic dissimilarity [12], which is defined in Def. 1 (c.f. [7]).

Definition 1. *Upward cotopic dissimilarity. The upward cotopic dissimilarity* $\delta : o \times o \to [0, 1]$ *is a dissimilarity over a hierarchy* $H = \langle o, \leq \rangle$, *such that:*

$$\delta(c, c') = 1 - \frac{|UC(c, H) \cap UC(c', H)|}{|UC(c, H) \cup UC(c', H)|}$$

where $UC(c, H) = \{c' \mid \forall c, c' \in H \land c \leq c'\}$ *and* $c \leq c'$ *means that* c' *is more general than* c.

The upward cotopic dissimilarity relates the number of shared hypernyms to the total number of hypernyms of two concepts to be matched according to the BO. The shared hypernyms of price and rate according to WordNet are highlighted in Fig. 5, which yields a dissimilarity value of $\delta = 1 - 5/10 = 0.5$.

The primitive type compatibility of the attributes is also taken into account when their dissimilarity is assessed. Accordingly, two attributes with numerical types are less dissimilar than a numerical and an alphabetical type. The dissimilarity of the types is encoded in a static look-up table. The upward cotopic dissimilarity and the type compatibility are aggregated into a single dissimilarity value according to Equation 1, which aggregates N different dissimilarity values δ_i, where each of them is weighted by ω_i. Fig. 6 shows the dissimilarity values of city to all the attributes of the other class model.

$$\hat{\delta} = \sum_{i=1}^{N} \delta_i \omega_i, \quad \sum_{i=1}^{N} \omega_i = 1, \quad \forall \omega_i : \omega_i > 0 \qquad (1)$$

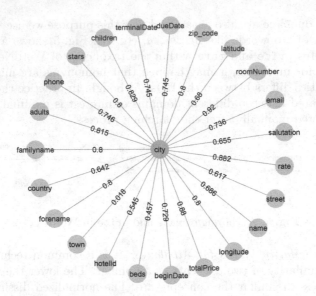

Fig. 6. Dissimilarity values for `city`

Compute Min. Weighted Attribute Assignment: After the dissimilarity values
have been computed for all attribute pairs, proper attribute mappings are created. We assume that most of the attributes represent atomic information, which
is why only 1:1 attribute mappings are considered in our approach. The mapping
of attributes is considered as an optimization problem with the aim to assign as
many attributes as possible while minimizing the sum of the dissimilarity values. The matching algorithm uses an existing algorithm for the minimum cost
flow problem [20] as a subroutine to find this minimal weighted assignment. A
solution for the assignment referring to the scenario is shown in Fig. 7.

Fig. 7. Min. Weighted Attribute Assignment

Anchor Class Pairs in Background Ontology: This step is analogous to the anchoring of attributes.

Compute Dissimilarity Values for Classes: The dissimilarity of the class pairs is
assessed by using the upward cotopic dissimilarity. In addition, the attribute mappings are also taken into account. The intuition is that classes that share many

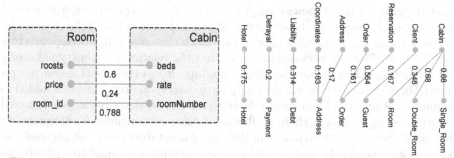

Fig. 8. Shared Attribute Dissimilarity   **Fig. 9.** Class Mappings

dissimilar attributes are also dissimilar for their part. The shared attributes dissimilarity relates the number of shared attributes to the maximal number of attributes. Fig. 8 shows the attribute mappings between Room and Cabin that are part of the optimal attribute assignment. Thus, the shared attribute dissimilarity is $\delta = \frac{0.6+0.24+0.788+3}{6} \approx 0.771$. The upward cotopic and the shared attributes dissimilarity are aggregated into a single dissimilarity value in accordance with Equation 1.

Match Classes Greedy: Contrary to the attribute matching, the classes are matched with a greedy strategy instead of calculating an optimal assignment. The class mappings are created in a ascending order according to the dissimilarity of the class pairs. At the same time, mappings are only created as long as the dissimilarity is below a threshold. If one of a pair's classes is already part of a mapping, the other is added to that mapping. That way 1:1 mappings can be expanded to complex 1:n, n:1, or n:m mappings. Fig. 9 shows the resulting set of complex class mappings. Consequently, the set of resulting class mappings is disjoint.

The set of attribute and class mappings that link the SR's and the SO's class models is the input for the VC normalization, which is the subject of the next section.

4 Visual Contract Normalization

As a preparation for the normalization of the VCs, a QVT [1] script is generated from the mappings obtained by the class model matching. Because of its relational character, the QVT script can be executed in both directions. Thereby the transformation direction is determined implicitly by selecting the target model. In our approach, we transform the VCs that conform to the class model of the SR into VCs that conform to the SO's class model. The LHS and the RHS of a VC are transformed separately and recomposed into a newly created, normalized VC. This section describe how the transformation script is generated. The generation process consists of three steps: Relations are (1) created for the class mappings, (2) enriched by attribute mappings, (3) connected with respect to associations.

Class Mappings: Fig. 10 shows the QVT relation that was generated from the 1:2 class mapping between the classes `Reservation` and `Order` of the SO's class model and the class `Order` of the SR's class model. Each class mapping corresponds to a **top relation**. The **top** keyword indicates that the relation is an entry point of a transformation, which means that object bindings from other relations are not required. For each of the classes of the mapping, a corresponding **domain** is added to the relation. A relation domain has a *domain pattern* that describes a specific model graph consisting of objects, their attributes, and association links. A relation holds, when all its domain pattern match in the source and target model respectively. In case a relation holds, the *root variables* of the domains are bound to concrete objects. The **enforce** keyword ensures that a relation holds when the domains of the source model can be bound. If necessary, new objects of the target model are created or existing objects are deleted. As a result, the source and target model are consistent in regard to that relation.

```
      top relation Reservation_Order_Order{
            var_totalPrice : ecore::EFloat;
            var_dueDate : String; ...
            enforce domain provider dom_reservation : provider::Reservation {
5             client = var_client : provider::Client {} ...
            };
            enforce domain provider dom_order1 : provider::Order {
                liability = var_liability : provider::Liability {},
                totalPrice = var_totalPrice,
10              dueDate = var_dueDate ...
            };
            enforce domain requester dom_order2 : requester::Order {
                debt = var_debt : requester::Debt {},
                total_charge = var_totalPrice ...
15          };
            when {
                var_dueDate = if dom_order1.oclIsUndefined()
                then dom_order2.debt.due_date
                else dom_order1.dueDate
20              endif;
                Client_Guest(var_client, requester::Guest.allInstances()->any(true)); ...
            }
      }
      top relation Address_Coordinates_Address{
25          enforce domain provider dom_address1 : provider::Address {
                coordinates = dom_coordinates
            };
            enforce domain provider dom_coordinates : provider::Coordinates {...};
            enforce domain requester dom_address2 : requester::Address {...};
30    }
```

Fig. 10. Excerpt of the Generated QVT Script

Attribute Mappings: After the generation of relations, we add appropriate QVT statements to the relations that take the attribute mappings into account. Each 1:1 attribute mapping corresponds to a *Property Template Item (PTI)* that is added to the respective domain pattern. In our approach, we use PTIs to instruct the transformation where to read attributes values from the source model and where to assign these values to attributes of the target model. Since classes and attributes were matched independently, it may happen that it is not possible to reflect class and attribute mappings at the same time. We identified two cases where we added PTIs to relations: (1) Both mapped attributes are owned by two classes that were mapped for their part. As shown in Fig. 10, the classes `Order` were mapped and are part of the same relation. Their attributes `totalPrice` and `total_charge` were also mapped. Hence, respective PTIs are added that bind these attributes to the same value over variable `var_totalPrice` (line 9 and 14). (2) Both mapped attributes are owned by two classes that have not been mapped for their part. For example, the attributes `dueDate` and `due_date` were mapped. Their owning classes `Order` and `Debt` have not been mapped for their part. However, `due_date` can be accessed over `dom_order2` because `Order` has an association to `Debt`. Hence, a PTI is added to the respective domain pattern that binds the value of `due_date` to the variable `var_dueDate` (line 10). Furthermore, `var_dueDate` is bound to an Object Constraint Language (OCL) [2] expression in the when clause of the relation. The expression represents the navigation path that accesses `due_date` (line 18). It should be noticed, that the navigation path depends on the transformation direction and that such a path may only exist in one direction. The transformation direction can be determined by calling the OCL function call *dom_order1.oclIsUndefined()*. Thus, `var_dueDate` is only bound to `due_date` if transforming from the SR's to the SO's class model. The else branch has no effect and is just for syntactical validity.

Associations: Until now, we considered classes in isolation during the QVT script generation. Here we examine associations between classes, i.e. association instances from the source model are transformed to links of the target model. During the class model matching (Sect. 3) no association mappings were established that could be translated to QVT statements. Instead, the link creation is exclusively derived from the class mappings. To simplify, we assume that classes have at most one unidirectional, single-valued association to another certain class. Links between objects are established by either referencing already bound variables that are available in the scope of a relation or by binding variables with relation calls. Similar to the attribute mappings, we distinguish two cases when and how to create links: (1) A complex class mapping maps n classes of a class models to m other classes. One of the n has an association to one of the other $n-1$ classes. For example, `Address` has an association to `Coordinates` and both classes are part of the same mapping. Hence, a PTI is added to the respective `Address` domain pattern, that binds the association `coordinates` and the root variable `dom_coordinates` (line 26). (2) A class has an association to another class and both classes were not mapped. For example, `Reservation` has an association to `Client` and both classes were not mapped. Hence, a PTI is added to the `Reservation` domain pattern that binds the association `client` to an *object template expression* which describes the characteristics of a specific `Client` object (line 5). The object template is empty, because its characteristics are already defined in the `Client` domain pattern, that occurs in another relation. Thus, the binding of the variable is delegated to the other relation by a *relation call expression* in the when statement (line 21). The parameter types of a *relation call* must conform to the types of the domains of the called relation. If conforming variables are available in the scope of the calling relation, they are also used as parameters in relation calls. Otherwise, any arbitrary instance of a required parameter type is used as a parameter. Exemplary, such arbitrary objects are determined by calling the OCL function *Guest.allInstances()->any(true)*.

To summarize, we have shown how a QVT transformation script can be generated automatically from the set of mappings. The next section introduces our implementation for the class model matcher and the QVT script generator.

5   Tool Support

We integrated our service description model normalization into the *Rich Service Description Language (RSDL) Workbench*, which allows to create, publish, and discover Rich Service Description Language (RSDL) specifications. The RSDL workbench is realized as a plug-in for the integrated development environment Eclipse and is under development at the University of Paderborn in the Collaborative Research Centre 901 *On-the-Fly Computing*. Our workbench uses the following third-party plug-ins: Papyrus[5] that provides a graphical editor for the UML parts of the specifications and Henshin[6] that provides a graphical editor that is used to model the VCs. The service discovery was realized as a Java API for RESTful Web Services (JAX-RS) by means of the Jersey framework[7].

Further, our class model matcher uses the Eclipse plug-in EMF Compare[8]. The indexing mechanism is based on the Jena framework[9] to read background ontologies, which are stored in a normalized form in a database. For the QVT script generation, the metamodel of the QVTd[10] project has been used. The transformation execution engine mediniQVT[11]

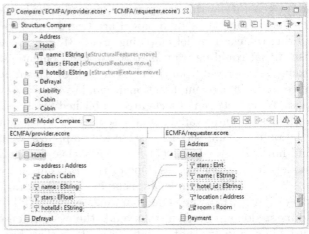

Fig. 11. Graphical User Interface (EMF Compare)

is leveraged to run the transformation in order to normalize the VCs. Fig. 11 shows the identified mappings between two class models of a service request and a service offer in the graphical user interface provided by EMF Compare.

---

[5] http://www.eclipse.org/papyrus/
[6] http://www.eclipse.org/henshin/
[7] https://jersey.java.net/
[8] http://www.eclipse.org/emf/compare/
[9] http://jena.apache.org/
[10] http://www.eclipse.org/mmt/qvtd
[11] http://projects.ikv.de/qvt

6   Related Work

Several research areas are related to the normalization of service description models: ontology and model matching, coupled model evolution, and service discovery. Concerning ontology matching, many approaches and systems have been (and still are) developed that allow to create mappings between heterogeneous ontologies or schemas. A nice overview of various approaches and the current state of research is provided by the survey [19].

A classification of matching approaches is provided by [11], which distinguishes between: static identity-based, signature-based, similarity-based, and language-specific matching approaches. According to this classification, our class model matching approach is a similarity-based matching approach, which additionally leverages background ontologies to identify synonyms, homonyms, as well as correspondences between classes with a similar ontological semantic.

In the following, we want to highlight three matching systems exemplary: EMF Compare identifies differences between different versions of the same Eclipse Modeling Framework (EMF) model and is therefore suited for an integration in version control systems to keep track of the model's evolution. The matching algorithm behind EMF Compare is related to [21]. However, without adaptations EMF Compare is not suited to match heterogeneous class models, because it does not recognize synonyms for example. The matching process of Scarlet [17] anchors the concepts to be matched in one or more background ontologies that were determined by external Semantic Web search engines. Next, a semantic relation between the matched concepts is inferred from the anchor concepts. However, similarity values are not computed. Furthermore, most of the matching systems consider only 1:1 mappings. An exception is e.g., AgreementMaker [4], which first computes all similarity values and afterwards a user selects the desired metrics and mapping cardinalities. Then, an algorithm is executed to compute an optimal solution on the weighted assignment problem. This algorithm is iteratively executed to obtain n:m mappings.

In the case of class models, Coupled Model Evolution (CME) addresses the problem, that object models become inconsistent when their class model evolves. In this regard, CME is related to the VCs normalization except that CME considers different versions of the class model, whereas VCs normalization considers heterogeneous class models. COPE [8] is an approach that keeps track of class model modifications and creates a history of changes. A migrator that is generated from this history applies the changes to the object models. COPE is not suited to normalize VCs, because typically no such change history is available for heterogeneous class models.

The service discovery approach that was introduced in this thesis relies on the approach of Huma et al. [10] that uses RSDL specifications [9]. Huma et al. also address heterogeneous data schemas: As a preparation for an automation of the heterogeneity resolution, the approach requires that local class models are manually mapped to a common global class model. Our approach aims to close this gap and automate this process as far as possible.

7   Conclusion and Future Work

In this paper, we introduced an holistic approach to overcome structural as well as terminological heterogeneity of service description models. Thereby, we enable the behavior-aware matching of service requests and services offers.

The main contributions of our work are as follows: In contrast to yet another structural model matcher, our class model matcher exploits domain-specific background ontologies that offer the opportunity to identify semantic relations between different class models. While the majority of existing matchers only consider 1:1 class correspondences, our matcher identifies also complex 1:n, n:1, and n:m correspondences that arise from different logical structuring or from different degrees of granularity. By representing identified class mappings in terms of QVT relations, we enable an automatic normalization of the behavioral model, which are typed over the class models.

In future work, we will conduct an extensive evaluation of our class model matcher in the course of the CRC 901 and by participating in the Ontology Alignment Evaluation Initiative (OAEI)[12] that aims for a systematic evaluation of matching systems.

Furthermore, we intent to address current limitations of our approach. Concerning the class model matcher these are the identification of mappings between attributes and classes as well as associations mappings. In the former case, an attribute in one class model does not necessarily correspond to another attribute, because the same information an attribute represents may be derived from a class. An example of the latter case is represented by a class that has more than one association to another class, where each represents a different role. In such situations association mappings are necessary.

Concerning the transformation script generation, multi-valued associations are not considered yet. The transformation allows to establish links to at most one object, whatever cardinality the respective association has. Furthermore, the class model matcher allows in fact to map attributes with different types. However, manual intervention is required to reasonably translate, e.g., an alphabetic to a numeric value. Finally, complex QVT relations appeared as a problem, because the more domains a relation has, the less likely it is that the domain patterns will match and the relation will hold. Further research is required to determine a proper number of maximal domains.

References

1. Meta Object Facility (MOF) 2.0 Query/View/Transformation Specification Version 1.1 (January 2011),
   http://www.omg.org/spec/QVT/1.1/PDF/
2. OMG Object Constraint Language (OCL) Version 2.3.1 (January 2012),
   http://www.omg.org/spec/OCL/2.3.1/PDF

---

[12] http://oaei.ontologymatching.org/

3. Aleksovski, Z., Klein, M., ten Kate, W., van Harmelen, F.: Matching Unstructured Vocabularies using a Background Ontology. In: Staab, S., Svátek, V. (eds.) EKAW 2006. LNCS (LNAI), vol. 4248, pp. 182–197. Springer, Heidelberg (2006)
4. Cruz, I.F., Antonelli, F.P., Stroe, C.: AgreementMaker: Efficient Matching for Large Real-World Schemas and Ontologies. Proc. of the VLDB Endowment 2(2), 1586–1589 (2009)
5. de Bruijn, J., Lausen, H., Polleres, A., Fensel, D.: The Web Service Modeling Language WSML: An Overview. In: Sure, Y., Domingue, J. (eds.) ESWC 2006. LNCS, vol. 4011, pp. 590–604. Springer, Heidelberg (2006)
6. Engels, G., Güldali, B., Soltenborn, C., Wehrheim, H.: Assuring Consistency of Business Process Models and Web Services Using Visual Contracts. In: Schürr, A., Nagl, M., Zündorf, A. (eds.) AGTIVE 2007. LNCS, vol. 5088, pp. 17–31. Springer, Heidelberg (2008)
7. Euzenat, J., Shvaiko, P.: Ontology Matching, vol. 18. Springer, Heidelberg (2007)
8. Herrmannsdoerfer, M., Benz, S., Juergens, E.: COPE - Automating Coupled Evolution of Metamodels and Models. In: Drossopoulou, S. (ed.) ECOOP 2009. LNCS, vol. 5653, pp. 52–76. Springer, Heidelberg (2009)
9. Huma, Z., Gerth, C., Engels, G., Juwig, O.: A UML-based Rich Service Description Language for Automatic Service Discovery of Heterogeneous Service Partners. In: CAiSE Forum, pp. 90–97 (2012)
10. Huma, Z., Gerth, C., Engels, G., Juwig, O.: Towards an Automatic Service Discovery for UML-based Rich Service Descriptions. In: France, R.B., Kazmeier, J., Breu, R., Atkinson, C. (eds.) MODELS 2012. LNCS, vol. 7590, pp. 709–725. Springer, Heidelberg (2012)
11. Kolovos, D.S., Ruscio, D.D., Pierantonio, A., Paige, R.F.: Different Models for Model Matching: An analysis of approaches to support model differencing. In: Proceedings of CVSM 2009 @ ICSE 2009, pp. 1–6. IEEE Computer Society (2009)
12. Maedche, A., Zacharias, V.: Clustering Ontology-based Metadata in the Semantic Web. In: Elomaa, T., Mannila, H., Toivonen, H. (eds.) PKDD 2002. LNCS (LNAI), vol. 2431, pp. 348–360. Springer, Heidelberg (2002)
13. Mendes, P.N., Jakob, M., Bizer, C.: DBpedia for NLP: A Multilingual Cross-domain Knowledge Base. In: Proc. of the 8th International Conference on Language Resources and Evaluation, LREC 2012 (2012)
14. Miller, G.A.: WordNet: A Lexical Database for English. Communications of the ACM 38(11), 39–41 (1995)
15. OWL-S Coalition. OWL-based Web Service Ontology (2006), http://www.ai.sri.com/daml/services/owl-s/1.2/
16. Rahm, E., Bernstein, P.A.: A survey of approaches to automatic schema matching. The VLDB Journal 10(4), 334–350 (2001)
17. Sabou, M., d'Aquin, M., Motta, E.: SCARLET: SemantiC RelAtion DiscoveRy by Harvesting OnLinE OnTologies. In: Bechhofer, S., Hauswirth, M., Hoffmann, J., Koubarakis, M. (eds.) ESWC 2008. LNCS, vol. 5021, pp. 854–858. Springer, Heidelberg (2008)
18. SAWSDL Working Group. Semantic Annotations for WSDL and XML Schema, SAWSDL (2007), http://www.w3.org/TR/2007/REC-sawsdl-20070828/
19. Shvaiko, P., Euzenat, J.: Ontology matching: State of the art and future challenges (2012)
20. Tarjan, R.E.: Data Structures and Network Algorithms, vol. 14. SIAM (1983)
21. Xing, Z., Stroulia, E.: UMLDiff: An Algorithm for Object-Oriented Design Differencing. In: Proc. of the 20th IEEE/ACM International Conference on Automated Software Engineering, pp. 54–65. ACM (2005)

Towards the Systematic Construction
of Domain-Specific Transformation Languages

Jesús Sánchez Cuadrado, Esther Guerra, and Juan de Lara

Universidad Autónoma de Madrid, Spain

Abstract. General-purpose transformation languages, like ATL or QVT, are the basis for model manipulation in Model-Driven Engineering (MDE). However, as MDE moves to more complex scenarios, there is the need for specialized transformation languages for activities like model merging, migration or aspect weaving, or for specific domains of wide use like UML. Such *domain-specific transformation languages* (DSTLs) encapsulate transformation knowledge within a language, enabling the reuse of recurrent solutions to transformation problems.

Nowadays, many DSTLs are built in an ad-hoc manner, which requires a high development cost to achieve a full-featured implementation. Alternatively, they are realised by an embedding into general-purpose transformation or programming languages like ATL or Java.

In this paper, we propose a framework for the systematic creation of DSTLs. First, we look into the characteristics of domain-specific transformation tools, deriving a categorization which is the basis of our framework. Then, we propose a domain-specific language to describe DSTLs, from which we derive a ready-to-run workbench which includes the abstract syntax, concrete syntax and translational semantics of the DSTL.

1 Introduction

Model transformations are central to MDE. Many transformation languages have been proposed and are widely used nowadays, e.g. ATL or QVT. We term these languages General-Purpose Transformation Languages (GPTLs), because their scope considers transformation of models, but they are not specific for particular tasks (like migration or refactoring) or domains (like UML or Petri nets).

We can use GPTLs to tackle a wide variety of scenarios, but in our experience, some transformation tasks become more natural and easier by using specialized transformation languages offering primitives tailored to the task to be solved. Examples of these tasks include model migration, promotion of models into meta-models, and aspect weavers for domain-specific languages. Similar to the benefits of using domain-specific languages over general-purpose ones in well-known domains, we claim that these transformation scenarios would benefit from Domain-Specific Transformation Languages (DSTLs). This is so as DSTLs make explicit domain knowledge that otherwise needs to be repeatedly embedded in transformations built with GPTLs or programming languages like Java.

Some works in the literature recognise the need for DSTLs [16,25,30]. However, there is a lack of methods and tools for their systematic engineering, including

J. Cabot and J. Rubin (Eds.): ECMFA 2014, LNCS 8569, pp. 196–212, 2014.

the definition of their abstract syntax, concrete syntax and semantics. While the design of domain-specific modelling languages is well understood and there is a plethora of workbenches to speed up their construction, this support is lacking for DSTLs. By offering such support, many transformation tasks can be recast as DSTLs instead of relying on ad-hoc solutions.

In this paper, we propose a design process and tool support for the systematic construction of DSTLs. First, we provide a suitable language to describe the DSTL abstract syntax. This language includes transformation-specific constructs like Mapping, ImperativeRule and Guard. From the description of the DSTL abstract syntax, we generate a MOF-based meta-model which is instantiated to describe concrete transformations, and an initial concrete syntax for the DSTL, tailored to the selected transformation constructs. Depending on the style of the DSTL (e.g. mapping-based or imperative), we also generate a scaffolding of the compilation into the Eclectic transformation virtual machine [7]. Eclectic is a family of transformation languages with different styles (e.g. target-oriented or mapping), and the languages to compile to are selected based on the primitives used in the DSTL description. Instead of relying on code generation to produce Eclectic code, we use model transformations, using a novel template-based technique. We illustrate our proposal with a DSTL for promotion transformations, showing the benefits w.r.t. a hand-made implementation of the DSTL.

Altogether, the contributions of the paper are: (i) the identification of domains and tasks where DSTLs make sense, based on a review of the literature, and (ii) a systematic process for the integral definition of DSTLs.

The paper is organized as follows. Sec. 2 presents an overview of different transformation tasks that would benefit from DSTLs, exposing useful features in each scenario. Sec. 3 introduces our approach and a running example. Sec. 4 presents our way to define the abstract and concrete syntax of DSTLs, while Sec. 5 explains how we specify their semantics. Sec. 6 shows tool support. Sec. 7 reviews related works and, finally, Sec. 8 concludes.

2   Domain Specific Transformation Languages

A DSTL is a transformation language designed for a specific transformation task (e.g. model merging), or restricted to work on special kinds of models (e.g., UML models). Its aim is not to be "universal", applicable to any transformation task, as languages like ATL or QVT are. On the contrary, DSTLs contain domain-specific primitives enabling a more succinct and intensional expression of the task to be performed, which frequently leads to simpler transformation models. Fig. 1 shows a scheme with the main features we require for DSTLs: restricted application context (fixed

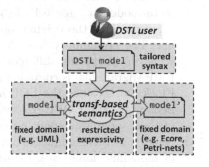

Fig. 1. DSTLs features

source or target) or expressivity (e.g. model migration), and syntax tailored to the specific task.

From the literature, we have identified two scenarios for DSTLs: a) transformation tools identified as DSTLs by their creators, built ad-hoc; and b) families of transformation tasks developed using GPTLs, which can be seen as an application area for creating a DSTL. In the first scenario, DSTLs are given semantics by building an interpreter, or by compiling into a general-purpose programming language (GPL), a GPTL or a virtual machine. Moreover, in either scenario, the source or target meta-model of the DSTL may be fixed. For instance, many applications have the recurrent need to transform from a variety of languages into a fixed one, like PROMELA or Petri nets [36] for verification purposes. The second scenario typically arises due to the recurrent need to transform from widely used languages, like UML or XML. These transformations are generally written from scratch using GPTLs or GPLs; however, developers would benefit from explicit linguistic support for the features and structure of the fixed language, which could be provided by DSTLs, leading to simpler transformations.

Next, based on a review of the literature (22 articles), we identify some specific transformation tasks where the availability of DSTLs and systematic means for their construction would be beneficial, pointing out the main features expected from such DSTLs. Table 1 shows a summary, gathering the two typical scenarios for DSTLs (DSTLs built in an ad-hoc way, and families of similar transformation tasks), whether the source or target meta-models of the DSTL should be fixed, if the DSTL is in-place, the main DSTL primitives, the kind of concrete syntax, and the language semantics given by the authors (i.e. the DSTL or tool has a compiler or interpreter, or a GPTL or GPL is used for execution).

1. *Promotion.* This kind of transformations transforms a model into a meta-model. When considering a particular meta-modelling technology, the target meta-model is fixed (e.g. Ecore). Most works in the literature [4,12,31] encode these transformations using textual GPTLs – like ATL or Tefkat [19] – or directly in Java. Based on these works, useful primitives in these DSTLs would be mappings, bindings and guards.

2. *Migration.* These transformations deal with the update of artefacts upon meta-model changes [6,15,26,34]. The source and target meta-models, which correspond to the original and evolved meta-models, are not fixed *a priori*. The community has identified the particularities and needs for this scenario, proposing different textual DSTLs for migration. For instance, EMFMigrate [34] is compiled into a transformation virtual machine, Epsilon Flock [26] extends the EOL imperative language to add migration-specific behaviour, and COPE [15] defines primitives for meta-model changes. Most of these languages adopt a mapping-based style for migration rules.

3. *Aspects.* Several languages have been proposed to define aspects for a variety of modelling languages, ranging from general-purpose like UML [17,35], to domain-specific ones like Petri nets [22,37] and Building Information Models (BIM) [18]. In most cases, aspects are defined using graphical patterns, thus pointcuts require pattern matching while advices and introductions imply

Table 1. Summary of features for DSTLs in different domains

	fixed src	fixed tar	in-place	main primitives	concrete syntax	semantics
scenario a: domain specific transformation languages, built ad-hoc						
Aspects [17,18,22,37]	√	√	√	pointcut (match) advice (creation) introduction (creation)	graphical patterns	interpreter
Bridges [5,9]	√	√		mapping queries, expressions	textual rules	interpreter
BIM [30]	√	√		aggregation	tabular	interpreter
Merging [2,11]				compare merge, compose	graphical mappings / textual rules	interpreter
Migration [6,15,26,34]	∼ᵃ			migrate differencing (default) copy guard	textual mappings with OCL expressions	interpreter / compilation to VM
Model inst. [1]				CRUD on refs.	tree-based editor	compilation to VM
scenario b: families of recurring transformation tasks						
Abstraction [28,29]	√	√	∼ᵇ	pattern-search merge, split filter	textual patterns / graphical patterns / imperative language	GPTL / GPL
HOT[33]	√	√	∼	queries, creation	textual rules	GPTL
Promotion [4,12,31]		√		mapping binding guard	textual mappings with OCL expressions	GPTL / GPL
Refactoring [20,21]	√	√	√	pattern-search merge, split pull, push	graphical patterns / imperative language	GPTL / GPL

ᵃ EMFMigrate uses a fixed source
ᵇ Some are in-place, some are out-place

pattern creation. In these works, the support for the application of aspects to models is ad-hoc or by compilation to graph transformation systems.

4. *Abstractions and refactorings.* Abstractions are model operations that produce simpler, higher-level views of a model. For example, [29] presents a catalogue of abstractions for workflow languages, and [28] for modelling languages. Abstractions need to identify relevant patterns (like sequences of nodes or connected components), and then filter, aggregate or merge those patterns. Similar needs are found in approaches for model refactoring [21] and model slicing [3]. While a few works use DSTLs [3], most approaches use GPTLs, like graph transformation [20].

5. *Model merging and composition.* These transformations merge two models through their common elements. There are specific DSTLs targeting this scenario [2,11], with primitives such as compare, merge or compose.

6. *Higher-order transformations (HOTs).* These are transformations of transformations, and they are developed using textual GPTLs or GPLs. HOT development would benefit from a DSTL specialized for a fixed input/output language (the meta-model of the transformation language, like ATL or QVT), and with higher-order primitives for the manipulation of the specific language (recurrent queries, concise creation of complex patterns, etc.). The proposal in [33], which adds a template language and a library of HOT-specific helpers to ATL, could be reified as a DSTL.

7. *Bridging technical spaces.* These works bridge a technical space, like grammarware [5] or databases [9], with the modelling space. Some authors use DSTLs [5,9] with specialised query languages for this purpose, but they are built in an ad-hoc manner. Other approaches use injectors and GPTLs (as in many examples of the ATL Transformation Zoo[1]).

8. *Others.* There are works describing DSTLs for other domains, like [30], which proposes a DSTL to calculate the budget for constructing a building from its model and its components' price. Another example is [1], which describes a DSTL for instantiating model templates using feature models. This DSTL permits specifying instantiation rules, like selecting or deleting references, and its semantics is given by a compilation into the ATC virtual machine.

In conclusion, many domain-specific transformations tasks are currently developed using GPTLs or programming languages, but may benefit from having a more specialized transformation language at hand. In fact, as discussed above, for some domains several DSTLs have already been built to facilitate developing such transformation tasks. This indicates a trend, which can be clearly witnessed in the domain-specific aspect languages area for which there is even an established dedicated workshop [10]. These DSTL approaches typically rely on subsets of the features of a GPTL (e.g. mappings, bindings), equipped with domain-specific constructs (e.g. support for special queries or expressions). The implementations range from totally ad-hoc approaches developed from scratch [5,9] to more systematic ones, e.g., based on compilation to a VM [34]. Most of the approaches try to reuse well-known syntaxes, such as OCL for queries or graph patterns for rewritings, but such syntaxes are normally encoded from scratch (notable exceptions are [26,34]). Likewise, the tool support quality varies (not shown in the table), but advanced features such as semantic autocompletion for textual editors and debugging support are missing since their implementation cost is high. Hence, we propose an approach to DSTL development in which the DSTL designer can mix and match features found in GPTLs, as well as adding special features of the domain. Then, our approach speeds up the development of the DSTL tooling using a model-driven approach.

3   Overview and Running Example

Building a DSTL involves the definition of its abstract syntax, concrete syntax (textual, graphical, tabular, or a mix of them), and execution semantics (typically, developing an interpreter or compiler). Additional elements may be needed, such as a scoping mechanism for variables and a type checker to ensure that the types used in a transformation belong to the meta-models being transformed.

These tasks are normally accomplished using an ad-hoc process without specialized tool support [16], which poses several inefficiencies. First, the abstract syntax has to be devised in terms of MOF constructs instead of using native

---

[1] http://www.eclipse.org/atl/atlTransformations/

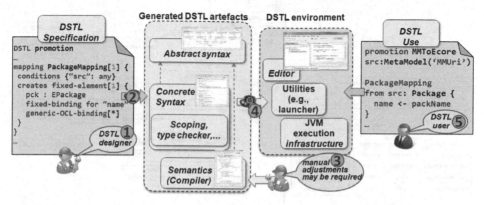

Fig. 2. Our proposal for the construction of domain-specific transformation languages

concepts of the transformation domain, like *rule* or *mapping*. Using these primitives facilitates defining the semantics of the DSTL. Secondly, reusing of typical transformation features, like the use of OCL to define navigation expressions or the integration of a type checker for meta-models has to be done manually. Finally, creating an efficient and stable execution infrastructure from scratch is a time consuming and error prone task.

Our solution to these problems is a framework for the development of DSTLs which provides automation for the generation of their abstract syntax, concrete syntax and execution semantics, specialised for the peculiarities of the DSTL. Fig. 2 shows the working scheme of our process. It illustrates the different steps in the construction of a DSTL for *promotion transformations* in order to facilitate the definition of this kind of transformations [4,12,31].

As a first step (*label 1*), the DSTL designer defines the primitives to be included in the DSTL. For this purpose, we make available a domain-specific language (DSL) which includes constructs close to the transformation domain. For instance, in the figure, the DSTL specification includes the definition of a mapping type that will be used to identify which source elements will be promoted into packages, and thus, the source of the mapping can be any element but the target is fixed (EPackage). The complete DSTL specification includes additional mapping types for the promotion of the other modelling elements.

Our DSL uses primitives of the transformation domain, facilitating the generation of several artefacts. In particular, from the DSTL specification, we generate an Ecore meta-model for the abstract syntax of the DSTL, a default implementation of its concrete syntax (including a scope resolutor and a type checker for the input/output meta-models), and an initial scaffolding of the compiler (*label 2*). The generated concrete syntax is tailored to the transformation primitives selected in the DSTL. The compiler synthesizes Eclectic code from the DSTL model, and this code is compiled into the Java Virtual Machine.

The designer can customize the default abstract syntax, concrete syntax and compiler (*label 3*), e.g., to add domain-specific functionality. Then, an environment for the language (*label 4*) is automatically created. The figure shows a DSTL user building a promotion transformation using the generated DSTL (*label 5*).

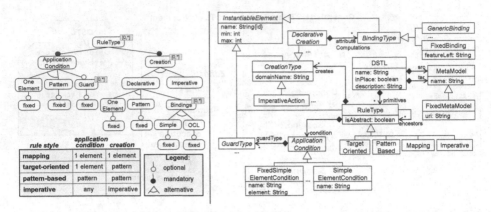

Fig. 3. Rule types (left). Meta-model for specifying DSTLs (excerpt) (right).

In the following two sections we detail the different steps in our framework.

4   Designing the Syntax

This section presents our DSL to define DSTLs (sec. 4.1), and the subsequent generation of the abstract and concrete syntax (secs. 4.2 and 4.3).

4.1   Describing the DSTL

As we have seen, DSTLs profit from native concepts of the transformation domain, and may combine features and operations found in GPTLs with domain-specific ones. Thus, the first step is choosing the required constructs for the language. For space reasons, in this paper, we focus on the selection and customization of suitable rule types, since it is normally the main construct of a DSTL, although in practice we have considered other aspects such as scheduling and tracing.

The left of Fig. 3 shows a feature diagram describing the kind of rules that could be constructed with our approach. All rule types have an application condition and creation directives. Application conditions identify the elements matched by the rule, which can be either a single element or a pattern, and can include guards. If the DSTL has a fixed source or target meta-model (as is the case in our running example for promotion transformations), then it is possible to use concrete types of the fixed meta-model in the DSTL definition; otherwise, the types are not fixed and should be specified in the transformation. Rule types also need to define the style of the creation directives, which can be either declarative or imperative. In the former case, the creation can be of a single element or of a graph pattern, and it is possible to define bindings for the attributes. For the elements marked with cardinality [0, *] in the feature diagram, the designer can fine-tune the number of times they can be instantiated (any number by default). The most common rule styles result from the combination of the features in this diagram (see the table at the bottom of the figure): *mappings* (rules that create one target element from one source element), *target-oriented rules* (creation of a target graph pattern from a source element), *pattern-based rules* (patterns in the rule source and target), and *imperative rules*.

We have realized these design choices in the meta-model shown to the right of Fig. 3. Its root class is DSTL, which defines if the transformation is in-place and the source and target meta-models. To indicate that a meta-model is fixed in the DSTL, we use the metaclass FixedMetaModel. A DSTL contains transformation primitives, which are instances of RuleType or its subclasses. A RuleType has an application condition (subclasses of ApplicationCondition) and creates elements (subclasses of CreationType). The application condition describes the conditions needed to apply the rule. For instance, FixedSimpleElementCondition is used for rule types having a single source element with a type from the fixed source meta-model. In this case, the rule will be applied to each element of type element. Conditions can also be of type SimpleElementCondition, and in this case, the rule will be applied to each element of the type specified in the specific transformation. Application conditions can have in addition a number of GuardTypes.

The elements a RuleType creates are configured through subclasses of Creation-Type, like ImperativeAction and DeclarativeCreation. The latter has subclasses for the creation of one or several elements of a fixed or variable type, and can be assigned BindingTypes for attribute computation. Two supported binding types are GenericBinding, where the target feature is specified in the particular transformation, and FixedBinding, which forces the binding of a particular feature of the created element.

The subtypes of RuleType force the use of specific combinations of application conditions, guards, creations and bindings, as shown in the feature diagram. For example, a Mapping has a FixedSimpleElementCondition or SimpleElementCondition, simple declarative creation, and any number of guards and bindings. It is possible to instantiate RuleType if no more specific rule type suits the needs of the DSTL.

Fig. 4 shows part of the definition of the promotion DSTL example, using a concrete syntax we have devised for the previous meta-model. Lines 1–3 declare the DSTL with a fixed target meta-model (ecore). Lines 5–7 declare an abstract mapping with a simple application condition (an element "src" of any available type from the input meta-model). Then, two concrete mapping types are declared that inherit from Common, and hence receive the same condition type. The PackageMapping mapping creates and element with fixed type EPackage from ecore, and has a fixed binding for the feature name and any number of arbitrary OCL bindings. Thus, a transformation using the DSTL will require providing the source type that will be transformed into an EPackage, a literal or an expression for the fixed binding, and any number of additional bindings.

4.2   Generating the Abstract Syntax

From the description of the desired primitives of the DSTL, we automatically generate a meta-model. As an example, Fig. 5 shows an excerpt of the generated meta-model for our promotion DSTL (package promotion). Each metaclass in this meta-model inherits from some base class in package dstlInst. This package

```
1  DSTL promotion                                    12      generic−OCL−binding[∗]
2  src: variable[name: "src" ]                       13   }
3  tar: fixed[name: "ecore", uri: "http://www.ecl..."]   14  }
4                                                     15  mapping ClassMapping[1..∗] extends Common {
5  abstract mapping Common {                          16    creates:
6    conditions { "src": any }                        17      fixed−element EClass[1] {
7  }                                                   18        fixed−binding for "name"
8  mapping PackageMapping[1] extends Common {          19        generic−OCL−binding[∗]
9    creates:                                         20      }
10     fixed−element EPackage[1] {                     21  }
11       fixed−binding for "name"                      22  ...
```

Fig. 4. Describing the promotion DSTL (excerpt)

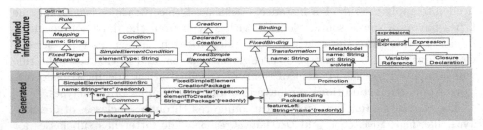

Fig. 5. Generated abstract syntax meta-model (excerpt)

contains infrastructure classes, like Mapping or Binding. For example, a root metaclass Promotion is added to the DSTL meta-model, which inherits from the infrastructure class Transformation. As the source meta-model is not fixed, the root metaclass includes a reference to MetaModel, to allow the specification of a source meta-model in the specific transformation. From the mapping PackageMapping in the DSTL definition, a metaclass with the same name is added to the meta-model. This metaclass inherits from FixedTargetMapping, which reflects the fact that it is a mapping and its target is fixed. The metaclass also inherits from Common in the same package, which defines the source application conditions for the mapping. Please note that our generator is able to select the base classes to inherit from based on the chosen primitives (e.g. Mapping in Fig. 3), but also on the selected rule features if the more general RuleType metaclass is used instead. For instance, a RuleType with one-element condition and one-element creation is automatically classified as a Mapping. Finally, we have a dedicated infrastructure package for OCL-like expressions. This is used in our running example, since the description of the promotion DSTL includes OCL-like bindings.

The rationale of this approach is that the simple description in Fig. 4 carries semantic information (e.g., on desired rule types), which can be automatically carried to a meta-model (see Fig. 5), and that is used to generate a default textual syntax (see Section 4.3), and a compiler for the DSTL (see Section 5).

4.3   Generating the Concrete Syntax

From the DSTL description, we also generate a concrete syntax. We support two styles: textual, and tabular for the case of DSTLs consisting of mappings only. The concrete syntax is based on Xtext, and is customized according to the transformation primitives used (mapping, pattern-based, imperative, etc.). For pattern-based rules, we generate a syntax for patterns similar to that of QVT-Relations. For mappings, we support two styles: one with simple rules (like the syntax of ATL) and another one with nested rules, available if the target meta-model is fixed. Nested rules follow the structure of composite associations of the target meta-model. Finally, if the DSTL uses an expression language (as in Fig. 5), the syntax of the expression language is integrated in the DSTL syntax.

Listing 1 shows an excerpt of a promotion transformation in concrete syntax, using the simple rules style generated by default. This syntax is more concise than e.g., ATL, as we have a fixed target language. Lines 4 and 9 instantiate the package and class mappings, where only the source of the mappings needs to be given. Lines 6 and 11 correspond to the mandatory name bindings.

```
1  promotion MM2Ecore
2  src: MetaModel("MetaModel")
3
4  PackageMapping
5  from src: MetaModel {
6     name <- packName
7  }
8
9  ClassMapping
10 from src: MetaClass {
11    name <- className
12 }
13 ...
```

Listing 1. Excerpt of promotion transformation in DSTL syntax.

```
1  eclectic promotion2ecore (src) -> (ecore)
2  navigation promotion_navigation (src)
3     def src!MetaModel.reachClasses
4        src!MetaClass.all_instances
5     end
6  end
7
8  mappings promotion ( src ) -> ( ecore )
9     from src : src!MetaModel to tgt : ecore!EPackage
10       tgt.eClassifiers <- src.reachClasses
11       tgt.name = src.packName
12    end
13
14    from src : src!MetaClass to tgt : ecore!EClass
15       tgt.name = src.className
16    end
17 end
```

Listing 2. Equivalent Eclectic transformation.

5 Designing the Semantics

To define the executable semantics of the DSTL, we establish a mapping to one or more languages of the Eclectic model transformation family [7]. In Eclectic, each language addresses a specific transformation concern, and can be combined with the other languages through composition mechanisms. Eclectic currently provides the following languages: *i)* a mapping language to define one-to-one and one-to-many correspondences, *ii)* a target-oriented language with object notation and explicit rule calls, *iii)* an attribution language to compute inherited and synthesized attributes, *iv)* a pattern matching language with object-notation, and *v)* a lower-level imperative language, which also plays the role of scheduling language and supports in-place transformation. Languages *i-iv* do not allow complex expressions, but these need to be encoded in navigation libraries. The combination of these languages covers many of the scenarios studied in Section 2.

Listing 2 shows the Eclectic transformation with equivalent semantics to the promotion transformation in Listing 1. The *mappings* language is naturally used to establish the correspondences declared in the promotion, where the target type is implicitly given by the rule type. Thus, the Eclectic mapping in lines 9–12 corresponds to the PackageMapping rule, while the mapping in lines 14–16 corresponds to the ClassMapping rule. Bindings for the name property have a direct correspondence in Eclectic. However, the promotion in Listing 1 does not specify how to relate classes to packages, that is, a binding to fill the reference eClassifiers in EPackage is missing. This is "domain knowledge" which gets inferred if no such binding is given. In this case, the default behaviour is generating the binding in line 10 (tgt.eClassifiers ← src.reachClasses), as well as the helper reachClasses within a navigation module which extends the source meta-model (lines 2–6).

To automate the generation of Eclectic code, we need a compiler from the abstract syntax of the promotion DSTL to Eclectic. The next subsection presents a novel facility to support the development of such compilers.

5.1   Code Generation by Template-Based Transformations

In the simplest case, a DSTL has a direct mapping to a language in Eclectic. A compiler would be conceptually straightforward to implement, but in practice, it is complex because it requires knowledge of the abstract syntax of Eclectic. An alternative is to generate plain-text (as in [16]), but this neither guarantees the syntactic correctness of the language, leading to a brittle solution, with cumbersome develop-generate-compile-test cycles, nor allows traceability between the DSTL and Eclectic (which is needed for a debugger).

To address this issue, we propose a *template language* targeting Eclectic. This is a model transformation language embedded into the Eclectic syntax, which facilitates specifying model-to-model transformations into Eclectic. In this way, transformation constructs are embedded in Eclectic syntax, like flow control constructs (iteration and condition) and placeholders, in the style of the Model-to-Text standard [23]. Most importantly, it is a safe template system, as the generated Eclectic programs are guaranteed to be syntactically correct. Hence, we obtain the benefits of model-to-text transformations (we use the concrete syntax of the target), and those of model-to-model transformations (we generate syntactically correct models).

Fig. 6 shows an excerpt of the compiler specification for the running example. Lines 2-3 declare the input and output meta-models that the generated transformation will use. The source meta-model in line 2 is obtained from the DSTL model using the expression between "[" and "/]". Line 5 defines a template to map each PromotionProgram to one or more Eclectic modules, so that we can use Eclectic syntax within the template to define a *mappings* transformation and a *navigation* module. The compiler specification does not process a promotion program, but it specifies the rules that the generated compiler will follow.

To create rules for packages, the specification iterates over the refPackageMapping reference to obtain all instances of PackageMapping (line 8). The target type EPackage is fixed (line 10), while the source type is given in the particular promotion transformation, and hence an expression is used (line 9). Lines 11–12 navigate the binding for name and generate the corresponding Eclectic binding. Lines 15-20 check whether a binding for reference eClassifiers has been provided (as it is optional), and if not, they generate a default behaviour to add classes (transformed by ClassMapping rules of the DSTL) to the package. This requires

```
 1  compiler spec promotion2ecore                 19        tgt.eClassifiers <- src.reachClasses
 2  input src : [ t.srcMeta.uri /]                20     [/if]
 3  output ecore : 'http://www.eclipse.org/emf/...'  21      // Generate OCL bindings...
 4                                                 22     [/for]
 5  [template createTransformation                 23     // Similar rules for classes, attributes, etc...
 6   (t : PromotionProgram) : EclecticModule]      24  end
 7    mappings promotion(src) -> (ecore)           25
 8     [ for m : t.refPackageMapping ]             26  navigation promotion_navigation(src)
 9        from src : src![ m.src.elementType /]     27   [ for m : t.refPackageMapping ]
10        to tgt : ecore!EPackage                  28      def src![ m.src.elementType /].reachClasses
11        [ b : m.CreatePackage.nameBinding /] ->  29        src![ t.refClassMapping.src.elementType /].
12          tgt.name = src.[ b.rightFeature /]     30          all_instances
13                                                 31      end
14      // Optional class binding                  32     // Helpers for expressions, OCL bindings...
15      [if b : m.CreatePackage.classBinding ]     33   [/for]
16        tgt.eClassifiers = src.[ b.rightFeature /] 34 end
17      [else]                                     35 [/template]
18        // Fixed behaviour to resolve classes
```

Fig. 6. Excerpt of the compiler specification for the promotion DSTL

generating a helper method, shown in lines 28-31, because Eclectic only allows complex expressions in navigation modules. This shows that the DSTL designer can provide sensitive defaults to simplify the common cases.

In our proposal, it is important to select the best suited Eclectic languages for the concerns of the DSTL, as a wise choice will facilitate the compiler specification, like in the example of Fig. 6. To help in this process, we have analysed how to map different DSTL features to Eclectic languages. Thus, given a DSTL specification, we generate a scaffolding of the compiler with a selection of languages. For instance, we generate most of the code in Fig. 6, except lines 19 and 28–31, which depend on design decisions of the DSTL designer. Even though we could generate the complete specification, we believe that the power of a DSTL comes from providing domain-specific constructs and sensible default behaviour. Such degree of generation coverage is possible because our DSL to specify DSTLs provides richer semantic information than a plain MOF meta-model.

6 Tool Support

We have developed a prototype tool demonstrating our approach. The left of Fig. 7 shows our workbench to build DSTLs, being used to define a more complete version of the promotion DSTL which includes application conditions with arbitrary patterns and guards. From this description, the workbench generates a configuration model (with similar purpose as the *genModel* in EMF) to fine-tune the generation process, e.g., giving names for packages, file extensions, and the type of concrete syntax. Currently, we support three styles for the concrete syntax: textual *simple rules* (like in ATL), textual *nested rules*, and tabular for mapping-based DSTLs. The configuration model contains sensible defaults, so that oftentimes there is no need for any adjustment.

Starting from the DSTL definition, an environment for it is generated using the configuration model. Fig. 7 shows the generated artefacts: an ecore meta-model, a compiler specification, and a fully functional Xtext project. The upper right of the figure shows the DSTL environment in action. It offers a customized

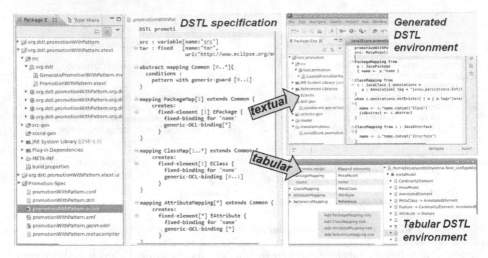

Fig. 7. DSTL workbench and generated environments

```
 1  mappings promotion (src) −> (ecore)          10  patterns promotion_pm(src)
 2  uses promotion_pm                            11    def classMappingPM() −> (c)
 3                                               12      c : in!JavaClass {
 4    from src : promotion_pm!classMappingPM     13        annotations = a : Annotation {
 5    to tgt : ecore!EClass                      14          tag = "javax.persistence.Entity"
 6      tgt.name = src.nameExpressionDelegate    15        }
 7    end                                        16      }
 8    ...                                        17    end
 9  end                                          18  end
```

Fig. 8. Excerpt of the Eclectic transformation for the example in Fig. 7

editor for promotion models, together with a compiler to synthesize Eclectic transformations from DSTL models.

In this example, the chosen rule types have patterns, guards and create fixed target elements. For this reason, we compile into the pattern-matching and mapping languages of Eclectic, which implies creating two transformation modules. To give an intuition of the composition style of Eclectic (detailed in [7]), Fig. 8 shows how the mapping transformation is seamlessly enriched with pattern matching. Line 2 imports the pattern matching module promotion_pm, used as a regular model where patterns are interpreted as types. In this way, the from part of the rule matches the pattern called classMappingPM (line 4), defined in the promotion_pm module (lines 10–18). Patterns use object-diagram syntax.

The tabular syntax shown in the bottom right of Fig. 7 permits configuring mappings by dragging types from the meta-model to the right to the appropriate mapping, and filling the required bindings.

While we are still working on a comprehensive evaluation of our approach, the preliminary results indicate that it can be used effectively to construct DSTL workbenches. As an estimation, from the specification for the running example, declaring 5 types of rules in 43 LOCs (without blank lines), we generate: a meta-model (15 classes and 31 features), a customized Xtext grammar (166 LOCS, 29 rules, and including an expression language), and a compiler specification (49 LOCS), which in turn becomes a compiler (250 LOCs). Thus, the advantage is that from a single compact specification, many heterogeneous complex artefacts are generated and integrated into a ready-to-run customized environment for the DSTL. Moreover, the generated compiler is guaranteed to generate syntactically correct transformations, as it is specified with a safe template system.

7 Related Work

Next, we review works targeting the construction of DSTLs. [16] proposes building a meta-model for the DSTL and its compilation into a GPTL (the Epsilon languages) using a model-to-text transformation. However, this work does not provide a systematic approach, or supports defining the abstract and concrete syntax of the DSTL, and there is no traceability between the DSTL models and the generated code. In [25], the authors propose a framework to generate Java-based execution engines for DSTLs, starting from en EBNF grammar. However, there is no description on how this can be achieved in practice.

The Epsilon languages can be seen as a set of DSTLs built atop the Epsilon Object Language [24]. While they leverage from EOL's concrete syntax and semantics, defining a new language needs from a manual extension of the ANTLR grammar and a manual Java encoding of the semantics. Instead, we provide model-driven support for the definition of the abstract syntax, concrete syntax and semantics, which does not restrict the DSTL to any specific concrete syntax, and specialised semantics can be given via compilation.

T-Core [32] is a set of scheduling primitives for model transformation, based on pattern-matching and rewriting. While T-Core's goal is to define flexible rule control languages, our approach describes DSTLs in an integral way. Nonetheless, T-Core's primitives could complement the ones in Eclectic. [27] proposes building DSTLs by mixing the concrete syntax of the involved DSLs (for the rule patterns), together with a transformation language. While that proposal leaves its realization to future work, it could be complemented with our approach, which focusses more on designing the transformation language itself.

Regarding the generation of transformation code, the ACG language is designed to generate bytecode for the ATL VM from a model. However, it is too low-level to use it for implementing DSTLs. Thus, in [33], a template language for ATL is proposed, with no implementation available. Even though still a prototype, our template language for Eclectic is, to our knowledge, the first safe template language to generate transformations (inspired by [13,14]).

Finally, [8] provided a feature-based survey of different transformation styles. Our work is based on a subset of common features found in GPTLs, focusing on those that are needed to implement DSTLs. Besides, we allow features to be chosen and combined into a DSTL.

8 Conclusions and Future Work

In this paper, we have proposed a systematic process and support for the creation of DSTLs. From a DSL-based description of the DSTL, several artefacts are generated: an abstract syntax, a (Xtext-based or tabular) concrete syntax and a compiler specification for an Eclectic language, or a combination of them. The proposal is supported by a prototype implementation.

This work opens a wide line of research, similar to the one initiated years ago by works dealing with the automated creation of environments for domain-specific modelling languages. In this respect, we plan to continue improving our prototype, and explicitly consider important aspects of transformations like bidirectionality or scheduling. We will also support other types of concrete syntax, including graphical ones, and plan to extend our template approach.

Acknowledgements. This work has been funded by the Spanish Ministry of Economy and Competitivity with project "Go Lite" (TIN2011-24139).

References

1. Avila-García, O., Estévez, A., Rebull, E.: Using software product lines to manage model families in model-driven engineering. In: SAC, pp. 1006–1011. ACM (2007)
2. Bézivin, J., Bouzitouna, S., Del Fabro, M.D., Gervais, M.-P., Jouault, F., Kolovos, D., Kurtev, I., Paige, R.F.: A canonical scheme for model composition. In: Rensink, A., Warmer, J. (eds.) ECMDA-FA 2006. LNCS, vol. 4066, pp. 346–360. Springer, Heidelberg (2006)
3. Blouin, A., Combemale, B., Baudry, B., Beaudoux, O.: Modeling model slicers. In: Whittle, J., Clark, T., Kühne, T. (eds.) MODELS 2011. LNCS, vol. 6981, pp. 62–76. Springer, Heidelberg (2011)
4. Brambilla, M., Fraternali, P., Tisi, M.: A metamodel transformation framework for the migration of WebML models to MDA. In: MDWE 2008, pp. 91–105 (2008)
5. Cánovas Izquierdo, J.L., García Molina, J.: Extracting models from source code in software modernization. SoSyM, 1–22 (2012)
6. Cicchetti, A., Di Ruscio, D., Pierantonio, A.: Managing dependent changes in coupled evolution. In: Paige, R.F. (ed.) ICMT 2009. LNCS, vol. 5563, pp. 35–51. Springer, Heidelberg (2009)
7. Sánchez Cuadrado, J.: Towards a family of model transformation languages. In: Hu, Z., de Lara, J. (eds.) ICMT 2012. LNCS, vol. 7307, pp. 176–191. Springer, Heidelberg (2012)
8. Czarnecki, K., Helsen, S.: Feature-based survey of model transformation approaches. IBM Systems Journal 45(3), 621–646 (2006)
9. Díaz, O., Puente, G., Izquierdo, J.L.C., Molina, J.G.: Harvesting models from web 2.0 databases. SoSyM 12(1), 15–34 (2013)
10. Domain-specific aspect languages workshop, http://www.dsal.cl/
11. Engel, K.-D., Paige, R.F., Kolovos, D.S.: Using a model merging language for reconciling model versions. In: Rensink, A., Warmer, J. (eds.) ECMDA-FA 2006. LNCS, vol. 4066, pp. 143–157. Springer, Heidelberg (2006)
12. Gallardo, J., Bravo, C., Redondo, M.A.: A model-driven development method for collaborative modeling tools. J. Net. Comp. App. 35(3), 1086–1105 (2012)
13. Heidenreich, F., Johannes, J., Seifert, M., Wende, C., Böhme, M.: Generating safe template languages. In: SIGPLAN Not, vol. 45, pp. 99–108. ACM (2009)
14. Hemel, Z., Visser, E.: PIL: A platform independent language for retargetable DSLs. In: van den Brand, M., Gašević, D., Gray, J. (eds.) SLE 2009. LNCS, vol. 5969, pp. 224–243. Springer, Heidelberg (2010)

15. Herrmannsdoerfer, M.: COPE – A workbench for the coupled evolution of meta-models and models. In: Malloy, B., Staab, S., van den Brand, M. (eds.) SLE 2010. LNCS, vol. 6563, pp. 286–295. Springer, Heidelberg (2011)

16. Irazábal, J., Pérez, G., Pons, C., Giandini, R.S.: An implementation approach to achieve metamodel independence in domain specific model manipulation languages. In: ICSOFT, pp. 62–69. SciTePress (2012)

17. Kienzle, J., Al Abed, W., Fleurey, F., Jézéquel, J.-M., Klein, J.: Aspect-oriented design with reusable aspect models. In: Katz, S., Mezini, M., Kienzle, J. (eds.) Transactions on AOSD VII. LNCS, vol. 6210, pp. 272–320. Springer, Heidelberg (2010)

18. Kramer, M., Klein, J., Steel, J.: Building specifications as a domain-specific aspect language. In: DSAL. ACM (2012)

19. Lawley, M., Steel, J.: Practical declarative model transformation with tefkat. In: Bruel, J.-M. (ed.) MoDELS 2005 Workshops. LNCS, vol. 3844, pp. 139–150. Springer, Heidelberg (2006)

20. Mens, T.: On the use of graph transformations for model refactoring. In: Lämmel, R., Saraiva, J., Visser, J. (eds.) GTTSE 2005. LNCS, vol. 4143, pp. 219–257. Springer, Heidelberg (2006)

21. Mens, T., Tourwé, T.: A survey of software refactoring. IEEE Trans. Software Eng. 30(2), 126–139 (2004)

22. Molderez, T., Meyers, B., Janssens, D., Vangheluwe, H.: Towards an aspect-oriented language module: Aspects for Petri nets. In: DSAL. ACM (2012)

23. OMG. MOFM2T 1.0, http://www.omg.org/spec/MOFM2T/1.0/

24. Paige, R.F., Kolovos, D.S., Rose, L.M., Drivalos, N., Polack, F.A.C.: The design of a conceptual framework and technical infrastructure for model management language engineering. In: ICECCS, pp. 162–171 (2009)

25. Reiter, T., Kapsammer, E., Retschitzegger, W., Schwinger, W., Stumptner, M.: A generator framework for domain-specific model transformation languages. In: ICEIS, pp. 27–35 (2006)

26. Rose, L.M., Kolovos, D.S., Paige, R.F., Polack, F.A.C.: Model migration with Epsilon Flock. In: Tratt, L., Gogolla, M. (eds.) ICMT 2010. LNCS, vol. 6142, pp. 184–198. Springer, Heidelberg (2010)

27. Rumpe, B., Weisemöller, I.: A domain specific transformation language. In: Models and Evolution (2011)

28. Selic, B.: A short catalogue of abstraction patterns for model-based software engineering. Int. J. Software and Informatics 5(1-2), 313–334 (2011)

29. Smirnov, S., Reijers, H.A., Weske, M., Nugteren, T.: Business process model abstraction: a definition, catalog, and survey. Dist. Par. Datab. 30(1), 63–99 (2012)

30. Steel, J., Drogemuller, R.: Domain-specific model transformation in building quantity take-off. In: Whittle, J., Clark, T., Kühne, T. (eds.) MODELS 2011. LNCS, vol. 6981, pp. 198–212. Springer, Heidelberg (2011)

31. Steel, J., Duddy, K., Drogemuller, R.: A transformation workbench for building information models. In: Cabot, J., Visser, E. (eds.) ICMT 2011. LNCS, vol. 6707, pp. 93–107. Springer, Heidelberg (2011)

32. Syriani, E., Vangheluwe, H.: De-/re-constructing model transformation languages. ECEASST, 29 (2010)

33. Tisi, M., Cabot, J., Jouault, F.: Improving higher-order transformations support in ATL. In: Tratt, L., Gogolla, M. (eds.) ICMT 2010. LNCS, vol. 6142, pp. 215–229. Springer, Heidelberg (2010)

34. Wagelaar, D., Iovino, L., Di Ruscio, D., Pierantonio, A.: Translational semantics of a co-evolution specific language with the EMF transformation virtual machine. In: Hu, Z., de Lara, J. (eds.) ICMT 2012. LNCS, vol. 7307, pp. 192–207. Springer, Heidelberg (2012)
35. Wimmer, M., Schauerhuber, A., Kappel, G., Retschitzegger, W., Schwinger, W., Kapsammer, E.: A survey on UML-based aspect-oriented design modeling. ACM Comput. Surv. 43(4), 28 (2011)
36. Winkler, U., Fritzsche, M., Gilani, W., Marshall, A.: Bob the builder: A fast and friendly model-to-petrinet transformer. In: Vallecillo, A., Tolvanen, J.-P., Kindler, E., Störrle, H., Kolovos, D. (eds.) ECMFA 2012. LNCS, vol. 7349, pp. 416–427. Springer, Heidelberg (2012)
37. Xu, D., Nygard, K.E.: Threat-driven modeling and verification of secure software using aspect-oriented petri nets. IEEE TSE 32(4), 265–278 (2006)

A MOF-Based Framework for Defining Metrics to Measure the Quality of Models

Tao Yue and Shaukat Ali

Certus Software V&V Center, Simula Research Laboratory, Norway
{tao,shaukat}@simula.no

Abstract. Controlled experiments in model-based software engineering, especially those involving human subjects performing modeling tasks, often require comparing models produced by experiment subjects with reference models, which are considered to be correct and complete. The purpose of such comparison is to assess the quality of models produced by experiment subjects so that experiment hypotheses can be accepted or rejected. The quality of models is typically measured quantitatively based on metrics. Manually defining such metrics for a rich modeling language is often cumbersome and error-prone. It can also result in metrics that do not systematically consider relevant details and in turn may produce biased results. In this paper, we present a framework to automatically generate quality metrics for MOF-based metamodels, which in turn can be used to measure the quality of models (instances of the MOF-based metamodels). This framework was evaluated by comparing its results with manually derived quality metrics for UML class and sequence diagrams and it has been used to derive metrics for measuring the quality of UML state machine diagrams. Results show that it is more efficient and systematic to define quality metrics with the framework than doing it manually.

Keywords: Quality Metrics, Controlled Experiments, Metamodel, and MOF.

1 Introduction

Empirical research in software engineering helps us understand how approaches, methodologies, tools, and techniques work. A controlled experiment is performed in a controlled environment (typically in a laboratory setting), to observe cause-effect relationships, where one or more variables are manipulated, other variables are controlled at fixed values and the effect is measured [1].

Controlled experiments in model-based software engineering often require the evaluation of models designed by human subjects (i.e., *Models Under Evaluation (MUE)*) by comparing them to models designed by experts (*reference models*). The comparison typically uses quality metrics that evaluate models from different quality aspects such as completeness and correctness. Based on the values of those metrics, calculated in those models, we determine how good the MUE is as compared to the reference model. A similar requirement arises when teachers of Software Engineering courses grade models designed by students. The assessment of those models is often done by comparing them to prepared solution models.

J. Cabot and J. Rubin (Eds.): ECMFA 2014, LNCS 8569, pp. 213–229, 2014.
© Springer International Publishing Switzerland 2014

In our recent works [2, 3] we conducted controlled experiments, which required manually defining metrics to compare MUEs with reference models for UML class and sequence diagrams. The definition of these metrics was found to be cumbersome and error-prone, mainly due to the complexity of the UML metamodel. Such a tedious experience encouraged us to simplify the definition of such metrics for any MOF-based modeling languages. MOF [4] is a standard defined by the Object Management Group (OMG) that allows defining metamodels. A metamodel describes the concepts and relationships of a modeling language (e.g., UML [5]) and guides the organization of data in models conforming to that language.

The main contribution of this paper is a generic framework to formally specify a number of quality measurements (*Completeness*, *Correctness*, *Redundancy*) for MOF-based modeling languages, which are sufficient to measure the quality of conforming models. The framework allows defining metrics at varying levels of complexity, ranging from coarse-grained metrics covering a subset of a metamodel to fine-grained ones covering an entire metamodel. The framework defines metrics using a language's metamodel, where there is access to the details of (possibly hundreds of) the language's concepts and their relationships. It allows selecting a subset of the metamodel (ignoring the rest) that should be considered for each metric. The framework also provides the flexibility to specify weights on the metamodel details, mainly for the purpose of prioritizing the importance of these details relative to the needs of the specific evaluation objectives of the controlled experiments.

We evaluate our framework in two ways. First, we used it to define a set of metrics for evaluating UML state machines, which were then applied to two experiments [6, 7]. Second, we defined metrics for UML class and sequence diagrams using the framework. Automatically generated metrics were then compared with the manual ones for two experiments [8]. Result show that the framework-defined metrics are consistent with the manually developed ones but much more efficient and systematic to define. The rest of the paper is organized as follows. Section 2 presents background, Section 3 presents the conceptual model of the framework, whereas Section 4 provides the framework. Section 5 presents our evaluation, and the related work is reviewed in Section 6 and Section 7 concludes the paper.

2   Background

In this section, we will give a background discussion on the Ecore metamodel [8]—a well-known implementation of the MOF metamodel. Then we discuss the simplified UML state machine metamodel, which will be used as the running example to illustrate our quality measurement framework (Section 4).

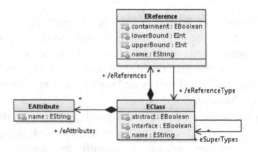

Fig. 1. A simplified Ecore model

A simplified subset of the Ecore metamodel is provided in Fig. 1. It contains three metaclasses: EClass, EAttribute, and EReference. EClass is identified by name and a set of contained EAttributes. EReference is used to model associations between classes. A reference is identified by its name and has a type that must be an instance of EClass (i.e., the association from EReference to EClass with role name eReference-Type). An important attribute of EReference is containment, which indicates whether an association is a composition association (when containment is 'true').

Fig. 2 shows a part of the EMF implementation of the UML2 state machine metamodel. It consists of different metaclasses such as StateMachine, Region, State, and Transition, which are instances of EClass, as indicated by the stereotype <<eClass>> applied. Each metaclass consists of instances of EAttribute. For example, the State metaclass has four instances of EAttribute: isComposite, isOrthogonal, isSimple, and isSubmachineState. A metaclass may have instances of EReference. For example, the StateMachine metaclass has an instance of EReference referring to the metaclass Region with the role name as region. This is shown as a composition association between StateMachine and Region.

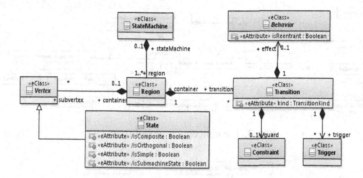

Fig. 2. EMF Implementation of the UML state machine metamodel (excerpt)

3   Conceptual Model

This section presents a conceptual model as UML class diagrams shown in Fig. 3 and Fig. 4, to define the key concepts of our quality framework and their relationships. As shown in Fig. 3, ModelUnderEvaluation (e.g., UML models) has different Views (e.g., UML sequence diagrams). An MUE contains a set of model elements (i.e., MUE ModelElement). If such a model element contains other model elements (e.g., via UML Composition), it is an instance of CompositeElement, otherwise it is an instance of AtomicElement. ReferenceModel is a model designed by experts and used to evaluate models designed by experiment subjects. We compare ModelUnderEvaluation with ReferenceModel using our framework. Similar to ModelUnderEvaluation, ReferenceModel is also composed of a set of REF ModelElements.

A model element in MUE can be evaluated as MatchedElement, CorrectElement, or RedundantElement. If a modeling element *partially or fully* matches with a modeling element in the corresponding reference model, then it is a MatchedElement. Interpretations of "matching" may be different in other contexts and are determined by experiment designers. For example, when evaluating class diagrams, a matched class means that this class has the same or similar name as a class in the reference class diagram [3]. Here, the class name is the key to determine whether the class is a matched element. It is also possible that several elements match to an element with a different type. For example, class A (e.g., "AccountName") and an association between it and another class (class B) (e.g., "BankAccount") in a class diagram under evaluation might match to an attribute of class B (i.e., "AccountName" is an attribute of "BankAccount" in the reference model). A `CorrectElement` means that the element under evaluation is *fully* matched to a model element in the reference model, which implies that all the properties of the element are all correctly matched to the properties of the matching element in the reference model. With this definition, `CorrectElement` is a special case of `MatchedElement`. A `RedundantElement` is a model element under evaluation that does not match to any element in the reference model.

The quality of a MUE is evaluated from three aspects: `Correctness`, `Completeness`, and `Redundancy` (Fig. 4). Note that our proposed evaluation framework only applies to controlled experiments with needs to compare MUEs with a reference model. Hence, the definition of these three evaluation aspects is based on this context.

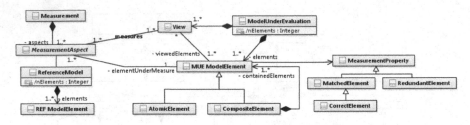

Fig. 3. The conceptual model (part 1)

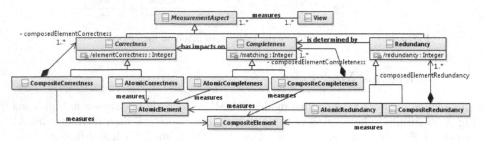

Fig. 4. The conceptual model (part 2)

The completeness of each model element contained by a view contributes to the overall `Completeness` of the view. For example, the completeness of a class diagram is calculated based on the completeness of each element contained in the class diagram. `AtomicCompleteness` measures the completeness of an atomic element while `CompositeCompleteness` measures the completeness of a composite element. An atomic element is a model element that does not contain any reference to any model element including self-references; otherwise it is a composite model element. The calculation of `CompositeCompleteness` of a composite element depends on the completeness of its contained model elements. The derivation of the attribute `matching` of `AtomicCompleteness` is formally specified using the OCL expression shown in Fig. 5.

If the atomic element is a matched element, then the value of matching is 1, else 0. Attribute matching of CompositeCompleteness is calculated as the average of the completeness of all of the modeling elements contained by the composite element.

```
Context AtomicCompleteness::matching:Integer
init:    -1
derive: if self.class.elementUnderMeasure.oclAsType(AtomicElement).
              measurementProperty.oclIsType(MatchedElement)
        then 1 else 0 endif
Context CompositeCompleteness::matching:Integer
init:    -1
derive: (self.class.elementUnderMeasure.oclAsType(CompositeElement).
           containedElements->select(c|c.measurementProperty.
           oclIsType(MatchedElement))->collect(mElement|mElement->
           oclAsType(Completeness).matching)->sum())
              /(self.class.composedElementCompleteness->size()))
```

Fig. 5. Formalization of AtomicCompleteness and CompositeCompleteness

Completeness has impact on Correctness. In other words, the calculation of correctness of a view relies on its completeness. This is because the measurement Correctness only makes sense when a model element under evaluation is a matched modeling element. Therefore, the overall correctness of a view is based on the proportion of the correctness of the matched elements, which is however determined by the measurement of Completeness. The Correctness of a view is measured by the correctness of each matched model element in the view. AtomicCorrectness measures the correctness of an atomic element, while CompositeCorrectness measures the correctness of a composite element. The calculation of CompositeCorrectness of a composite element depends on the correctness of its contained model elements. The derivation of the attribute elementCorrectness of AtomicCorrectness is formally specified using the OCL expression as shown in Fig. 6: If the atomic element is a correct element, then the value elementCorrectness is 1, else 0. Attribute elementCorrectness of CompositeCorrectness is calculated as the average of the correctness of all of its contained modeling elements.

```
Context AtomicCorrectness::elementCorrectness:Integer
init:    -1
derive: if self.class.elementUnderMeasure.oclAsType(AtomicElement).
           measurementProperty.oclIsType(CorrectElement) and
            self.class.elementUnderMeasure.measurementProperty.oclIsType(MatchedElement)
        then 1 else 0 endif
Context CompositeCorrectness::elementCorrectness:Integer
init:    -1
derive: (self.class.elementUnderMeasure.oclAsType(CompositeElement).
           containedElements->select(c|c.elementUnderMeasure.measurementProperty.
           oclIsType(MatchedElement) and c.elementUnderMeasure.measurementProperty.
           oclIsType(CorrectElement))->collect(mElement|mElement.
           oclAsType(Correctness).elementCorrectness)->sum())
              /(self.class.composedElementCorrectness->size()))
```

Fig. 6. Formalization of AtomicCorrectness and CompositeCorrectness

Redundancy of a view is measured by the number of redundant model element in the view. AtomicRedundancy measures the redundancy of an atomic element while CompositeRedundancy measures the redundancy of a composite element. The calculation of CompositeRedundancy of a composite element depends on the redundancy of its contained model elements. The derivation of attribute redundancy of AtomicRedundancy and CompositeRedundancy is formally specified using the OCL expressions as shown in Fig. 7. If the atomic element is redundant, the value of `redundancy` is 1, else 0. Attribute `redundancy` of `CompositeRedundancy` is calculated as the average of the redundancy of all of the modeling elements contained by the composite element.

```
Context AtomicRedundancy::redundancy:Integer
init:    -1
derive:  if self.class.elementUnderMeasure.oclAsType(AtomicElement).
             measurementProperty.oclIsType(RedundantElement)
         then 1 else 0 endif
Context CompositeRedundancy::redundancy:Integer
init:    -1
derive:  (self.class.elementUnderMeasure.oclAsType(CompositeElement).compositeElement
         .containedElements->select(c|c.elementUnderMeasure.measurementProperty.
         oclIsType(RedundantElement))->collect(mElement|mElement.redundancy)->sum()
             )/(self.class.composedElementRedundancy->size())
```

Fig. 7. Formalization of AtomicRedundancy and CompositeRedundancy

4   Quality Measurement Framework

An overview of our framework is shown as a UML activity diagram in Fig. 8. The first activity (A1) is that experts define the QMM3 metrics on the MOF metamodel. In the second activity (A2), a user is asked to select a subset of the MOF-based metamodel (M2), whose model elements will be used to derive the QMM2 metrics. This step provides the user an opportunity to select only important model elements to evaluate and omit the others. If the user decides to keep all the model elements in the M2 level metamodel for evaluation, then this step can be skipped. Step A3 provides the user an opportunity to define weights for model elements of the selected subset of the MOF-based metamodel. For example, if the user considers that `Class` is more important than `Association` when UML class diagrams are evaluated, then more weight can be

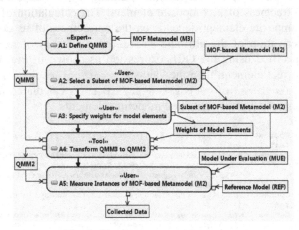

Fig. 8. The measurement framework

assigned to `Class` than to `Association`. Step A4 takes the user selected subset of the MOF-based metamodel and the user specified weights as input and automatically transforms the QMM3 metrics into QMM2 metrics. This step will be described in detail in Section 4.2. In A5, the user takes input QMM2, a model under evaluation (MUE) and a reference model (REF), which are both instances of the MOF-based metamodel, measures the quality of MUE against REF, and generates values for the QMM2 metrics (*Collected Data*).

In the rest of the section, we first define the QMM3 metrics (A1) (Section 4.1), followed by detailed discussion of the transformation from QMM3 to QMM2 (activities A2, A3 and A4) (Section 4.2).

4.1   Definition of QMM3

The MOF level metrics, also called QMM3, are specified in Fig. 9, Fig. 10, and Fig. 11 using UML class diagrams and OCL expressions. The definition of QMM3 is based on the Ecore metamodel (Fig. 1). An instance of EClass consists of a set of instances of EAttribute and/or EReference; therefore, the calculation of the formula for QMM3 metric EClassCompleteness (or EClassCorrectness) depends on the QMM3 metrics EAttributeCompleteness and EReferenceCompleteness (or EAttributeCorrectness, and EReferenceCorrectness). Each instance of EReference refers to an instance of EClass as its reference type; therefore the calculation of the formula of the QMM3 metric EReferenceCompleteness (or EReferenceCorrectness) depends on EClassCompleteness (or EClassCorrectness).

In Fig. 9, each Completeness metric has an attribute representing the formula used to calculate formula::Real. EAttributeCompleteness and EReferenceCompleteness have another attribute (value:Integer) representing the value of the completeness of an instance of EAttribute or EReference. If an instance of EAttribute matches to an instance of EAttribute of the reference model, the value of the attribute value of EAttributeCompleteness is assigned to be 1, otherwise 0. Metric EClassCompleteness has five operations, defined for the convenience of specifying the formulas of the metrics and they should be executed when transforming QMM3 to QMM2. These five operations are specified using OCL expressions below:

```
context EClassCompleteness::getNumberOfEAttributes (): Integer
pre      init: 0
post     result: self.class.eAttributeCompleteness->size()
context EClassCompleteness::getNumberOfEReferences (): Integer
pre      init: 0
post     result: self.class.eReferenceCompleteness->size()
context EClassCompleteness::getAttributeCompleteness (): Integer
pre      init: 0
post     result: self.class.eAttributeCompleteness->collect().value->sum()
                 /getNumberOfEAttributes()
context EClassCompleteness::getReferenceCompleteness (): Integer
pre      init: 0
post     result: self.class.eReferenceCompleteness->collect().value->sum()
                 /getNumberOfEReferences()
context EClassCompleteness::caculateFormula() : Real
pre      init: 0.0
post     result: (getNumberOfEAttributes()*getAttributeCompleteness()+
                 +getNumberOfEReferences()*getReferenceCompleteness())
               /(getNumberOfEAttributes()+getNumberOfEReferences())
```

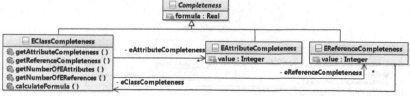

Fig. 9. Definition of Completeness (QMM3)

The first two operations of class `EClassCompleteness` obtain the total number of the instances of `EAttribute` and `EReference`, contained by an instance of `EClass`. Operations `getAttributeCompleteness()` and `getReferenceCompleteness()` obtain the values of the completeness of all the instances of `EAttribute` and `EReference` contained by the instance of `EClass`, respectively. The formula of `EClassCompleteness` is calculated, through operation `calculateFormula()`, based on the proportions of the completeness of all the instances of `EAttribute` and `EReference` contained by the instance of `EClass`.

Fig. 10 specifies the definition of correctness. The same pattern as for the metrics on completeness (Fig. 9) is followed. The only difference is that operation `getClassCompleteness()` is defined to obtain the completeness of an instance of `EClass` for the purpose of calculating the correctness of the instance, based on the reason explained in Section 3. The specification of the six operations of `EClassCorrectness` is provided below as OCL expressions:

```
context EClassCorrectness::getNumberOfEAttributes (): Integer
pre     init: 0
post    result: self.class.eAttributeCorrectness->size()
context EClassCorrectness::getNumberOfEReferences (): Integer
pre     init: 0
post    result: self.class.eReferenceCorrectness->size()
context EClassCorrectness::getAttributeCorrectness (): Integer
pre     init: 0
post    result: self.class.eAttributeCorrectness->collect().value->sum()
               /getNumberOfEAttributes()
context EClassCorrectness::getReferenceCorrectness (): Integer
pre     init: 0
post    result: self.class.eReferenceCorrectness->collect().value->sum()
               /getNumberOfEReferences()
context EClassCorrectness::getClassCorrectness (): Real
pre     init: 0.0
post    result: self.class.eClassCorrectness.formula
context EClassCorrectness::caculateFormula() : Real
pre     init:    0.0
post    result: ((getNumberOfEAttributes()*getAttributeCorrectness()+
               +getNumberOfEReferences()*getReferenceCorrectness())
              /(getNumberOfEAttributes()+getNumberOfEReferences()))*
               getClassCompleteness()
```

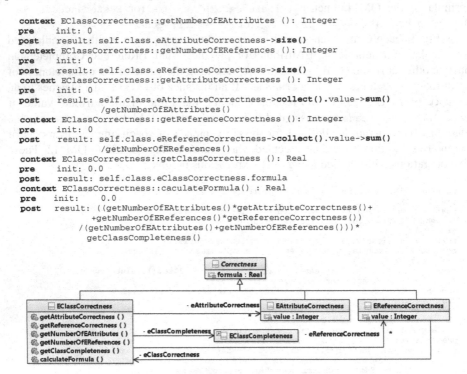

Fig. 10. Definition of Correctness (QMM3)

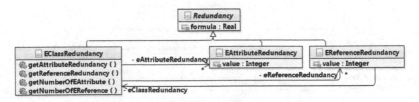

Fig. 11. Definition of Redundancy (QMM3)

Fig. 11 shows the definition of redundancy of QMM3. `EClassRedundancy` is very similar to `EClassCompleteness`. The only difference is that we check redundancy in an `EClass` (contained elements that do not match to any model element in a reference model) based on the redundancy in its contained `EAttribute` and `EReference`. The specification of the five operations of `EClassRedundancy` is provided below:

```
context EClassRedundancy::getNumberOfEAttributes (): Integer
pre    init: 0
post   result: self.class.eAttributeRedundancy->size()
context EClassRedundancy::getNumberOfEReferences (): Integer
pre    init: 0
post   result: self.class.eReferenceRedundancy->size()
context EClassRedundancy::getAttributeRedundancy (): Integer
pre    init: 0
post   result: self.class.eAttributeRedundancy->collect().value->sum()
                /getNumberOfEAttributes()
context EClassRedundancy::getReferenceRedundancy (): Integer
pre    init: 0
post   result: self.class.eReferenceRedundancy->collect().value->sum()
                /getNumberOfEReferences()
context EClassRedundancy::caculateFormula() : Real
pre    init: 0.0
post   result: (getNumberOfEAttributes()*getAttributeRedundancy()+
                +getNumberOfEReferences()*getReferenceRedundancy())
             /(getNumberOfEAttributes()+getNumberOfEReferences())
```

4.2 Transformation of QMM3 to QMM2

We use the UML state machine metamodel (Section 2) as a running example to illustrate the automated transformation of QMM3 to QMM2. The QMM2 metrics for evaluating the completeness of UML state machines (named as QMM2-SM) is partially presented as the class diagram in Fig. 12. The class diagram is derived from the UML state machine metamodel (Fig. 2) and was extended with additional QMM3 quality metric information through stereotypes: <<EClassCompleteness>>, <<EAttributeCompleteness>> and <<EReferenceCompleteness>>.

The transformation from the QMM3 metrics to M2 level metrics for MOF-based metamodels contains the following three steps: 1) Our tool automatically identifies instances of `EClass` and their relationships, 2) User manually selects model elements in the MOF-based metamodel to be measured and specifies their weights, and 3) Our tool automatically transforms the QMM3 metrics into M2 level metrics (QMM2) for the MOF-based metamodel. In the rest of the section, we discuss each of these steps.

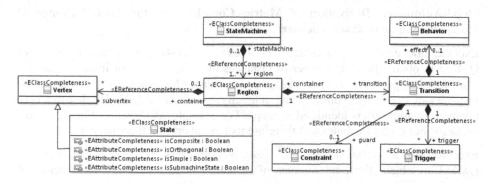

Fig. 12. QMM2 for UML State Machine (QMM2-SM)

Step1-Automated Identification of Instances of EClass and their Relationships.
First, identify instances of EClass ($S_{InstancesOfEClass}$) of the MOF-based metamodel.
For example, as shown in Fig. 2, all the classes in the class diagram are instances of
EClass (i.e., stereotyped with <<eClass>>). Second, for each instance I belonging to
$S_{InstancesOfEClass}$, identify the instances of EAttribute and EReference, either directly or
indirectly contained by I. By 'indirectly', we mean the instances of EAttribute and
EReference that are inherited from the direct and indirect superclasses of I if there are
any. For example, if I is State then it indirectly inherits, for instance, the association
between Region and Vertex which is a direct superclass of State. Direct model elements are the ones that are directly contained in an instance of EClass. For example,
if I is State then it has a direct attribute called isComposite, which is an instance of
EAttribute. One can see that these two steps can be easily automated by simply querying the MOF-based metamodel.

Step2-User Inputs. In this step, a user has an option to get involved in the transformation process by selecting model elements to be measured and assigning weights to
them. For example, if the completeness of Transition is measured as the average
completeness of Guard, Trigger, and Effect, then the weights assigned to each of the
three model elements contained by Transition is 1. Otherwise, if this set of values
{0.5, 1.5, 1} is assigned to Guard, Trigger, and Effect, respectively, then it means
that Trigger (weight =1.5) is considered more important than Effect (weight = 1)
and Guard (weight = 0.5). Notice that the sum of the weights should always be equal
to the number of weighted model elements. If the user does not assign any weights,
then all weights are automatically assigned to be 1. Notice that the containment relationship between Transition and all its contained elements (e.g., Guard, Trigger,
and Effect) is automatically derived in Step1. Based on the instantiation algorithm
specified in Step1, we can make sure that all the contained elements of a composite
element are automatically derived and metrics can therefore be systematically defined. No single element would be left out. The user can also select the model elements to be measured. For example, the user might think it is not important to take
attribute isComposite of State into the account when calculating the completeness or
correctness of State, then the user can unselect this attribute and therefore our algorithm will not take it into the account when the metrics are generated (Step3). By
default, all model elements are taken into the account.

**Step3-Automated Derivation of Metric Completeness for Each Instance of
EClass belonging to SInstancesOfEClass.**

Execute operation getNumberOfEAttributes() of class EClassCompleteness of
QMM3 to obtain the total number of instances of EAttribute, for instance I of EC-
lass belonging to SInstancesOfEClass. $I\_numberOfEAttributes$ = number of the
instances of EAttribute directly and indirectly contained by I. Notice that this containment relationship is identified in Step1. For example, as shown in Fig. 12, State
contains four direct attributes and therefore its I_numberOfEAttributes = 4.

Execute operation getNumberOfEReferences() of class EClassCompleteness of
QMM3 to obtain the total number of instances of EReference for instance I.
I_numberOfEReferences = number of the instances of EReference contained by I. For

example, as shown in Fig. 12, `Transition` contains four instances of `EReference` (e.g., the association to `Constraint`), which are all stereotyped with <<EReference-Completeness>>, then I_numberOfEReferences = 4.

Execute operation `getAttributeCompleteness()` of class `EClassCompleteness` of QMM3 to obtain the completeness of all the instances of `EAttribute` for instance I.

$$I_{eAttributeCompleteness} = \frac{\sum_{a=1}^{I_{numberOfEAttributes}} W_a * Completeness_a}{I_{numberOfEAttributes}}, \text{ where } Completeness_a$$

denotes the completeness of attribute a. W_a denotes the weight assigned to attribute a. As we discussed in the conceptual model (Section 3), an instance of `EAttribute` must be an atomic element; therefore its completeness is determined by `AtomicComplete-ness`. For example, the completeness of `State` can be calculated as the average value of the completeness of all its contained attributes (e.g., `isComposite`), if the weight assigned to each of the attributes is 1. For example, the following formula can be generated for calculating the completeness of all the attributes of `State` (stereotyped with <<EAttributeCompleteness>>), based on the metamodel shown in Fig. 12.

$$S_a = \frac{W_{isComposite} * C_{isComposite} + W_{isOrthogonal} * C_{isOrthogonal} + \cdots}{4}, \text{ where } W_{isComposite} \text{ and}$$

$W_{isOrthogonal}$ are the weights assigned to attributes `isComposite` and `isOrthogonal`. $C_{isComposite}$ and $C_{isOrthogonal}$ are their completeness, respectively. The sum of the weights assigned to the four attributes should be equal to the number of the attributes.

Execute *operation* `getReferenceCompleteness()` of class `EClassCompleteness` of QMM3 to obtain the completeness of all the instances of `EReference` for instance

$$I. I_{eReferenceCompleteness} = \frac{\sum_{r=1}^{I_{numberOfEReferences}} W_r * Completeness_r}{I_{numberOfEReferences}}, \text{ when the value of}$$

the attribute `composition` of the instance of `EReference` is true, then $Completeness_r$ denotes the completeness of the instances of the `EClass` (c) referred to by the reference r and W_r is the weight assigned to it. In other words, $Completeness_r$ is equal to the average value of `EClassCompleteness` of each instance of c. Otherwise, $Completeness_r$ denotes the completeness of the reference r and W_r is the weight assigned to it. For example, the following formula can be generated for the completeness of all the references of `Transition`, based on the metamodel in Fig. 12. $S_r = \frac{W_{effect} * C_{effect} + W_{trigger} * C_{trigger} + W_{guard} * C_{guard} + W_{container} * C_{container}}{4}$, where

W_{effect}, $W_{trigger}$, W_{guard} and $W_{container}$ are the weights assigned to effect, trigger, guard and the reference to `Region` (with role name `container`), respectively. C_{effect}, $C_{trigger}$, C_{guard} and $C_{container}$ are the average values of the completeness of the effect, triggers, guard of a transition and its containment by a region. The sum of the weights assigned to the attributes should be equal to the number of the attributes.

Execute operation `getFormula()` *of class* `EClassCompleteness` *of QMM3 to obtain the completeness of the instance I.*

$$I_{eClassCompleteness} = \frac{I_{numberOfEAttributes} * I_{eAttributeCompleteness} + I_{numberOfEReferences} * I_{eReferenceCompleteness}}{I_{numberOfEAttributes} + I_{numberOfEReferences}}$$

Step4-Automated Derivation of Metric `Correctness` for Each Instance of `EClass` belonging to `sInstancesOfEClass`. This step is very similar to the step of deriving metric `Completeness` for instances of `EClass`, described previously.

Execute *operation* `getNumberOfEAttibute()` of class `EClassCorrectness` of QMM3 to obtain the total number of instances of `EAttribute` for instance I of `EClass` belonging to `SInstancesOfEClass`. *I_numberOfEAttributes* = number of the instances of `EAttribute` directly and indirectly contained by I. Notice that this containment relationship is identified in Step1.

Execute *operation* `getNumberOfEReferences()` of class `EClassCorrectness` of QMM3 to obtain the total number of instances of `EReference` for instance I. *I_numberOfEReferences = number of the instances of* `EReference` *contained by I.*

Execute *operation* `getAttributeCorrectness()` of class `EClassCorrectness` of QMM3 to obtain the `correctness` of all the instances of `EAttribute` for instance I.

$$I_{eAttributeCorrectness} = \frac{\sum_{a=1}^{I_{numberOfEAttributes}} W_a * Correctness_a}{I_{numberOfEAttributes}}$$, where Correctness$_a$ denotes the correctness of attribute a. W_a denotes the weight assigned to a. Correctness of an instance of `EAttribute` is determined by `AtomicCorrectness` (Section 3).

Execute operation `getReferenceCorrectness()` of class `EClassCorrectness` of QMM3 to obtain the completeness of all the instances of `EReference` for instance I.

$$I_{eReferenceCorrectness} = \frac{\sum_{r=1}^{I_{numberOfEReferences}} W_r * Correctness_r}{I_{numberOfEReferences}}$$, when the value of attribute `composition` of the instance of `EReference` is true. *Correctness$_r$* denotes the correctness of the instance of the `EClass` (*c*) referred to by reference *r*, and W_r is the weight assigned to it. In other words, *Correctness$_r$* equals to the average value of `EClassCorrectness` of each instance of *c*. Otherwise, *Correctness$_r$* denotes the correctness of the reference *r* and W_r is the weight assigned to it.

Execute *operation* `getFormula()` of class `EClassCorrectness` of QMM3 to obtain the correctness of for the instance I. $I_{eClassCorrectness} = I_{eClassCompleteness} *$ $$\frac{I_{numberOfEAttributes} * I_{eAttributeCorrectness} + I_{numberOfEReferences} * I_{eReferenceCorrectness}}{I_{numberOfEAttributes} + I_{numberOfEReferences}}$$

Step5-Automated Derivation of `Redundancy` for Each Instance of `EClass` belonging to `SInstancesOfEClass`. This step follows the similar procedure as we did for metric `Completeness`, except that metric `Completeness` is checked against matched elements while metric `Redundancy` is checked against redundant elements (Section 3).

5   Evaluation

Section 5.1 presents our evaluation, where we compare the metrics generated by our framework for UML class and sequence diagrams with the ones manually developed, followed by the application of the metrics generated by our framework for UML state machine diagrams in Section 5.2.

5.1   Metrics for UML Class and Sequence Diagrams

This work was motivated by the experience of our manual development of two sets of quality metrics for UML class and sequence diagrams (Section 1) for two controlled experiments [2]. These experiments evaluated the applicability of a use case modeling approach, called RUCM [3], in terms of its impact on the quality of UML class and sequence diagrams, by comparing with a traditional use case modeling approach. The UML class and sequence diagrams designed by the experiment subjects (MUE) were evaluated against manually developed experts' solutions (REF).

Diagrams were evaluated from three aspects: completeness, correctness, and redundancy. Three main types of model elements contribute to the measurement of class diagrams: Class, Association, and Generalization. The quality of classes in class diagrams is further measured based on three properties: stereotypes, attributes, and operations. Additionally three extra measuring aspects were introduced to evaluate classes, which are the metrics that were impossible to be automatically generated because they are not related to either the syntax or semantics of UML class diagrams, but are the indicators of a good object-oriented design. These extra metrics are: 1) A class does not represent one and only one logical concept, 2) A class does not give a cohesive set of responsibilities, and 3) A class does not represent the intended meaning of the class. It is worth noticing that users are welcomed to introduce this type of metrics and it can be easily done. The users only need to indicate to which model elements these metrics should be applied and what are their weights.

Messages, interaction uses, and combined fragments are the three main types of model elements of sequence diagrams and they contribute to the measurement of sequence diagrams in our controlled experiments. One measuring aspect *Message Sequence Correctness* was introduced to evaluate whether the sequence of messages along lifelines is correct according to the use case specification of the system under study. This metric contributes to the overall correctness of sequence diagrams. However it cannot be automatically generated due to the same reason we discussed earlier.

We compared the generated metrics for UML class and sequence diagrams by our measurement framework with the manually developed metrics of the experiment designers. Results show that most of the metrics are matched, except the ones we discussed above, which cannot be generated automatically as they are not related to the syntax and semantics of the modeling language. This type of metrics is usually related to the quality of a good object-oriented design.

5.2   Metrics for UML State Machine Diagrams

Our framework was applied to generate quality metrics for UML state machines to evaluate the "applicability" of state machines when modeling crosscutting behavior using AspectSM [9], a UML profile extending UML state machine to provide mechanisms to define and weave aspects into state machines. With AspectSM, crosscutting behavior is modeled using "aspect state machines". Their applicability was compared with that of standard state machines directly modeling crosscutting and standard behavior. In other words, aspects combined with state machines modeling standard behavior are compared with state machines modeling the entire system behavior, including its crosscutting one. Applicability is defined based on the completeness, correctness, and redundancy of state machines when compared to their corresponding reference state machines. Metrics to measure aspect state machines and standard UML state machines were automatically generated using our framework. We applied these metrics to two controlled experiment [6, 7] to measure quality of subject-derived state machines with the ones developed by experts (reference state machines).

Two main model elements (i.e., State and Transition) of state machine diagrams were measured by the experiment designers. A state was measured by its name only. A transition was measured by its contained triggers, guards, and effects. Each model element was assigned the same weight such that all model elements are considered equally important. According to experiment needs, users are encouraged to select only appropriate elements to evaluate. By doing so the resulted metrics derived from our framework can be significantly simplified and additionally these metrics would be more meaningful for experiments. For instance, in the experiment design, we decided not to include Region and any of its properties because in the experiment subjects were not required to model regions when they designed the state machine diagrams. Therefore, no region appeared in the state machine diagrams designed by the students.

6   Related Work

Many metrics for Object-Oriented (OO) design have been proposed to help evaluating and subsequently improving the quality of a design. For instance, SDMetrics [10] provides a set of measures to quantify the structural quality of OO code and design such as size, coupling, and complexity. SDMetrics also provides a tool support to automatically collect data for these measures. This tool implementation is based on a series of research results like [11, 12]. There also exist other works (e.g., [13, 14]) proposing similar kinds of software quality measures (e.g., size, cohesion). Such measures help in assessing individual software's quality, instead of comparing software designs with reference designs to conduct empirical studies, as we do here. Intensive empirical studies (e.g., [15-17]) have been conducted to investigate the connections of OO quality metrics with software characteristics such as maintainability.

There exist some works on quality measures of UML models. Xu et al. [18] proposed a structural complexity measure for UML class. The proposed approach only considers the complexity of classes and relationships between them. Each model element of a class diagram can be assigned a weight, which is taken in consideration while calculating complexity of class diagrams. Reißing [19] proposed a model, based on UML metamodel, for OO design measurement. This model defines structural metrics of a class diagram for the purpose of automating evaluation of UML class diagrams. The definitions of all the metrics are based on the UML metamodel, which makes the tool implementation for calculating metrics easy. Marchesi [20] proposed a set of metrics for UML use case and class diagrams. The objective is to allow early estimate of development efforts and implementation time, etc. Genero et al. [21] summarized and analyzed a set of existing OO metrics that can be applied for assessing the complexity of class diagrams and based on the analysis results, they proposed some new metrics on relationships (e.g., number of associations of a class). The authors also conducted an empirical evaluation on these class diagram metrics [22] to investigate whether these metrics are related to the maintainability of class diagrams. Notice that all these related works are mainly limited their scope to quality metrics of UML class diagrams. Kim and Boldyress [23] proposed a set of metrics for UML class and use case diagrams. They also proposed metrics for messages in UML sequence diagrams. A tool has been implemented to obtain data for their proposed metrics automatically. Similar tools (e.g., [24, 25]) have been developed to automatically collect data based on metrics from different UML diagrams. A set of metrics are proposed in [26] to measure the complexity of UML state machine diagrams based on measures such as 'Number of Transitions' and 'Number of Guards'.

To compare with the above existing works, our framework defines metrics at the MOF metamodel level, and automatically transforms them to obtain metrics for MOF-based metamodels (M2 level). The motivation of our work is not to derive quality metrics like what the related work does, but for evaluating a model by comparing it with a reference model, which is considered as an "Oracle" and usually designed by an expert. This kind of comparison is very important in the context of empirical studies (e.g., [2]) for assessing, for example, a model designed by an experiment subject by comparing it with an expert solution. Besides, as we define metrics in the M3 level, our proposed measurement framework can be used not only for UML models, but also other MOF-based modeling languages such as Knowledge Discovery Meta-Model (KDM) [27] and Business Process Definition Metamodel (BPDM] [28].

7   Conclusion

In this paper, we presented a quality measurement framework for defining quality metrics at the MOF metamodel (M3) and a (semi-automated) instantiation with a tool support to obtain quality metrics for MOF-based metamodels (e.g., UML metamodel). The motivation of this work arose from a series of controlled experiments we conducted [3], where it was required to define quality metrics to measure quality of experiment subjects' solutions by comparing them with the reference solutions developed by experts. Manually developing such metrics is an error-prone task since the metamodels at the M2 level can be extremely complex. Using our framework such metrics can be defined once at the MOF metamodel (e.g., Ecore metamodel) and a tool can automatically transform them into quality metrics for any M2 metamodel.

We evaluated our automatically generated metrics for UML class and sequence diagrams by comparing them with the manually developed metrics for two controlled experiments. We found two sets of metrics consistent with each other. We further used the framework to generate metrics for UML state machines and used them in two controlled experiments to determine the applicability of an aspect-oriented state machine modeling approach. In the future, we plan to extend our tool to provide a use interface support for defining metrics that are independent of the syntax or semantics of any MOF-based language. Such examples include metrics that check whether a model meets a good object-oriented design. We also plan to use our framework to generate metrics for other MOF-based metamodels, besides for the UML metamodel.

References

1. Claes Wohlin, P.R.: Martin Höst: Experimentation in software engineering: An introduction. Kluwer Acdamic Publisher, London (2000)
2. Yue, T., Briand, L., Labiche, Y.: Facilitating the Transition from Use Case Models to Analysis Models: Approach and Experiments. ACM Transactions on Software Engineering and Methodology (TOSEM) 22 (2013)

3. Yue, T., Briand, L.C., Labiche, Y.: A Use Case Modeling Approach to Facilitate the Transition Towards Analysis Models: Concepts and Empirical Evaluation. In: Schürr, A., Selic, B. (eds.) MODELS 2009. LNCS, vol. 5795, pp. 484–498. Springer, Heidelberg (2009)
4. OMG: MOF 2.0 Core Specification (formal/2006-01-01).
5. OMG: UML 2.2 Superstructure Specification (formal/2009-02-04).
6. Ali, S., Yue, T., Briand, L.: Assessing Quality and Effort of Applying Aspect State Machines for Robustness Testing: A Controlled Experiment. In: International Conference on Software Testing, Verification and Validation (2013)
7. Ali, S., Yue, T.: Comprehensively Evaluating Conformance Error Rates of Applying Aspect State Machines for Robustness Testing. In: International Conference on Aspect-Oriented Software Development (AOSD 2012), pp. 155–166. ACM (2012)
8. http://www.eclipse.org/modeling/emf/
9. Ali, S., Briand, L., Hemmati, H.: Modeling Robustness Behavior Using Aspect-Oriented Modeling to Support Robustness Testing of Industrial Systems (2010)
10. http://www.sdmetrics.com/index.html
11. Briand, L., Melo, W., Wüst, J.: Assessing the applicability of fault-proneness models across object-oriented software projects. IEEE Transactions on Software Engineering, 706–720 (2002)
12. Briand, L., Wüst, J.: Empirical studies of quality models in object-oriented systems. Advances in Computers 56, 97–166 (2002)
13. Chidamber, S.R., Kemerer, C.: Towards a Metrics Suite for Object Oriented design. In: Object-Oriented Programming: Systems, Languages and Applications (OOPSLA 1991), pp. 197–211. SIGPLAN Notices (1991)
14. Bieman, J., Kang, B.: Cohesion and reuse in an object-oriented system. In: The 1995 Symposium on Software Reusability, pp. 259–262. ACM (1995)
15. Briand, L., Bunse, C., Daly, J.: A controlled experiment for evaluating quality guidelines on the maintainability of object-oriented designs. IEEE Transactions on Software Engineering 27, 513–530 (2002)
16. Harrison, R., Counsell, S., Nithi, R.: Experimental assessment of the effect of inheritance on the maintainability of object-oriented systems. Journal of Systems and Software 52, 173–179 (2000)
17. Lange, C.F.J.: Assessing and improving the quality of modeling: A series of empirical studies about the UML. Technische Universiteit Eindhoven (2007)
18. Xu, B., Kang, D., Lu, J.: A Structural Complexity Measure for UML Class Diagrams. In: Bubak, M., van Albada, G.D., Sloot, P.M.A., Dongarra, J. (eds.) ICCS 2004. LNCS, vol. 3036, pp. 421–424. Springer, Heidelberg (2004)
19. Reißing, R.: Towards a model for object-oriented design measurement. In: ECOOP Workshop on Quantative Approaches in Object-Oriented Software Engineering, pp. 71–84 (2001)
20. Marchesi, M.: OOA metrics for the Unified Modeling Language. In: The 2nd Euromicro Conference on Software Maintenance and Reengineering, pp. 67–73 (1998)
21. Genero, M., Piattini, M., Calero, C.: Early measures for UML class diagrams. L'Objet 6, 489–505 (2000)
22. Genero, M., Piattini, M., Calero, C.: Empirical validation of class diagram metrics. In: International Symposium on Empirical Software Engineering, pp. 195–203. IEEE (2002)
23. Kim, H., Boldyreff, C.: Developing software metrics applicable to UML models. In: The 6th International Workshop on Quantitative Approaches in Object–Oriented Software Engineering. Citeseer (2002)

24. Lavazza, L., Agostini, A.: Automated Measurement of UML Models: an open toolset approach. Journal of Object Technology 4, 114–134 (2005)
25. Carbone, M., Santucci, G.: Fast&&Serious: a UML based metric for effort estimation. In: 6th ECOOP Workshop on Quantitative Approaches in Object-Oriented Software Engineering. Citeseer (2011)
26. Cruz-Lemus, J., Maes, A., Genero, M., Poels, G., Piattini, M.: The impact of structural complexity on the understandability of UML statechart diagrams. Information Sciences 180, 2209–2220 (2010)
27. OMG: OMG Knowledge Discovery Meta-Model (KDM) (formal/2009-01-02)
28. OMG: OMG Business Procee Definition Metamodel (BPDM) (formal/2008-11-03)

Neo4EMF, A Scalable Persistence Layer for EMF Models

Amine Benelallam[1], Abel Gómez[1], Gerson Sunyé[1], Massimo Tisi[1], and David Launay[2]

[1] AtlanMod, Inria, Mines-Nantes, & Lina, France
{amine.benelallam,abel.gomez-llana,gerson.sunye,massimo.tisi}@inria.fr
[2] Mia-Software Nantes, France
dlaunay@mia-software.com

Abstract. Several industrial contexts require software engineering methods and tools able to handle large-size artifacts. The central idea of abstraction makes model-driven engineering (MDE) a promising approach in such contexts, but current tools do not scale to very large models (VLMs): already the task of storing and accessing VLMs from a persisting support is currently inefficient. In this paper we propose a scalable persistence layer for the de-facto standard MDE framework EMF. The layer exploits the efficiency of graph databases in storing and accessing graph structures, as EMF models are. A preliminary experimentation shows that typical queries in reverse-engineering EMF models have good performance on such persistence layer, compared to file-based backends.

1 Introduction

With large-scale software engineering becoming a compelling necessity in several industrial contexts, companies need tools that are capable to scale efficiently. One of such companies is MIA Software, part of the group Sodifrance, working in the field of software modernization.

The emergence of new techniques and tools for building complex, adaptive and distributed systems has raised a need for the modernization of existing software. A software modernization process follows a systematic approach by first building high level abstractions from source code through reverse engineering, and then using these abstractions to understand, evaluate the quality, extract enterprise architectures and finally, improve the system. A natural approach to reverse engineering is to use Model-Driven Engineering (MDE) tools and in particular those based on the Eclipse Modeling Framework (EMF).

Indeed, EMF has become a *de facto* standard for building MDE tools, providing a common base for different purposes: reverse engineering [6, 26], model transformation [14,19], and code generation [5,18]. However, EMF was designed to support modeling activities in the first place and has shown clear limits when dealing with large models, which is often the case of automatically generated models.

J. Cabot and J. Rubin (Eds.): ECMFA 2014, LNCS 8569, pp. 230–241, 2014.

While several solutions to persist EMF models exist, they are limited for two reasons. First, most of them do not allow partial model load and unload, and hence, the size of the models they can handle is limited by the memory size; and second, models are structurally graphs and most of the existing solutions are based on relational databases, which are not fully adapted to store graphs.

In this paper we identify specific large-model requirements, discuss the limitations of EMF with this respect, and present a scalable persistence layer for EMF models that meets these requirements. Our persistence layer, Neo4EMF, is built on top of the popular graph database Neo4j. Neo4EMF is open-source, publicly available at [3] and it can be immediately used by existing EMF-based tools, without modifying them, to improve their applicability to complex industrial contexts.

Neo4EMF provides two main benefits to the state-of-the-art MDE tools: (i) a scalable access to very large models – a. k. a. large-scale models – with on-demand loading of model elements, (ii) the possibility to exploit the enterprise features of Neo4j, like online backups, horizontal scalability and advanced monitoring. To evaluate this aspect we perform a set of queries in the domain of software modernization, and we compare the execution performance of these queries with the *de facto* standard persistence layers for EMF: XMI and CDO [13].

The paper is organized as follows. Section 2 introduces the concept of persistence layer and graph database, Section 3 describes our proposed persistence layer, Section 4 experimentally evaluates the performance of our layer. Section 5 compares our proposal to existing related work, and finally Section 6 concludes and draws the future perspectives of the tool.

2   Background

2.1   Persistence Layers

Software developers often need to persist the state of one or more objects using an existing storage support: relational databases, XML files, etc. There are two main approaches to achieve object persistence. The first one is to hard code the persistence behavior in the class. This approach is efficient and adapted to small applications, but increases the coupling between the class and the storage support. The second approach is to use a persistence layer [2], i. e., a robust and adaptable mechanism that hides storage details from developers and reduces coupling between the storage support and classes. The adaptability of this approach is ensured by a mapping that binds the object model, composed of classes, references, and attributes to the storage model: tables, columns, etc. The object and the storage models can evolve independently, provided a mapping between their concepts is possible. The mapping reduces the development cost of persistent classes, but has a significant impact on the performance.

The emergence of code generation techniques allows developers to adopt a third approach that combines the advantages of the two others. It consists on automatically generating an efficient code for persistence using the correspondence mapping as a generation parameter. Contrary to a persistent layer, the adaptability is not ensured at runtime, but at generation time.

Persistence Layers for EMF. Since the publication of the XMI standard [20], XML-based serialization has been the preferred format for storing and sharing models and metamodels. Some tools, such as EMF [12], have even adopted it as their canonical representation. However, XMI-based serialization in EMF results to be extremely inefficient: (i) XMI files sacrifice compactness in favor of human-readability and (ii) XMI files need to be completely parsed to obtain a navigational model of their contents. The first factor greatly reduces the efficiency in I/O accesses, while the second greatly increases the memory required to load and query models and limits the use of proxies and on-demand loading to inter-document relationships. Moreover, XMI-based implementations do not provide advanced features such as concurrent modifications, model versioning, or access control out-of-the-box.

The design of CDO [13], built on top of EMF, solves most of these problems. CDO was initially envisioned, among other things, as a framework to manage large models in a collaborative environment with a low memory footprint. CDO implements a client-server architecture with transactional and notification facilities where model elements are loaded on demand. CDO servers (usually called *repositories*) are built on top of different data storage solutions. However, in practice, only relational databases are commonly used. Indeed, only *DB Store* [8], which uses a proprietary Object/Relational mapper, supports all the features of CDO and is regularly released in the *Eclipse Simultaneous Release* [9–11].

2.2   Graph Databases

The volume of data that organizations gather has grown explosively in recent years, showing a need for solutions that scale-out, as well as the limits of relational databases. To overcome these limits, new technologies for data management have raised, the so-called NoSQL databases [25]. Despite their non-respect of the ACID properties, these database are able to manage large-scale data on highly distributed environments.

Among the different data models used on NoSQL databases (e. g.column, document, or key-value), graph databases are particularly adapted to store EMF models. The graph data model uses graph structures with nodes, edges, and properties to store data and provides index-free adjacency. Although this data model is not new—the research on graph databases was popular back in the 1990s—it became again a topic of interest due to the large amounts of graph data introduced by social networks and the web in general.

3   Neo4EMF

Neo4EMF is our proposal for scalable model persistence built on top of the EMF framework. Neo4EMF is an open source project that aims at providing a compatibility layer between the EMF API and a graph-based storage subsystem. Specifically, Neo4EMF is built on top of Neo4j [23], a NoSQL database which is distributed under the terms of the (A)GPLv3.

EMF-based models can easily be described in terms of graph concepts, since there is a natural mapping between the two representations. This natural translation is the main motivation that lead us to choose a native graph database instead of another NoSQL database. Since graph databases like Neo4j have shown good performance for connected data operations, we argue that they are a promising platform for model manipulation.

In this section we first briefly provide an overview of the underlying mapping between EMF models and Neo4j artifacts through a running example, then we describe the main design principles of Neo4EMF.

3.1   Mapping EMF Models and Neo4j Graphs

Figure 1 shows a small excerpt of the *Java* metamodel provided by MoDisco [26]. This metamodel describes *Java* programs in terms of *Packages*, *ClassDeclarations*, *BodyDeclarations* and *Modifiers*. A *Package* is a named container that groups a set of *ClassDeclarations* through the *ownedElements* composition. A *ClassDeclaration* contains a *name* and a set of *BodyDeclarations*. Finally, a *BodyDeclaration* contains a *name*, and its *visibility* is described by a single *Modifier*.

Figure 2 shows a simple instance of this metamodel. This instance contains a single *Package* (`package1`), containing only one *ClassDeclaration* (`class1`). The *Class* contains only the `bodyDecl1` *BodyDeclaration*, which is `public`. Figures 1, 2, and 3 show that:

- MODEL ELEMENTS are represented as *nodes*. *Nodes* p1, c1, d1 and m1 are examples of this, and correspond to the elements p1, c1, d1 and m1 shown in Figure 2. A ROOT element denotes the model element(s) that directly or indirectly references all the other elements in the model.
- ELEMENT ATTRIBUTES are represented as *node properties* – a pair of ⟨*property name, property value*⟩ contained in the corresponding *node*. This can be observed in *nodes* p1, c1, d1, and m1 again.
- METAMODEL ELEMENTS are also represented as *nodes*. *Nodes* representing metamodel elements are indexed to ease their access. These kind of *nodes* also contain two node properties. As it can be seen in *nodes* P, C, B, and M (which correspond to *Package*, *ClassDeclaration*, *BodyDeclaration*, and *Modifier* on Figure 1), the first property holds the name of the metamodel element, and the second property the metamodel unique identifier (a. k. a. *nsURI*).

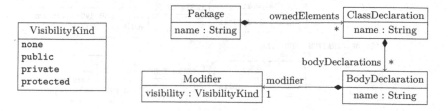

Fig. 1. Excerpt of the *Java* metamodel

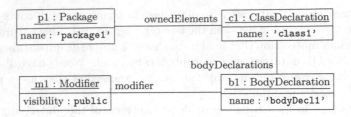

Fig. 2. Sample instance of the *Java* metamodel (nsURI: `http://java`)

- CONFORMANCE RELATIONSHIPS are represented as an outgoing *relationship* of type `INSTANCE_OF` pointing to the node representing the corresponding metamodel element, as exemplified by the horizontal arrows of Figure 3.
- REFERENCES are represented as *relationships*. To avoid naming conflicts in *relationships*, we use the following convention for assigning names: `CLASS_NAME__REFERENCE_NAME`. Vertical arrows in Figure 3 are examples of references. Bidirectional references would be represented with two separate directed graph *relationships*.

3.2 Neo4EMF Design Principles

Figure 3 shows the high-level architecture of Neo4EMF. In this section we introduce the different design principles that we respected in the development of Neo4EMF.

Compliance with Standard APIs. In order to keep compliance with EMF, Neo4EMF provides a feature to generate an adapted Java code implementation

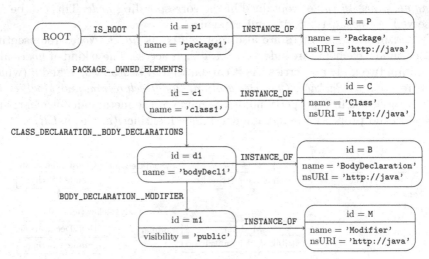

Fig. 3. Representation of the sample instance of the *Java* metamodel in Neo4j

allowing a refined on-demand loading. To allow for a fine-grained on-demand load mechanism even when using the Java generated API, Neo4EMF provides an adapted code generator supporting all the kinds of EMF generation (reflective, virtual, and dynamic). Neo4EMFObject extends the EMF *EObject* class with additional metadata such as the *id*. In addition to the default package organization, we generate a Java class containing a map from the model references to the Neo4j Relationships.

On Demand Loading. Neo4EMF uses an on-demand loading mechanism that reduces memory footprint and allows programs to load and query large models in systems with limited memory. This capabilities are provided for both the Neo4EMF dynamic API and the Neo4EMF generated Java API. These APIs are kept fully compliant with the standard EMF methods to load, navigate, modify, and save models. When a resource is loaded, only the root elements of the model are charged in memory, without any reference to their features. Depending on the user's query, the rest of the model is to be loaded. Thus, when a feature is queried, Neo4EMF checks if the elements already exist in the *cache memory*, if not they are loaded from the backend store.

Lightweight Model Change Tracking. Saving model changes in XMI is time consuming, especially when dealing with in large models. The standard serialization mechanisms must traverse the whole resource to save a file. Neo4EMF uses an event-driven change notification approach to keep track of the model changes. Every Neo4EMFObject contains an adapter that sends a notification for each change to a shared listener. Notifications are stored in a *ChangeLog model*, which is asynchronously analyzed to optimize persistence operations. In this case, instead of traversing the whole resource to save the changes, Neo4EMF queries a *ChangeLog model*, and saves only the modified elements. Here, a model change can either be a creation of a new element, an edition of feature(s) of an existing one, or a deletion. Figure 4 shows the metamodel of the *ChangeLog model*.

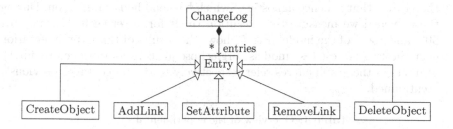

Fig. 4. Neo4EMF ChangeLog

Lightweight First Time Loading. Neo4EMF Java code generation separates objects data from their objects, in the sense that, every generated class references to an inner class holding all the class features. This allows a light-weight first time loading of Neo4EMF Objects.

4   Experimental Evaluation

In this section, we evaluate how the access time of Neo4EMF scales in increasingly large scenarios, and we compare it against CDO (with H2 as relational database backend) and XMI. These experiments are performed over 3 EMF models that conform to the Java Metamodel proposed in MoDisco [26] and reverse-engineered from existing code using the MoDisco Java Discoverer. As starting code we used 3 sets of Eclipse plugins, of increasing size. Table 1 details how the experiments vary in size and thus in the number of elements:

4.1   Execution Environment

Experiments are executed in a laptop computer running Windows 7 Enterprise 64. The most significative hardware elements are: an Intel Core i7 processor 3740QM (2.70GHz), 16 GB of DDR3 SDRAM (800MHz), and a Samsung SM841 SATA3 SSD Hard Disk (6GB/s). Experiments are executed on Eclipse version 4.3.1 running Java SE Runtime Environment version 1.7 (specifically, build 1.7.0_40-b43).

In order to compare the three technologies, we generate three different EMF access APIs, starting from the Java MoDisco Metamodel respectively with 1) EMF standard parameters, 2) CDO parameters, and 3) Neo4EMF generator. We import the 3 experimental models, originally in XMI format to CDO and Neo4EMF, and we verify that all the imported models contain the same data.

Experiment I : Model Traversal. In a first experimentation we execute a model visitor that starting from the root of the model traverses the full containment tree in a depth-first order. At each step of the traversal the visitor loads the element content from the backend, and modifies the element (changing its name). Only the standard EMF interface methods are used by the visitor, that is hence agnostic of which backend he is running on. During the traversal we measure the execution times for covering 0.1%, 1%, 10% 50% and 100% of the model. Fig. 5 shows the results of this experimentation over the two largest test models (org.eclipse.jdt.core and org.eclipse.jdt.*). Markers in the graph curves refer respectively to the percentages previously mentionned.

Table 1. Overview of the experimental sets

#	Plugin	Size	Number of elements
1	org.eclipse.emf.ecore	24.2MB	121.295
2	org.eclipse.jdt.core	420.6MB	1.557.007
3	org.eclipse.jdt.*	984.7MB	3.609.454

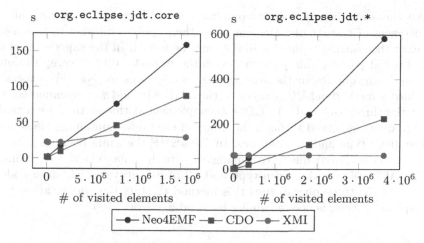

Fig. 5. Results for model traversal on test models 2 and 3

Experiment II : Java Reverse Engineering. In a second experimentation – see results in Fig.6 – we execute a set of three simple queries on the Java metamodel that originate from the domain of reverse-engineering Java code. While the first of these queries is a well-known scenario in academic literature, the other two have been selected to mimic typical model access patterns in reverse engineering, according to the experience of our industrial partner.

1. Grabats (GB): it returns the set of classes that holds static method declarations having as return type the holding class (e. g., Singleton) [15].
2. Unused Method Declarations (UnM): it returns the set of method declarations that are private and not internally called.
3. Class-Attribute Map (CA-M): it returns a map associating each Class declaration to the set of its attribute declarations.

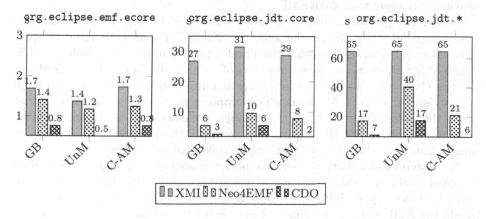

Fig. 6. Results for scenario 2

All these queries start their computation by accessing the list of all the instances of a particular element type, then apply a filtering to this list to select the starting points for navigating the model. In the experience of our industrial partner this pattern covers the quasi-totality of computational-demanding queries in the reverse-engineering domain. For this reason we added a method *getAllInstances* to the EMF API and we implemented it in all the three back-ends. In CDO we implemented this method by a native SQL query, achieved through the union of the tables containing elements of the given type and its subtypes. In Neo4EMF the same result is achieved by a native Neo4j query traversing the graph nodes via the relationship `INSTANCE_OF`, for the given type and all of its subtypes. The user-code of each of the three queries uses this method to start the computation in all implementation, hence remaining backend-agnostic.

4.2 Discussion

The results of the two experimentations are consistent with each other. Fig. 5 shows that while in XMI the access time to each model element is negligible with respect to the initial model-loading time (since the whole model is loaded in memory), the two backends with on-demand loading mechanisms have a constant access time (giving linear complexity to the query). This shows that the backends can scale well for even larger sizes. In both experiments in Fig. 5 the backends with on-demand loading mechanisms outperform XMI when the part of the model that needs to be accessed is lower than a certain ratio of the full model. The graphs show that this ratio is approximately constant, independently of the size of the model and it amounts to 14.12% and 12.46% for Neo4EMF and 29.54% and 27.84%. for CDO. The CDO backend performs better than Neo4EMF, by an approximately constant factor that in the two experiments is respectively of 1.38 and 2.6.

The results from Fig. 6 show that both Neo4EMF and CDO outperform XMI. The test also confirms the previous result, showing execution times from CDO consistently lower than Neo4EMF.

Summarizing, while resulting a better solution than XMI for the industrial use case under study, the current version of Neo4EMF does not exhibit the performance optimizations in caching and prefetching of more mature solutions like CDO. CDO has two complementary ways of caching, one of CDOObjects placed on the client side, and two other caches maintaining CDORevisions (through the revision manager). Moreover CDO supports partial collection loading that gives the possibility to manage the number of elements to be loaded when an elements is fetched for the first time. Likewise, CDO provides a mechanism to decide how and when fetching the target objects asynchronously.

We also remark that the acceptable performances of XMI may be misleading in a real-world scenario: the amount of memory we used allowed to load the whole models in memory, avoiding any swapping in secondary memory that would have made the XMI solution completely unusable for the scenario. Moreover the use of an SSD hard disk significantly improved the loading & saving times from file.

On-demand loading allows to use only the necessary amount of primary memory, extending the applicability of MDE tools to these large scenarios.

We did not measure significant differences in memory occupation between CDO and Neo4EMF, but we noticed several problems in importing large models in CDO. For instance CDO failed to import the test model 3 from its initial XMI serialization on a 8Go machine, as a `TimeOutException` was raised.

Finally, the comparison with relational databases backend should also take into account several other features, besides execution time and memory in a single processor configuration. Neo4EMF allows existing MDE tools to make use from now of the characteristics of graph databases like Neo4j, including clustering, online backups and advanced monitoring.

5   Related Work

The interest on scalable model persistence has grown significantly in recent years, especially with the advent of new solutions for Model-Driven Reverse Engineering (MDRE) and Software Modernization (MDSM). Tools built on top of the EMF, such as MoDisco [6,17,26] have shown that models obtained from reverse-engineering processes can normally be composed of millions of elements [15]. Existing approaches are not suitable to manage this kind of artifacts both in terms of processing and memory consumption requirements.

CDO is the *de facto* standard solution to handle large models in EMF by storing them in a relational database. However, different experiences have shown that CDO does not scale well to very large models [21,22,24]. Barmpis and Kolovos [4] suggest that NoSQL databases would provide better scalability and performance than relational databases due to the interconnected nature of models.

Morsa [21] was one of the first approaches to provide persistence of large scale EMF models using NoSQL databases. As Neo4EMF, Morsa is based on a NoSQL database. Specifically, Morsa uses MongoDB, a document-oriented database, as its persistence backend. Morsa can be used seamlessly to persist large models using the standard EMF mechanisms. As CDO, it was built using a client-server architecture. Morsa provides on-demand loading capabilities together with incremental updates to maintain a low workload. Performance of the storage backend and their own query language (MorsaQL) has been reported in [21] and [22]. Neo4EMF is similar to Morsa in several aspects (notably in on-demand loading) but it aims at exploiting the optimized navigation performance offered by graph-databases w.r.t. document-oriented databases.

Mongo EMF [7] is another alternative to store EMF models in MongoDB databases. Mongo EMF provides the same standard API than previous approaches. However, according to the documentation, the storage mechanism behaves slightly different than the standard persistence backend (for example, for persisting collections of objects or saving bi-directional cross-document containment references). For this reason, Mongo EMF cannot be used without performing any modification to replace another backend in an existing system.

EMF fragments [16] is another NoSQL-based persistence layer for EMF aimed at achieving fast storage of new data and fast navigation of persisted models. Supported backends are MongoDB, Apache Hbase and regular files on the file system. EMF fragments principles are simpler than in other similar approaches and those principles are based on the proxy mechanism used by EMF for inter-document relationships. In EMF fragments, models are automatically partitioned in several chunks (fragments). Unlike Neo4EMF, CDO, and Morsa, all data from a single fragment is loaded at a time, and only links to another fragments are loaded on demand. Another difference with other approaches is that artifacts should be specifically adapted: metamodels have to be modified to indicate where the partitions should be made to get the partitioning capabilities. While our approach has the advantage of not requiring metamodel-specific user manipulation or tool adaptation, fragmentation may provide performance benefits that we plan to investigate in future versions of Neo4EMF.

6 Conclusions and Future Work

In this paper we present the first version of Neo4EMF, a tool that can improve the applicability of MDE to large-scale scenarios, where on-demand loading, high-performance access and enterprise-level data-management features are needed. Our preliminary experimentation shows that, while Neo4EMF is a beneficial alternative to XMI for these scenarios, its raw performances do not surpass a more mature solution like CDO.

In our future work we plan to improve the tool by implementing performance optimization strategies, starting from a definition of model partitions, i.e., elements that are loaded in a single transaction, to reduce the total number of transactions during execution. We then plan to study the problem of memory unloading, by deriving unloading strategy from a definition of the possible uses of the persisted model. Finally we want to extend the applicability of Neo4EMF to other graph databases by exploiting recent proposals of common APIs among graph-databases [1], making of Neo4EMF a generic graph-database backend like CDO is for relational databases.

References

1. Blueprints (2014), https://github.com/tinkerpop/blueprints/wiki
2. Ambler, S.W.: The design of a robust persistence layer for relational databases. Technical report (2000)
3. AtlanMod. Neo4EMF (2014), http://www.neo4emf.com/
4. Barmpis, K., Kolovos, D.S.: Comparative analysis of data persistence technologies for large-scale models. In: Proceedings of the 2012 Extreme Modeling Workshop, XM 2012, pp. 33–38. ACM, New York (2012)
5. Bettini, L.: Implementing Domain-Specific Languages with Xtext and Xtend (2013)
6. Bruneliere, H., Cabot, J., Jouault, F., Madiot, F.: Modisco: A generic and extensible framework for model driven reverse engineering. In: Proceedings of the IEEE/ACM International Conference on Automated Software Engineering, ASE 2010, pp. 173–174. ACM, New York (2010)
7. Hunt, B.: MongoEMF (2014), https://github.com/BryanHunt/mongo-emf/wiki/

8. Eclipse Foundation. CDO / DB Store (2014),
   http://wiki.eclipse.org/CDO/DB_Store/
9. Eclipse Foundation. CDO / Hibernate Store (2014),
   http://wiki.eclipse.org/CDO/Hibernate_Store/
10. Eclipse Foundation. CDO / MongoDB Store (2014),
    http://wiki.eclipse.org/CDO/MongoDB_Store/
11. Eclipse Foundation. CDO / Objectivity Store (2014),
    http://wiki.eclipse.org/CDO/Objectivity_Store/
12. Eclipse Foundation. Eclipse Modeling Framework Project, EMF (2014),
    http://www.eclipse.org/modeling/emf/
13. Eclipse Foundation. The CDO Model Repository, CDO (2014),
    http://www.eclipse.org/cdo/
14. INRIA and LINA. ATLAS transformation language (2014)
15. Jouault, F., Sottet, J., et al.: An AmmA/ATL Solution for the GraBaTs 2009
    Reverse Engineering Case Study. In: Grabats 2009 5th International Workshop on
    Graph-Based Tools, Zurich, Switzerland (July 2009)
16. Scheidgen, M.: EMF fragments (2014),
    https://github.com/markus1978/emf-fragments/wiki/
17. Modeliosoft Solutions (2014), http://www.modeliosoft.com/
18. Musset, J., Juliot, É., Lacrampe, S., Piers, W., Brun, C., Goubet, L., Lussaud, Y.,
    Allilaire, F.: Acceleo user guide (2006)
19. O.: MOF 2.0 QVT final adopted specification (ptc/05-11-01) (April 2008)
20. OMG. OMG MOF 2 XMI Mapping Specification version 2.4.1(August 2011)
21. Espinazo Pagán, J., Sánchez Cuadrado, J., García Molina, J.: Morsa: A scalable
    approach for persisting and accessing large models. In: Whittle, J., Clark, T.,
    Kühne, T. (eds.) MODELS 2011. LNCS, vol. 6981, pp. 77–92. Springer, Heidelberg
    (2011)
22. Pagán, J.E., Molina, J.G.: Querying large models efficiently. Information and Soft-
    ware Technology (in press, 2014) (accepted manuscript),
    http://dx.doi.org/10.1016/j.infsof.2014.01.005
23. Partner, J., Vukotic, A., Watt, N.: Neo4j in Action. O'Reilly Media (2013)
24. Scheidgen, M., Zubow, A., Fischer, J., Kolbe, T.H.: Automated and transpar-
    ent model fragmentation for persisting large models. In: France, R.B., Kazmeier,
    J., Breu, R., Atkinson, C. (eds.) MODELS 2012. LNCS, vol. 7590, pp. 102–118.
    Springer, Heidelberg (2012)
25. Stonebraker, M.: Sql databases v. nosql databases. Communications of the
    ACM 53(4), 10–11 (2010)
26. The Eclipse Foundation. MoDisco Eclipse Project (2014),
    http://www.eclipse.org/MoDisco/

Towards an Infrastructure for Domain-Specific Languages in a Multi-domain Cloud Platform

Thomas Goldschmidt

ABB Corporate Research Germany
thomas.goldschmidt@de.abb.com

Abstract. Recently, cloud computing gained more and more traction, not only in fast moving domains such as private and enterprise software, but also in more traditional domains like industrial automation. However, for rolling out automation software as a service solutions to low-end, long-tail markets with thousands of small customers important aspects for cloud scalability such as easy self service for the customer are still missing. There exists a large gap between the engineering efforts required to configure an automation system and the effort automation companies and their customers can afford. At the same time, tools for implementing Domain-Specific Languages (DSLs) have recently become more and more efficient and easy to use. Tailored DSLs that make use of abstractions for the particular (sub-)domains and omitting other complexities would allow customers to handle their applications in a SaaS-oriented, self-service manner. In this paper, we present an approach towards a model-based infrastructure for engineering languages for a multi-domain automation cloud platform that make use of modern DSL frameworks. This will allow automation SaaS providers to rapidly design sub-domain specific engineering tools based on a common platform. End-customers can then use these tailored languages to engineer their specific applications in an efficient manner.

1 Introduction

Recently, cloud computing gained more and more traction not only in fast moving domains such as private and enterprise software but also in more traditional domains like industrial automation. For example, offering automation software as Software-as-a-Service (SaaS) allows companies to reach customers that could not afford to maintain a complete on-premise system automation. The type of automation software which this targets is level 3 (defines the activities of the work flow to produce the desired end-products) and selected areas of level 2 (defines the activities of monitoring and controlling the physical processes) of the ISA-95 standard [7], i.e., activities of manufacturing execution systems (MES). Typical sub-domains for this low end automation are building automation or different areas in the smart grid domain such as renewable power generation and electronic vehicle charging. Furthermore, with the advent of the Internet of Things (IoT) traditional automation tasks such as monitoring and control also broaden their scope to more and more smaller and privately deployed applications.

J. Cabot and J. Rubin (Eds.): ECMFA 2014, LNCS 8569, pp. 242–253, 2014.
© Springer International Publishing Switzerland 2014

However, in these low-end markets there exists a large gap between the engineering efforts required to configure an automation system and the effort automation companies and their customers can afford. On one hand, automation companies cannot offer engineering to tens of thousands of customers which are the target for their automation SaaS. Therefore, a prerequisite for SaaS to work on a large scale is that customers can do self-service on their applications, i.e., do engineering tasks on their own. On the other hand such customers do not have the expertise and cannot afford the expenses for engineering the automation system themselves based on the current complexity of engineering. Current generic engineering languages such as the languages defined by the IEC 61131-3 standard are designed for expert automation engineers and are thus often too complex for non-experts. Furthermore, for most of the tasks in these low-end domains, where an automation SaaS solution is a good fit, such complex capabilities are not needed. A tailored Domain-Specific Language (DSL) [4] that makes use of abstractions for the particular (sub-)domain and omitting other complexities would allow customers to handle their applications in a SaaS-oriented, self-service manner.

At the same time, tools for implementing domain-specific languages have recently become more and more efficient and easy to use. For example, for the embedded systems domain an extensible platform called *mbeddr* [15] was created that allows for extensibility and modularity [13] based on an underlying base language, which is based on C. Such platforms allow to tailor languages to specific needs in sub-domains or even individual projects. A main advantage of modern DSL systems such as MPS [8](on which mbeddr is based) is that the DSL development environment and the runtime environment for the created languages are based on common IDE. This allows for rapid prototyping and development of the DSLs and the editors for the DSLs. Created languages can be tested and used on the spot and do not require an extensive generation and compilation procedure. Additionally, the coupling between the metamodel and views on that metamodel becomes more and more loose. For example, MPS now allows to have multiple textual, graphical or tabular view types on the same metamodel. Using these mechanisms, a DSL for the specific sub-domain can be produced based on the needs of the intended users.

In this paper, we present an approach towards a model-based infrastructure for engineering languages for a multi-domain automation cloud platform. A central model repository based on an industry standard information model (OPC UA [10]) serves as storage for all metamodels, language definitions and engineering models. A web-enabled DSL framework (MPS [8]) provides language engineering functionality on top of these models. Finally, the platform supports different roles in a domain's ecosystem: domain expert, language engineer, domain-specific engineer and operator. Hence, the complete life-cycle of a DSL ands its corresponding engineering system is supported in the platform, starting from the definition of the domain's metamodel, the language definition, up to the use of the language by engineers and its runtime environment. We implemented a proof of concept prototype showing the technical feasibility of the system.

The contribution of this paper is twofold. First, by presenting our envisioned approach we give practitioners a basis on how domain-specific engineering on scalable, multi-domain cloud platform can be realized. Second, we raise conceptual and technical challenges that we identified to the attention researchers to provide indications for future research.

This paper is structured as follows. Section 2 gives a background on OPC UA [10] which is one of the main concept/technology used in our platform. In Section 3 we present the conceptual architecture of the platform. We give an overview of the proof-of-concept prototype we implemented in Section 4. Conceptual and technical challenges encountered are presented in Section 5. Finally, Section 6 summarizes related work and Section 7 concludes and presents future work.

2   OPC Unified Architecture

OPC UA is a well established industrial standard in the automation domain for communication as well as for making information models accessible. As it already provides basic building blocks for describing runtime systems as well as the domain-specific engineering artifacts (e.g., control programs, device configurations, etc.) it is a good candidate to serve as technical foundation for the common information model within our platform. This section explains the technical features of OPC UA and tries to highlight parts that might still be missing to work in our platform.

OPC UA provides a secure, reliable, high-performance communication infrastructure to exchange different types of data in industrial automation. That includes current data like measurements (e.g. from a temperature sensor) and setpoints (e.g. for defining the desired level in a tank), events (e.g. device lost connection) and alarms for abnormal conditions (e.g. a boiler reached a critical level). In addition, it provides the history of current data (e.g. the temperature trend for the previous day or the last ten years) and of events (what events of a certain type occurred the last five days). In order to provide semantic with the data, also meta data is exchanged in terms of an information model. In Figure 1 depicts an example of an OPC UA address space using the standard graphical representation defined by the OPC UA specification [11].

On the right hand side in Figure 1 the type system is shown, with object types in a type hierarchy. For example, the *DeviceType* is an abstract object type representing all kinds of devices. It defines a variable called *SerialNumber*. A subtype *TemperatureSensorType* adds the *Temperature* variable, including the *EngineeringUnits*. Variables are typed as well, like the *Temperature* of type *AnalogItemType* defined by the OPC Foundation. This type adds a property to the variable containing the *EngineeringUnits*. On the left hand side in Figure 1 an instance of the *TemperatureSensorType*, *TempSensor1*, is shown. The instances contain the concrete values, like the temperature measured by *TempSensor1*.

OPC UA is based on a client server model where the client asks for data and the server delivers the data. The client has the option to read and write the data,

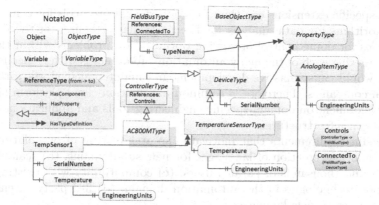

Fig. 1. Example of an Address Space in OPC UA

but also to subscribe to data changes or event notifications. In addition, the client can browse the address space of the server and read the meta data information. For large and complex address spaces the client also has the capability to query the address space for information, for example asking for all temperature sensors that are currently measuring a temperature larger than 25 °C.

The most prominent set of engineering languages, namely the 5 languages defined by the IEC 61131-3 standard, has an official OPC UA representation defined by PLCOpen [12]. The standard defines different domain-specific languages, i.e., Structured Text, Instruction Lists, Function Block Diagrams, Ladder Diagrams and Sequential Function Charts. The languages are partially interchangeable and overlap to a certain extent. For example, the Function Block Diagrams language can be used to connect and orchestrate existing executable code blocks which, in turn, can be implemented by the Structured Text language.

Based on the function block (CTU_INT) and program code (MyTestProgram) in Listings 1.1 and 1.2 the corresponding OPC UA representation is given in Figure 2. Using this kind of information model the programs running in a PLC can be monitored just as any other variable. Generic, OPC UA based program visualizations can then be used to monitor the state of programs using the same way as for their primary variables. This eases the maintenance of the programs and helps engineers, for example, during debugging.

However, the current specification of the PLCopen OPC UA representation does not include the executable parts of the function blocks and programs. For example, the OPC UA representation in Figure 2 shows that it only includes the variables (e.g., CU, R, PV) specified in Listings 1.1 and 1.2 but not the dynamic code parts such as if-then-else blocks. For a complete representation of the control programs in OPC UA this would be required.

3   Conceptual Architecture

The proposed common platform can provide basic automation functionality such as acquiring data from the field as well as storing, analyzing and visualizing it.

Domain-specific extensions can then focus on special protocols for communication, algorithms for data analysis for the particular semantics of the data, or approaches for doing control or solving optimization problems within that domain. Targeting each of the many automation sub-domains with a specific SaaS solution would cause massive development and maintenance efforts within automation companies. Therefore, a common automation cloud platform helps to focus development on domain-specific engineering tools and applications on top of a common infrastructure.

The main requirements that motivate the architecture of our platform are (a) easy and fast creation of languages for new sub-domains, (b) scalability to hundreds and thousands of parallel users, (c) compatibility with existing communication technologies in the automation domain, (d) 3rd party extensibility for the creation of new languages.

```
1  FUNCTION_BLOCK CTU_INT
2  VAR_INPUT
3      CU: BOOL;
4      R: BOOL;
5      PV: INT;
6  END_VAR
7  VAR
8      PVmax: INT := 32767;
9      CU_OLD: BOOL;
10 END_VAR
11 VAR_OUTPUT
12     CU: BOOL;
13     Q: BOOL;
14     CV: INT;
15 END_VAR
16     IF R THEN
17        CV := 0;
18     ELSEIF ((NOT CU_OLD)
19         AND CU
20         AND (CV < PVmax)) THEN
21            CV := CV + 1;
22     END_IF;
23     Q := (CV >= PV);
24     CU_OLD := CU;
25 END_FUNCTION_BLOCK
```

Listing 1.1. Example function block implementation.

```
1  PROGRAM MyTestProgram
2  VAR_INPUT
3      Signal: BOOL;
4  END_VAR
5  VAR
6      MyCounter: CTU_INT;
7  END_VAR
8  VAR_TEMP
9      QTemp: BOOL;
10     CVTemp: INT;
11 END_VAR
12     MyCounter(CU := Signal,
13        R:= FALSE, PV := 24);
14     QTemp := MyCounter.Q;
15     CVTemp := MyCounter.CV;
16 END_PROGRAM
```

Listing 1.2. Example 61131-3 program.

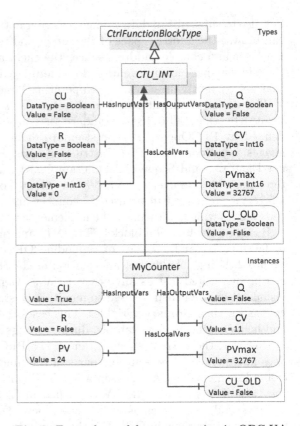

Fig. 2. Example model representation in OPC UA

By providing customizable domain-specific engineering languages as a building block we facilitate self-service engineering and enable the platform to scale to a large number of customers. A DSL infrastructure that has a common way of creating and using languages as well as engineering, accessing the artifacts created with the language can form this building block. To achieve this we propose a model-based approach based on a common model repository that is deployed in the automation cloud platform. Figure 3 gives an overview on how we envision our model-based DSL infrastructure for a multi-domain automation cloud platform could look like.

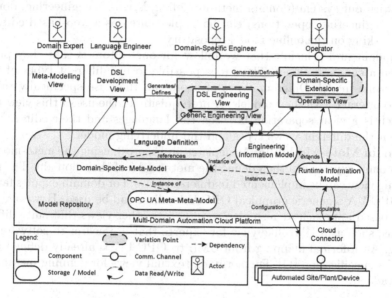

Fig. 3. Architecture of the language and modeling environment of a multi-domain automation cloud platform

Model Repository: A main component of the infrastructure is the common model repository that hold, metamodels, language definitions, engineering models as well as runtime information models. As introduced in Section 2, OPC UA provides a meta-metamodel tailored for the automation domain, as well as a common way of accessing all models on all meta levels. Furthermore, OPC UA is prepared to serve as a basis for building DSLs on top of it [5]. These capabilities make OPC UA a good foundation for the common model repository. Additionally, OPC UA does not imply a storage format for the models but rather defines the way on how models are exposed. Therefore, we combine an OPC UA information model access layer with a scalable cloud database (such as NoSQL databases). This combination provides a scalable, multi-tenant model repository for our system.

Furthermore, OPC UA specifies a query interface for browsing and finding nodes within the information model but does not prescribe the underlying query implementation. Thus, it is possible to map model queries to the underlying persistence technology and its efficient query mechanisms.

As all models are then available in the OPC UA address space and have the corresponding links between each other a cross-model navigation can easily be implemented. Furthermore, OPC UA allows platform developers to store, browse, and manage all models the same way. Thus, making it easy to add generic services for all the above phases. For example, versioning services or social/community sharing services can be built that work for all created languages at once.

Web-based Editors: Modern web-based editors[1] can be used as an efficient way to interact with an online development system. Therefore, all user interaction with our system (domain meta-modeling, language engineering, domain-specific engineering, operations) can be implemented as a web-based editor directly working on the online model repository.

A fundamental principle that we follow for our editors is that they present views on a common model. Thus, it is possible to use different types of views on the same model. Different types of users can then use specifically tailored views to interact with their models. A prerequisite for the use of this view-based approach is a clear separation between the languages and their editors which represent the different views types and the underlying model.

Domain Meta-Modeling: As depicted in Figure 3, using the meta-modeling view domain experts can then define the metamodel of their domain. The meta-modeling view can be implemented in different ways. For domain experts familiar with OPC UA a generic graphical OPC UA editor can be used. However, being a view-based approach we also plan to integrate other views that suite different domains, such as a UML-like view for experts that are nearer to software engineering. An informal mapping from UML to OPC UA is already defined in the OPC UA specification [11]. Furthermore, textual views for defining metamodels can be added.

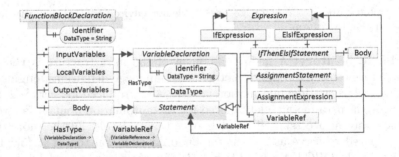

Fig. 4. Excerpt from a metamodel defined using OPC UA for the IEC 61131-3 languages

Figure 4 depicts an example metamodel defined using OPC UA. It shows an excerpt of different concepts of the IEC 61131-3 specification, such as a function block that has input and output variables but also the actual control algorithm (body having statements) can be represented in that way.

Language Engineering: Based on the domain-specific metamodel, language engineers use the DSL development view to define one or more languages that

---
[1] E.g., Cloud9 IDE (https://c9.io/)

implement the views that are tailored for the targeted domain-specific engineers' needs. The resulting editor can then be plugged into the engineering view extending it with domain-specific capabilities.

To achieve a representation of languages on top of our common model repository we require a DSL framework that has an interchangeable storage layer. Furthermore, the language specification metamodel (having constructs like *language specifications, view type definitions, templates*, etc.) needs to be mappable to our OPC UA based information model. Finally, the generated editors have to be web-enabled so that we can run them on our cloud platform.

Additionally, we envision the DSL infrastructure to support extensible views so that tailored domain-specific languages can be created on top of base languages that are executable (such as Java or a 61131-3 language where we have a cloud based interpreter). An example extension language, a simple cause and effect matrix editor for the building automation domain could be created as a tabular view on the domain-specific metamodel. E.g., associating light switches with room lights can be easily mapped by selecting the appropriate cells in the matrix. A mapping of such matrices to 61131-3 was introduced in [1] and could be implemented for this editor as well.

Domain-Specific Engineering: The role of the domain-specific engineer can now be taken over in self-service by the SaaS customer. Such engineers will then develop and configure the customer specific applications which in turn is also stored as an instance (engineering information model) of the domain-specific metamodel. This engineering model is also input to the cloud connector component which is responsible for handling the data coming from or going to the automated site, plant or device(s). This data then populates the runtime information model which is the basis for functionality such as history, analysis, control and visualization. Finally, operators can use the operations view, including domain specific extensions also coming from the DSL to interact with the system. Figure 5 shows an editor that we created based on the OPC UA metamodel given in Figure 4. It defines a textual view type for the function blocks based on the syntax definition given in the IEC 61131-3 specification.

Runtime System: Other components, for history, analysis and execution control algorithms are also part of the automation cloud system but are out of scope of this paper. However, it is important to note that all real-time critical control software will have to remain local to the plant. Only higher level control and optimization task with longer cycle times (e.g., greater than a second) will be part of the automation SaaS.

4 Prototype

Based on a survey we executed earlier[2], which was based on a tool-oriented taxonomy of view-based modeling [6], we analyzed different technologies for implementing a proof-of-concept prototype for our platform. We needed a tool that

---

[2] An earlier but published version of this is available here:
http://sdqweb.ipd.kit.edu/burger/mod2012/

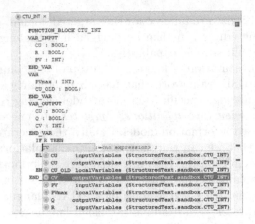

Fig. 5. Editor created for the example metamodel defined in Figure 4

supports both textual as well as graphical syntaxes in a projectional, view-based manner. Furthermore, we selected projectional partiality (allowing different view types to work on different parts of a metamodel), view overlap as well as intra/inter view type overlap (allowing different views at the same time on the model as well as different view types on the same model) as main required features. In addition to the selection properties from the taxonomy, the tool shall support web-based views and have an exchangeable storage layer.

The JetBrains Meta Programming System (MPS) [8] is an approach for the creation of textual modeling languages. MPS provides the possibility to internally map the language to Java where it can then be executed just like an internal DSL. However, MPS also allows to define a mapping to other base languages. The biggest difference to most other textual modeling language approaches is that MPS persists a kind of Abstract Syntax Tree (AST) of the language's instances instead of persisting the concrete syntax representation as text file. The editors manipulating the AST are projectional editors that create the textual representation on the fly. For upcoming versions (3.1) also graphical representations are be supported. The use of the AST as the main underlying model allows for the use of multiple, alternative concrete representations of a model. These representations may also project only a certain part of the underlying model to the concrete syntax. The projections created based on the AST are not persisted, thus MPS does not support custom formatting.

Currently, to the best of our knowledge MPS [8] fulfills or will eventually fulfills our previously posed requirements. It supports textual and tabular views already and is on the way of supporting graphical views [3]. Furthermore, web-based views are also supported[4]. Therefore, our current proof-of-concept prototype is based on this technology. Another important feature which we require for our platform,

---

[3] MPS [3] roadmap: Q1 2014: MPS 3.1 Support for diagrams in editor

[4] Early version available here: https://github.com/JetBrains/jetpad-projectional; Roadmap Q2 2014: MPS 3.5 Web-based projectional editor

i.e., the exchangeable storage layer, is also supported by MPS as it supports custom persistence.

As mentioned earlier we envision our platform to be based on a common OPC UA based model repository. We implemented a prototypical MPS persistence provider for OPC UA. Additionally, we created an implementation that allows us to store OPC UA models in a cloud based database. Furthermore, we started implementing a set of editors for the 61131-3 languages based on MPS. The example editor presented in Figure 5 is one of these editors.

5   Conceptual and Technical Challenges

We currently see a several conceptual and technical challenges on our way towards the envisioned platform. Some of them are specific technical questions where we aim to extend our proof-of-concept prototype to evaluate them. Others, are on a conceptual level where more and broader research would be required. The challenges we see so far are given in the list below. We do not deem this list as being a complete picture, new challenges might arise over time as we further develop the platform.

(1) The mapping between the abstract syntax tree (AST) as defined by MPS and OPC UA has to be validated more extensively. Can all constructs used in the DLS tool be represented in OPC UA. Is reference handling done in a consistent way? (2) A great advantage of online editors is concurrent model editing. Meaning, multiple users can work in parallel on the same content and receive immediate updates from one another. For collaborative engineering this might give real benefits regarding the engineering efficiency. Cloud applications such as Google Drive already nicely support this feature for office documents. However, it remains to be evaluated how big these benefits really are and how good the combination of an MPS-based web-editor and the underlying OPC UA-based persistency support this kind of feature. (3) The usability of the web-editors may be a crucial point for the acceptance of the platform to a large number of customers. Therefore, we plan to employ metrics that assess the usability of the editors for different types of users. (4) Another challenge we see is the validation of the created languages. How can we ensure that the languages and abstract view types that are developed, also by 3rd parties can be mapped to the underlying execution engines correctly. We would need to do verification on the language definitions and the transformations to ensure this. However, there exists limited related work in this area which could serve as a basis for this task.

6   Related Work

A multitude of approaches for the creation of domain-specific languages exists. To mention a few of them: The Graphical Modelling Framework (GMF) [2], which is part of the Eclipse Modelling Project provides means for creating graphical modeling languages based on Ecore metamodels. Language engineers may specify which elements of a metamodel should be editable through a specific diagram. This allows for projectional view types. MetaEdit+ [14] is a commercial tool for creating graphical domain specific modeling languages. Support for the integration of multiple languages has also been investigated using this approach. This also enables the approach for multi view type modeling, as different languages may cover different parts of an interconnected, common metamodel.

Spoofax [9] is a language workbench based on scannerless parser generator Stratego/SDF. Due to the scannerless parsing mechanism it features extensive support for modularization of languages. However, explicit support for view-based modeling, is not given in this approach. There will be still one main view type, i.e., the textual one that needs to be complete. Other, additional view types then may be partial and also have a different representation.Xtext [3], is the official textual modeling approach of the Eclipse Modelling Project. Its primary use case is the integrated definition of concrete and abstract syntax based on a grammar-like specification. Additionally existing metamodels may be imported and and enriched with a view type definition. A language engineer may define different syntax elements for the same class allowing for intra view type overlaps.

However, none of the above mentioned tools provide support for textual as well as graphical projectional views and web-based editors at the same time. Only this would allow for a deployment on a cloud platform. For us this justifies the choice of MPS as a core technology in our platform. Regarding a cloud-based DSL platform very little related work exists. Cloud based editors, such as Cloud9 IDE (https://c9.io) or WriteLatex (http://writelatex.com) provide online editors for specific languages. However, they do not allow their tenants to define own languages and can therefore not be considered a complete cloud-based DSL infrastructure.

7   Conclusions and Future Work

In this paper, we presented a conceptual architecture for a multi-domain engineering cloud platform for the automation domain. The platform is based on a central model repository implemented on top of the OPC UA meta-metamodel and supports the entire life-cycle of a domain-specific language from metamodel definition to operations of the engineered system. Furthermore, we raised conceptual and technical challenges we encountered that give researchers hints for future research.

Based on the proposed architecture we aim to complete our proof-of-concept implementation that facilitates a combination of an OPC UA based model repository, MPS [8] as language engineering workbench and web-based views for the different roles. We plan to use the building automation domain as case study to implement domain-specific languages and the corresponding protocol connectors (e.g., KNX and EnOcean) for the cloud connector. Furthermore, we intend to build a full-fledged IEC 61131-3 web-based editor based on our existing proof-of-concept prototype to evaluate if and how a complex system of languages can be built on top of the proposed infrastructure.

References

1. Drath, R., Fay, A., Schmidberger, T.: Computer-aided design and implementation of interlock control code. In: 2006 IEEE Computer Aided Control System Design, 2006 IEEE International Conference on Control Applications, 2006 IEEE International Symposium on Intelligent Control, pp. 2653–2658 (October 2006)
2. Eclipse Foundation. Graphical Modeling Project (GMP) Homepage, http://www.eclipse.org/modeling/gmp/ (last retrieved December 17, 2013)
3. Eclipse Foundation. Xtext Homepage, http://www.eclipse.org/Xtext/ (last retrieved January 08, 2014)
4. Fowler, M.: Domain-Specific Languages. Addison-Wesley Professional (2010) ISBN 0321712943
5. Goldschmidt, T., Mahnke, W.: Evaluating domain-specific languages for the development of OPC UA based applications. In: 7th Vienna International Conference on Mathematical Modelling, Special Session Modelling and Model Transformation in Automation Technologies, MATHMOD (2012)
6. Goldschmidt, T., Becker, S., Burger, E.: Towards a tool-oriented taxonomy of view-based modelling. In: Modellierung, pp. 59–74 (2012)
7. ISA. International standard for the integration of enterprise and control systems, http://www.isa-95.com/
8. JetBrains. Mcta programming system - DSL development environment (2013), http://www.jetbrains.com/mps/
9. Kats, L.C., Visser, E.: The spoofax language workbench: Rules for declarative specification of languages and ides. In: ACM Sigplan Notices, vol. 45, pp. 444–463. ACM (2010)
10. Mahnke, W., Leitner, S.H., Damm, M.: OPC Unified Architecture. Springer Press (2009)
11. OPC Foundation. OPC UA Specification: Part 3 - Address Space Model, http://opcfoundation.org/UA/Part3 (2010)
12. PLCopen and OPC Foundation. Explanation of the combined technologies of plcopen and opc foundation (2009)
13. Ratiu, D., Voelter, M., Molotnikov, Z., Schaetz, B.: Implementing modular domain specific languages and analyses. In: Proceedings of the Workshop on Model-Driven Engineering, Verification and Validation, MoDeVVa 2012, pp. 35–40. ACM, New York (2012) ISBN 978-1-4503-1801-3
14. Tolvanen, J.-P., Kelly, S.: Metaedit+: Defining and using integrated domain-specific modeling languages. In: Proceeding of OOPSLA 2009, pp. 819–820 (2009) ISBN 978-1-60558-768-4
15. Voelter, M., Ratiu, D., Kolb, B., Schaetz, B.: mbeddr: Instantiating a language workbench in the embedded software domain. Automated Software Engineering 20(3), 339–390 (2013)

Experiences with Business Process Model and Notation for Modeling Integration Patterns

Daniel Ritter

HANA Platform, SAP AG
Dietmar-Hopp-Allee 16, 69190 Walldorf, Germany
daniel.ritter@sap.com

Abstract. *Enterprise Integration Patterns* (EIP) are a collection of widely used best practices for integrating enterprise applications. However, a formal integration model is missing, such as *Business Process Model and Notation* (BPMN) from the workflow domain. There, BPMN is a "de-facto" standard for modeling business process semantics and their runtime behavior.

In this work we present the mapping of integration semantics represented by EIPs to the BPMN syntax and execution semantics. We show that the resulting runtime independent, BPMN-based integration model can be applied to a real-world integration scenario through compilation to an open source middleware system. Based on that system, we report on our practical experiences with BPMN applied to the integration domain.

Keywords: Business Process Model and Notation (BPMN), Enterprise Integration Patterns, Message-based Integration, Middleware.

1 Introduction

Integration middleware systems address the fundamental need for application integration by acting as the messaging hub between applications. As such, they have become ubiquitous in service-oriented enterprise computing environments in the last years. These systems control the message handling during service invocations and are at the core of each Service-Oriented Architecture (SOA) [8]. Since their implementation and operation remains challenging, best practices for building those systems, called *Enterprise Integration Patterns* (EIP), were collected by [7]. Later other practitioners (e.g., [18,1]) and researchers (e.g., [17]) added further patterns. Although these patterns describe typical concepts in designing a messaging system, they cannot be considered a modeling language. A modeling language would allow for the formal, runtime independent specification of integration scenarios and verification.

More precisely, the requirements that are important for developing integration systems, however, not covered by current approaches like the EIPs are collected subsequently. The EIPs propose a visual notation, which allows composition of patterns, while the notation does not specify a semantic model for integration (*REQ-1*: Define a semantic model for message-based integration as foundation

J. Cabot and J. Rubin (Eds.): ECMFA 2014, LNCS 8569, pp. 254–266, 2014.

of a Domain-specific Language (DSL) for integration). A semantic model for integration shall cover a human and computer readable, syntactical notation (*REQ-2*: Specify the syntax) as well as a behavioral runtime specification, which shall be independent of the specific runtime platform implementations (*REQ-3*: Define a platform independent behavioral semantics). The integration DSL shall consider the control flow (*REQ-4*: Support control flow modeling), similar to previous work on Coloured Petri Nets [4] that is used for verification of the EIPs' control flow [6], as well as the data flow for message exchange (*REQ-5*: Allow for data flow modeling for message exchange). The formal integration model shall allow for validation of integration programs and the verification of runtime systems (*REQ-6*: Validate programs and verify the runtime systems).

In this paper, these shortcomings (cf. *REQ*) are addressed by proposing a language for message-based integration grounded on a standard from the related workflow domain, called *Business Process Model and Notation* (BPMN) [15]. For instance, Figure 1 shows an asynchronous integration scenario of a corporate with its bank and business monitoring via SAP Cloud to Cash[1] (CTC), syntactically expressed in BPMN according to the definition proposed in this paper. The incoming message is of type "FSN" (short for Financial Services Network[2]), which has to be translated to its canonical data model incarnation "FSN:CDM" for further processing, using a *Message Translator* pattern. Through an adapted *Claim Check* pattern, the message is stored for later use and handed over to the *External Service* pattern as request to the bank (no further translation required). On successful execution, the original message is restored from the claim check, translated to an ISO format "FSN-ISO" and sent to the CTC application, which tracks the message exchange from a business perspective.

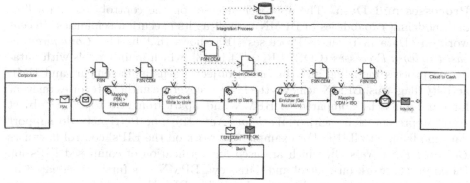

Fig. 1. Business Monitoring: Messages sent from Corporate to Bank are routed to SAP Cloud to Cash (CTC) for monitoring purpose (cf. [16])

The contribution of this paper is the syntactic and semantic formalization of common integration patterns using BPMN (cf. *REQs-1–3*). Due to the manifold collection of patterns, we focus on some hand-picked, core patterns. The complete list of pattern to BPMN mapping can be found in supplementary material [16]

---

[1] http://www.sap.com/pc/tech/cloud/software/cloud-applications/index.html
[2] http://scn.sap.com/docs/DOC-40696

(not mandatory). With the EIPs as business process building blocks, integration semantics can be expressed as implementation independent BPMN syntax. From this formal model, we show the realization of the sample integration scenario in Figure 1 to Apache Camel [1], which is a widely used, open-source system for message-based integration and event processing [5] (cf. *REQs-4-5*). Based on the interaction with customers and integration domain experts, we report on experiences with our modeling approach and discuss advanced integration modeling techniques.

Section 2 discusses the contribution of the paper in the context of related work. Section 3 introduces general integration semantics and defines the syntactic and semantic mapping from selected EIPs to BPMN. In Section 4 we apply our approach to an open-source ESB for the "business monitoring" scenario. In Section 5 we share our experiences, before concluding in Section 6.

2   Related Work

The patterns described by [7,17,18,1] are not building blocks of a modeling language, however, they describe typical concepts in designing a messaging system; thus they are an informal specification language. For that, there are elaborated modeling techniques like the *Business Process Model and Notation* (BPMN) [15], the *Workflow Patterns* defined by [20] or *Service Integration Patterns* [2]. Enterprise Integration Patterns (EIPs) complement these notations by a set of typical designs found in a messaging infrastructure.

Processes and Data. The approach stresses on the control flow, data flow and modeling capabilities of BPMN as well as its execution semantics. Recent work on "Data in Business Processes" [10] shows that besides *Configuration-based Release Processes* (COREPRO) [14,12,13], which mainly deals with data-driven process modeling and (business) object status management, and UML activity diagrams, BPMN achieves the highest coverage in the categories relevant for our approach. Compared to BPMN and apart from the topic of "object state" representation, neither *Workflow Nets* [19] nor Petri nets do support data modeling at all [10]. For example, the work on the EIPs' control flow uses *Coloured Petri Nets* [4], which are used for verification of composed EIPs [6]. Based on the work on control and data flow, BPMN was further evaluated by [9,11] with respect to data dependencies within BPMN processes, however, not towards a combined control and data flow as in our approach.

Process Languages for Integration. The work builds on this foundation and combines it with executable integration patterns, their configuration and mapping to the *Web Services Business Process Execution Language* (WSBPEL) proposed by [17] and leverages the work of [18] that started to map the EIPs to the BPMN syntax and some semantics by example. In this document, we provide a systematic continuation of this work by defining a comprehensive syntax and model for widely-used patterns.

3   The BPMN Integration Pattern Language

Before defining the mapping of some selected EIPs to BPMN, we discuss the relevant BPMN syntax (mainly taken from the *BPMN Collaboration Diagram* [15]) directly in the context of core integration concepts.

3.1   Core Integration Concepts and BPMN

The main syntactical artifacts in BPMN denote process steps, sequences and the representation of messages that are exchanged between processes during runtime. The core concepts of message-based integration are *Message*, *Message Channel* and *Integration Adapters* (cf. *Message Endpoint*) [7].

A message is informally defined as a piece of information to be exchanged between sender and receiver. This information can be a piece of data (i. e., EIP *Document Message*), a command for execution (i. e., EIP *Command Message*), or an event for logging (i. e., EIP *Event Message*). This notion is shared by BPMN, in which the sender and receiver applications are *Participant* elements. In BPMN a participant may have internal details, in the form of an executable process.

The connection between sender and receiver participants is called message channel, which is the fundamental infrastructure of a messaging system. For example, there are EIP *Point-to-Point Channels*, connecting exactly one sender with one receiver, and one-to-many channels like EIP *Publish-Subscribe* or *Broadcast/Multicast*. A message sent to such a channel can be received by multiple receivers, while for n receivers, n copies of the original message have to be provided. In general, channels specify non-functional qualities like the *Quality of Service* (QoS; best-effort, exactly once), *Message Exchange Pattern* (MEP: In-Only or InOut), and *Capacity* (e. g., maximum message size). For instance, a file poller acts one-way (InOnly), since it cannot handle response messages and can be configured to ensure the delivery of messages (exactly once).

On the other hand, most document message exchange works according to the *Request-reply Pattern*, which specifies a two way communication (InOut). This corresponds to the *Process* flow in BPMN, which is controlled by a combination of flow objects (e. g., events, activities, gateways) and connections. We consider BPMN *Start Event* and *End Event* that initiate the process flow with a "message-receive" semantic or terminate the flow, thus terminates a process or part of a process, after having sent the message. The BPMN throwing/catching *Intermediate Event* is used to express message events, errors, and timed message processing. The BPMN *Activity/Task* represents process steps that allow to manipulate a message within the channel and has to be executed, before the flow can proceed. BPMN *Gateway* elements are able to handle multiple process flows, where they route or fork the flow. For that, BPMN *Sequence Flow* definitions connect flow elements within a channel. Besides the control flow, the message channel requires a data flow, which is expressed as a sequence of BPMN *Data Object* and BPMN *Data Store* definitions that are associated to the flow elements. More formally, these BPMN execution semantics for messaging are defined as process model in Definition 1. In a nutshell, a process is initiated by a start event, i. e., a message that contains data according to a specified format (e. g., XML Schema). Then a sequence flow is fired that moves the control in form of a *Token* to the next flow element in the process (e. g., activity, gateway, event) and puts it into ready state. The data flow is handled by associated data objects from one element to the next one. More precisely, a flow element in the ready state gets activated, if all associated data is supplied, and executes its inherent behavioral semantics on the data (e. g., script, service call). The process ends through the invocation of a message end event firing the outgoing message before the process context stops.

Definition 1 (Process model). *A process model $M = (N, SF, DO, DF)$ consists of a finite non-empty set $N \subseteq A \cup G \cup E$ of nodes being activities A of types ServiceTask, ScriptTask and MessageTask, gateways G of types Exclusive-Gateway and ParallelGateway, and events E of types StartEvent, EndEvent and Intermediate Event, where A, G, E are pairwise disjunct.*

The finite non-empty set of SequenceFlow relations $SF \subseteq (N \setminus EndEvent) \times (N \setminus StartEvent)$ represents the control flow. The finite, non-empty set of data objects DO represents data associated to N and $DF \subseteq (N \cup DO) \times (DO \cup N)$ is the data flow relation.

For the Process and Sub-Process instantiation, a Message Start Event or Receiving Message Task is required comparable to a `constructor`. The instances can be terminated by (Message) End Events, the `destructor`. An already instantiated process can be re-invoked using the BPMN correlation mechanism, similar to a `factory pattern`.

Finally, a message endpoint connects an application to a messaging system. In BPMN, the *Message Flow* specifies message exchange (e. g., process status information, error messages, data) between participants or participants and process elements. When mapped to messaging systems, the message flow represents a message endpoint by specifying the message with its structure, operation and interface (e. g., WSDL) that can be routed to the message channel. The model that describes the complete system for an integration flow is specified in Definition 2.

Definition 2 (Integration Flow). *An integration flow $IFlw = (CO, PO, MF)$ consists of a Collaboration CO containing a finite non-empty set of Pool $PO \subseteq P \cup M$ of Participant P and process model M (cf. Definition 1), where $M \subseteq P_{int}$ and P_{int} is the participant referencing the (integration) process steps, and the Message Flow relation for the sender $MF_S \subseteq P_s \times (P_{int} \cup E_s)$ and the receiver $MF_r \subseteq P_s \times (P_{int} \cup E_e)$, where P_s denotes an arbitrary amount of sender participants, E_s and E_e represent sets of start and end events of an integration process P_{int} and P_r denotes the set of receiving participants. The message MS is part of the message exchange from sender to receiver via the MF relation.*

3.2 Mapping Enterprise Integration Patterns to BPMN

The definitions of a *Process Model* and an *Integration Flow* (IFlow) are used to map some selected EIPs to BPMN. We have selected basic integration patterns like *Request-Reply, Content Enricher,* the two antipodes *Splitter* and *Aggregator,* and the *Message Translator.* The other patterns from the literature we covered in [16] as non-mandatory supplementary reading.

The basic message exchange patterns are one-way or two-way communication on an end-to-end IFlow level. These patterns are fundamental, since they let the sender participant communicate synchronously (InOut) or asynchronously (InOnly). Figure 2 (a) shows a two-way integration flow in BPMN using a synchronously "waiting" *Service Task.* Definition 3 specifies the pattern's runtime behaviour. The definitions of the subsequently discussed patterns and the "business monitoring" integration scenario can be expressed in the same way, however, is informally described due to brevity.

Definition 3 (Request-Reply (synchronous)). *The control flow CF is defined as* $CF = E_s \times ServiceTask \times MF_{req} \times P_r \times MsgFlow_{res} \times ServiceTask \times E_e,$ *where the set of ServiceTask of type A, while the process instantiation* **constructor**, E_s *and termination* **destructor** $= E_e \cup E_{err},$ *where* E_{err} *denote error events. The data flow DF is* $E_s \times DO_{in} \times ServiceTask \times MF_{req} \times P_r \times MF_{resp} \times ServiceTask \times DO_{out} \times E_e,$ *where* MF_{req} *and* MF_{resp} *denote message flows for request, response, respectively. If an exceptional situation occurs during the execution of the ServiceTask, a separate channel* Exc *is instantiated to handle the error:* $Exc = ServiceTask \times E_e.$

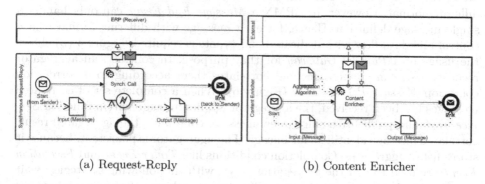

(a) Request-Reply   (b) Content Enricher

Fig. 2. Request-Reply Pattern synchronous (a), Content Enricher Pattern (b) (cf. [16])

A pattern that adheres to Definition 3 is the content enricher. The content enricher consumes messages from the channel and merges additional information into the header or body of the original message according to an *Aggreg. Algorithm,* shown in Figure 2 (b). The data can come from local tables or remote services (not shown). The content enricher is non-persistent by default: if any operation during or after the enrichment operation fails, intermediate results of the operation are lost and the operation has to be re-processed from the latest persistence state onwards. The enricher uses a *Service Task* to map the incoming message (Input) to a request understandable to the external participant, waits for the response and aggregates it to the original message resulting to the output message (Output) according to an aggregation algorithm denoted by a *Data Object.*

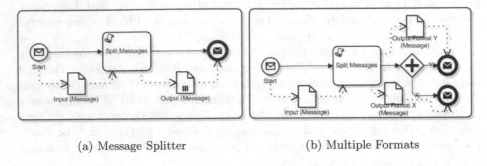

(a) Message Splitter   (b) Multiple Formats

Fig. 3. Message Splitter Pattern (a), with differing output messages (b) (cf. [16])

An interesting pair of patterns are the antagonists *Splitter* and *Aggregator*. Both patterns have a channel cardinality of 1:1, however, the splitter is message creating (1:n message cardinality) and the aggregator is also message creating, while the new message is an aggregate of multiple incoming messages (message cardinality n:1) The splitter breaks one original message into multiple (smaller) messages. For that, the splitter creates as many new messages as the split function (*Script Task*) results to. Figure 3 (a) denotes a splitter, whose split results are of the same format. The split function could result to multiple messages of different format. However, in BPMN a *Message End Event* can only handle a single message definition. Hence, for each message with differing format a new control and data flow with dedicated end events is required. Figure 3 (b) shows the usage of a *Parallel Gateway* for that purpose. In contrast, an aggregator receives a stream of messages and correlates them according to a correlation condition *Message Receive Task* (Figure 6). When a complete set of correlated messages has been received, the aggregator applies an aggregation function *Service Task* and publishes a single, new message containing the aggregated result correlated message identifiers for lineage. The aggregator is persistent, because it stores list of aggregates. Completion conditions like *Timer Event* and *Escalation Event* are used to end the aggregation, e.g., with the following strategies: wait for all, wait for first best, timeout. The outer workings of the aggregator are shown in Figure 4 (a). The first message instantiates a stateful aggregator that can only be ended through its completion conditions or an exceptional situation. The inner workings and the instantiation mechanics are shown in Figure 6 and discussed in detail later.

The message translator, shown in Figure 4 (b), converts an incoming message (format) into a data format expected by its corresponding receiver. Therefore it does not create new messages, but changes the original message. The translator is stateless and has a channel cardinality of 1:1. The message translator is structurally similar to the enricher, while the translator calls an internal mapping program (not shown), instead of an external one.

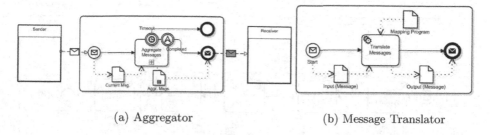

(a) Aggregator   (b) Message Translator

Fig. 4. Aggregator Pattern (collapsed) (a), Message Translator Pattern (b) (cf. [16])

4 Case Study: BPMN Integration Patterns in Action

We demonstrate the practicability of our integration modeling approach through the application to the "business monitoring" scenario from the *Financial Service Network* domain (cf. Figure 1). The scenario features messages sent from a corporate to one or multiple banks, while all messages are passed to the "Cloud to Cash" application, which correlates the technical messages to their business contexts and provides an overview.

The technical implementation uses a well-known open source integration middleware system called *Apache Camel* [1], to which we "compile" our BPMN-based IFlow definitions. In Apache Camel the basic concepts are implemented in a proprietary way. A message consists of a set of name-value pair headers, a variable body or payload and a set of attachments. The addressable message endpoints are defined within *Component* runtime artifacts, which represent a factory for endpoint objects. The inbound and outbound message adapters are part of the component as *Consumer* (`camel:from`) and *Producer* (`camel:to`) objects. A Camel *Route* realizes a concrete implementation of a channel. The *Camel Context* is the container for runtime services (e. g., mapping program, aggregation algorithm) and (multiple) routes.

Figure 5 illustrates the compilation from an IFlow model to Apache Camel artifacts. For better understanding, we used BPMN *Group* elements, which we annotated with the Camel syntax, to overlay the BPMN integration scenario. Hereby, the integration flow is represented by a `camel:context` with exactly one assigned `camel:route`. Between the `camel:from` inbound the two outbound calls `camel:to uri="cfx:"`, several Camel components `camel:to` are executed. The compilation of this definition results in an executable runtime, if all runtime services are attached to the Camel context.

The execution semantics of Camel differ from Definition 2, since Camel has no separation of data and control flow during the execution of a route and behaves rather like a call stack, i. e., the Camel components remain active during the complete route processing. The BPMN workings involve a token-based state model including associated data that lets activities finish after processing. In this case study we mapped the BPMN to the Camel execution semantics by synthesising the control and data semantics to Camel route processing.

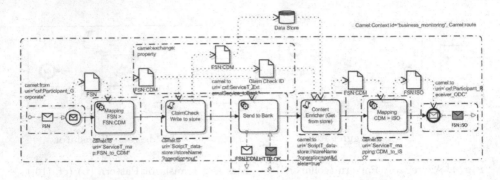

Fig. 5. Translating Business Monitoring: Messages IFlow to Apache Camel. The Camel representation is shown as *Group* overlay for better understanding only. *Message Flow* elements denote Message Endpoint definitions.

Listing 1.1. Message Processing Log for "Business Monitoring (anonymized)"

```
1  Entering CXF Inbound Request{
2      contextName = business_monitoring, MessageGuid =
           iXGKWlUtoQPl0xg..., OverallStatus = COMPLETED,
           ReceiverId = ctc, SenderId = corporate, ...
3      Entering Camel route route27 {
4      Processing exchange ID-0001 in
               To[map:FSN_to_CDM] {...}, To[data-store
               ?op=put] {...}, To[cxf:toBank] {...},
               To[data-store ?op=get&delete=true] {...},
               To[map:CDM_to_ISO] {...}, To[cxf:bean:ODC]
               {...}
5      }
6  }
```

When instrumenting the camel runtime with a technical "Message Processing Log" (MPL) monitoring capabilities, we can follow the message during the route processing. Listing 1.1 shows a shortened and anonymized MPL for our scenario, marking the most relevant steps during the processing of the Camel route. As discussed, the log illustrates the slightly different execution semantics of Camel.

5 Experiences and Limitations

During customer user studies and extensive, hands-on sessions with integration domain experts, we gained practical insight in the usage of our modelling approach. Subsequently, we discuss some technical aspects of the usage of the proposed syntax and semantics and list practical and conceptual limitations, for which we give solutions in the context of BPMN.

Business vs. Technical View. The Business Process Model and Notation was originally defined for business users (e. g., business analysts, business experts): the technical developers implement and use the processes and the business experts monitor and manage the processes [15]. However, the more complex examples within this document (e. g., Fig. 6) show that bridging the gap between the business process design and process implementation in the domain of EIPs with BPMN can become difficult, if not impossible. For complex integration problems, the composition of EIPs quickly leads to technical BPMN syntax, which becomes intractable for business users.

(Sub-) Process Instantiation, Instance Handling. The instantiation of processes and sub-processes in BPMN is statically defined. This is sufficient for stateless, short-running processes. However, there are cases of stateful patterns (e. g., resequencer (not shown), aggregator), for which a more dynamic, conditional instance handling would be required.

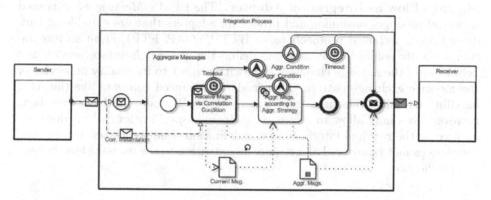

Fig. 6. Aggregator with timeout on sequence sub-process instance and conditional start mechanism for instance correlation per sequence

For instance, if for different messages sequences (i. e., consisting of correlation, sequence identifiers and a sequence termination information) separate aggregation sub-processes shall be started and independently interrupted by a *Timer* during an aggregation, the resulting BPMN syntax becomes tricky and the instantiation semantic seems violated. Figure 6 shows one possible syntactic approach to sequence-based timeouts in BPMN. An aggregator is a complex pattern and requires an embedded sub-process to define its tasks. Using a mechanism known as "Conditional Start" [3] combined with the BPMN correlation makes the instantiation tractable. When a message arrives, to which no aggregate is assigned, a new instance of an aggregator sub-process is created and the message is dispatched to this new instance. The subsequent messages for an existing, active aggregate are dispatched to the respective sub-process instance. For each correlated message sequence, an active sub-process instance exists and can be terminated through time out or if the aggregate is complete. The aggregated message is sent and the sub-process is closed for further messages. In case new messages arrive for a closed sequence, a new sub-process is created.

Although the combination of BPMN correlation and conditional start makes the dynamic instantiation of sub-processes tractable, the mechanism comes with the implication of "redundant" syntax. Let's assume before the messages are aggregated (in Figure 6), a message translator has to transform them to a specific format (preprocessing) and the aggregated message has to be mapped to the target format (post-processing). The latter can be clearly added between the aggregator sub-process and the message end event. However, the preprocessing would be either executed in the parent process before the sub-process execution for the first message and copied to the aggregator sub-process for subsequent messages, or directly "in-lined" into the sub-process.

The topic of (sub-) process instantiation applies to all other complex patterns with sub-processes (e. g., inline synch/asynch bridge, resequencer).

Message Flow as Integration Adapter. The BPMN *Message Flow* is used to model message-consuming and producing adapters that are capable of handling various technical protocols (e. g., HTTP, SOAP, FTP). From an integration semantic point-of-view, adapters define the message interface/service and behaviour of the message channels, e. g., with respect to its quality of service or the message exchange pattern. That leads to advanced concepts like the retry handling for failed messages from a persistence. The standard message flow, however, does only allow to reference a *Message* specification, which does not even cover the required interface/service definition. The mentioned behavioural concepts cannot be covered and require an extension to the message flow beyond its specification.

6   Concluding Remarks

The Enterprise Integration Patterns are a set of widely used patterns denoting the building blocks for a structured implementation of a messaging system. In this work we proposed a syntactic mapping to the Business Process Model and Notation (BPMN) (cf. *REQ-2*); thus each pattern is a set of elements in a BPMN Process, which can be composed to sets of message channels from the senders to the receivers of a message. In contrast to [18] we showed that an extension of BPMN for the integration domain with specific EIP constructs is not necessary.

Together with the syntax we defined corresponding execution semantics (cf. *REQ-3*). We developed the concept of composed patterns further to a complete definition of an *Integration Flow* (*REQ-1*). Although the syntax is compliant to BPMN, the BPMN execution semantics had to be slightly changed for *Message Endpoint* represented as *Message Flow*. The result is an integration domain specific language, with which integration aspects of messaging systems and their execution semantics can be expressed independent of the runtime implementation (cf. *REQs-5–6*). The approach allows for validation of integration programs and runtime systems (cf. *REQ-6*).

The "Business Monitoring" case study shows that our runtime independent modelling approach can be successfully compiled to the well-known, open source integration middleware *Apache Camel* and lets us assume that the application to other runtime systems is possible.

Acknowledgments. We thank Volker Stiehl and Ivana Trickovic for their support on BPMN and the formalization of integration semantics.

References

1. Anstey, J., Zbarcea, H.: Camel in Action. Manning (2011)
2. Barros, A., Dumas, M., ter Hofstede, A.H.M.: Service interaction patterns. In: van der Aalst, W.M.P., Benatallah, B., Casati, F., Curbera, F. (eds.) BPM 2005. LNCS, vol. 3649, pp. 302–318. Springer, Heidelberg (2005)
3. Bihari, S., Fischer, R., Loos, C., Reddy, P., Stiehl, V.: Sap netweaver process orchestration–build a complete integration scenario (sap teched 2013). Technical report. SAP AG (2013)
4. Gierds, C., Fahland, D.: Using petri nets for modeling enterprise integration patterns. Technical Report BPM Center Report BPM-12-18. BPMcenter.org. (2012)
5. Emmersberger, C., Springer, F.: Tutorial: Open source enterprise application integration - introducing the event processing capabilities of apache camel. In: DEBS, pp. 259–268 (2013)
6. Fahland, D., Gierds, C.: Analyzing and completing middleware designs for enterprise integration using coloured petri nets. In: Salinesi, C., Norrie, M.C., Pastor, Ó. (eds.) CAiSE 2013. LNCS, vol. 7908, pp. 400–416. Springer, Heidelberg (2013)
7. Hohpe, G., Woolf, B.: Enterprise Integration Patterns: Designing, Building, and Deploying Messaging Solutions. Addison-Wesley Longman Publishing Co., Inc., Boston (2003)
8. Josuttis, N.M.: SOA in Practice. O'Reilly Media (2007)
9. Meyer, A., Pufahl, L., Fahland, D., Weske, M.: Modeling and enacting complex data dependencies in business processes. In: Daniel, F., Wang, J., Weber, B. (eds.) BPM 2013. LNCS, vol. 8094, pp. 171–186. Springer, Heidelberg (2013)
10. Meyer, A., Smirnov, S., Weske, M.: Data in business processes. EMISA Forum 31(3), 5–31 (2011)
11. Meyer, A., Weske, M.: Data support in process model abstraction. In: Atzeni, P., Cheung, D., Ram, S. (eds.) ER 2012. LNCS, vol. 7532, pp. 292–306. Springer, Heidelberg (2012)
12. Müller, D.: Management datengetriebener Prozessstrukturen. PhD thesis (2009)
13. Müller, D., Reichert, M., Herbst, J.: Flexibility of data-driven process structures. In: Eder, J., Dustdar, S. (eds.) BPM Workshops 2006. LNCS, vol. 4103, pp. 181–192. Springer, Heidelberg (2006)
14. Müller, D., Reichert, M., Herbst, J.: Data-driven modeling and coordination of large process structures. In: Meersman, R., Tari, Z. (eds.) OTM 2007, Part I. LNCS, vol. 4803, pp. 131–149. Springer, Heidelberg (2007)
15. O.M.G. (OMG). Business process model and notation (bpmn) version 2.0. Technical report (January 2011)

16. Ritter, D.: Using the business process model and notation for modeling enterprise integration patterns. CoRR, abs/1403.4053 (2014)
17. Scheibler, T.: Ausführbare Integrationsmuster. PhD thesis (2010)
18. Stiehl, V.: Prozessgesteuerte Anwendungen entwickeln und ausführen mit BPMN: Wie flexible Anwendungsarchitekturen wirklich erreicht werden können. dpunkt.verlag GmbH (2012)
19. van der Aalst, W.M.P.: The application of petri nets to workflow management. Journal of Circuits, Systems, and Computers 8(1), 21–66 (1998)
20. van der Aalst, W.M.P., ter Hofstede, A.H.M., Kiepuszewski, B., Barros, A.P.: Workflow patterns. Distributed and Parallel Databases 14(1), 5–51 (2003)

Author Index